D1460613

HANDBOOK OF RESEARCH ON INTERNATIONAL ENTREPRENEURSHIP STRATEGY

Handbook of Research on International Entrepreneurship Strategy

Improving SME Performance Globally

Edited by

Pervez N. Ghauri

Birmingham Business School, University of Birmingham, UK

V.H. Manek Kirpalani

Distinguished Professor Emeritus, John Molson School of Business, Concordia University, Canada and Honorary Professor, University of the West Indies at St. Augustine, Trinidad & Tobago

Cheltenham, UK • Northampton, MA, USA

Published by
Edward Elgar Publishing Limited
The Lypiatts
15 Lansdown Road
Cheltenham
Glos GL50 2JA
UK

Edward Elgar Publishing, Inc.
William Pratt House
9 Dewey Court
Northampton
Massachusetts 01060
USA

A catalogue record for this book
is available from the British Library

Library of Congress Control Number: 2015943124

This book is available electronically in the **Elgar**online
Business subject collection
DOI 10.4337/9781783471584

ISBN 978 1 78347 157 7 (cased)
ISBN 978 1 78347 158 4 (eBook)

Typeset by Servis Filmsetting Ltd, Stockport, Cheshire
Printed and bound in Great Britain by TJ International Ltd, Padstow

Contents

About the editors

Pervez N. Ghauri completed his PhD at Uppsala University in Sweden where he also taught for several years. After Uppsala, he has worked at the Norwegian School of Management, Oslo, University of Groningen, Netherlands and Manchester Business School, UK. He was Professor of International Business at King's College London before joining Birmingham Business School, University of Birmingham, UK. He is also Visiting Professor at University of Vaasa, Finland and British Hispanic Foundation Chair for Postgraduate studies at Complutense University in Madrid, Spain for 2014–15. He served as Vice President for the Academy of International Business (AIB-Worldwide) from 2008 to 2010 and is a Fellow of the European International Business Academy (EIBA). Recently he was awarded an honorary doctorate by Turku School of Economics and Management, Finland.

Pervez has published more than 25 books and numerous articles in journals such as the *Journal of International Business Studies*, *Journal of World Business*, *Management International Review*, *British Journal of Management*, *Journal of Business Research*, *Industrial Marketing Management*, *European Journal of Marketing* and *International Marketing Review*. He consults and offers training programmes to a number of organizations such as BP, Airbus Industries and Ericsson. He is the founding editor in chief for *International Business Review* and series editor for the Emerald book series *International Business and Management*.

V.H. Manek Kirpalani, DSc HEC University of Montreal, MA and BA Honours Oxford University, is a widely recognized authority in the field of international business and marketing. He is Distinguished Professor Emeritus of Marketing and International Business at John Molson School of Business, Concordia University, Montreal where he also was a member of the Board of Governors. Further, he is Honorary Professor at the University of the West Indies, and was Director, CIBER, at Bloomsburg University, Pennsylvania. Furthermore, he is Visiting Distinguished Professor at the Aalto University School of Economics, Finland, the Faculty of Management, Warsaw University, Poland, has been Visiting Fellow Templeton College, Oxford, and Visiting Professor at other well-known universities in the USA, Europe, Hong Kong and India.

He is a Distinguished Fellow of the Academy of Marketing Science (one of 40), where he was also a governor and Vice-President. He was a member of the Board of Directors of the American Marketing Association for four years, and head of their Global Marketing Division. He is the author of over 220 publications. These include 21 books and a number of articles in renowned journals such as *Industrial Marketing Management*, *International Business Review*, *Journal of International Business Studies* *Journal of Marketing*, and *Journal of the Academy of Marketing Science*, *Journal of International Marketing* and *Journal of Business Research.* Prior to joining academe, he was managing director of an Electrolux AB subsidiary and manager of a trading company subsidiary of the Swedish Match Company.

Contributors

Pál Belyó was educated at the Corvinus University Budapest (CUB), where he received his MSc and Dr oec. (Economics) degrees. In 1981, he received his CSc (PhD) degree in Economic Sciences from the Hungarian Academy of Sciences. Between 1997 and 2009, he was the founder and Chief Executive Director of the Institute for Economic Analysis and Information Technology (ECOSTAT) of the Hungarian Central Statistical Office (HCSO), following which, between 2009 and 2010 he served as President of the HCSO. Dr Belyó is a renowned expert on the Hungarian economy and has published extensively on this subject. He was awarded the CUB Kaldor prize (Economist of the Year 2002) and the HCSO Fényes Elek prize in 2007. Currently, he is Director of the Policy Agenda Research Company in Budapest and Professor at Budapest College of Management in Hungary.

Funda Celikel Esser is a policy analyst at the Joint Research Centre of the European Commission. Prior to joining the Commission, she held research posts at the European Foundation for the Improvement of Living and Working Conditions (Eurofound) in Dublin, Jean Monnet Centre of Excellence and Capgemini Consulting in Berlin and Centre for European Policy Studies (CEPS) in Brussels. Funda has co-authored several science and policy papers and articles on innovation efficiency, the link between innovation performance and governance, European innovation policies, born global enterprises, flexicurity measures, public sector restructuring and its effects on the workforce and labour markets, and has presented her work at high-level academic conferences such as the 2014 World Entrepreneurship Conference and 2014 Industrial Relations in Europe Conference.

Nuno Fernandes Crespo holds a PhD in Management from ISEG – School of Economics and Management of the University of Lisbon, Portugal. Currently, he is Assistant Professor at ISEG and teaches courses related to entrepreneurship and entrepreneurial marketing. His main research areas are international business, entrepreneurship and international entrepreneurship, with a focus on firm actions that facilitate the internationalization process. He has presented his research at several international academic conferences.

Kalanit Efrat (PhD, 2008, University of Haifa, Israel) is a senior lecturer of marketing and head of the marketing programme at the Ruppin Academic

Center, Israel. She serves as a visiting lecturer at the University of Haifa, Israel, and at the University of Agder, Norway. Her research focuses on subjects relating to international marketing management and marketing strategy with a strong emphasis on innovation. Her research has been published in the *Journal of World Business*, *Technovation*, and *International Marketing Review*, among others.

Margarida Fontes is a researcher at the National Laboratory of Energy and Geology (LNEG) and associate researcher at DINÂMIA'CET-IUL, the Centre for Socioeconomic Change and Territorial Studies in Portugal. She has a PhD in Management of Innovation from the University of Manchester, UK. Her main research interests are knowledge dynamics, sustainability transitions and scientific entrepreneurship. She conducts research on the process of knowledge production and dissemination in emerging fields (biotechnology, renewable energies), with particular emphasis on the roles played by new firms and by scientists, and on networks as locus of knowledge circulation and innovation. She has published and participated in national and international research projects in these fields.

Susan Freeman, Associate Professor, is the Director of the International Business Research Group (IBRG) and is the Discipline Leader for International Business in the Adelaide Business School, at the University of Adelaide, Australia. She is the Vice-President of the Australian New Zealand International Business Association (ANZIBA). Susan took on the role as co-editor of *International Marketing Review (IMR)* in 2013. Susan holds a PhD in international marketing (Monash University, Australia) and her research focus is international business strategy including early accelerated internationalizing smaller firms, international entrepreneurship, services internationalization, CSR and emerging markets, with a particular interest in the Asian region, and on qualitative research methodologies.

Mika Gabrielsson is Professor of International Business and Sales Management at the University of Eastern Finland. Prior to this position he served for ten years as Professor at Aalto University, where he is now an Adjunct Professor. Also, he is affiliated as a Visiting Professor at the University of Portsmouth, UK. His teaching covers areas such as international business and sales management in the global context, and research interests include, among others, rapid globalization. He has published over 150 articles in refereed international journals and other publications. He is a frequent reviewer in many journals and serves, for instance, on the editorial board of *Industrial Marketing Management*. Before joining the academic world he held several senior positions in purchasing and marketing of global high-tech companies.

Peter Gabrielsson is Professor of International Marketing at the University of Vaasa and Adjunct Professor of International Business at Aalto University School of Business, Finland. His teaching covers areas such as export and global marketing and his research interests include international entrepreneurship, globalization process of firms, born globals, globalizing internationals and global marketing strategies. He has led several large research projects such as the 'Born Globals: Growth Stages and Survival Project', financed by TEKES and published in journals including the *Journal of International Marketing*, *Industrial Marketing Management*, *International Business Review*, *Management International Review* and *International Marketing Review* as well as serving as editorial board member for the *Journal of International Marketing* and a reviewer in a number of international journals. He has extensive experience in senior management positions at Nokia and other global ICT firms.

Valeska V. Geldres is Professor of Marketing and is currently the Dean of the Law and Business Faculty at Universidad de La Frontera (Chile). Professor Geldres earned her PhD in Business Administration and Marketing from Universidad de Sevilla (Spain) and BA in Business Administration from Universidad Austral de Chile. She also completed a postdoctoral programme at the University of São Paulo (Brazil). Her research interests include international business, entrepreneurship, human capital and business history. She developed a born global firm and served as its export manager for Chilean products to Europe and the Middle East and currently serves as the CEO of this venture.

Geir Gripsrud has been Professor of Marketing at the BI Norwegian Business School since 1990. He has for several years served in various management positions in the school (e.g., Dean of Bachelor Studies, Dean of Master of Science Studies). His research interests initially focused on retailing and distribution channels, but he later turned more towards international business–related topics like exporting, FDI and country image. His research has appeared in journals such as *International Journal of Research in Marketing*, *International Journal of Physical Distribution & Logistics Management*, *Journal of International Business Studies* and *Journal of Business Research*.

Birgit Hagen is Assistant Professor of International Entrepreneurship and International Marketing at the University of Pavia. She received her PhDs from the Vienna University of Economics and Business and from the University of Pavia. Her research interests fall at the intersection of small firm internationalization and international entrepreneurship. Her work has been published in the *International Business Review*, *Management International Review* as well as in several book chapters. She received the Palgrave Macmillan award for the best paper at the 2011 conference of the UK Chapter of the Academy of International Business, Edinburgh for a paper co-authored with Antonella Zucchella.

Auke Hunneman is Associate Professor at BI Norwegian Business School, Oslo and Adjunct Associate Professor at the University of Stavanger, Norway. He also is Associate Dean for the Bachelor of International Marketing at BI Norwegian Business School. He obtained his PhD at the University of Groningen, the Netherlands. His research interests are retailing, store image, market response models, spatial econometrics, social networks, network dynamics, strategic alliances and marketing accountability.

Seung Hoon Jang, PhD (in Business, University of Nebraska-Lincoln), is an Assistant Professor of Management at the Bloomsburg University of Pennsylvania. He has served with the Samsung Economic Research Institute (SERI), the largest private think tank in Korea, as a research analyst. He has published several journal articles, led conference proceedings and presentations, discussing strategic management, technological innovation, entrepreneurship and global leadership practices. He is currently a member of Beta Gamma Sigma and Decision Science Institute.

Marian V. Jones is full Professor of International Business and Entrepreneurship at the Adam Smith Business School at the University of Glasgow, Scotland. Her research concerns the international growth and development of new and small firms. Her theoretical contributions reflect temporal and spatial aspects of internationalization, and draw on knowledge, capabilities and cognitive reasoning theories.

Saara Julkunen holds a DSc in Management of SMEs from the University of Eastern Finland (UEF). Currently, she is an Assistant Professor in International Sales and the Deputy Head of the Business School at UEF. Her teaching focuses on an extensive view of multifaceted international sales work and sales management in different kinds of companies and cross-cultural environments. She also does research related to sales processes, customer–seller relationship development, interorganizational collaboration and entrepreneurship in different sales organizations. She has participated in several EU projects established to fund sales education at the University of Eastern Finland. She has a business background as a hypermarket retailer and entrepreneur.

Jung Seek Kim, PhD (University of Texas at Dallas) is Associate Professor of Marketing at the College of Business at Bloomsburg University of Pennsylvania. His research interests include e-commerce/digital marketing, international marketing/emerging markets, information search/decision rules/choice behaviour, and cross-cultural difference in consumer behaviour.

Salman Kimiagari is a PhD candidate at the Business School of Laval University (FSA), Canada. He earned his Bachelor's degree in Industrial Management from the Faculty of Management of University of Tehran and MBA from the College of Engineering of the University of Tehran. He is a student member of the Interuniversity Research Centre on Enterprise Networks, Logistics and Transportation (CIRRELT). Since 2012, he is affiliated as lecturer with FSA in several courses such as operation management, international business and strategic management. For over six years he also served as a consultant to industries, ministries and organizations in Iran. His research interest areas are focused on international business, market engineering, business design and operation research. He has published several articles in refereed international journals and conferences. He is a frequent reviewer for several international conferences.

Olli Kuivalainen, DSc (Economics), is Professor of International Marketing and Entrepreneurship at the School of Business at Lappeenranta University of Technology (LUT), Finland. His expertise covers broad areas of international business, marketing, entrepreneurship and technology management and their interfaces. He has published in journals such as *Journal of World Business*, *Journal of International Marketing*, *Technovation*, *International Marketing Review*, *International Business Review*, *International Journal of Production Economics* and *Journal of International Entrepreneurship*, among others.

Miria Lazaris was awarded her PhD in International Business from Monash University, Australia in 2011. Her research interests include born global SMEs, internationalization, top management, networks, food and beverage sector, entrepreneurship and international business theory. Miria is a Teaching Associate within the Faculty of Business and Economics at Monash University. In addition to her work at Monash University, Miria is an Adjunct Lecturer for the Master of International Business programme at the University of Adelaide.

Leonidas C. Leonidou (MSc, PhD University of Bath, UK) is a Professor of Marketing at the University of Cyprus and a Visiting Principal Research Fellow in Marketing at Leeds University Business School, UK. Before joining academia, he worked as a marketing analyst/consultant for many companies in the Middle East, Eastern Europe and Eastern Mediterranean. His current research interests are in the areas of international marketing/purchasing, relationship marketing, strategic marketing, socially responsible marketing and marketing in emerging economies. He has published extensively in these fields and his articles appeared in both academic journals and practitioner journals. He has also written chapters and books on marketing. He is on the editorial boards of various journals.

Nicolas Li has recently received his PhD in Management from the University of Glasgow Adam Smith Business School, where he grew his research interests in international entrepreneurship and SMEs internationalization. He also attended the University of Aberdeen, UK (MSc), and the University of British Columbia, Canada (BA). He has recently published in the *International Marketing Review*.

Irene Mandl is Research Manager at the European Foundation for the Improvement of Living and Working Conditions (Eurofound). She works in policy-oriented socioeconomic research in the field of employment and the labour market as well as entrepreneurship. Some of her major research topics refer to small and medium-sized enterprises (SMEs), restructuring and structural change, business start-ups and transfers, internationalization, specific forms of entrepreneurship (e.g., one-person enterprises, family businesses, ethnic entrepreneurship, born globals), corporate social responsibility and HR management (e.g., skills development, age management, financial employee participation etc.). She investigates policies and strategies of public authorities and social partners related to a wide spectrum of employment issues as well as on company practices regarding labour aspects.

Izaias Martins (PhD) is Associate Professor at EAFIT University, Colombia. He received his PhD in Entrepreneurship and Business Management and his Master's in Entrepreneurship, Strategy and Management from the Autonomous University of Barcelona (Spain). He has participated in several research projects of recognized institutions such as the Global Entrepreneurship Monitor (GEM), the Institute of Regional and Metropolitan Studies of Barcelona and the Latin American Association of Schools of Management and Accounting (ALAFEC). Research interests include entrepreneurship, intrapreneurship, international entrepreneurship and informal venture capital.

István Molnár was educated at the Corvinus University Budapest (CUB), Hungary, where he received his MSc and Dr oec. (Economics) degrees. He completed his postdoctoral studies in Darmstadt, Germany, and took part in different research projects in Germany in the 1980s and 1990s. In

1996, he received his CSc (PhD) degree in Economic Sciences from the Hungarian Academy of Sciences, and in 2012 his Dr Habil. in Informatics Science from the CUB. His main fields of interest are mathematical modelling, software technology and application of IT/IS in business and education. Dr Molnár's educational activities include teaching in different higher educational institutions in Europe, the Middle East and in the USA.

Benoit Montreuil is Professor in the Faculty of Business at Université Laval in Québec, Canada, since 1988. He holds the Canada Research Chair in Interconnected Business Engineering. He has previously held positions at UQTR, Canada and Purdue University, USA. He is a member of the Interuniversity Research Centre on Enterprise Networks, Logistics and Transportation (CIRRELT). He teaches global business design in Laval's MBA programme. His main research interests lie in developing concepts, methodologies and technologies for creating, optimizing, transforming and enabling businesses and value creation networks to thrive in a fast-evolving world. He has published 250 scientific publications and delivered 240 scientific communications. He has extensive advisory, entrepreneurial and collaborative research experience with industry.

Nurul Efifi Mohamad Ngasri (Fifie) is a PhD student of International Business (IB) supervised by Associate Professor Susan Freeman (IB), Dr Chris Medlin (Marketing) at the University of Adelaide and Dr Miria Lazaris (IB), Monash University, Australia. Her primary research interest revolves around international entrepreneurship, more importantly on SMEs from the emerging markets and how their survivability factors may differ from SMEs from the developed markets. As a consequence, her research is primarily driven by network dynamics of SMEs, effectuation and causation principles of entrepreneurship and dynamic capabilities of firms.

Alojzy Z. Nowak, PhD, is a Professor of Economics, educated in Poland, USA, England, Belgium and Germany. He is currently Vice-Rector of the University of Warsaw. He teaches in Poland, France, England, South Korea, Nepal, China, Taiwan and USA and is on the editorial boards of Polish and international journals. He is author or co-author of more than 200 publications, and former adviser to the Polish prime minister. He is currently on the supervisory boards of several Polish and international banks and businesses, adviser of many Polish and international PhD students and leader and primary investigator of many EU and NATO grants.

Jonathan Ohn, PhD (Lehigh University, USA), is a Professor and Department Chair of Finance at the College of Business of Bloomsburg University of Pennsylvania. His teaching areas include investments, financial management and international finance and he has appeared twice each in *Who's Who Among America's Teachers?* and *Who's Who in American Education?* He has publications in finance and economics both in national and international journals – *Economics Letters, The Econometrics Journal, Business and Economic Review, New York Economic Review, Journal of Business and Economics, Northeastern Journal of Business, Economics, and Technology*, and *International Journal of Manpower*, among others.

Kaisu Puumalainen, DSc (Technology), is Professor in Technology Research in the School of Business at Lappeenranta University of Technology, Finland. Her areas of research interest include entrepreneurship, innovation, strategic orientations, sustainability and internationalization. She has published more than 50 articles on these issues in *Journal of the Academy of Marketing Science, International Journal of Research in Marketing, International Business Review, European Journal of Marketing* and *Technovation*, among others.

Markus Raatikainen is a project researcher and lecturer at the University of Eastern Finland. He holds a Master's degree in Economics and Business Administration, and since 2013 he has been a PhD student in the International Business and Sales Management programme. His main research interests are decision-making logic and networking in international new ventures, and he is especially interested in the internationalization processes of high-technology firms originating in small, open economies. He has presented his research at international conferences such as the annual conferences of the European International Business Academy and the Industrial Marketing and Purchasing Group. Based on these conference research papers, he is currently finishing his first article for publication.

Alex Rialp-Criado (PhD) is Associate Professor in Business Organization at the Business Department of Universitat Autònoma de Barcelona, Spain. His research focuses on strategic internationalization of SMEs, export marketing management and international entrepreneurship (born globals/international new ventures) from both developed and emerging/transition economies, and also investigates knowledge and IT management. He is author and/or co-author of different books, book chapters and articles published in both leading national and international academic journals such as *Journal of International Marketing, International Business Review, International Marketing Review, European Management Journal, Transformations in Business and Economics, European Journal of International Management, Advances in International Marketing, Journal of International Entrepreneurship, Journal of Knowledge Management*, and

Journal of Global Marketing, among others. Dr Rialp-Criado also serves as editorial review board member and ad hoc reviewer for different academic journals.

Sami Saarenketo is Professor of International Marketing at the School of Business, at Lappeenranta University of Technology, Finland. His primary areas of research interest are international marketing and entrepreneurship in technology-based small firms. He has published on these issues in *Journal of World Business*, *International Business Review*, *Management International Review*, *European Business Review*, *European Journal of Marketing* and *Journal of International Entrepreneurship*, among others.

Saeed Samiee (PhD, Ohio State University) is the Collins Professor of Marketing and International Business at the University of Tulsa, USA. Prior to joining TU as the Director of the International Management Center, he was a member of the faculty at the University of South Carolina. His research is focused on topics related to international marketing and business. His most recent research addresses deliberate product cannibalization by Western and Chinese firms operating in China. He has contributed to scholarly journals in marketing and international business as an author and a member of 13 editorial review boards. He has been a visiting scholar and has lectured at business schools in over a dozen countries.

Rotem Shneor is an Associate Professor in International Management at the University of Agder's School of Business and Law in Norway. He also serves as the Academic Director of the Centre for Entrepreneurship at the University of Agder, and as the Head of the Nordic Crowdfunding Alliance. His research focuses on subjects relating to international and cross-cultural marketing, Internet marketing, and internationalization, as well as cognitive aspects of entrepreneurship, entrepreneurship education, new venture finance and crowdfunding. His research has been published in *Cross Cultural Management*, *Entrepreneurship and Regional Development* and *Journal of Product & Brand Management*, among others.

Vítor Corado Simões is Professor at ISEG – Lisbon School of Economics and Management, University of Lisbon, Portugal. His main research areas are international management and innovation management, namely MNCs, MNC subsidiaries and born globals. He coordinated the research project on 'COTEC Portugal: The Innovative SME Network' (2010), and been member of the international evaluation team of research at the University of Uppsala, Sweden (2012). He has great international experience as consultant to OECD, UNIDO and the European Commission (chair of the CREST/EU Working Group on SMEs and Innovation, and member of the advisory team to Directorate-General for Research and Innovation on Regional Innovation Strategies – 2013). He has been involved in PROINNO/TrendChart on Innovation and is now correspondent to the Research & Innovation Observatory policies. Professor Simões served as President of the European International Business Academy in 1993 and is now member of the Fellows of the Academy.

Carl Arthur Solberg entered academia after ten years in business. His PhD was earned at Strathclyde University, Glasgow. His publications centre on internationalization and international marketing and more specifically strategy development in globalizing markets. He has won best paper awards in the *Journal of International Marketing* (1997 and 2002) and European International Business Academy (EIBA) (2008) and was ranked the second most prolific researcher in international marketing in 2008 in *Asia Pacific Journal of Management*. He sits on the board of directors of several SMEs engaged in international markets.

M. Cristina Stoian is a lecturer in International Business at Brunel University, London. Her research interests include SME internationalization, international entrepreneurship, international business-to-business relationships and professional business advisers for SMEs.

Lasse Torkkeli is a post-doctoral researcher since 2014 at the School of Business, in Lappeenranta University of Technology, Finland. His PhD dissertation, completed in 2013, examined the concept of network competence in internationally operating small and medium-sized enterprises (SMEs), in particular its development and influence on internationalization outcomes of Finnish and Russian SMEs. His current research interests relate to SME internationalization, dynamic capabilities in the context of international business, business networks and networking, and cultural aspects in international business, particularly in business-to-business interaction. He has previously published, for example, in the *Journal of International Entrepreneurship* and in the *European Management Journal*.

Yancy Vaillant (MA, PhD) is Associate Professor at ESC-Rennes School of Business (EQUIS, AMBA, AACSB), France and the Universitat Autònoma de Barcelona, Spain. He directed the Global Entrepreneurship Monitor (GEM) for Catalonia and has collaborated with the OECD on topics related to territorial policy and governance. He has participated in several research projects for the European, Spanish or Catalan administrations that study and formulate policy recommendations in areas related to territorial strategy, entrepreneurship and the promotion of innovation-based development. Vaillant is a graduate of Concordia University (Canada) and earned his PhD from the University of Barcelona. He has postgraduate certificates from both Växjö University (Sweden) and the

MIT Sloan School of Management (USA). He was also trained as an entrepreneurship educator at Babson College (USA).

Antonella Zucchella is Full Professor of Marketing at the University of Pavia, Italy and Senior Scholar at the Anglia Ruskin University in Cambridge, UK. She is also visiting Professor at the University of Strasbourg, France. She is the author of several articles and books on firm internationalization and entrepreneurship and is involved both in national and in European research projects on international marketing and on entrepreneurship.

Foreword
Michael R. Czinkota

It is a pleasure to write this foreword for the *Handbook of Research on International Entrepreneurial Strategy: Improving SME Performance Globally*, edited by my good friends V.H. Manek Kirpalani and Pervez N. Ghauri. This work makes an important contribution to the knowledge and literature of the international plans and activities of smaller-sized corporations. These smaller-sized firms are different from the larger players and deserve such specially focused research.[1]

We hear much about the growth of world trade, globalization and imbalanced distribution of incomes. Yet, how does one understand all the issues, thoughts and arguments involved? Who decides what information and approaches to use and how to use them? How does one develop a time frame and context for addressing entrenched or novel issues? Misunderstandings can be rife. Only a few decades ago, Bill Gates of Microsoft, on a visit to Georgetown University, pronounced that there was no need for his company to have a Washington office. Oh ye of little faith – today the firm has 'seen the light' and supports a major operation in Washington, DC.

In order to learn from the past, we must understand what was done before us, appreciating the context in which changes occur. Over the past half-century, international business and trade have mushroomed in importance, and, in the last two decades, have reached and passed a tipping point. Social and economic shifts have taken international business issues from the backroom discussions of experts to highly public and visible discussions around the world. From ignorance, we have often entered into the stage of too much information.[2] A new sense of transparency and accountability offers new directions to businesses and their executives.

The role of governments has changed drastically, first shrinking in the 1980s and 1990s, but now coming back with a vengeance, dictating the direction and strength of international business activities. After decades

---

[1] Czinkota, M.R. and W. Johnston (1985), 'Exporting: does sales volume make a difference – reply', *Journal of International Business Studies*, **16**(2), 157–61.

[2] Czinkota, M.R. (2015), 'Marketing Management: TMI', Summer, www.ama.org/publications/MarketingNews/Pages/tmi.aspx.

of aiming for more open markets, even the liberal trading nations and the trade-supporting politicians within them, develop a tendency to restrict imports and encourage exports. In blatant disregard to the fact that someone's export has to be someone else's import, governments expect to be able to protect home industries and keep their own economies stable and revitalized, without any repercussions from abroad.[3]

Over the long haul, we can distinguish patterns of ebb and flow in the international business and trade arena. Publicly, we are often told one thing – such as the need for the free flow of international trade – but when looking at actual decision patterns, actions often differ from pronouncement. Just like Saint Augustin who prayed in about 400 AD, 'Lord, make me chaste, but not yet', policy-makers and government executives often develop strong, non-transparent measures to delay or even defeat the easing of international trade flows and innovations. There are also times when change cannot happen quickly enough, when everyone aims to streamline and fast-track legislation and international accords by limiting the influence of insightful and deliberate legislative votes.

There are the subtle and not so subtle efforts at sanctions and disruptions of trade flows, yet they are often met by opposing interest levels, which try to negate such restrictions. Repeatedly we see one side that is losing contracts blaming it all on the corruption and nepotism of the winners. Particularly in the international arena, cultural differences can lead to very different ways of doing business. Just think of countries where competitiveness plays a key role, and compare them to nations where closeness to and support of family members is crucial for business. Business decisions and partners are likely to be evaluated in a very different fashion. In such instances, administrative actions and laws can be seen either as rigorous structural supports for economic development, or as substantial barriers to growth.

The use and meaning of terminology also has major effects. For example, for decades, the award of the term 'most favoured nation (MFN)' status in international trade negotiations has led to complaints, demonstrations and even street battles because it was seen (incorrectly) as special pereferential treatment. In spite of no substantial changes, the problem has now gone away, since governments have changed the terminology and only speak of 'normal trade relations' (NTR), a goal that seems to be acceptable to all. Definitions that shape our understanding of core issues such as 'fairness', 'market gaps', 'dumping' and 'natural' can be

---

3 Czinkota, M.R. and I. Ronkainen (2012), *International Marketing* (10th edition), Cincinnati, OH: Cengage.

changed or amended, and thus present us with new realities. Terminology can also be used to demonize or alienate trading partners, with terms such as 'freedom fries' which, in years of US–French alienation substituted for 'French fries'.

Nowadays, one discusses and often repositions the meaning of key business pillars such as risk, competition, profit and ownership, which perhaps gradually prepares us for a new environment. Many of today's business executives discover that their activities are but one integral component of society. Politics, security and religion are only some of the other dimensions that historically, and maybe again in the future, are held in possibly higher esteem by society at large than economics and business. Those who neglect holistic perspectives and argue based on business principles alone may increasingly find themselves on the losing side.

We all need to work on including the context of the future in our considerations. Just consider how different things will be in a mere 25 or 50 years – keeping in mind that the ballpoint pen only came to the US market in 1945, the computer game Pong only entered the market in 1972, and email on personal computers only advanced in the late 1980s. Will we look as retro to our descendants as our ancestors appear to us today (if we bother to look)? Yet, at the same time we all are only a brief constant in a world of change, and even then we reserve the right to change our mind.

We complain about the new phenomenon of pirates in Somalia, though that profession was very popular during Roman times in Sicily (which is where Pompeius earned his early public spurs when he brought about the pirate's demise). We highlight the disruptions from terrorism but neglect that in 1100 the Crusaders had been writing home about their fear of terror. We debate new approaches to teaching and communication, but don't stop to think what effect Gutenberg's printing press, wireless telegraphy or the introduction of radio had on monks, business and society respectively. We deplore the differentiation of groups based on religion, but conveniently forget the impact of Torquemada and the Inquisition, of Luther's theses nailed on the church doors of Wittenberg, and of the persecution of Jews or Mormons.

One of former Secretary of Defense Donald Rumsfeld's policy pronouncements was: 'There are known knowns, which are things we know that we know. There are known unknowns; that is to say, there are things that we now know we don't know. But there are also unknown unknowns; these are things of which we do not know that we don't know'. For each individual the applicability of these categories depends on personal context, knowledge and exposure. This book by Ghauri and Kirpalani allows the reader to partake in all of these three categories, by providing insights into the structure and strategies of smaller-sized firms from a policy, academic and business perspective. In addition, the perspectives presented are not unilaterally based on one nation alone, but are broad based to include countries such as Finland, Hungary, Italy, Scotland, Spain and South Korea. To paraphrase the philosopher Ludwig von Wittgenstein: 'If you are not part of the discussion you are like a boxer who never goes into the ring'. It is important to be in the ring. This very special book lets you view and understand the crucial nexus of international marketing, particularly market entry, growth and government activities, and allows you an opportunity to become part of the thinking, planning and discussion. Ghauri and Kirpalani have done very important work. The opportunities offered by this book are substantial and you can make them part of your personal sphere. Happy Reading!

Georgetown University
Washington, DC
March 2015

Foreword

Stefan Schmid

When academics, practitioners or journalists refer to internationalization and globalization, they often have large multinational corporations (MNCs) in mind, such as General Electric, Volkswagen or L'Oréal. However, many small and medium-sized enterprises (SMEs) represent international or global players as well. Being the backbone of most economies and societies, SMEs are not only affected by intensified competition, they are also drivers of cross-border trade and foreign direct investment.

The present volume puts SMEs and their internationalization at the focus of our interest. Under the editorship and guidance of Pervez N. Ghauri and V.H. Manek Kirpalani, nearly 40 researchers have contributed to a better understanding and explaining of crucial facets of SME internationalization. Hence, the *Handbook of Research on International Entrepreneurial Strategy: Improving SME Performance Globally* can provide scholars and managers with highly valuable insights and experiences drawn from a wide spectrum of countries, such as Finland, Israel, Italy, Norway, Poland, Scotland or Spain.

The book chapters cover the initial phase of firm foundation, including many fundamental aspects, such as the personality of the founder, his or her entrepreneurial mindset, or his or her innovative behaviour. They also discuss the subsequent phases of growth, resulting from many decisions such as how, where and when to expand. The international dimension of growth is particularly important to the editors and to the authors of the single chapters, covering phenomena such as the seemingly simple (but often neglected) exporting firm, the born international firm, the born regional firm or the born global firm. Be it in the foundation or the growth phase, SMEs, even more than large corporations, are dependent on individuals who inspire the firm, who provide guidance to the firm and who manage the firm. Therefore, it is often the individual decision-maker or the group of individual decision-makers, such as a family, who matter much more to performance than in other types of firms.

SMEs are usually also embedded in a set of relationships helping them to expand. In various chapters of this volume, the authors show in an excellent way that many SMEs strongly depend on social relationships with other individuals and that they benefit from the tacit knowledge accumulated from their respective social networks. Many contributions also stress the fact that SMEs are part of wider networks, including alliance partners, governments, political institutions, or export promotion agencies. Neglecting the importance of embeddedness would mean not to fully understand the antecedents and consequences of SME internationalization.

If you are interested in recent findings in the field of entrepreneurship or international business (or even both), this is essential reading for you. I am sure that you will enjoy studying the chapters of this volume and that you will appreciate the thoughtful inspiration you will receive for your practical action, your scholarly research or your thinking about SMEs and their role in the global economy.

ESCP Europe Business School
Berlin
March 2015

Preface

The *Handbook of Research on International Entrepreneurial Strategy: Improving SME Performance Globally* is the result of a book project undertaken after discussion with Ben Booth of Edward Elgar Publishing. All three of us recognized that the SME international entrepreneurial strategy and performance research field had reached a growth point where definitions, parameters and more theory needed to be developed for the field to expand. Researchers, practitioners and policy-makers were increasingly showing keen interest in such expansion. Also, we had been working and publishing articles in this field and were widely known for our work.

This Handbook offers very good coverage of the origin and evolution of SME international entrepreneurial strategy and performance, definitions and the changing history of this sector. It goes on to discuss the importance of internationalizing SMEs in different parts of the world, and various research areas still to be investigated in this field, including the effects of different cultures on the origin and growth of SMEs. Thereafter, the international entrepreneurial strategies that SMEs can adopt are outlined. The text focuses on the different types of internationalizing SMEs that have emerged, ranging from the traditional to born globals, including international new ventures.

The text also analyses internationalizing growth paths of SMEs as affected by different factors. These factors include the interactions of entrepreneurship and internationalization growth, aspects of knowledge accumulation, application and management, and the influence of the Internet. Also, the impact of utilization of large channels, of alliances and networks, and of large partner MNCs is covered. Further, the institutional support available in selected countries is discussed.

A chosen group of leading scholars and researchers have written contributions to this book. They were invited due to their expertise and to reflect the diversity of perspectives. The book has two main parts. The first part begins with a chapter giving an intellectual overview and synopsis of the sector. The second part contains a wide-ranging chapter on conclusions and future research areas. These two chapters are written by us, the two author/editors of the book.

Part I of the book deals with international entrepreneurial behaviour of the SME and the development of theoretical and empirical research. The overview chapter mentioned above is followed by nine contributor chapters. The sub-areas covered are international entrepreneurial causation strategy versus effectuation based on internal founder and firm-specific strategy; the influence of marketing intelligence and adaptation efforts on international performance; international networking strategies; marketing strategies of international new ventures and the export behaviour of new ventures from small and open economies; the simultaneous effects of innovativeness and export behaviour; managerial attitude as an antecedent of network development for internationalizing SMEs, outlining a process view of the internationalization of new ventures; and last how to enhance the competitiveness of an East European economy using SME innovativeness as a stimulator.

Part II of the book covers internationalization of EU SMEs, using export promotion programmes to assist internationalizing SMES, and the role of government in the same endeavour in emerging economies. Then there are four chapters on international entrepreneurship among Finnish, Italian, Scottish and Hungarian firms respectively, followed finally by the conclusions and future research chapter.

Overall we are happy to present the book to all academics, practitioners, policy-makers and others who are interested in the growing recognition of the importance of internationalizing entrepreneurial SMEs, specifically to those who wish to learn more about how these SMEs confer a multipronged and beneficial impact on economic growth, innovativeness, knowledge, human skill and ability development on the societies and global networks in which they flourish.

Pervez N. Ghauri and V.H. Manek Kirpalani
2015

Acknowledgements

Our deepest appreciation is expressed to the people who have helped in the development of this book. The first group are the numerous talented professionals who have contributed various chapters and whose names are cited in the text. We also wish to thank our institutions, the John Molson School of Business, Concordia University, Montreal, Aalto University School of Economics, and the University of the West Indies, St. Augustine, Trinidad and Tobago, King's College London and Birmingham Business School.

We are indebted to Susan Krieger, Associate Professor, Mansfield University of Pennsylvania, who helped to organize the manuscript. Our sincere appreciation and thanks to Ben Booth, Commissioning Editor Edward Elgar Publishing for his continuous encouragement of our ideas and thoroughness in helping us to bring the manuscript to publication.

Finally our warmest thanks to our families: V.H. Manek Kirpalani to his wife Prakash, children Tara and Arjun, Tara's husband Sundeep, her children Siona, Rahul and Sarina, and Arjun's children Melina and Natasha; and Pervez N. Ghauri to Tyaba and Saad Ghauri for their understanding throughout the project.

PART I

INTERNATIONAL ENTREPRENEURIAL STRATEGY AND BEHAVIOUR

1. Overview

V.H. Manek Kirpalani and Pervez N. Ghauri

DEFINING THE TERMS

Internationalization and Globalization

Internationalization is the expansion of economic activities beyond a country's border. Internationalization has been underway for centuries, but the pace is quickening. Prior to the days of empires, international trade had been about final goods and based on absolute advantage. Finished final products that were not produced or were produced in insufficient quantities in one's own country were imported, and products produced abundantly were exported (Vernon, 1966; Ghauri and Cateora, 2014). The advent of empires changed the balance of benefits. Conquered colonies supplied cheap resources on which value was added in dominant 'mother' countries. The finished products were partially consumed at home, while the rest were exported, thus creating wealth in the mother countries. Many firms in the mother countries became large and controlled operations abroad, for example the East India Company and the British American Tobacco Company. These firms became the precursors of what became known as MNEs – multinational enterprises.

After World War II, there was a surge of foreign direct investment (FDI). Many parts of Europe were devastated. As North American firms were untouched by such ravages, they saw a window of opportunity. FDI flowed to Western Europe and Latin America. Resources and product development gave them an internally transferable advantage that allowed them to overcome competition from local firms. Also, they became the main study of much international business literature. Basically, internationalization is the natural consequence of the growth of the firm. As the firm grows, it grows out of the home market and looks for further growth by crossing national borders. Internationalization has thus been subject to many studies and the topic has been studied from several angles: rate, speed, gradual stepwise approach versus born global and advantages and disadvantages of different entry modes (Buckley and Ghauri, 1999 and 2015).

Gradually, internationalization has converted into globalization for most MNEs. Advances in information technology and an increasing interdependence in the world have made foreign markets a vital part of the strategic planning for large organizations, the MNEs. The infrastructure that permits globalization is becoming more powerful. There are several pillars of this infrastructure that are mutually reinforcing this trend. The first pillar is the expanding scale, liquidity, mobility and integration of the capital markets. Second is the growing ability worldwide to leverage on knowledge, talent and technology. Firms like Coca-Cola, Microsoft and Hyatt Hotels are gaining much from a business model that minimizes their investment in fixed assets and maximizes their ability to leverage brands, standards, management skills and intellectual property across the global arena (Underwood, 2004). Third is the liberalization of national regulations and lowering of economic barriers to trade, capital flows and technology links. Fourth, is the worldwide deregulation of the telecommunication industry that has cut the marginal cost of computing and communication almost to zero. Fifth, is the growth of the global labour pool that in the next 10–12 years will absorb nearly two billion workers from emerging markets, who will cost less, and will not be much less productive than their counterparts in rich lands. Therefore, the unit cost of production will go down dramatically. Sixth, is the economic restructuring that followed the integration of Central and Eastern Europe into the EU, as well as the expansion of markets in China, India and Asia, specifically in the ASEAN group. Globalization is thus a phenomenon mainly driven by economic forces, which has resulted in liberalization and integration of capital markets, spatial reorganization of production and international trade. The slicing of the manufacturing process into multiple partial operations can be carried out at different locations and consumed globally (Buckley and Ghauri, 2004).

It is estimated that today the motivation of reaching new customers or looking for optimal locations for different parts of their value chain explains perhaps the bulk of FDI. Many are in industries such as autos and fast-moving consumer goods (FMCGs) where foreign firms set up locally to do better business or in service industries where a local presence is beneficial. MNEs have been building plants in low-wage countries and also then exporting the finished goods to other countries including the home market in addition to producing products for local consumers in the host country. Although business is the primary engine driving globalization, international organizations have arisen to coordinate policy among nations on global issues such as trade, the environment, sustainable development, health and crisis management. Further the global marketplace is being institutionalized through the creation of a series of multilateral entities. Overall, globalization is leading to integrated global markets, intensifying competition, diminishing control, shortening product cycles and increasing uncertainty. The new global economy is one in which most firms are continuously vulnerable.

Strategy

Very few organizations these days would admit to lacking a strategy. If they are not doing well, the usual statement is that we lack a good strategy. But over time the word 'strategy' seems to have been drained of focused meaning by overuse. A foremost historian of military strategy has tried to find a workable definition (Freedman, 2013). A recurrent theme is the dichotomy between strategies based on the application of superior force and those based on the application of guile, the latter signifying cleverness that defeats brute force. *The Art of War*, an ancient Chinese military treatise attributed to Sun Tzu, a high-ranking military general and strategist, has had an influence on Eastern and Western military thinking, business tactics, legal strategy and beyond; his theme was that 'all war is based on deception' (Sun Tzu, 2003). He advocated stratagem and finesse rather than the 'chance of arms' (Ghauri and Fang, 2001). His teachings are still used in business schools and military academies today. Another great strategist who advocated deceit and psychological manipulation is Niccolò Machiavelli ([1532] 1961), who is also still studied.

But the concept of strategy as it was usually understood by the end of the twentieth century was as a way of uniting operational ability in the military sphere with political objectives. As Carl von Clausewitz, a great Prussian strategist put it: 'War is not merely an act of policy but continuation of political intercourse carried on with other means' (von Clausewitz [1932–43] 1984, p. 87). The belief is in the centrality of a victory that compels an opponent to submit to one's will. This is examined in its three main forms, one being the 'strategy of force' from von Clausewitz to nuclear game theory and the rise of asymmetric warfare. The second is 'strategy from below', which looks at political varieties such as Karl Marx, who saw himself as the 'General Staff' of the downtrodden. The third is 'strategy from above', which examines the development of big business strategy.

In modern times the pursuit of decisive victory has been undermined by the mutual destructive power of nuclear weapons and the frustrations from counterinsurgency operations. The same is true in politics and business; initial success is hardly ever decisive. Strategy is not a grander name for a plan that moves you forward in predetermined steps. A German general, Moltke, said 'No plan survives contact with the enemy'. Or as boxer Mike Tyson said 'Everyone has a plan 'til they get punched in the mouth'. The present authors conclude that it may be better to look at strategy as a form of script, which incorporates the possibility of chance events, attempts to anticipate the interactions of many players over a long time, and is open-ended.

Global business strategies in the twentieth century

Let us now turn to global business strategies. In the earlier twentieth century, firms expanding internationally were categorized as resource seekers, market seekers and efficiency seekers (Dunning, 1988, 2000). At a later time, firms emerged that were market adaptors and market integrators. In the former case, firms gained the ability to adapt to specific geographic areas to obtain the benefits of scope and specialization. At the core of the multilocal approach is the privileged local access stemming from large local investments. ABB, Nestlé, Shell and Unilever took this approach internationally. One of the first multilocals was arguably the Swedish Match Company, who owned or controlled match factories in many different countries.

Later, in the 1960s a different type of firm, the global marketer, began to emerge, one aiming to create global markets for specific products. These global marketers created global demand and established global standards (Levitt, 1983). Boeing used scale in airframes and Canon used specialization in 35 mm cameras to satisfy foreign markets without making large foreign investments (Bryan and Fraser, 1999). More recently, firms have been converging around a global or transnational model that combines the best aspects of each approach (Buckley and Ghauri, 2004). This model relies on greater internal integration to capture global specialization and scale advantages, and on local approaches to gain privileged access. However, in spite of the 'think global, act local' rhetoric, there appears to be little empirical evidence that this approach has led to regional market penetration levels similar to the ones obtained in the home region (Rugman and Verbeke, 2004). Therefore, MNEs holding differing market positions in various regions of the world indicates the need for different competitive strategies. It implies that international markets are characterized by incomplete integration that is regional and not global.

Global economic growth has resulted in a shift from capital-intensive to technology-intensive production to marketing-intensive strategies. Many historic determinants of cost and value advantages are disappearing, and are replaced by intangibles such as talent, intellectual property, brands and networks. Intangibles now enable a firm to 'buy' the access that used to come with geographical privilege. Intangibles lie at the heart of specialization and will be the scarce resources. These will be the branding, configuration and entrepreneurial capabilities that generate enormous competitive advantage (Ghauri et al., 2011). Thus Microsoft wins large returns from Windows and Apple generates huge profits from iPhone.

SMEs and Globalization

There is a wide range of definitions and measures of SMEs, varying between many countries and also between different sources reporting SME (small and medium-sized company) statistics. However, the most common basis for definition is employment, and here again, there is variation in defining the upper and lower size limit of an SME. Despite this variance, a large number of sources, including the European Union, define an SME as having a cut-off range of 0–250 employees. Some of the other commonly used criteria are total net assets, sales and investment level. SMEs account for 60 to 70 per cent of jobs in most OECD countries, with a particularly large share in Italy and Japan, and a relatively smaller share in the United States (Ghauri and Park, 2012). Throughout they also account for a disproportionately large share of new jobs, especially in those countries that have displayed a strong employment record, including the United States, United Kingdom and the Netherlands. Some evidence also points to the importance of age, rather than size, in job creation: young firms generate more than their share of employment (OECD, 2000). Table 1.1 indicates that SME employees are around two-thirds of the total labour force in the majority of countries. Further, that the SME sector's contribution to GDP is significant in most countries.

Obviously very few SMEs can be termed global companies in the sense of having a significant market share in many countries of the world. The word *globally* in the context of the title of this book refers to the comparative study of the international performance of SMEs from different countries. We believe that the comparative study of such SMEs will add immense value for researchers and managers, who will be able to compare the performance and the reasons for SMEs internationalizing in different ways and at different levels and speeds from different nations. The parameters defining SMEs vary in many countries. It is useful to draw these out as they often influence the type and extent to which strategies can be developed.

Born Globals

Around the turn of the millennium, several studies appeared on 'born globals' (BGs) (see, for example, Gabrielsson and Kirpalani, 2004). These studies refer to small firms with unique technology, superior design or innovative products/services, know-how, systems or other specialized

Table 1.1 Firm size and employment/GDP share

Nation	(1) GDP/Capita in US$	(2) SME250	(3) SMEOFF	(4) SME_GDP	(5) INFORMAL	(6) INFO_GDP
Albania	744.077	9.49				
Argentina	7483.77	70.18	70.18	53.65		21.80
Australia	20930.40	50.60		23.00		15.30
Austria	29619.35	66.10	66.10	16.00		10.45
Azerbaijan	558.29	5.34	5.34			47.20
Belarus	2522.94	4.59	4.59	9.00		16.65
Belgium	27572.35	69.25	69.25			18.65
Brazil	4326.55	59.80	59.80	49.21		33.40
Brunei	17983.77					69.40
Bulgaria	1486.74	50.01	50.01	39.29	63.00	31.25
Burundi	170.59		20.51			
Cameroon	652.67	20.27	20.27		61.40	
Canada	19946.50		58.58	57.20		11.75
Chile	4476.31	86.00	86.50		40.00	27.60
Colombia	2289.73	67.20	67.20	38.66	53.89	30.05
Costa Rica	3405.37		54.30			28.65
Côte d'Ivoire	746.01	18.70	18.70		59.6	
Croatia	4453.72	62.00	62.00		70.00	23.50
Czech Republic	5015.42	64.25	64.25			12.35
Denmark	34576.38	68.70	78.40	56.70	15.40	13.60
El Salvador	1608.91		52.00	44.05	46.67	
Estonia	3751.59	65.33	65.33			17.85
Finland	26813.53	59.15	59.15			13.30
France	27235.65	67.30	62.67	61.80	9.00	12.10
Georgia	736.79	7.32	7.32		36.67	53.10
Germany	30239.82	59.50	70.36	42.50	22.00	12.80

Ghana	377.18	51.61	51.61		71.76	
Greece	11593.57	86.50	74.00	27.40		24.20
Guatemala	1460.47	32.30	32.30	50.25		55.70
Honduras	706.01		27.60			46.70
Hong Kong, China	21841.82		61.50			13.00
Hungary	4608.26	45.90	45.90	56.80		29.85
Iceland	27496.90		49.60			
Italy	19218.46	79.70	73.00	58.50	39.00	22.20
Japan	42520.01	71.70	74.13	56.42		11.10
Kazakhstan	1496.16		12.92		40.00	28.25
Kenya	340.85	33.31	33.31		41.10	
Korea, Rep.	10507.69	76.25	78.88	45.90	19.62	38.00
Kyrgyzstan Rep.	972.25	63.22	63.22		40.00	
Latvia	2418.82	20.63				29.80
Luxembourg	45185.23	70.90	70.90	76.30		
Mexico	3390.17	48.48	48.48			38.05
Nicaragua	432.34		33.90			
Nigeria	256.55	16.72	16.72		48.85	76.00
Netherlands	27395.01	61.22	58.50	50.00		12.65
New Zealand	16083.78		59.28	35.00	9.20	10.15
Norway	33657.02		61.50			11.30
Panama	2998.63	72.00	72.00	60.12		51.05
Peru	2162.12	67.90	67.90	55.50	54.56	50.95
Philippines	1099.31	66.00	66.00	31.50	30.63	50.00
Poland	3391.08	63.00	61.81	48.73		16.45
Portugal	11120.81	79.90	81.55	67.25		16.20
Romania	1501.08	37.17	37.17	33.60	42.73	17.55
Russian Federation	2614.38	13.03	13.03	10.50	42.18	34.30
Singapore	22873.66		44.00			13.00
Slovak Rep.	3651.45	56.88	32.07	37.10		10.00

Table 1.1 (continued)

Nation	(1) GDP/Capita in US$	(2) SME250	(3) SMEOFF	(4) SME_GDP	(5) INFORMAL	(6) INFO_GDP
Slovenia	9758.43		20.26	16.65	31.00	
South Africa	3922.60		81.53			
Spain	15361.80	80.00	74.95	64.70	21.90	20.00
Sweden	27736.18	61.30	56.50	39.00	19.80	13.80
Switzerland	44716.54		75.25			8.55
Taiwan, China	12474.00	68.60	68.60		14.50	16.50
Tajikistan	566.44		35.91			
Tanzania	182.85	32.10	32.10		42.24	31.50
Thailand	2589.83	86.70	86.70			71.00
Turkey	2864.80	61.05	61.05	27.30		
Ukraine	1189.84	5.38	5.38	7.13		38.65
United Kingdom	19360.55	56.42	56.42	51.45		10.40
United States	28232.07		52.54	48.00		12.20
Vietnam	278.36	74.20	74.20	24.00		
Yugoslavia, Fed. Rep.	1271.12	44.40	44.40			
Zambia	418.93	36.63	36.63			
Zimbabwe	643.84	15.20	15.20		33.96	

Notes: The variables are defined as follows (values for variables 2 to 6 are 1990–99 averages): GDP/Capita is the real GDP per capita in USD; SME250 is the SME sector's share of formal employment when 250 employees is used as the cut-off for the definition of SME; SMEOFF is the SME sector's share of formal employment when the official country definition of SME is used; SME_GDP is the SME sector's contribution to GDP when the official country definition of SME is used; INFORMAL is the share of the shadow economy participants as a percentage of the formal sector labour force; INFO_GDP is the share of the shadow economy participants as a percentage of GDP.

Source: Ayyagari, M., T. Beck and A. Demirgüç-Kunt (2003), 'Small and medium enterprises across the globe: a new database', *World Bank Open Knowledge Repository*, Washington, DC. © World Bank; accessed 6 May 2015 at https://openknowledge.worldbank.org/handle/10986/18131. License: CC BY 3.0 IGO.

competence and had the vision to globalize rapidly. For born global firms the realization of entrepreneurial activities cannot be separated from the international business context and market in which they are being created. But the BG start-up lacks resources compared to the requirement of reaching world markets. Such resources include managerial and financial resources required for globalization and global marketing. These resources are difficult to gain from conventional sources because the BG has yet to prove its credibility as a profitable entity. The risk of not gaining profitability is even higher and these firms face even bigger challenges. Born globals probably fit in to Solberg and Askeland's description framework where theories of networks and alliances are seen as most useful to explain firms' internationalization strategies (Solberg and Askeland, 2006).

Performance

The word *performance* in context refers to success/failure in international markets. Such performance measurement is a combination of indicators relating to growth and to profitability – that is, a judgement on the mix of volume, value, rate of advancement and of sustainability of the operations. It is known that growth and profitability do not always correlate positively (Moreno and Casillas, 2008). The relationships between differentiated international strategic orientations leading to different strategic behaviours and the subsequent international performance of SMEs is a very important question for entrepreneurs and policy-makers. Our approach is that the international growth of an SME is derived from strategic behaviour, which is influenced by its entrepreneurial orientation. Operationally this is influenced by the SME's internal factors and those related to the external business environment (Elg et al., 2014).

Porter's model (1980) offers strategies of leadership and differentiation. These strategies seek to obtain sustainable competitive advantage, which will allow the business unit to obtain high levels of profitability. Compared to this typology two others can be considered for SMEs. The first one was proposed by Ansoff (1965): growth through new products or technologies, and growth through attention to new needs or new markets. The second one by Miles and Snow (1978) made a significant contribution about differentiated strategic orientations. They outline four strategic behaviour types:

- prospectors;
- analysers;
- defenders;
- reactors.

Prospectors emphasize innovations, explore new market opportunities, trends and technologies. Defenders have a conservative strategy – they follow the successful leader. Analysers are in between. Reactors have no consistency. The type of strategic orientation influences organizational behaviour that creates distinctive competencies that to varying degrees enable innovation or efficiency or quality or customer responsiveness, each of which can be leveraged to create a cost or differentiation advantage that influence growth and total performance.

An empirical analysis has aimed at finding different strategic types amongst internationalizing SMEs and their resulting international performance differentials (Hagen et al., 2012). The study found that a combination of customer orientation and niche strategy was effective in international performance (Luostarinen and Gabrielsson, 2006), and as a successful route to small firm internationalization (Zucchella et al., 2007). Cluster analysis and logistic regression showed that the probability of being a high performer in foreign markets for the entrepreneurial/growth-oriented type, the customer niche group and the production-oriented SMEs are almost five time higher as for firms lacking orientation and strategy. These high-performing SMEs are characterized by higher export ratios and more consistent growth rates and also measure things such as product performance and profits realized abroad (Hagen et al., 2012). In general, the results were corroborated by the findings from earlier internationalization literature (Buckley and Casson, 1976; Cavusgil, 1984).

Entrepreneurial Strategies

We think the word *entrepreneurial* is best understood in this context in conjunction with defining the words entrepreneurship and entrepreneur. Schumpeter, arguably the most famous economist in the field of entrepreneurship, focuses on the entrepreneurial function and not on the attributes of the person. His concepts include the introduction of new products, new production methods, the opening of new markets, new sources of supply and raw materials and the reorganization of an industry (Schumpeter and Clemence, 1989). Traditionally, researchers explain firms' growth through their opportunity seeking and entrepreneurial behaviour (Hayek, 1945; Penrose, 1959). It is thus the opportunity seeking that creates dynamics for firms and markets (Ghauri et al., 2005). Researchers such as Kirzner (1997) and Shane and Venkataraman (2000) ground their perspective in the behaviour of entrepreneurs instead of market mechanisms, thus turning from external market devices to internal factors such as opportunity-seeking behaviour.

In summary, the literature has brought out four main attributes of an entrepreneur. These are innovation capability, internal focus of control, risk-taking propensity and energy level. Innovation refers to creative thinking and acting in all sectors. Internal focus indicates the ability of a person to be self-reliant. The other two attributes are self-explanatory. Innovation is well recognized as an entrepreneurial capability. Research indicates that the other three attributes decrease in importance with increasing cultural distance from the Protestant model of independent achievement to collectivist group cultures.

THEORIES AND MODELS OF INTERNATIONALIZATION

Traditionally, internationalization and global research approaches have evolved around two schools of thought: the process school and the economic school. The former assumes the firm follows a behavioural approach (Cyert and March, 1963); the latter relies on the rational economics-dominated firm utilizing transaction costs (Williamson, 1975). Research emanating from the process approach focuses on the question of how internationalization happens. The rationale for a stage-wise development is very reasonable: via the export mode, the firm can test foreign market acceptance with minimal risk. If demand proves promising, the firm increases market power by establishing a sales unit abroad. Then through non-investment foreign production operations, manufacturing conditions can be tested before establishing a production unit abroad (Johanson and Vahlne, 1977). The economic-based internationalization model assumes the firm policy-maker is 'homo economicus'. He or she has access to perfect information and will select the rational solution. This leads to approaches such as transaction cost and/or an eclectic paradigm: the OLI (ownership, location, internationalization) paradigm (Dunning, 1988, 2000). The 'homo economicus' view is useful in establishing production facilities during the later stages of a firm's internationalization but it sidesteps the process aspects of internationalization. Both the process- and economics-based theories are micro-level approaches, which imply that the firm and the market are two modes that can be used to accomplish an economic function. A macro-level framework was provided by Porter's national competitiveness model. From that stemmed the micro-model of the globalizing firm, which gains from industry globalization drivers and its own globalizing levers. The firm gains competitive advantage from value adding in its supply chain (Porter, 1980).

Based on the process theory model an SME's internationalization can be analysed through using a network perspective as the starting point.

It can be argued that firms internationalize because the firms in their international network are doing so. Within any system firms engaged in the production, distribution and use of goods and services depend on each other due to their specialization. Certain industries or markets are more likely to be internationalized given the configuration of the world economy (Buckley and Ghauri, 1999; Hadjikhani and Ghauri, 2001). Firms are interdependent both through cooperation and competition. From a micro-perspective, complementary as well as competitive direct relationships involving partners in the network are crucial elements of the internationalization process. From the macro-perspective, both direct and indirect relationships need to be taken into account. The indirect ones involve firms that are not partners in the network. For a firm both the strength of the network ties and the size of its international network influence its decision to diversify internationally. However, some research shows that the strength of the ties is more important than the size of the network. From the network perspective, the internationalization strategy of a firm can be shown as the need to lower the need for knowledge development, for adjustment and to exploit established network positions (Johanson and Mattsson, 1993; Elg et al., 2013). Much of the network-based research on international business focuses on the management of international relationships. Issues with regard to networks include different types of relationships, trust, control and interdependency.

Knowledge is often concentrated in one person in an SME who will have a substantial impact on internationalization through close social relationships with other individuals in other firms. These social relationships are extremely important for entrepreneurs. This social network is effective and is being affected by the business network of gained resources and the operational mode of internationalization. From the entrepreneurial perspective, networks of individuals and the tacit knowledge they integrate, the accumulation of social capital of entrepreneurs connected with each other, leads to entrepreneurs getting access to resources and information for entrepreneurial actions. Networks can increase firm legitimacy and legitimacy leads to greater access to customers, suppliers and other resources needed to be successful internationally (Hoang and Antoncic, 2003; Hadjikhani et al., 2008). Ceteris paribus the larger the network size the greater the possibility of gaining resources and information, both in volume and in variety. The process approach, like the economic approach, overlooks the possibility of individuals making entrepreneurial strategic choices. Thus they are less appropriate for understanding radical strategic change, where entrepreneurs play an important role (Reid, 1981; Andersson, 2000).

The importance of entrepreneurs is widely recognized as main variables in the SME's internationalization. However, to create the most value, entrepreneurs also need to act strategically. Therefore, entrepreneurs can be seen as strategists who find a successful match between what a firm can do given its organizational strengths and weaknesses and what it might do given its environmental opportunities and threats. This is the research at the interface of entrepreneurship and international business research called 'international entrepreneurship' (McDougall and Oviatt, 2000). Such entrepreneurs have individual-specific resources that facilitate the recognition of new opportunities and assembling of resources for the venture (Schumpeter, 1950; Ghauri et al., 2005). They are one of the most important agents of change. These entrepreneurs establish ventures that operate across national borders. They are alert to the possibilities of combining resources from different national markets because of the competencies they have developed in terms of knowledge, background and networks.

DISCUSSION ON MAIN GLOBAL BUSINESS STRATEGIES

Traditional theories and models of internationalization have been based on research examining the international activities of large, mature firms. Broadly speaking, the resource-based view suggests that firms seek to capitalize on and increase their capabilities and endowments, whereas organizational economics asserts that firms focus on minimizing costs of organizing. Much of international business research has developed around resource-based theories. MNEs have large resources and the question was, what strategies to use for deploying them? Although these theories explain a substantial amount of international business activity of large, mature firms, these theories and models do not always explain the formation and operation of international new ventures, especially in today's dynamic environment. It has also been pointed out that the economic theories appear to be too narrow to cope with the complexity of volatile global competition (Solberg and Askeland, 2006).

When applied in a global market the resource-based theory builds on the international trade theory of comparative advantage and is seen as analogous to the organizational capability approach (Malhotra et al., 2003). A firm enters global markets when it can exploit and develop its comparative advantage, capabilities and societal resources for a sustainable competitive advantage (Andersen, 1997). The entry mode chosen for foreign markets, however, depends on the type of resource advantage. If the firm-specific advantage for instance, is superior knowledge based on tacit information, the firm should pursue a hierarchical governance structure, for example internalization, rather than a market structure. In contrast, if the firm faces capability constraint in an unfamiliar area of activity, collaborations are a useful vehicle for enhancing knowledge (Madhok, 1997; Park and Ghauri, 2014).

The organizational capability perspective, with its focus on both the firm's capabilities of which knowledge is one component and relationships is the other, covers both the internal and the external aspects of the international development of firms. This theory may be seen to follow naturally from first the international process theory, where building knowledge through own experience is central, and then the network theory where the importance of relationships for knowledge transfer is central (Andersen, 1993; Chiva et al., 2014).

As regards SMEs one could argue that the language of strategy and structure, which is often prescribed by many models of international business to enable firms to survive in competitive global markets, is somewhat limited for explaining SME internationalization. Close consideration of SME practice highlights the importance of multifaceted frameworks of analysis that go beyond the economic, strategic and behavioural and that take account of the often chaotic, opportunistic and incremental process through which entrepreneurs build international relationships and transactions (Buckley, 1991; Andersen, 1993; Calof and Beamish, 1995). This means that when evaluating the international activity of SMEs, there is a closer relationship to entrepreneurship than there is to international strategy and structure that have tended to dominate research (Eren-Erdogmus et al., 2010). International entrepreneurship is a tightly integrated process whereby entrepreneurs envision and realize the emergence of their business as an international entity.

An important difference between theories of multinational enterprise and a theory of international ventures seems to be the unit of analysis. Theories of international entrepreneurship argue that some firms start out internationally because of certain entrepreneur-specific capabilities versus firm-specific (Knight and Cavusgil, 1996; McDougall and Oviatt, 1996). When the entrepreneur creates the enterprise, there are no routines in place, but the entrepreneur has a vision and a network of contacts that he or she is going to build up further. Thus, the study of international ventures has to be concerned with individual learning by the entrepreneur as well as with organizational learning of the emerging entrepreneurial firm. Entrepreneurial behaviour in large, established companies, often referred to as 'corporate intrapreneurship', is not included in the discussion here; we are concerned only with SMEs. The remainder of the discussion is encompassing but not exhaustive and it does not cover all interactions among constructs. We start with stating a significant point that practitioners must constantly keep in mind – that they need to hone all the competencies and management know-how of the entrepreneur in order to keep internationalizing with a high-performance trajectory.

At the heart of entrepreneurial activity is innovation. Schumpeter distinguished between invention and innovation, with invention being the discovery of an opportunity and innovation being the exploitation of this opportunity. International entrepreneurial success requires not just the discovery of a valuable innovation but also that the innovation be introduced successfully to international markets. Schumpeter suggested five possible situations where new innovations can occur (Schumpeter, 1934): (1) the entrepreneur revolutionizes the pattern of production by exploiting an innovation or an untried technology for producing a new commodity, or (2) producing an old commodity in a new way, (3) by opening a new source of supply of materials, (4) opening a new outlet for products, or (5) by reorganizing the industry.

INTERNATIONAL ENTREPRENEURSHIP AND RELATED STRATEGY CONCEPTS FOR SMEs

Our next step is to delineate the range of *international entrepreneurial strategies* that SMEs feasibly adopt and the reasons that limit the range. 'International entrepreneurship is a combination of innovative, proactive, and risk-seeking behaviour that crosses national borders and is intended to create value in organizations' (McDougall et al., 2003, p.45; see also McDougall and Oviatt, 2000). The recognition of entrepreneurship as a significant force in the formulation of strategy has grown from the 1990s (Oviatt and McDougall, 1994). Controlled vision must be allowed to dominate rational calculations. The forerunners were the concepts of strategic stretch and leverage. Companies with the new thinking can rapidly grow internationally, jumping over stages as outlined in the process theory. They can even extend beyond the tight straitjacket of their own transaction costs by joining networks abroad. The conventional wisdom starts changing away from strategic fit and resource allocation towards a strategic stretch approach based on a gap between the resources available and the aspiration of the firm. The allied concept of leverage suggested a means of reaching these aspirations without changing the level of internal resources.

Entrepreneurial behaviour may occur at the individual, group or organizational levels. Once the entrepreneur paradigm is introduced, new concepts emerge. Thus, one can have a technical entrepreneur who focuses on a path that can create an international pull strategy where a network links with the firm. There is the other possibility of a marketing entrepreneur who implements an international push strategy. Further, one can have an entrepreneur who drives towards an international restructuring of an industry. Social capital can be defined as the goodwill that is engendered by the fabric of social relations and that can be mobilized to facilitate action (Adler and Kwon, 2002; Liu et al., 2010). It has earlier been an implicit assumption in resource-based theory that competitive advantage comes as a result of resources and capabilities owned and controlled by a single firm, but this view is changing – interfirm cooperation permits firms to share resources and thereby overcome resource-based constraints to growth. SMEs can thus gain advantages from social capital networks they participate in. Moreover, some researchers maintain that social networks are used at a personal level. Entrepreneurs can choose and manage the network they belong to (Oviatt and McDougall, 1994).

The international strategy an SME chooses is assumed to depend upon the firms' key employees' experience and network, the characteristics of the industry, how global it is and the characteristics of the product(s) It was concluded that the SMEs that may be recommended to venture abroad at an early stage are the ones with a unique product or process. These are ones that can be termed 'born globals'. In addition what can be very helpful are founders or other key employees with extensive experience and networks from previous employment in similar industries. In particular, the ones with good and well-established relations to certain actors in the industry supporting them with knowledge and insight to areas they themselves are lacking. Further, the pace by which a firm enters new markets and the increase in the firm's export share are a result of the industry being global; thus it makes foreign markets more accessible for internationalizing firms (Karlsen, 2007). For these firms, internationalization is not an extension of what has already occurred or 'has been' in the home market but is in fact a trajectory that can lead to their being classified as 'born globals'.

For SMEs that internationalize some years after start-up on the other hand, the international arena is seen as another 'site' in which entrepreneurial activities are tried out or practised. Internationalization is seen as an extension of what has already occurred in the domestic market and in this sense is also local or regional. This means that in staged or gradual internationalization, international entrepreneurship is characterized by the extension and broadening of entrepreneurial capabilities that have already been developed at home.

REFERENCES

Adler, P.S. and S.-W. Kwon (2002), 'Social capital: prospects for a new concept', *Academy of Management Review*, **27**(1), 17–40.

Andersen, O. (1993), 'On the internationalization process of firms: a critical analysis', *Journal of International Business Studies*, **24**(2), 209–31.

Andersson, S. (2000), 'The internationalization of a firm from an entrepreneurial perspective', *International Studies of Management and Organization*, **30**(1), 63–93.

Ansoff, H.I. (1965), *Corporate Strategy: An Analytic Approach to Business Policy for Growth and Expansion*, New York: Penguin Books.

Ayyagari, M., T. Beck and A. Demirgüç-Kunt (2003), 'Small and medium enterprises across the globe: a new database', *World Bank Open Knowledge Repository*, Washington, DC.

Bryan, L.L. and J.N Fraser (1999), 'Getting to global', *The McKinsey Quarterly*, No. 4.

Buckley, P.J. (1991), 'The frontiers of international business research', *Management International Review*, **31**(Special Issue), 7–20.

Buckley, P.J. and M. Casson (1976), *The Future of Multinational Enterprise*, London: Macmillan.

Buckley, P.J. and P.N. Ghauri (1999), 'Introduction and review', in P.J. Buckley and R.N. Ghauri (eds), *The Internationalization of the Firm: A Reader*, London: Academic Press.

Buckley, P.J. and P.N. Ghauri (2004), 'Globalisation, economic geography and the strategy of multinational enterprises', *Journal of International Business Studies*, **35**(2), 81–98.

Buckley, P.J. and P.N. Ghauri (2015), *International Business Strategy: Theory and Practice*, London: Routledge.

Calof, J.C. and P. Beamish (1995), 'Adapting to foreign markets: explaining internationalization', *International Business Review*, **4**(2), 115–31.

Cavusgil, S.T. (1984), 'Differences among exporting firms based on their degree of internationalization', *Journal of Business Research*, **12**(2), 195–208.

Chiva, R., P. Ghauri and J. Alegre (2014), 'Organizational learning, innovation and internationalization: a complex system model', *British Journal of Management*, **25**(4), 687–705.

Cyert, R.M. and J.G. March (1963), *A Behavioral Theory of the Firm*, Englewood Cliffs, NJ: Prentice-Hall.

Dunning, J.H. (1988), 'The eclectic paradigm of international production: a restatement and some possible extensions', *Journal of International Business Studies*, **19**(1), 1–15.

Dunning, J.H. (2000), 'The eclectic paradigm as an envelope for economics and business theories of MNE activity', *International Business Review*, **9**(2), 163–90.

Elg, U., P. Ghauri and J. Schaumann (2014), 'Internationalization through socio-political relationships: MNEs in India', *Long Range Planning* [online], accessed 12 May 2015 at http://www.sciencedirect.com/science/article/pii/S0024630114000752.

Elg, U., J. Schaumann and P.N. Ghauri (2013), 'Internationalization through social exchange relationships' conference paper at Emerging Markets, 39th Annual Conference of the European International Business Academy (EIBA), Bremen, Germany.

Eren-Erdogmus, I., E. Cobanoglu, M. Yalcin and P.N. Ghauri (2010), 'Internationalization of emerging market firms: the case of Turkish retailers', *International Marketing Review*, **27**(3), 316–37.

Freedman, L. (2013), *Strategy: A History*, New York: Oxford University Press.

Gabrielsson, M. and V.H.M. Kirpalani (2004), 'How to reach new business space rapidly', *International Business Review*, **13**(5), 555–71.

Ghauri, P. and P.R. Cateora (2014), *International Marketing* (4th edition), New York: McGraw-Hill Higher Education.

Ghauri, P. and T. Fang (2001), 'Negotiating with the Chinese: a socio-cultural analysis', *Journal of World Business*, **36**(3), 303–25.

Ghauri, P. and B. Park II (2012), 'The impact of turbulent events on knowledge acquisition', *Management International Review*, **52**(2), 293–315.

Ghauri, P., A. Hadjikhani and J. Johanson (2005), *Managing Opportunity Development in Business Networks*, Basingstoke, UK: Palgrave Macmillan.

Ghauri, P., U. Elg. V. Tarnovskaya and F. Wang (2011), 'Developing a market driving strategy: internal capabilities and external activities', *Schmalenbach Business Review*, **11**(3), 1–23.

Hadjikhani, A. and P. Ghauri (2001), 'The behaviour of international firms in socio-political environment in the European Union', *Journal of Business Research*, **52**(3), 263–75.

Hadjikhani, A., J.W. Lee and P. Ghauri (2008), 'A network view of MNCs' socio-political behavior', *Journal of Business Research*, **61**(3), 912–24.

Hagen, B., A. Zucchella, P. Cerchiello and N. De Giovanni (2012), 'International strategy and performance – clustering strategic types of SMEs', *International Business Review*, **21**(3), 369–82.

Hayek, F. (1945), 'The use of knowledge in society', *American Economic Review*, **35**(4), 519–30.

Hoang, H. and B. Antoncic (2003),'Network-based research in entrepreneurship: a critical view', *Journal of Business Venturing*, **18**(2), 165–87.

Johanson, J. and L.G. Mattson (1993), 'Internationalization in industrial systems – a network approach, strategies in global competition', in P.J. Buckley and R.N. Ghauri (eds), *The Internationalization of the Firm: A Reader*, London: Academic Press.

Johanson, J. and J.-E. Vahlne (1977), 'The internationalization process of the firm – a model of knowledge development and increasing foreign market commitments', *Journal of International Business Studies*, **8**(1), 23–32.

Karlssen, S.M.F. (2007), 'The born global – redefined: on the determinants of SMEs' pace of internationalization', Dissertation No. 2/2007, Oslo: BI Norwegian School of Management, Department of Marketing.

Kirzner, I. (1997), 'Entrepreneurial discovery and the competitive market process: an Austrian approach', *Journal of Economic Literature*, **35**(1), 60–85.

Knight, G.A. and S.T. Cavusgil (1996), 'The born global firm: a challenge to traditional internationalization theory', in T.K. Madsen (ed.), *Advances in International Marketing* (Vol. 8), Greenwich, CT: JAI Press Inc, pp. 11–26.

Levitt, T. (1983), 'The globalization of markets', *Harvard Business Review*, May–June, 92–102.

Liu, C.-L., P. Ghauri and R. Sinkovics (2010), 'Understanding the impact of relational capital and organizational learning on alliance outcome', *Journal of World Business*, **45**(3), 237–49.

Luostarinen, R. and M. Gabrielsson (2006), 'Globalization and marketing strategies of born globals in SMOPECs', *Thunderbird Business Review*, **48**(6), 773–80.

Machiavelli, N. ([1532] 1961), *The Prince*, London: Penguin Classics.

Madhok, A. (1997), 'Cost, value and foreign market entry mode: the transaction and the firm', *Strategic Management Journal*, **18**(1), 39–61.

Malhotra, N.K., J. Agarwal and F.M. Ulgado (2003), 'Internationalization and entry modes: a multitheoretical framework and research propositions', *Journal of International Marketing*, **11**(4), 1–31.

McDougall, P.P. and B.M. Oviatt (1996), 'New venture internationalization, strategic change, and performance: a follow-up study', *Journal of Business Venturing*, **11**(1), 23–40.

McDougall, P.P. and B.M. Oviatt (2000), 'International entrepreneurship: the intersection of two research paths', *Academy of Management Journal*, **43**(5), 902–8.

McDougall, P.P., B.M. Oviatt and R.C. Shrader (2003), 'A comparison of international and domestic new ventures', *Journal of International* Entrepreneurship, **1**(1), 59–82.

Miles, R.E. and C.C. Snow (1978), *Organization Strategy, Structure and Process*, New York: McGraw Hill.

Moreno A.M. and J.C. Casillas (2008), 'Entrepreneurial orientation and growth of SMEs: a causal model', *Entrepreneurial Theory and Practice*, **32**(3), 507–28.

OECD (2000), *Small Businesses, Job Creation and Growth: Facts, Obstacles and Best Practices*, Paris: OECD, accessed 15 May 2015 at http://www.oecd.org/cfe/smes/2090740.pdf.

Oviatt, B.M. and P.P. McDougall (1994), 'Toward a theory of international new ventures', *Journal of International Business Studies*, **25**(1), 45–65.

Park, B.-I. and P. Ghauri (2014), 'Determinants influencing CSR practices in small and medium sized MNE subsidiaries: a stakeholder perspective', *Journal of World Business* [online], accessed 12 May 2015 at http://www.researchgate.net/publication/262526613_Determinants_influencing_CSR_practices_in_small_and_medium_sized_MNE_subsidiaries_A_stakeholder_perspective.

Penrose, E. (1959), *The Theory of the Growth of the Firm*, New York: Wiley.

Porter, M.E. (1980), *Competitive Strategy: Techniques for Analyzing Industries and Competitors*, New York: The Free Press.

Reid, S.D. (1981), 'The decision-maker and export entry and expansion', *Journal of International Business Studies*, **12**(2), 101–12.

Rugman, A. and A. Verbeke (2004), 'A perspective on regional and global strategies of multinational enterprises', *Journal of International Business Studies*, **35**(1), 3–18.

Schumpeter, J. (1934), *The Theory of Economic Development*, *Cambridge*, MA: Harvard University Press.

Schumpeter, J. (1950), *Capitalism, Socialism and Democracy*, New York: Harper.

Schumpeter, J.A. and R.V. Clemence (1989), *Essays on Entrepreneurs, Innovations, Business Cycles and the Evolution of Capitalism*, New Brunswick, NJ: Transaction Publishers Corp.

Shane, S. (2000), 'Prior knowledge and discovery of entrepreneurial opportunity', *Organization Science*, **11**(4), 448–79.

Shane, S. and S. Venkataraman (2000), 'The promise of entrepreneurship as a field of research', *Academy of Management Review*, **25**(1), 217–26.

Solberg, C.A. and V. Askeland (2006), 'The relevance of internationalization theories: a contingency framework', in F.M. Fai and E.J. Morgan (eds), *Managerial Issues in International Business* (Vol. 13), New York: Palgrave Macmillan.

Sun Tzu (2003), *Sun Zi Art of War: An Illustrated Translation with Asian Perspectives and Insights*, translated and annotated by C.-H. Wee, Hong Kong: Pearson Education Asia.

Underwood, B. (2004), 'Capitalism, meet globalism', *Fast Company*, No. 78, January, 27–8.

Vernon, R. (1966), 'International investment and international trade in the product cycle', *Quarterly Journal of Economics*, **80**(1), 190–207.

Von Clausewitz, C. ([1932–43] 1984), in M.I. Howard and P. Paret (eds), *On War* (*Vom Kriege*, 3 vols, Berlin), Princeton, NJ: Princeton University Press.

Williamson, O.E. (1975), *Markets and Hierarchies: Analysis and Antitrust Implications*, New York: The Free Press.

Zucchella, A., G. Palamara and S. Denicolai (2007), 'The drivers of the early internationalization of the firm', *Journal of World Business*, **42**(3), 268–80.

2. Reactive and proactive international entrepreneurial behaviour: causation and effectuation

Miria Lazaris, Nurul Efifi Mohamad Ngasri and Susan Freeman

INTRODUCTION

In the past decade, international entrepreneurship (IE) has emerged as a new field of study that intersects international business and entrepreneurship in an effort to examine and explain the cross-border entrepreneurial activities of small and medium-sized enterprises (SMEs) (Jones et al., 2011). The growth of IE as a field of study has been largely attributed to the growth of studies examining the proliferation of early internationalizing firms, referred to as born globals (Knight and Cavusgil, 2004), born international SMEs (Kundu and Katz, 2003), early internationalizing firms (Mathews and Zander, 2007) and international new ventures (INVs) (Oviatt and McDougall, 1994). Unlike firms that increase their involvement in international markets gradually over time, born global SMEs can enter a number of markets within three years of inception (Madsen, 2013), often using a range of different entry service modes such as strategic partnerships involving little or no equity by SMEs (Freeman and Cavusgil, 2007; Kuivalainen et al., 2007; Di Gregorio et al., 2008). This chapter uses the term *born global SMEs* to refer to those SMEs that have engaged in early internationalization – that is, have internationalized within three years of inception.

Internationalization is defined as the 'process of increasing involvement in international operations' (Welch and Luostarinen, 1988, p. 36). The internationalization of SMEs, particularly born global SMEs, has received much attention in recent years. Several dimensions of internationalization have been used to encapsulate the international activities of born global SMEs including time of internationalization, or pace. However, while initial research effort was focused on reporting and explaining the early and rapid internationalization of born global SMEs, emphasizing the role of time, recent efforts have also highlighted differences within this group of early internationalizing SMEs (Kuivalainen et al., 2012). The suggestion that there are several patterns of internationalization among early internationalizing firms has theoretical and practical implications, relating in part to the comparability and generalizability of research in the international business and IE fields. For example, Jones et al. (2011) identify the challenges of cross-study comparisons due to operational issues and point out that 'the global start-up is only one form of INV, and the INV is not necessarily a BG' (p. 642). Similarly, Kuivalainen et al. (2012) argued that, while it is acknowledged that early internationalizing firms have different features, the absence of a rigid classification poses challenges for researchers.

The early internationalization of born global SMEs has been attributed to new market conditions, technological developments, growing significance of global networks and alliances, and skilled entrepreneurs (Rialp-Criado et al., 2010). However, some argue that internationalization is an accidental consequence of a firm's actions (Hennart, 2014). For example, Johanson and Vahlne (2009) argue that internationalization is a by-product of the firm's attempt to achieve a better network position. Similarly, evidence from small, advanced economies such as Australia suggest that internationalization (both rapid and gradual) is a path-dependent opportunity recognition process shaped by networks (Chandra et al., 2012). More recently, Hennart (2014) argued that the early internationalization of INVs can be attributed to three categories of factors: (1) unique firm-specific resources, (2) non-equity modes of entry and (3) reduction of transportation and communication costs. These three factors largely dispel two assertions relating to rapid internationalization. First, that rapid internationalization is driven by knowledge-intensive products and second, the importance of top management's experience, orientation and education. He argues instead that early internationalization and the original Uppsala model present distinct business models and that the former is explained by its approach to 'sell niche products and services to internationally dispersed customers using low-cost information and delivery methods' (p. 32). While we acknowledge the importance of product adaptations in this chapter we propose a complementary argument – that entrepreneurs play an important and undisputable role in the internationalization of born global SMEs. Specifically, we argue that our understanding of why and how internationalization differs among firms is enhanced when we take into consideration decision-making processes.

Specifically, this chapter discusses the initial internationalization of born global SMEs, particularly those from small, developed economies, using effectuation theory to explain how entrepreneurs identify and exploit international opportunities. We note the different approaches adopted by early born global SMEs as evidenced by the numerous typologies

(Freeman and Cavusgil, 2007; Kuivalainen et al., 2007; Di Gregorio et al., 2008) and we argue that more research is needed to explain differences in the way early internationalizing firms identify and pursue initial international opportunities. Taking as given that internationalization is a path-dependent process (Chandra et al., 2012), we argue that the early approach taken by firms to enter and compete in international markets has a significant influence on their subsequent behaviour. However, there is a paucity of research on and theoretical development in these processes. Although the literature recognizes several antecedents of early and rapid internationalization, we explore further the role of knowledge and networks, especially as they relate to the previous international experience of founders.

Jones et al. (2011) suggest that research could examine how knowledge is created and how opportunity recognition emerges as a result of entrepreneurial learning and changes in firm networks and internationalization patterns. Theoretical perspectives have traditionally drawn upon the resource-based view (RBV) (Barney, 2001), dynamic capabilities (Teece et al., 1997), knowledge-based view (KBV) of the firm (Grant, 1991) and social network theory (Coleman, 1988) to explain SME internationalization. While each have made meaningful contributions to the field of IE, these theories have failed to clearly elucidate the processes by which these small and new firms make decisions relating to which opportunities to pursue. As a result, it has been argued that the phenomenon of early internationalization still lacks comprehensive theoretical explanations and causal models (Rialp-Criado et al., 2010). This chapter responds to suggestions that few studies claiming to examine IE are in fact underpinned by entrepreneurship and international business theories (Jones et al., 2011). Specifically, we draw on effectuation theory to examine both the knowledge and networks of the SME to explain the process by which international opportunities are identified and pursued, thus contributing to the relatively new and growing IE research that has applied effectuation theory to the examination of early internationalizing SMEs, including born global SMEs (Schweizer et al., 2010; Andersson, 2011; Evers and O'Gorman, 2011).

Throughout this chapter, links are drawn between the tenets of effectuation theory and the observed behaviour of born global SMEs from Australia, a market well known for the early observance of the born global phenomenon (Rennie, 1993). Australian SMEs have limited resources, and operate in a small domestic market that is geographically isolated. In addition, recent years have presented Australian SMEs with high levels of uncertainty relating to the appreciation of the Australian dollar and natural disasters (Department of Industry Innovation, Science and

Research, 2011). Theoretical perspectives that do not account for decisions under such uncertainty may not sufficiently explain internationalization of Australian SMEs, particularly born global SMEs. Our chapter will provide a foundation upon which effectuation theory (Schweizer et al., 2010; Sarasvathy et al., 2014) can be utilized to further theoretical development in the field of IE.

This chapter is structured as follows. First we draw on effectuation theory, and argue that compared to causation theories it can provide valuable new insights on the process by which born global SMEs approach internationalization. Next, the principles of effectuation theory are applied to extant research on born global SMEs, particularly what we know about the development and utilization of knowledge, networks and international opportunities, especially in small and developed economies such as Australia. We argue that while effectuation logic prevails during initial internationalization of born global SMEs, internationally experienced managers are more likely to engage in proactive behaviours based on causation logic. Surprisingly, we observe that the latter are also likely to use both approaches simultaneously. We develop a conceptual framework to explain the process by which initial and subsequent internationalization of born global SMEs are underpinned by the effectual and causation approaches to internationalization. Finally, theoretical contributions are discussed as well as practical and managerial implications.

THEORETICAL APPROACHES TO SME INTERNATIONALIZATION

It is widely accepted that internationalization and entrepreneurship are related and that entrepreneurship theories can help further our understanding of firms' internationalization (Andersson, 2011, p. 628). A plethora of studies have emerged to explain the internationalization patterns of SMEs. Rialp-Criado et al. (2010) purport that born global behaviour is best explained by integrating theoretical frameworks from strategic management. Studies underpinned by these theories (i.e., RBV, dynamic capabilities and KBV; Grant, 1991; Teece et al., 1997) have identified several salient factors including the experience and orientation of top managers, personal and business networks (Yu et al., 2011), and knowledge (De Clercq et al., 2012) that influence the time, pace and scope of internationalization. However, these theories are largely causation based and explain means by which organizational outcomes, such as competitive advantage (Grant, 1991; Barney, 2001) are attained. Causation models assume pre-defined goals, maximization of expected returns, business planning and competitive analysis, and exploitation of resources and capabilities (Harms and Schiele, 2012). However, causation models do not address how managers make decisions in highly uncertain and unpredictable environments. Interestingly, such issues are addressed in the entrepreneurship literature, most recently with effectuation theory.

Sarasvathy et al. (2014) argue that the common characteristic of turbulent environments requires flexible approaches to exit and re-entry of the market. Sarasvathy (2008) suggests that in environments of volatility and unpredictability, as is often the case with SMEs in small, open and highly competitive markets like Australia, entrepreneurs may be more focused on survival of the firm rather than achieving competitive advantage over rivals. Often in cases where new ventures are established in unknown industries or industries that do not yet exist, typically found in high-technology sectors frequented by born global SMEs (Freeman and Cavusgil, 2007), theories that suggest step-by-step planning (Johanson and Vahlne, 1977) or towards long-term performance outcomes (Teece et al., 1997) do not account for early stage venture dynamics. For instance, the complexity surrounding how entrepreneurs manage to launch their product or services successfully, with unknowable market response rates, is not easily understood from traditional theories (Sarasvathy, 2008). Therefore, relying on traditional theories, originating from the strategic management literature, to explain complex and dynamic phenomena in IE may be confounding. Essentially, Sarasvathy (2008) suggests that effectuation may be a more suitable theoretical underpinning to explain entrepreneurial opportunity creation in comparison to the exploitation of pre-existing opportunities, as commonly contended by traditional views from the strategic management literature. According to Sarasvathy et al. (2014), three characteristics of IE that make effectuation theory particularly useful compared to traditional theories include: (1) cross-border uncertainty, (2) limited resources and (3) network dynamics.

EFFECTUATION, CAUSATION AND INTERNATIONALIZATION

IE is fundamentally concerned with the identification and exploitation of opportunities that cross national borders (Jones et al., 2011). However, scholars are divided with regard to the entrepreneurial opportunity identification process. Scholars from the entrepreneurship literature tend to suggest that opportunities pre-exist in the market and therefore entrepreneurs capitalize their resources to exploit existing opportunities (Shane and Venkataraman, 2000). This is explained by conventional economics literature that suggests the market mechanism is fully functional (i.e., at equilibrium) and that entrepreneurship activities come into being as an outcome of interacting market mechanisms to meet changing supply and demand conditions (Kleindorfer and Wu, 2003).

To the contrary, effectuation theory suggests that opportunities are created as a result of entrepreneurs' exploitation of their means (Sarasvathy, 2008). It argues that this happens because the market mechanism can be inefficient and therefore entrepreneurship activities are encouraged to assist in re-achieving equilibrium of the market by the exploitation of non-existent opportunities (Sarasvathy, 2001). Sarason et al. (2006) provide support for this understanding of opportunities through effectuation theory by suggesting that opportunities need to be understood from the perspective of the entrepreneurs as well as the social context in which opportunities are being co-created with other players. Without a thorough understanding of the operational mechanism of the market, the explanation of entrepreneurial opportunity exploitation is inadequate as opportunities may be embedded in the social context and are waiting to be explored (ibid.).

At the heart of this argument is the assumption surrounding the competing paradigms that treat opportunities as a central construct, and which challenge the current theoretical approach of SME internationalization studies. This is reflected by Alvarez and Barney (2010, p. 572) who suggest that 'most of the tools and frameworks that are applicable in the formation and exploitation of discovery opportunities have limited utility for those seeking to exploit creation opportunities'.

Effectuation theory as a theoretical lens for the study of internationalization is already emerging as a relevant theory for SME internationalization and has been incorporated in a recent adaptation of the original U-model in an article by its original authors (Schweizer et al., 2010). Nevertheless, the response by IE scholars has been inadequate and Perry et al. (2012, p. 838) observe that 'only a few researchers have attempted to empirically model and test effectuation'. In her seminal article, Sarasvathy (2001) argued that entrepreneurial decision-making is guided by effectual logic, which is essentially about 'entrepreneurial opportunity formation under uncertainty' (Bhowmick, 2011, p. 52). Effectuation takes as given a set of means so that the entrepreneur's task is to choose between effects that can be created with that given set of means (Sarasvathy, 2001). In contrast, the causation approach requires the entrepreneur to take an effect as given and select between means to create that effect. Effectuation, therefore, takes into account the impact of the entrepreneur's actions on his or her new venture (Read et al., 2009). We argue that this theory provides a useful theoretical lens with which to examine and understand disparity in the literature regarding the initial internationalization process of born global SMEs as reactive or proactive. More recently, Sarasvathy et al. (2014) draw on and extend the work by Schweizer et al. (2010) to argue that effectuation theory may be particularly useful in explaining how firms internationalize, with respect to *why*, *when*, *where* and *how fast*, as opposed to questions relating to *whether* to internationalize and call for the future combination of effectuation and IE frameworks.

According to Sarasvathy (2008), there are five principles that characterize effectuation: (1) bird-in-hand, (2) affordable loss, (3) lemonade, (4) crazy quilt and (5) pilot-in-the-plane. These principles of effectuation are discussed below.

Bird-in-hand

Effectuation suggests creation of effect with a given set of means. In this situation, means are explained as understanding who I am, who I know and what I know (Sarasvathy, 2001). In contrast, causal reasoning suggests a predetermined set of goals by which the entrepreneur constructs a specified plan to be executed and therefore plans on the needed means to achieve the desired goal. The distinguishing characteristic between maintaining flexibility in the generalized aspiration and being stringent in the specified outcome therefore differentiates causal versus effectual reasoning in explaining entrepreneurship strategies (Perry et al., 2012). In particular, the theory of effectuation suggests that understanding the entrepreneurs (i.e., bird-in-hand principle) is important to explain the first stage of entrepreneurship. This is consistent with Van Gelderen et al. (2006) who contend that different characteristics of entrepreneurs and non-entrepreneurs explain the success of the venture in the pre-start-up phase.

Since the 1990s, a large body of research has emerged to examine the characteristics and resources of founders of born global SMEs, including international experience, orientation, knowledge and social networks. This research can explain the bird-in-hand principle that supports early internationalization. For instance, Davidsson and Honig (2003) found that an entrepreneur's identification of tacit and explicit knowledge enables greater opportunity discoveries in the nascent stage. Tacit knowledge is represented by work experience whilst explicit knowledge is governed by the level of education (ibid.). In addition, the significance of 'who I know' is explained by Harris and Wheeler (2005). They found that access to resources and knowledge is only a complementary attribute that explains the necessity to form network relationships early in the venture with other industry players. Instead, 'for these entrepreneurs, the relationships do much more, they direct strategy, and can transform the firm' (ibid., p. 204). Accordingly, this chapter examines closely factors relating to the previous experience of founders, specifically knowledge and networks.

Affordable Loss

Affordable loss is contrasted with expected return in that entrepreneurs who start a venture with resources available in hand would approximate how much they are willing to lose from their initial investment (Sarasvathy, 2001). On the other hand, expected return is a primary motive for entrepreneurs adopting causal reasoning by estimating the value outcome of their venture capital (Amit et al., 1998). By accepting loss affordable for probable unsuccessful investment outcomes, the entrepreneurs are able to remain flexible in changing the course of the venture towards something that is more profitable in the future. Changing the course of the business is not a characteristic of failure, rather an indication of loss affordability and remaining flexible in the face of circumstances that equate to environmental volatility. This principle is also related to bird-in-hand by leveraging on 'who I know' and sharing inspirational ideas to mitigate potential losses.

Rather than adopting sophisticated tools to estimate maximized returns, effectual entrepreneurs adopt affordable loss heuristics to lessen potential losses (Dew et al., 2009). They argue that particularly in a turbulent environment of information asymmetries, firms are often at a disadvantage if solely relying on market information. Therefore, individual judgement on the current occurrences of the market is essential to address unpredictable market behaviour. In addition, entrepreneurs mitigate losses by leveraging the resources of their network partners. One illustration of a risk minimization strategy by rapidly internationalizing firms is illustrated in the study by Andersson (2011). He found that born global SMEs enter into multiple markets in a short time span by leveraging on network relationships rather than conducting extensive market research in the selection of foreign markets. This indicates that loss affordability strategy is tightly connected to relational activities among network partners. This is consistent with Sarasvathy (2001, p. 252) who suggests that 'effectuation emphasizes strategic alliances and pre-commitments from stakeholders as a way to reduce and/or eliminate uncertainty'. As a consequence, firms are able to mitigate potential losses and accelerate their expansion to foreign markets.

Recently, Freeman et al. (2013) contributed to this argument by demonstrating that born global SMEs exit and re-enter markets as a crucial strategy to maintain survivability of the firm in highly volatile environments. Often in the case where firms exit the market, their commitment to and relationship with previous partners are maintained (ibid.). This counterintuitive phenomenon indicates the importance of networks. Networks ensure that they remain flexible within the venture. Maintaining long-standing relationships and commitment with key network partners is a key attribute towards loss affordability, particularly in the case of rapidly internationalizing firms.

Lemonade

In causal-based strategies, the effect of contingencies that may result in deviation from the initial plan is generally unwelcome. Often contingencies are perceived as a situation of undesirability; rather, entrepreneurs minimize the risk of contingencies with execution plans that are put in place in advance. On the other hand, effectuation suggests contingencies as unavoidable especially in a turbulent environment of high degrees of unpredictability (Sarasvathy, 2001). In recent news reports by *The Telegraph*, UK (e.g., Evans-Pritchard, 2013), economists forecast that the big emerging markets (BEMs) such as China will soon be faced with economic downturn. Over the past few months, there has been some evidence of high levels of domestic lending and interbank loans that are not being channelled appropriately to strengthen the economy, and worsened with the strengthening of US dollar. These events have resulted in a lack of confidence by foreign investors to invest in the BEMs. In the last decade, this trend was the reverse as multinational corporations and foreign investors were bringing a large amount of capital to invest into the BEMs. This recent trend of capital flight out of the BEMs has been referred to as de-globalization (for emerging economies) and re-globalization (for developed economies). These recent changes emphasize entrepreneurial inability to accurately predict long-term cross-border business outlooks, a trait typically important in the case of causal reasoning (Sarasvathy, 2001). To the contrary, effectual entrepreneurs are not discouraged by bad news in the business environment. Rather, they choose to seize every opportunity in the course of their venture. Sarasvathy (2008) suggests that effectual entrepreneurs maintain control of the environment through their network relationships rather than working around their limited predictive capacity.

Entrepreneurs who adopt effectual reasoning are more concerned with the phrase 'to the extent we can control future, we do not need to predict it' (Sarasvathy, 2001, p. 251). This is consistent with the conventional view in entrepreneurship that autonomous decision-making power is essential to exploit the entrepreneurial capabilities of the founding partners (Antoncic and Hisrich, 2003). This brings the focus (and unit of analysis) back to the entrepreneur rather than the firm level. The importance of autonomy is acknowledged in the additional dimensions of the entrepreneurial orientation (EO) construct that was developed by Lumpkin and Dess (1996), along with competitive aggressiveness. They expanded the construct from the initial dimensions proposed by Covin and Slevin (1989) that consist of innovativeness, proactiveness and risk-taking behaviour. Despite this, Lumpkin et al. (2009) observe that entrepreneurial autonomy is distinguishable from corporate autonomy because (1) it is perceived as the bottom-up rather than top-down approach (Krueger and Brazeal, 1994) and (2) it is characterized by an autonomous decision-making process aided by a group of individuals (i.e., colleagues or stakeholders) working on similar outcomes rather than based on hierarchical individualistic decision-making processes (Dess and Lumpkin, 2005). Therefore, from an international business point of view, a degree of environmental control is achievable due to the entrepreneurs' perceived desirability to maintain close relationships with key stakeholders, thus minimizing the need to predict the uncertainties (Perry et al., 2012; Sarasvathy et al., 2014).

Crazy Quilt

The ability to leverage on contingencies (i.e., lemonade) is closely related to the partnership ties built with key stakeholders in the early stages of the venture (i.e., crazy quilt). With limited capacity from scarce resources to expand on the business, effectual entrepreneurs see the need to convince trusted partners in the early stages (Goel and Karri, 2006) to cooperate on the generalized vision. Nevertheless, as the venture evolves, the entrepreneur remains flexible in the achievement of the generalized aspiration. Trust is built early, therefore facilitating open communication with key partners in situations of contingencies (Karri and Goel, 2008). In the early stages of the venture entrepreneurs may over-trust their key partners, as entrepreneurs may be willing to compromise a degree of their vision to accommodate mutual commitment by the stakeholders (Goel and Karri, 2006). Nevertheless, this is not necessarily detrimental to the company if the entrepreneur is able to exert the highest degree of control and influence on the business (Goel and Karri, 2006; Karri and Goel, 2008).

Not surprisingly, in the study of IE, the importance of networks is widely recognized to explain the behaviour of rapidly internationalizing firms. For instance, Knight and Cavusgil (2004, p. 137) demonstrate that in addition to a strong global focus, rapidly internationalizing firms are able to outperform their competitors in multiple overseas markets due to 'strong relationships that born globals develop with competent foreign distributors'. This illustration demonstrates the crazy quilt principle of effectuation that emphasizes that relationship building with key stakeholders in the early stages of the venture is already in line with the current positioning of the accelerated internationalization literature (Chetty and Campbell-Hunt, 2004; Freeman and Cavusgil, 2007).

Pilot-in-the-plane

In the causation-based model, entrepreneurs are focused on minimizing environmental dynamism by engaging with logics of prediction. On the other hand, effectuation suggests that entrepreneurs take control and act to shape the market according to their needs (Sarasvathy, 2001). In contrast to the original internationalization process (IP) model (Johanson and Vahlne, 1977) that suggests a linear model of internationalization, entrepreneurs may face the need to exit and re-enter a market due to some unavoidable contingencies and rapidly unpredictable market realities (Freeman et al., 2013). A linear process view of internationalization is argued to be too simplistic to capture the real dynamics of cross-border transactions necessitating firms to cope with rapid and volatile global economic shifts (Ahuja et al., 2012). In the recent observation published in *The New York Times* (Barboza, 2014), developed economies such as the USA are witnessing recovery in their economies, referred to as reglobalization in the West, whilst the opposite is happening in China where their renminbi continues to decline relative to the US dollar. Therefore, a processual model that enables a more thorough explanation of the internationalization behaviour of firms is timely, consistent with the most recent international business phenomenon. The need for moving in and out of markets, sometimes very quickly, therefore characterizes entrepreneurs' agility to control the environment (Yang and Liu, 2012). Being sensitive to loss affordability and remaining flexible while managing contingencies, effectual entrepreneurs react to declining market performance by shifting from unprofitable markets to the more profitable ones (Sarasvathy et al., 2014). In their study of Australian born global SMEs, Freeman et al. (2013, p. 175) observe that internationalization 'includes outward and inward-oriented activities, which rely on alliances and partnerships to increase the firm's international experience, overcome resource deficiencies and continue growth for survival'. The dynamic internationalization process model (Welch and Luostarinen, 1993) adopted in their study is already consistent with the effectuation principle that emphasizes flexibility as one of its key strategies for firm survival (Sarasvathy, 2008).

DRIVERS OF INTERNATIONAL OPPORTUNITIES AMONG BORN GLOBAL SMEs: THE ROLE OF KNOWLEDGE AND NETWORKS

Internationalization is a complex, multidimensional process that changes over time (Melén et al., 2014). While there are many dimensions on which to compare the internationalization of born global SMEs (Freeman and Cavusgil, 2007; Kuivalainen et al., 2007; Di Gregorio et al., 2008), we focus on initial internationalization and examine why and how some born global SMEs are able to pursue proactive internationalization whereas others adopt a more reactive approach. The proactive approach to internationalization is theoretically based on the assumption that internationalization is a planned process, by which firms actively search, identify and exploit opportunities in international markets (Chetty and Campbell-Hunt, 2004; Gabrielsson et al., 2008; Johanson and Vahlne, 2009). This body of literature assumes that early and rapid internationalization is the result of proactive efforts of managers to either exploit existing networks and/or develop new networks for the purpose of exploiting foreign market opportunities. As we discuss further below, proactive born global SMEs are able to internationalize early because they are founded by internationally experienced managers who have the knowledge (Nordman and Melén, 2008), capabilities (Weerawardena et al., 2007) and/or networks (Evers and O'Gorman, 2011) to actively develop international markets from inception.

This second approach, which we argue is grounded in effectuation theory, is a reactive response to unplanned or serendipitous opportunities (ibid.). While Crick and Spence (2005) found that initial internationalization among high-performing, high-technology SMEs was the outcome of planned efforts, the authors reported that subsequent internationalization was unplanned and the result of serendipitous encounters. The basic premise of this stream of research is that firms do not have an intention to internationalize. However, they do so in order to exploit international opportunities. Thus, internationalization is posited as reactive. Consistent with this logic is empirical evidence that SMEs' initial internationalization is driven by new or existing networks that 'pull' firms into foreign markets (Bell et al., 2003; Freeman et al., 2006). Thus the time, mode and market selection decisions are not the result of purposeful planning by management, but rather a reactive response to opportunities, as explained by effectuation theory.

Importantly, previous literature identifies both planned (proactive) and unplanned (reactive) approaches to internationalization and several typologies of internationalization have attempted to capture both the reactive and proactive approaches to early internationalization, demonstrating the complexities of early internationalizing SMEs. For example, Freeman and Cavusgil's (2007) study of Australian born global SMEs distinguishes reactive approaches to internationalization such as the responder from more proactive approaches such as the strategist. However, while available typologies tend to focus on identifying behavioural characteristics among early internationalizing SMEs, we argue that a better understanding of internationalization requires a closer examination of the decision-making processes. We argue that entrepreneurs of born global SMEs can use a combination of reactive and proactive behaviours. More recent research does confirm that entrepreneurs can use both approaches as internationalizing born global SMEs (Freeman et al., 2013). Interestingly, the previous international experience of founders, prior to founding their firms, enables them to plan the development of networks and critically evaluate international opportunities (Harms and Schiele, 2012).

The Role of Networks

Integral to effectuation processes is the importance of networks (Sarasvathy et al., 2014). Networks increase the resources available to ventures (expanding means) and converging goals throughout stakeholder self-selection (ibid.). However, when examining the role of networks in internationalization using effectuation, the focus switches to the dynamics of the networks, rather than on static features (i.e., structure and composition) (ibid.). The importance of networking activities is often reflected in the literature as a consequence of the need for SMEs to access resources. Nevertheless, networking activities could also be seen as a process 'of the owner–manager interacting naturally with actors in his network' (O'Donnell, 2014, p. 182). Therefore, the underlying effectual process undertaken by entrepreneurs in their networking activities is illustrated implicitly in the literature.

For instance, O'Donnell (2014) suggests that entrepreneurs do not directly calculate the potential gain from networking with specific types of network partners. Rather, they estimate the probable exchange of resources as a consequence of networking. In other words, entrepreneurs do not necessarily network to gain access to resources but may gain access to resources due to the consequential benefits of regular networking activities with other industry players. Schweizer et al. (2010) argue that internationalization is essentially a by-product of efforts by the firm to improve their position in a network. In addition, literature also highlights the importance of network relationships (i.e., who I know) to enhance international market knowledge (i.e., what I know). Fernhaber and Li (2013) suggest that informal and formal network relationships may foster better familiarity with cross-border transactions if the entrepreneur has some international educational and work experience. This suggests that the applicability of the bird-in-hand principle should be viewed as a multidimensional construct, in that 'who I am' influences 'who I know', which therefore influences 'what I know'.

With regard to born global SMEs, Sarasvathy et al. (2014) refer to the earlier work by Coviello (2006) to highlight the significance of the entrepreneur's role in networks. Drawing on effectuation theory, we argue that internationally experienced entrepreneurs have both international networks prior to founding the firm, as well as relevant knowledge to manage and further develop those networks. Because of this, they are perhaps more likely to engage in proactive development of networks, explained by causation models. Thus, we argue the following proposition:

P1: Effectual logic explains the development of networks for internationalization. However, the higher the international experience of the founder, the more likely it will be that he or she will also use causation logic.

The Role of Knowledge

The concept of knowledge is generally discussed in the internationalization literature as a consequence of opportunity *seeking behaviour* (Ardichvili et al., 2003). Nevertheless, there have been studies that demonstrate knowledge as readily embedded within the individual entrepreneur and therefore result in the *creation* of opportunities (Alvarez and Barney, 2007; Cohen and Winn, 2007). Opportunity identification is influenced by the previous experience and knowledge of the entrepreneur and is facilitated when the entrepreneur has prior complementary information (McMullen and Shepherd, 2006) such as resulting from previous international experience. In such a situation, entrepreneurs have complex mental models with which to interpret the external environment (Nadkarni and Perez, 2007), which may facilitate a more active search for information, knowledge and opportunities. Some authors have explicitly attributed the ability of some firms to internationalize early to the previous international experience of founders and thus their personal experiential knowledge (Weerawardena et al., 2007; Zucchella et al., 2007). This relates to the knowledge acquired from previous experience. For example, De Clercq et al. (2012) argue that early internationalization can be proactive and this is explained by taking into consideration their sources of knowledge. Consistently, it has been argued that born global SMEs have learning advantages that older, domestic SMEs may lack (Autio et al., 2000). Absorptive capacity, defined as 'the ability of the firm to recognize the value of new, external information, assimilate it, and apply it to commercial ends' (Cohen and Levinthal, 1990, p. 1) explains this. According to Cohen and Levinthal (1990), individuals gain more knowledge when it is related to their current stock of knowledge. Chetty et al. (2006) have shown that different experiences have different influences on managerial cognition in terms of the perceived importance of institutional knowledge. It follows that born global SMEs are more likely to have founders with previous international experience in comparison to traditional SMEs. Therefore, born global SMEs are better able to recognize relevant knowledge with which to actively plan their internationalization strategy.

Child and Hsieh (2014) suggest that entrepreneurs have varying approaches towards systematic or cognitive-based decision-making related to their educational experience. For instance, entrepreneurs who lack formal higher education will be more inclined to adopt cognitive reasoning (i.e., effectual) rather than systematic calculation in managing risk (i.e., causal). This implies that understanding of the entrepreneurs' background (i.e., who I am) is essential to distinguish different approaches firms undertake towards their internationalization activities (ibid.). Without a thorough understanding of the entrepreneur's background that eventually leads to their unique decision-making process, the explanation of how some firms are able to rapidly internationalize in comparison to others remains incomplete. Therefore, we argue that the bird-in-hand principle is essential in providing a nuanced understanding from the viewpoint of the entrepreneur to ease the current tension in the IE literature surrounding opportunity seeking versus creation.

In contrast to entrepreneurs with international experience, we argue that entrepreneurs lacking international experience are forced to focus on short-term experiments to identify international business opportunities. Schweizer (2012) explored the rationality of internationalization decisions among SMEs, using Lindblom's muddling-through approach (1959, as cited in Schweizer, 2012), which resembles an incremental and disjointed root process, which can be aligned with effectuation. Although there was evidence of rational decision-making (planning approach/causation), decisions relating to the internationalization process were made in complex conditions where the clarification of goals was lacking, so muddling-through processes were also evident, especially during the early stages of the internationalization process. His findings support those of Chandler et al. (2009) who argued that 'SMEs in the early stages of the internationalization process follow a spontaneous, effortless, and heuristic type of reasoning, but in the later stages tend to use clearer criteria when evaluating internationalization opportunities and to become more selective in terms of partners' (in Schweizer, 2012, p. 751). Schweizer (2012) attributes the change from muddling through to rational decision-making to experience, increased knowledge, and lower levels of goal ambiguity.

It has been suggested that experience provides a framework by which to process information, but which novice entrepreneurs lack (Westhead et al., 2005). It follows that managers lacking relevant international experience and international knowledge would focus on short-term opportunities to identify international opportunities. Indeed, Nordman and Melén (2008) found that born global SMEs with internationally experienced entrepreneurs at the helm proactively searched for opportunities. However, those with internationally inexperienced founders lacked a clear strategic approach, evidenced by the lack of specific objectives relating to the choice of foreign markets. Similarly, Evers and O'Gorman (2011) found that internationally inexperienced entrepreneurs were not necessarily proactive as regards their internationalization, nor did they follow a causation-based process. They argued that while prior knowledge and experiences shape their decisions and the opportunities they identify, international experience and related knowledge is not necessarily a precursor to early internationalization. More recently, Norwiński and Rialp (2013) reported effectuation logic among firms whose entrepreneurs had less prior international and business exposure. The experimental nature of the early internationalization of these firms, characterized by effectuation logic, was explained by a lack of knowledge about foreign markets, and an inability to engage in formal market research methods. This leads to the following proposition:

P2: Effectual logic explains the role of knowledge in internationalization. However, the higher the international experience of the founder, the more likely he or she will also use causation logic.

CONCEPTUAL FRAMEWORK

The conceptual framework we present is based on the extant literature and propositions. Our discussion supports a simple model of effectuation and causation for SME internationalization. Several studies support the argument that internationalization is a process characterized by serendipity (Crick and Spence, 2005), muddling through (Schweizer, 2012), improvisation (Evers and O'Gorman, 2011) and experimentalism (Freeman and Cavusgil, 2007) all of which align with the notion of effectuation. However, we also note suggestions that internationalization can also be a proactive process (Crick and Spence, 2005; Freeman and Cavusgil, 2007).

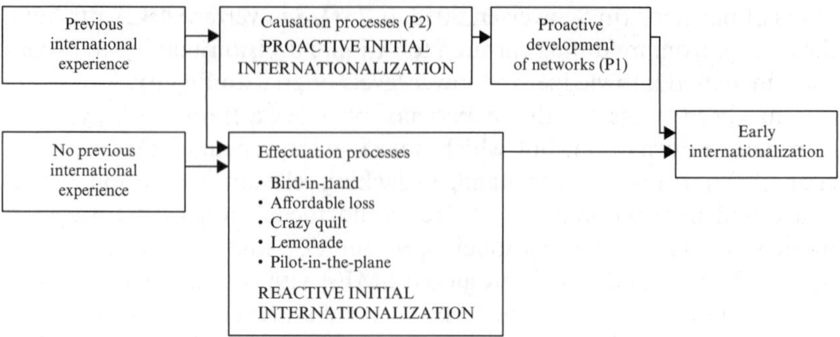

Figure 2.1 Conceptual framework

We argue that decisions relating to the early internationalization of born global SMEs are inherently laced with uncertainty, and therefore effectuation processes are important. However, born global SMEs whose founders have previous international experience are better able, and thus likely to also engage in proactive internationalization, which includes the proactive development of international networks, consistent with the causation process of decision-making. This is depicted in Figure 2.1.

DISCUSSION

In this chapter, we address the paucity of IE research with theoretical underpinnings from the field of entrepreneurship (Jones et al., 2011). Drawing on effectuation theory, we discuss the reactive and proactive initial internationalization of born global SMEs in terms of knowledge and networks resulting from the previous international experience of founders. In doing so, we acknowledge suggestions by Sarasvathy et al. (2014) that effectuation theory may be particularly useful in explaining how SMEs internationalize with respect to *why*, *when*, *where* and *how fast*. Specifically, we address *why*, *when* and *how* born global SMEs engage in proactive and/or reactive internationalization behaviour during initial internationalization. We suggest that while effectuation is an integral part of internationalization, due to the uncertain contexts of most cross-border transactions (Schweizer et al., 2010), causation processes are also evident (Harms and Schiele, 2012) and can be explained by the prior international experience of founders. When the previous international experience provides enhanced knowledge structures and complex cognitive models, managers are better able to engage in proactive internationalization consistent with causation. The previous international experience of the firms' founders facilitates early internationalization because it improves their ability to leverage existing networks and identify and positively evaluate international opportunities (DeClerq et al., 2012).

Throughout this chapter, and consistent with others (Schweizer et al., 2010; Harns and Schiele, 2012), our arguments highlight the important role of the founders of born global SMEs and their decision-making processes. Our work complements and extends the previous work by Schweizer et al. (2010), who argue that entrepreneurial capability is a state variable and experiential learning represents dynamism. However, we apply effectuation to the specific context of initial internationalization of born global SMEs to explain how previous international experience of founders impacts on reactive and proactive initial internationalization. While Schweizer et al. (2010) argue that network insiders are better able to exploit opportunities, we argue that some founders, by virtue of their previous international experience, are able to manage their networks, and therefore engage in planned behaviour consistent with causation models. Importantly, we do not suggest that international experience negates effectuation processes; rather we support the view that effectuation and causation can co-exist (Sarasvathy, 2001). We posit that internationally experienced managers are better able and more likely to apply causation processes. The ability to actively and purposefully search for new resources, markets and opportunities because of previous international experience intuitively makes sense. However, we make theoretical contributions to this relatively nascent field of enquiry (Perry et al., 2012). Thus we deem our contribution a valuable step towards the extrapolation of effectuation theory to IE phenomena.

In writing this chapter, we make several contributions. First, we have attempted to explain the reactive and proactive approaches taken by born global SMEs as they begin internationalization. Second, we show how effectuation theory can provide insights, helping to address inconsistencies and problems with extant IE research. In doing so, we contribute towards the promotion of effectuation theory as a useful perspective for examining internationalizing SMEs. It is worth mentioning at this point that we do not suggest that effectuation theory makes redundant other strategic management theories that have informed research in the field of IE such as the RBV, dynamic capabilities, KBV, network perspective and social network theory to explain SME internationalization. Rather, we support arguments for multitheoretical approaches (Crick and Spence, 2005), and we argue that effectuation, when combined with other theories, can enhance our understanding of SME internationalization.

DIRECTIONS FOR FURTHER RESEARCH

This chapter has some limitations relating to its theoretical nature and narrow focus; however, we hope our efforts demonstrate opportunities for future research. Entrepreneurs can, and do, use both effectuation and causation processes simultaneously (Sarasvathy, 2001; Freeman and Cavusgil, 2007; Freeman et al., 2013), thus future research should examine when and under what other conditions effectuation and causation processes are more likely to manifest during internationalization. Biographies can also be used to trace the previous experience of managers in an effort to understand other possible drivers of effectuation and causation processes. Future research might be able to refine, extend and empirically examine our propositions, using large sample qualitative and quantitative studies. While we argue in this chapter that previous international experience influences the knowledge and networks underlying causation and effectuation processes, researchers can examine other factors.

Any of the principles of effectuation, as they apply to SME internationalization, can also be further explored. For example, future research can examine exogenous factors to identify environmental contingencies and to explain how and when they impact on the internationalization process. Internationalization is a dynamic process that changes over time (Schweizer et al., 2010), and effectuation theory can be used to identify how and why firms change paths towards internationalization. Finally, we suggest that future research examines the constraints of internationalization in an effort to explain the domestic focus of some SMEs. Indeed, effectuation theory could be used to better understand how born global SMEs differ from their domestic counterparts.

REFERENCES

Ahuja, G., G. Soda and A. Zaheer (2012), 'The genesis and dynamics of organizational networks', *Organization Science*, **23**(2), 434–48.

Alvarez, S.A. and J.B. Barney (2007), 'Discovery and creation: alternative theories of entrepreneurial action', *Strategic Entrepreneurship Journal*, **1**(1–2), 11–26.

Alvarez, S.A. and J.B. Barney (2010), 'Entrepreneurship and epistemology: the philosophical underpinnings of the study of entrepreneurial opportunities', *The Academy of Management Annals*, **4**(1), 557–83.

Amit, R., J. Brander and C. Zott (1998), 'Why do venture capital firms exist? Theory and Canadian evidence', *Journal of Business Venturing*, **13**(6), 441–66.

Andersson, S. (2011), 'International entrepreneurship, born globals and the theory of effectuation', *Journal of Small Business and Enterprise Development*, **18**(3), 627–43.

Antoncic, B. and R.D. Hisrich (2003), 'Clarifying the intrapreneurship concept', *Journal of Small Business and Enterprise Development*, **10**(1), 7–24.

Ardichvili, A., R. Cardozo and S. Ray (2003), 'A theory of entrepreneurial opportunity identification and development', *Journal of Business Venturing*, **18**(1), 105–23.

Autio, E., H.J. Sapienza and J.G. Almeida (2000), 'Effects of age at entry, knowledge intensity, and imitability on international growth', *Academy of Management Journal*, **43**(5), 909–24.

Barboza, D. (2014), 'Currency of China continues to decline', *The New York Times*, accessed 7 May 2015 at http://www.nytimes.com/2014/03/01/business/chinese-currency.html?_r=0.

Barney, J.B. (2001), 'The resource-based view of the firm: ten years after 1991', *Journal of Management*, **27**(6), 625–41.

Bell, J., R.B. McNaughton, S. Young and D. Crick (2003), 'Towards an integrative model of small firm internationalisation', *Journal of International Entrepreneurship*, **1**(4), 339–62.

Bhowmick, S. (2011), 'Effectuation and the dialectic of control', *Small Enterprise Research*, **18**(1), 51–62.

Chandler, G.N., D.R. DeTienne, A. McKelvie and T.V. Mumford (2011), 'Causation and effectuation processes: a validation study', *Journal of Business Venturing*, **26**(3), 375–90.

Chandra, Y., C. Styles and I. Wilkinson (2012), 'An opportunity-based view of rapid internationalization', *Journal of International Marketing*, **20**(1), 74–102.

Chetty, S. and C. Campbell-Hunt (2004), 'A strategic approach to internationalization: a traditional versus a "born global" approach', *Journal of International Marketing*, **12**(1), 57–81.

Chetty, S., K. Eriksson and J. Lindbergh (2006), 'The effect of specificity of experience on a firm's perceived importance of institutional knowledge in an ongoing business', *Journal of International Business Studies*, **37**(5), 699–712.

Child, J. and L.H. Hsieh (2014), 'Decision mode, information and network attachment in the internationalization of SMEs: a configurational and contingency analysis', *Journal of World Business*, **46**(2), 135–42.

Cohen, W.M. and D.A. Levinthal (1990), 'Absorptive capacity: a new perspective on learning and innovation', *Administrative Science Quarterly*, **35**(1), 128–52.

Cohen, B. and M.I. Winn (2007), 'Market imperfections, opportunity and sustainable entrepreneurship', *Journal of Business Venturing*, **22**(1), 29–49.

Coleman, J.S. (1988), 'Social capital in the creation of human capital', *American Journal of Sociology*, **94**(S), S95–S120.

Coviello, N.E. (2006), 'The network dynamics of international new ventures', *Journal of International Business Studies*, **37**(5), 713–31.

Covin, J.G. and D.P. Slevin (1989), 'Strategic management of small firms in hostile and benign environments', *Strategic Management Journal*, **10**(1), 75–87.

Crick, D. and M. Spence (2005), 'The internationalisation of "high performing" UK high-tech SMEs: a study of planned and unplanned strategies', *International Business Review*, **14**(2), 167–85.

Davidsson, P. and B. Honig (2003), 'The role of social and human capital among nascent entrepreneurs', *Journal of Business Venturing*, **18**(3), 301–31.

De Clercq, D., H. Sapienza, R. Yuvuz and L. Zhou (2012), 'Learning and knowledge in early internationalization research: past accomplishments and future directions', *Journal of Business Venturing*, **27**(1), 143–65.

Department of Industry Innovation, Science and Research (2011), *Key Statistics: Australian Small Business*, accessed 6 May 2015 at http://workspace.unpan.org/sites/internet/Documents/UNPAN92675.pdf.

Dess, G.G. and G.T. Lumpkin (2005), 'The role of entrepreneurial orientation in stimulating effective corporate entrepreneurship', *The Academy of Management Executive*, **19**(1), 147–56.

Dew, N., S. Sarasvathy, S. Read and R. Wiltbank (2009), 'Affordable loss: behavioral economic aspects of the plunge decision', *Strategic Entrepreneurship Journal*, **3**(2), 105–26.

Di Gregorio, D.M. Musteen and D.E. Thomas (2008), 'International new ventures: the cross-border nexus of individuals and opportunities', *Journal of World Business*, **43**(2), 186–96.

Evans-Pritchard, A. (2013), 'China braces for capital flight and debt stress as Fed tightens',

The Telegraph, accessed 6 May 2015 at http://www.telegraph.co.uk/finance/china-business/10120716/China-braces-for-capital-flight-and-debt-stress-as-Fed-tightens.html.
Evers, N. and C. O'Gorman (2011), 'Improvised internationalization in new ventures: the role of prior knowledge and networks', *Entrepreneurship and Regional Development*, **23**(7–8), 549–74.
Fernhaber, S.A. and D. Li (2013), 'International exposure through network relationships: implications for new venture internationalization', *Journal of Business Venturing*, **28**(2), 316–34.
Freeman, S. and S.T. Cavusgil (2007), 'Toward a typology of commitment states among managers of born-global firms: a study of accelerated internationalization', *Journal of International Marketing*, **15**(4), 1–40.
Freeman, S., S. Deligonul and S.T. Cavusgil (2013), 'Strategic re-structuring by born-globals using outward and inward-oriented activity', *International Marketing Review*, **30**(2), 156–82.
Freeman, S., R. Edwards and B. Shroder (2006), 'How smaller born-global firms use networks and alliances to overcome constraints to rapid internationalization', *Journal of International Marketing*, **14**(3), 33–63.
Gabrielsson, M., V.H.M. Kirpalani, P. Dimitratos, C.A. Solberg and A. Zucchella (2008), 'Born globals: propositions to help advance the theory', *International Business Review*, **17**(4), 385–401.
Goel, S. and R. Karri (2006), 'Entrepreneurs, effectual logic, and over-trust', *Entrepreneurship Theory and Practice*, **30**(4), 477–93.
Grant, R.M. (1991), 'The resource-based theory of competitive advantage: implications for strategy formulation', *California Management Review*, **33**(3), 114–35.
Harms, R. and H. Schiele (2012), 'Antecedents and consequences of effectuation and causation in the international new venture creation process', *Journal of International Entrepreneurship*, **10**(2), 95–116.
Harris, S. and C. Wheeler (2005), 'Entrepreneurs' relationships for internationalization: functions, origins and strategies', *International Business Review*, **14**(2), 187–207.
Hennart, J. (2014), 'The accidental internationalist: a theory of born globals', *Entrepreneurship Theory and Practice*, **38**(1), 117–35.
Johanson, J. and J.E. Vahlne (1977), 'The internationalization process of the firm – a model of knowledge development and increasing foreign market commitments', *Journal of International Business Studies*, **8**(1), 23–32.
Johanson, J. and J. Vahlne (2009), 'The Uppsala internationalization process model revisited: from liability of foreignness to liability of outsidership', *Journal of International Business Studies*, **40**(9), 1411–31.
Jones, M.V., N. Coviello and Y. Yang (2011), 'International entrepreneurship research (1989–2009): a domain ontology and thematic analysis', *Journal of Business Venturing*, **26**(6), 632–59.
Karri, R. and S. Goel (2008), 'Effectuation and over-trust: response to Sarasvathy and Dew', *Entrepreneurship Theory and Practice*, **32**(4), 739–48.
Kleindorfer, P.R. and D. Wu (2003), 'Integrating long- and short-term contracting via business-to-business exchanges for capital-intensive industries', *Management Science*, **49**(11), 1597–615.
Knight, G.A. and S.T. Cavusgil (2004), 'Innovation, organizational capabilities, and the born-global firm', *Journal of International Business Studies*, **35**(2), 124–41.
Krueger, N.F. and D.V. Brazeal (1994), 'Entrepreneurial potential and potential entrepreneurs', *Entrepreneurship Theory and Practice*, **18**(1), 91–104.
Kuivalainen, O., S. Saaranketo and K. Puumalainen (2012), 'Start-up patterns of internationalization: a framework and its application in the context of knowledge-intensive SMEs', *European Management Journal*, **30**(4), 372–85.
Kuivalainen, O., S. Sundqvist and P. Servais (2007), 'Firms' degree of born-globalness, international entrepreneurial orientation and export performance', *Journal of World Business*, **42**(3), 253–67.

Kundu, S.K. and J.A. Katz (2003), 'Born-international SMEs: BI-level impacts of resources and intentions', *Small Business Economics*, **20**(1), 25–47.

Lindblom, C.E. (1959), 'The science of "muddling through"', *Public Administration Review*, **19**(2), 79–88.

Lumpkin, G.T. and G.G. Dess (1996), 'Clarifying the entrepreneurial orientation construct and linking it to performance', *Academy of Management Review*, **21**(1), 135–72.

Lumpkin, G.T., C.C. Cogliser and D.R. Schneider (2009), 'Understanding and measuring autonomy: an entrepreneurial orientation perspective', *Entrepreneurship Theory and Practice*, **33**(1), 47–69.

Madsen, T.K. (2013), 'Early and rapidly internationalizing ventures: similarities and differences between classifications based on the original international new venture and born global literatures', *Journal of International Entrepreneurship*, **11**(1), 65–79.

Mathews, J.A. and I. Zander (2007), 'The international entrepreneurial dynamics of accelerated internationalisation', *Journal of International Business Studies*, **38**(3), 387–403.

McMullen, J.S. and D.A. Shepherd (2006), 'Entrepreneurial action and the role of uncertainty in the theory of the entrepreneur', *Academy of Management Review*, **31**(1), 132–52.

Melén, S., R.E. Nordman and D. Sharma (2014), 'The continued internationalisation of an international new venture', *European Business Review*, **26**(5), 471–90.

Nadkarni, S. and P.D. Perez (2007), 'Prior conditions and early international commitment: the mediating role of domestic mindset', *Journal of International Business Studies*, **38**(1), 160–76.

Nordman, E.R. and S. Melén (2008), 'The impact of different kinds of knowledge for the internationalization process of born globals in the biotech business', *Journal of World Business*, **43**(2), 171–85.

Nowiński, W. and A. Rialp (2013), 'Drivers and strategies of international new ventures from a Central European transition economy', *Journal for East European Management Studies*, **18**(2), 191–231.

O'Donnell, A. (2014), 'The contribution of networking to small firm marketing', *Journal of Small Business Management*, **52**(1), 164–87.

Oviatt, B.M. and P.P. McDougall (1994), 'Toward a theory of international new ventures', *Journal of International Business Studies*, **36**(1), 29–41.

Perry, J.T., G.N. Chandler and G. Markova (2012), 'Entrepreneurial effectuation: a review and suggestions for future research', *Entrepreneurship Theory and Practice*, **36**(4), 837–61.

Read, S., M. Song and W. Smit (2009), 'A meta-analytic review of effectuation and venture performance', *Journal of Business Venturing*, **24**(6), 573–87.

Rennie, M. (1993), 'Global competitiveness: born global', *The McKinsey Quarterly*, No. 4, 45–52.

Rialp-Criado, A., I. Galvan-Sanchez and S. Suarez-Ortega (2010), 'A configurational approach to born-global firms' "strategy formation process"', *European Management Journal*, **28**(2), 108–23.

Sarason, Y., T. Dean and J.F. Dillard (2006), 'Entrepreneurship as the nexus of individual and opportunity: a structuration view', *Journal of Business Venturing*, **21**(3), 286–305.

Sarasvathy, S.D. (2001), 'Causation and effectuation: toward a theoretical shift from economic inevitability to entrepreneurial contingency', *Academy of Management Review*, **26**(2), 243–63.

Sarasvathy, S.D. (2008), *Effectuation: Elements of Entrepreneurial Expertise*, Cheltenham, UK and Northampton, MA, USA: Edward Elgar Publishing.

Sarasvathy, S.D., K. Kumar, J.G. York and S. Bhagavatula (2014), 'An effectual approach to international entrepreneurship: overlaps, challenges, and provocative possibilities', *Entrepreneurship Theory and Practice*, **38**(1), 71–93.

Schweizer, R. (2012), 'The internationalization process of SMEs: a muddling-through process', *Journal of Business Research*, **65**(6), 745–51.

Schweizer, R., J.-E. Vahlne and J. Johanson (2010), 'Internationalization as an entrepreneurial process', *Journal of International Entrepreneurship*, **8**(4), 343–70.

Shane, S. and S. Venkataraman (2000), 'The promise of entrepreneurship as a field of research', *Academy of Management Review*, **25**(1), 217–26.

Teece, D.J., G. Pisano and A. Shuen (1997), 'Dynamic capabilities and strategic management', *Strategic Management Journal*, **18**(7), 509–33.

Van Gelderen, M., R. Thurik and N. Bosma (2006), 'Success and risk factors in the pre-startup phase', *Small Business Economics*, **26**(4), 319–35.

Weerawardena, J., G. Sullivan-Mort, P.W. Liesch and G. Knight (2007), 'Conceptualizing accelerated internationalization in the born global firm: a dynamic capabilities perspective', *Journal of World Business*, **42**(3), 294–306.

Welch, L.S. and R. Luostarinen (1988), 'Internationalization: evolution of a concept', *Journal of General Management*, **14**(2), 34–55.

Welch, L.S. and R.K. Luostarinen (1993), 'Inward–outward connections in internationalization', *Journal of International Marketing*, **1**(1), 44–56.

Westhead, P., D. Ucbasaran and M. Wright (2005), 'Experience and cognition: do novice, serial and portfolio entrepreneurs differ?', *International Small Business Journal*, **23**(1), 72–98.

Yang, C. and H.-M. Liu (2012), 'Boosting firm performance via enterprise agility and network structure', *Management Decision*, **50**(6), 1022–44.

Yu, J., B. Gilbert and B.M. Oviatt (2011), 'Effects of alliances, time, and network cohesion on the initiation of foreign sales by new ventures', *Strategic Management Journal*, **32**(4), 424–46.

Zucchella, A., G. Palamara and S. Denicolai (2007), 'The drivers of the early internationalization of the firm', *Journal of World Business*, **42**(3), 268–80.

3. The influence of market intelligence and marketing mix adaptation efforts on the performance of Israeli born globals

Rotem Shneor and Kalanit Efrat

INTRODUCTION

Born globals (BGs) are often viewed as a unique breed of international entrepreneurial small and medium-sized enterprises (SMEs), with the potential for accelerated internationalization and a global market vision (Gabrielsson et al., 2008; Gabrielsson and Kirpalani, 2012). Thus far, much of the research on BGs has focused on the early stages of international new venture creation, the challenges it poses to earlier conceptualizations of an internationalization process, as well as on the motivations and drivers for its creation and emergence (Kirpalani and Gabrielsson, 2012; Leonidou and Samiee, 2012).

More specifically, when considering international marketing strategy of international new ventures, a review by Aspelund et al. (2007) has revealed that research has mainly concentrated on the speed of the internationalization process, niche versus commodity focus in product strategy, entry into few versus multiple markets simultaneously, elements influencing market selection choices, and entry mode decisions. Surprisingly enough, however, the critical international marketing strategy question concerning the standardization versus adaptation/localization of marketing mix elements (Ryans et al., 2003; Theodosiou and Leonidou, 2003) has largely been ignored.

This question is of particular importance, both due to the effects international marketing strategy has on international firm performance in general (Cavusgil and Zou, 1994; Leonidou et al., 2002; Knight et al., 2004), and the effect standardization and/or adaptation strategy has on firm performance in particular (Zou et al., 1997; Shoham, 1999). Furthermore, understanding of such effects is of added value in the BGs' context, which are firms that are pressured to perform under conditions of fierce competition and customer demands in multiple markets, while having access to limited resources and market knowledge (Knight and Cavusgil, 2004; Aspelund et al., 2007).

Since BGs often need to deal with operations in dynamic and volatile markets (Efrat and Shoham, 2012), as well as with liabilities of newness, smallness and foreignness (Zahra, 2005), they must also exhibit strong abilities to learn, adapt and change (McDougall and Oviatt, 1996). Earlier studies have linked these abilities to both market and learning orientations (Kropp et al., 2006; Kocak and Abimbola, 2009). More specifically, marketing orientation is defined as organization-wide generation, dissemination and responsiveness to market intelligence (Kohli and Jaworski, 1990). As such, market intelligence serves as both the core element and starting point of marketing orientation. In this respect, authors suggested that successful BGs devote active efforts to collecting and generating market-related intelligence through their engagements with their channels, networks and lead customers (Zhou et al., 2007; Gabrielsson et al., 2008). Nevertheless, the relationship between BGs' market intelligence efforts and their performance has, thus far, largely gone unstudied.

Hence, the current chapter presents a study seeking to address these gaps, while contributing to the understanding of BGs' post-establishment performance. In particular, the study examines potential effects of BGs' choices concerning adaptation of marketing mix elements, as well as market intelligence generation efforts, on their performance. This is done through an analysis of survey data collected from 69 Israeli BGs during 2012–13.

The chapter first provides an overview of studies at the intersection of BG internationalization, international marketing and firm performance. This is further extended to the standardization–localization dilemma in particular, and concludes with a list of hypotheses linking localization of marketing mix elements and BG performance. Next, methodology and analysis are presented, and findings are highlighted. The discussion section will then revisit findings vis-à-vis existing literature, and both contributions and limitations will be highlighted. Finally, the chapter will conclude with revisiting the main insights emerging from the study, as well as suggested implications for research and practice.

PERFORMANCE OF BORN GLOBALS

The phenomenon of an early and rapidly internationalizing entrepreneurial SME has been capturing the attention of international business scholars for the past two decades, who refer to it as either an 'international new venture' (Zahra et al., 2000; Oviatt and McDougall [1994] 2005; Zahra, 2005; Hallbäck and Larimo, 2007), 'early internationalizing firm' (Rialp et al., 2005), 'born glocal' (Svensson, 2006), or more commonly as the 'born global' firm (Knight and Cavusgil, 1996; Madsen et al., 2000; Moen,

2002; Gabrielsson and Kirpalani, 2004; Gabrielsson et al., 2008). While extensive conceptual discussions and typologies have been suggested in earlier reviews (Svensson, 2006; Hallbäck and Larimo, 2007; Gabrielsson et al., 2008; Gabrielsson and Kirpalani, 2012; Leonidou and Samiee, 2012), we use the term *born global* (BG) with reference to what Gabrielsson et al. (2008) are referring to as an international entrepreneurial SME, with the potential for accelerated internationalization and a global market vision.

Studies linking BGs (in this broad) term and performance have been limited, and can be grouped into two: first, studies comparing BGs and other types of firms in terms of their international performance; and, second, studies seeking to identify factors that impact BGs' international performance in particular. Here, regardless of study focus, researchers have been using both objective or subjective measurements for capturing performance (Aspelund et al., 2007). Objective measurements included firm survival, growth rates, share of international sales, export growth rates, sales growth rates and profitability growth rates relative to industry figures, number of employees, or number of markets served (as in McDougall and Oviatt, 1996; Autio et al., 2000; Zahra et al., 2000; Gleason et al., 2006; Zhou et al., 2007). And subjective measurements often included self-reported satisfaction with, or judgement of, achieved levels of these indicators in the various firms studied (as in Kropp et al., 2006; Efrat and Shoham, 2012). Sometimes both objective and subjective measurements were used in the same study (as in Kuivalainen et al., 2007).

When comparing BGs to other type of firms, as well as among different types of BGs, in terms of their performance, research highlights some interesting findings. Autio et al. (2000) have shown that early internationalizing firms have a higher share of international sales, growth in international sales and total sales than later internationalizing Finnish firms in the electronics industry. Also in Finland, Kuivalainen et al. (2007) have shown that, among Finnish exporters, BGs exhibited better export performance than born internationals (or gradual globalizers). Furthermore, based on a sample of NASDAQ listed firms, Gleason et al. (2006) showed that 12 and 18 months post-IPO, returns were significantly higher for BGs than for firms that did not engage in rapid internationalization. And, in addition, they also showed that, within the first six years since their inception, BGs with joint ventures or acquisitions in several countries performed better than BGs that only engaged in exports.

Studies that sought to identify factors impacting performance of BGs also came up with valuable findings. Here, in their analysis of US high-technology new ventures, McDougall and Oviatt (1996) found that internationalization is only profitable for organizations that can accommodate strategic changes. And Zahra et al. (2000) showed that technological learning (in terms of breadth, depth and speed), international diversity (in terms of number of countries in which foreign sales occur, as well as the technological and cultural diversity of these markets), and mode of entry (in terms of number of transactions going through acquisition arrangements, licensing agreements and export agreements) all impacted the international performance of US high-technology ventures.

More recently, some studies also emerged from outside the USA. Here, Kropp et al. (2006) found that innovativeness, market orientation and learning orientation all had positive impacts on the performance of export-oriented entrepreneurial firms from South Africa. Furthermore, Zhou et al. (2007) showed that due to their informational benefits, home-based social networks mediate the effects of both outward and inward internationalization orientation strategies on the international performance of Chinese BGs. Finally, and most recently, Efrat and Shoham's (2012) analysis of Israeli BGs has shown that their survival is impacted by operation in high-risk countries, as well as by their technological capabilities, marketing effectiveness and management capabilities. In addition, the same study also showed that the strategic performance of Israeli BGs is influenced by the levels of market growth and technological turbulence in the markets they were operating in, as well as by their market knowledge and management capability.

However, when reviewing these studies at an aggregate level, one may suggest that various aspects associated with market orientation and strategy can be identified as two of the common threads passing through all, directly or indirectly. These are evident in the identified effects of market orientation, market knowledge, marketing effectiveness, the informational value of social network relations, the value of ability to engage in strategic change, as well as in entry mode choices. Accordingly, the current study focuses on these two aspects and their relations to BGs' performance, while narrowing the focus on one critical aspect of market orientation (market intelligence), as well as one critical aspect of market strategy (the standardization–adaptation dilemma).

Market Intelligence Generation

Market orientation, defined as organization-wide generation, dissemination and responsiveness to market intelligence (Kohli and Jaworski, 1990), has been shown to affect organizational performance in general (Morgan et al., 2004; Wang et al., 2009), and BGs' performance in particular (Kropp et al., 2006; Kocak and Abimbola, 2009). Building on the resource-based view, research suggests that firms exhibiting higher levels of market orientation also exhibit superior performance thanks to better understanding of customers' needs and wants, competitor moves and strategies, channel requirements and the broader market environment, in comparison to others (Kohli and Jaworski, 1990; Jaworski and Kohli, 1993; Morgan et al., 2004).

However, it is market intelligence generation that lies at the core of market orientation, and represents its critical starting point (Kohli and Jaworski, 1990). When taking the specific characteristics of BGs into consideration, we posit that it is primarily market intelligence generation and the responsiveness to it, which poses the greatest challenge for BGs, due to their significant claims on the limited resources at the disposal of BGs. However, internal dissemination of market intelligence is less of a challenge in small-scale ventures, especially in comparison to larger organizations that were at the focus of earlier studies. This is mainly thanks to the relative flat structure, informal management style, dominant manager-owner and/or cohesion of the entrepreneurial team, which often characterize entrepreneurial SMEs (Mazzarol, 2011).

First, in terms of market intelligence generation, we posit that its importance for BGs is further exacerbated by their need to operate in dynamic and volatile markets (Efrat and Shoham, 2012), while overcoming challenges associated with liabilities of newness, smallness and foreignness (Zahra, 2005), under conditions of significant resource limitations (Knight and Cavusgil, 2004). Taken jointly, all these pressures push BGs towards tapping into what was labelled as 'know-what advantages', enabling them to be more effective and efficient, by allowing their management to select the most productive available resource combinations to match market conditions (Morgan et al., 2004). This point is further stressed in Knight and Cavusgil's (2004) claim that owing to limited traditional resources, BGs must succeed in foreign markets earlier, and with superior efficiency and effectiveness, as they cannot afford to make mistakes that may have afflicted other firms.

Accordingly, the current study focuses specifically on the effects of market intelligence generation efforts on BGs' performance, while proposing the hypothesis that firms exhibiting higher levels of commitment to market intelligence generation will also exhibit superior performance:

H1: The higher the commitment of BGs to market intelligence generation efforts, the better their international performance.

Responsiveness and Marketing Mix Adaptation

According to Kohli and Jaworski (1990), responsiveness is the set of actions taken in response to generated and disseminated market intelligence, often manifesting itself in more informed target market selection, the designing and offering of products/services that excel at catering to customers' current and anticipated needs, as well as in producing, distributing and promoting products/services in a way that elicits favourable end-customer response.

When brought into an international marketing strategy context, responsiveness is closely related to the dilemma surrounding the extent to which market mix elements are standardized or adapted locally (Ryans et al., 2003; Theodosiou and Leonidou, 2003). At the heart of this dilemma are two conflicting approaches and forces. The first approach assumes that consumers' wants and needs are, to a large extent, similar across markets, and that through economies of scale, firms employing a standardization strategy may lower costs and achieve greater margins. The second approach assumes heterogeneity of wants and needs across markets, and that through careful accommodation of these differences, firms employing an adaptation strategy may achieve greater margins through offering superior products and services that are better suited to each individual market. Suggestions to bridge the divide have also been suggested, mostly through a contingency approach indicating that the feasibility and desirability of adaptation strategy is dependent on timing and market circumstances (Theodosiou and Leonidou, 2003), as well as firm size and some of its other strategies (Schilke et al., 2009). And, others suggest, such decisions are also part of an ongoing negotiation with the market. Here, while markets cannot be forced to accept foreign firms' standardized marketing strategy, they may still be persuaded to do so, on a base of mutual interest (Solberg, 2000).

Studies examining the effects of standardization and/or adaptation marketing strategies on firm performance present inconclusive findings (Ryans et al., 2003; Theodosiou and Leonidou, 2003). Nevertheless, Leonidou et al.'s (2002) meta-analysis, incorporating 36 studies published between 1964 and 1998 on marketing strategy determinants of export performance, has shown that, overall, product, price, promotion and distribution strategy adaptations were all significantly correlated with superior overall export performance, though variations based on specific measurements of export performance were evident. Similar evidence also emerged in later studies as well. Lee and Griffith (2004) showed that product and price adaptations positively influenced performance of Korean exporters. Calantone et al. (2006) showed significant positive effect of product adaptation strategy on export performance of US, Japanese and Korean firms.

However, some later studies have also found opposite results. Here, O'Cass and Julian's (2003) study revealed that configurations of adaptation–standardization strategy didn't impact performance of the Australian exporters in their sample. And Navarro et al. (2010) showed that marketing tactic adaptations didn't directly impact export performance in their sample of Spanish exporters. A possible explanation for these conflicting results is in the treatment of marketing mix adaptation as a single confounded variable, rather than a set of discrete adaptation strategies for different components of the marketing mix (O'Cass and Julian, 2003; Navarro et al., 2010). Evidence supporting such argumentation may be found in Shoham (1999) who showed that price and promotion adaptations enhanced performance of Israeli exporters, while price and distribution standardization rather than adaptation have achieved the same.

Nevertheless, responsiveness implies more adaptation than standardization, as it puts premium on value generated through superior customer satisfaction. Accordingly, we posit that adaptation of the marketing mix elements will positively impact BGs' performance. This argument is mainly drawing on the fact that BGs, by definition, are new market entrants that, at least initially, have little influence vis-à-vis customers, existing market players and suppliers. Challenged with overcoming liabilities of newness, smallness and foreignness (Zahra, 2005), BGs are dependent on network relationships with multiple stakeholders, not only as source of knowledge, but also as source of legitimacy in their industry and markets (Sharma and Blomstermo, 2003; Freeman et al., 2006; Zhou et al., 2007; Karra et al., 2008). Here, legitimacy-seeking behaviour, in accordance with institutional theory proponents, implies adherence to accepted principles, rules, norms, standards and ways of doing things (Aldrich and Fiol, 1994; Delmar and Shane, 2004). And when brought into an international marketing context, also implies adherence to local preferences, tastes and conditions for doing commerce, across markets that differ in terms of geographical conditions, commercial infrastructure, technological infrastructure, legal and regulatory environment, purchasing power, and so on.

Based on the above we propose the following hypotheses:

H2(a): The greater the extent of product adaptation in BGs' international marketing strategy, the better their international performance.

H2(b): The greater the extent of price adaptation in BGs' international marketing strategy, the better their international performance.

H2(c): The greater the extent of promotion adaptation in BGs' international marketing strategy, the better their international performance.

METHODOLOGY

For analysing the effects of marketing research and localization efforts on BGs' performance we have collected data from Israeli BGs. In line with Knight et al.'s (2004) operational definition for BGs, the target participants of the study are firms that entered foreign markets within three years of inception and at least 25 per cent of whose sales were from exports. We approached firms that are included in the IVC – Israeli Venture Capital database. The sampling frame initially included 609 firms. After excluding R&D centres of foreign firms, the usable list comprised 426 relevant firms.

We then approached each firm by phone, ending up with 294 firms that met our criteria. Based on the information received from the phone survey, we sent an online questionnaire to a member of the managerial team (CEO, chief of marketing, head of business development), using the Qualtrics application. Three weeks after the initial approach this was followed by a phone reminder. We received 106 usable questionnaires, representing a response rate of 36 per cent. Eventually, 69 of these had complete data necessary for running the regression analysis presented in the current chapter.

Measures

Measures in the current study were adopted from earlier research with minor adaptations as specified in Table 3.1.

The multiple item constructs were assessed based on a factor analysis. Here, in order to choose proper statistical procedures we first checked our data for normal distribution. Since normality of item distribution was not supported in a Kolmogorov-Smirnov test, the extraction method chosen was principle axis factoring. Items loading on more than one factor were removed. At the end of this process, a six-factor solution emerged, with each item only loading on one factor (Table 3.2). The rotated solution suggested six factors with eigenvalues greater than 1, including – performance (7.092), product adaptation (4.554), promotion adaptation (3.101), price adaptation (2.368), market intelligence generation (1.615), and sales force adaptation (1.201). Cumulative variance explained by the extraction was 71.18. Later, the reliability of each factor was further assessed using Cronbach's alphas, which are reported for each variable. Finally, for allowing correlations between the constructs, their scores were saved as averages of all their related items.

Table 3.1 Variable measurements and sources

Variable	Items	Source
Performance	Please evaluate your major international market performance, based on the following aspects: Has been very profitable Has generated a high volume of sales Has achieved a high growth rate Has improved our global competitiveness Has strengthened our strategic position Has significantly increased our global market share The performance of this export venture has been very satisfactory This export venture has been very successful This export venture has fully met our expectations	Zou et al. (1998)
Market intelligence generation	Please answer the following questions regarding your organization: In this business we meet with customers at least once a year to find out what products/services they will need in the future Individuals from our manufacturing department interact directly with customers to learn how to serve them better[a] We do a lot of in-house market research[a] We are slow to detect changes in our customers' product preferences[a] We poll end users at least once a year to assess the quality of our products/services We often talk with or survey those who can influence our customers We collect industry information through informal means[a] Intelligence on our competitors is generated independently by several departments[a] We are slow to detect shifts in our industry[a] We periodically review the likely effect of changes in our business environment	Jaworski and Kohli (1993)
Marketing adaptation	For the list of marketing variables listed below, please indicate whether they are standardized (the same in all markets), or not: Product positioning Product design/style Product quality	Lages et al. (2008)

Table 3.1 (continued)

Variable	Items	Source
Marketing adaptation	Product features/characteristics	
	Brand/branding	
	Warranty[a]	
	Items/models in product line	
	Price	
	Profit margins	
	Discounts	
	Advertising	
	Media allocation	
	Sales force structure/management	
	Sales force role	
	Public relations	
	Advertising/promotion budget	

Note: a. Items removed following factor analysis.

Dependent variable

Performance was measured using the EXPERF scale developed by Zou et al. (1998). The scale includes nine items that are divided into three subscales of three items each measuring financial, strategic and satisfaction aspects of firm's performance. Here respondents were required to indicate the extent to which they agree with each item's statement on a five-point Likert scale, where 1 was labelled 'strongly disagree' and 5 was labelled as 'strongly agree'. Following the factor analysis, all nine items were retained, jointly loading on a single factor with Cronbach's alpha = 0.930.

Independent variables

Market intelligence generation was measured using items from Jaworski and Kohli's (1993) scale for the intelligence generation aspect of market orientation. The scale includes ten items capturing various aspects of firms' efforts towards customer and market reviews and surveys. Here as well respondents were required to indicate the extent to which they agree with each item's statement on a five-point Likert scale, where 1 was labelled 'strongly disagree' and 5 was labelled 'strongly agree'. Following factor analysis, only four of the original ten items were retained, jointly loading on a single factor with Cronbach's alpha = 0.750.

Marketing adaptation was measured based on Lages et al.'s (2008) STRATADAPT scale. While the original scale includes 30 items, we have included only 16 of these items, incorporating items representing product,

Table 3.2 Rotated factor matrix and reliability indicators

Items	Factors					
	Performance	Product adaptation	Price adaptation	Promotion adaptation	Sales force adaptation	Market intelligence generation
Performance-financial1	0.770					
Performance-financial2	0.889					
Performance-financial3	0.790					
Performance-strategic1	0.778					
Performance-strategic2	0.604					
Performance-strategic3	0.814					
Performance-satisfaction1	0.823					
Performance-satisfaction2	0.916					
Performance-satisfaction3	0.733					
Adaptation-product1		0.641				
Adaptation-product2		0.690				
Adaptation-product3		0.896				
Adaptation-product4		0.788				
Adaptation-product5		0.577				

Table 3.2 (continued)

Items	Factors					
	Performance	Product adaptation	Price adaptation	Promotion adaptation	Sales force adaptation	Market intelligence generation
Adaptation-product7		0.786				
Adaptation-price1			0.783			
Adaptation-price2			0.903			
Adaptation-price3			0.768			
Adaptation-promotion1				0.751		
Adaptation-promotion2				0.709		
Adaptation-promotion3					0.715	
Adaptation-promotion4					0.822	
Adaptation-promotion5				0.776		
Adaptation-promotion6				0.727		
Market Intelligence1						0.572
Market Intelligence5						0.722
Market Intelligence6						0.786
Market Intelligence10						0.613
Cronbach's alpha	0.930	0.874	0.905	0.843	0.835	0.750

Note: Extraction method: principal axis factoring. Rotation method: Varimax with Kaiser normalization. Loadings below 0.50 not shown.

price and promotion elements of the marketing mix. Here respondents were required to indicate, on a five-point Likert scale, the extent to which each marketing mix aspect (as stated in each item) was the same in all international markets their firm was operating in: 1 was labelled as 'the same' and 5 was labelled as 'completely different'. Following factor analysis, six of the seven product adaptation items were retained, loading on a single factor with Cronbach's alpha = 0.874; all three price adaptation items were retained, loading on a single factor with Cronbach's alpha = 0.905; however, the six promotion adaptation items loaded on two separate factors – one was labelled as 'promotion adaptation', measured by four items loading on a single factor with a Cronbach's alpha = 0.843; and the other was labelled as 'sales force adaptation', measured by two items loading on a single factor with a Cronbach's alpha = 0.835.

Control variable

Earlier studies either showed mild effects of firm age on degree of internationalization (Autio et al., 2000), or no effect on export performance (Zhou et al., 2007). However, these studies used a continuous variable of years since establishment. If a BG lifecycle is to follow a more punctuated stage approach, it may be worthwhile exploring this variable through an ordinal variable. In this respect, Gabrielsson et al. (2008) have suggested that BGs go through three key stages, namely – introduction, growth and breakout. Accordingly, we have included a *BG maturity* control variable, aimed at capturing these developmental stages. In the absence of concrete numerical earlier guidelines we have created an ordinal variable, capturing three levels of maturity: '1' representing firms five years or younger (as reflecting introduction stage), incorporating 35 per cent of firms in our sample; '2' representing firms between six and ten years in existence, incorporating 40 per cent of firms in our sample; and '3' representing firms 11 years or older, incorporating 25 per cent of firms in our sample.

ANALYSIS

Since our data violated the assumptions of normal distribution for all variables included, with the exception of the promotion adaptation, as made evident by significant values of the Kolmogorov-Smirnov tests, we have opted for non-parametric statistics (Field, 2005). Performance, $D(77) = 0.121$, $p < 0.01$; product adaptation, $D(77) = 0.163$, $p < 0.001$; price adaptation, $D(77) = 0.115$, $p < 0.05$; promotion adaptation, $D(77) = 0.092$, n.s.; sales force adaptation, $D(77) = 0.170$, $p < 0.001$; and market intelligence generation, $D(77) = 0.100$, $p < 0.1$.

Table 3.3 Descriptive statistics and Pearson correlations

	Mean	s.d.	1	2	3	4	5	6
Performance	52.46	28.76						
1 Product adaptation	46.43	27.45	–					
2 Price adaptation	45.43	28.59	0.342**	–				
3 Promotion adaptation	47.61	27.68	0.138	0.547***	–			
4 Sales force adaptation	48.04	27.62	0.196†	0.423***	0.437***	–		
5 Market intelligence generation	48.77	28.53	0.056	–0.113	0.027	–0.074	–	
6 BG maturity	1.99	0.81	0.052	0.100	–0.014	0.234*	0.086	–

Notes: N = 69; †$p < 0.1$; *$p < 0.05$; **$p < 0.01$; ***$p < 0.001$.

Accordingly, we have followed Conover and Iman's (1981) suggestion for using rank transformation procedures, where usual parametric procedures are used on the ranks of the data instead of the data themselves. Accordingly, a multiple regression is used for assessing the impact of ranked data of the marketing mix adaptation and market intelligence generation on ranked data of BGs' performance:

$$\begin{aligned}\text{Performance} = {} & \beta 0 + \beta 1\text{Product Adaptation} + \beta 2\text{Price Adaptation} \\ & + \beta 3\text{Promotion Adaptation} + \beta 4\text{Sales Force} \\ & \text{Adaptation} + \beta 5\text{Market Intelligence Generation} \\ & + \beta 6\text{BG Maturity}\end{aligned}$$

Checking for the potential threats of multicollinearity variance inflation factors (VIF) analyses were conducted (Table 3.4). The maximum VIF value obtained was 1.722, well within recommended levels and below ten, suggesting that multicollinearity was not an issue (Field, 2005). Moreover, the correlation table (Table 3.3) shows that none of the correlation coefficients are above 0.6, thereby indicating that there is no problem of excessive multicollinearity (ibid.).

Table 3.4 Regression results

	B	s.e.	Exp (β)	VIF
Intercept	7.445	11.672	–	–
Product adaptation	0.077	0.122	0.074	1.160
Price adaptation	0.031	0.144	0.031	1.722
Promotion adaptation	–0.079	0.143	–0.076	1.621
Sales force adaptation	0.302*	0.135	0.290	1.422
Market intelligence generation	0.380***	0.112	0.377	1.059
BG maturity	5.404	4.019	0.153	1.100
R2	0.272 (*R2*); 0.201 (*R2* adjusted)			
F statistic	3.854**			
N	69			

Notes: Significance levels: †$p < 0.1$; *$p < 0.05$; **$p < 0.01$; ***$p < 0.001$.

FINDINGS AND DISCUSSION

Table 3.4 shows the results of a linear regression analysis. The test result is significant ($F = 3.854$, df $= 6$, $p < 0.01$) thereby indicating adequate fit of the data to the model. The adjusted R^2 indicates that 20 per cent of the variance is explained by the independent variables.

First, in terms of our control variable, BG maturity as captured by our stage classification did not impact the performance of BGs in our sample. When viewed jointly with earlier findings concerning firm age in years (Autio et al., 2000; Zhou et al., 2007), one can conclude that BGs' age regardless of measurement, does not influence their performance. Alternatively, the objective five year periods' framework may have proven to be a weak indication of BG developmental stage. And alternative measurements, based on subjective self-reporting on the status of the firm, which may differ in terms of objective number of years between firms, may be a better way to capture it in future studies.

Second, our analysis shows that market intelligence generation efforts positively and significantly affect BGs' performance ($p < 0.001$). In this sense, our findings are consistent with earlier findings suggesting that market orientation in general impacts firm performance (Morgan et al., 2004; Kropp et al., 2006; Kocak and Abimbola, 2009; Wang et al., 2009). In this sense, our findings show that the market intelligence generation dimension of market orientation carries such an effect, even when examined separately from other aspects of market orientation.

Third, and surprisingly, our analysis shows that while the sales force dimension of promotion adaptations impact BGs' performance ($p < 0.05$), neither adaptation nor standardization in product, price and the advertising dimension of promotions impact BG performance. Here, with respect to promotion, our findings may be somewhat similar to those by Zou et al. (1997), who showed that adaptation of customer service was significantly correlated with export intensity, while standardized promotion was not, in their sample of Colombian exporters. More specifically, with respect to adaptation of sales force, our findings are also similar to Shoham's (1996), who identified a significant effect of sales force management adaptation on sales, profits and profit change in his sample of US manufacturing exporters.

Moreover, the finding of non-significant effects of marketing mix elements on performance supports earlier studies showing similar results (Samiee and Roth, 1992; O'Cass and Julian, 2003; Navarro et al., 2010), while further exhibiting that such findings also hold when breaking them into the specific components of product, price and advertising dimensions of promotions. Nevertheless, they also contradict other findings of significant effect of product adaptation on certain performance indicators (Johnson and Arunthanes, 1995; Zou et al., 1997; Shoham, 1999; Lee and Griffith, 2004; Calantone et al., 2006), price adaptation on certain performance indicators (Shoham, 1996; Lee and Griffith, 2004), and advertising-related elements of promotion on certain performance indicators (Shoham, 1996, 1999).

Faced with these conflicting findings, we concur with earlier calls for more nuanced analysis acknowledging potential contingencies (Theodosiou and Leonidou, 2003; Katsikeas et al., 2006; Schilke et al., 2009). More specifically, more detailed analysis of particularities associated with specific target markets, industries, timing and co-alignment with other firm strategies may all be relevant to understanding discrepancies in results, especially, when evaluating effects of marketing adaptation and standardization strategies on firm performance.

Moreover, the same logic can also explain an additional interesting observation indicating that market intelligence generation efforts do not significantly correlate with any of the marketing mix adaptation elements, as shown in Table 3.3. Here, one may again suggest that marketing intelligence informs both adaptation and standardization of marketing mix elements at the same time, and that both occur simultaneously with respect to different specific elements and market contexts.

Acknowledging Limitations

While the current study presents interesting findings, it also incorporates some limitations that should be acknowledged. First, our data are collected in the small, open and developed economy of Israel, which has some unique characteristics including inherent cultural diversity, dependence on distant markets versus neighbouring ones, as well as a strong bias towards high-technology and knowledge-intensive start-ups. Accordingly, similar studies of BGs are encouraged in different contexts such as larger home markets, more culturally homogeneous home markets, markets enjoying healthy trade relations with neighbouring economies, and a more industrially diversified start-up pool.

Second, one may question the relevance of using all nine items of the EXPERF scale, as developed by Zou et al. (1998), especially with respect to evaluations of strategic performance in the context of relatively young firms. This was done in the current study because interviews we held with 12 managers of born global firms, before the survey data collection effort, revealed concern and consideration of strategic performance by these managers. Moreover, since analysis of survey data shows that all items loaded nicely on the performance scale, it was decided to use the scale as is. Nevertheless, in future research, one may experiment with potential modifications to items of strategic performance, so as to better reflect realities specific to young firms.

Third, our survey did not include all of Lages et al.'s (2008) STRATADAPT scale items, only using 16 of the 30 original items. This was done in order to capture core dimensions of the construct with respect to product, price and promotions, while at the same time constraining the survey length, for increasing response rate and the share of complete data forms out of overall responses. Nevertheless, such choice may influence both factor structure and measured effects. Accordingly, studies that may accommodate all items can help evaluate the extent to which results were affected by the use of a shorter list of items.

Finally, our measurement of BG developmental stage was based on fixed periods set by number of years since establishment. However, maturity and developmental stage depend on more than the objective amount of time passed. Future studies may consider the potential merits of an alternative measurement, which can be based on subjective self-reporting along a list of items reflecting aspects of the organization's developmental status.

CONCLUSION

The current chapter presented a study seeking to contribute to the understanding of BGs' post-establishment performance. Based on the analysis of survey data collected from Israeli BGs, the study reveals that marketing adaptation efforts with respect to sales force significantly impacts BGs' performance. However, adaptation efforts with respect to product, price and promotions do not affect BGs' performance. In addition, the study also shows that marketing intelligence generation also has significant impact on BGs' performance. Finally, the developmental stages achieved by the BGs, as captured by pre-defined firm age groups, also did not affect their performance.

Accordingly, the study contributes to a body of research shifting focus towards BGs' performance, while highlighting the importance of marketing intelligence generation and responsiveness, as captured by adaptation of their sales force for enhancing BGs' performance. Moreover, by examining the relevance of marketing adaptation strategies for BGs, the current study also extends our understanding of born global marketing practices in particular. Finally, with the exception of sales force management, our study supports earlier studies showing that neither adaptation nor standardization are uniquely associated with BGs' performance (O'Cass and Julian, 2003; Navarro et al., 2010). And, similar to earlier studies, we also propose that both adaptation and standardization are evident in BGs' operation, while their contribution to performance is pending on firm, market and timing particularities (Theodosiou and Leonidou, 2003).

Accordingly, the current study serves as an invitation for further research examining these particularities and their potential mediating effects. Such studies can build on the logic outlined in earlier efforts by Katsikeas et al. (2006) and Schilke et al. (2009) studying multinational companies in general. Here, future studies should constrain data collection to the BG context, and include specific indicators of adaptation levels for all marketing mix elements.

Furthermore, while it is assumed that marketing intelligence efforts may suggest adaptation requirements or standardization opportunities, due to the superior understanding of the market, our own data exhibited insignificant correlations between the two. Hence, future studies are also encouraged to explore the potential moderating effects of market, firm and product particularities on the effect market intelligence generation is expected to have on adaptation extent of marketing mix elements.

Finally, when considering BG developmental stages, while our numerical framing of five years proved not to have an effect on BG performance, this may be more due to weak measurement than lack of real impact. Accordingly, authors are encouraged to develop a measurement, reflecting more subjective reporting on the firm's status on a list of items, for capturing BG developmental stages following the three-stage approach suggested by Gabrielsson et al. (2008).

REFERENCES

Aldrich, H.E. and C.M. Fiol (1994), 'Fools rush in? The institutional context of industry creation', *The Academy of Management Review*, **19**(4), 645–70.

Aspelund, A., T.K. Madsen and Ø. Moen (2007), 'A review of the foundation, international marketing strategies, and performance of international new ventures', *European Journal of Marketing*, **41**(11–12), 1423–48.

Autio, E., H.J. Sapienza and J.G. Almeida (2000), 'Effects of age at entry, knowledge intensity, and imitability on international growth', *Academy of Management Journal*, **43**(5), 909–24.

Calantone, R.J., D. Kim, J.B. Schmidt and S.T. Cavusgil (2006), 'The influence of internal and external firm factors on international product adaptation strategy and export performance: a three-country comparison', *Journal of Business Research*, **59**(2), 176–85.

Cavusgil, S.T. and S. Zou (1994), 'Marketing strategy–performance relationship: an investigation of the empirical link in export market ventures', *Journal of Marketing*, **58**(1), 1–21.

Conover, W.J. and R.L. Iman (1981), 'Rank transformations as a bridge between parametric and nonparametric statistics', *The American Statistician*, **35**(3), 124–9.

Delmar, F. and S. Shane (2004), 'Legitimating first: organizing activities and the survival of new ventures', *Journal of Business Venturing*, **19**(3), 385–410.

Efrat, K. and A. Shoham (2012), 'Born global firms: the differences between their short- and long-term performance drivers', *Journal of World Business*, **47**(4), 675–85.

Field, A. (2005), *Discovering Statistics Using SPSS* (2nd edition), London: Sage Publications Ltd.

Freeman, S., R. Edwards and B. Schroder (2006), 'How smaller born-global firms use networks and alliances to overcome constraints to rapid internationalization', *Journal of International Marketing*, **14**(3), 33–63.

Gabrielsson, M. and V.H.M. Kirpalani (2004), 'Born globals: how to reach new business space rapidly', *International Business Review*, **13**(5), 555–71.

Gabrielsson, M. and V.H.M. Kirpalani (2012), 'Overview, background and historical origin of born globals: development of theoretical and empirical research', in M. Gabrielsson and V.H.M. Kirpalani (eds), *Handbook of Research on Born Globals*, Cheltenham, UK and Northampton, MA, USA: Edward Elgar Publishing, pp. 3–15.

Gabrielsson, M., V.H.M. Kirpalani, P. Dimitratos, C.A. Solberg and A. Zucchella (2008), 'Born globals: propositions to help advance the theory', *International Business Review*, **17**(4), 385–401.

Gleason, K.C., J. Madura and J. Wiggenhorn (2006), 'Operating characteristics, risk, and performance of born-global firms', *International Journal of Managerial Finance*, **2**(2), 96–120.

Hallbäck, J. and J. Larimo (2007), 'Variety in international new ventures – typological analysis and beyond', *Journal of Euromarketing*, **16**(1–2), 37–57.

Jaworski, B.J. and A.K. Kohli (1993), 'Market orientation: antecedents and consequences', *Journal of Marketing*, **57**(3), 53–70.

Johnson, J.L. and W. Arunthanes (1995), 'Ideal and actual product adaptation in US exporting firms: market-related determinants and impact on performance', *International Marketing Review*, **12**(3), 31–46.

Karra, N., N. Phillips and P. Tracey (2008), 'Building the born global firm: developing entrepreneurial capabilities for international new venture success', *Long Range Planning*, **41**(4), 440–58.

Katsikeas, C.S., S. Samiee and M. Theodosiou (2006), 'Strategy fit and performance consequences of international marketing standardization', *Strategic Management Journal*, **27**(9), 867–90.

Kirpalani, V.H.M. and M. Gabrielsson (2012), 'Born globals: research areas that still need to be covered more fully', in M. Gabrielsson and V.H.M. Kirpalani (eds), *Handbook of Research on Born Globals*, Cheltenham, UK and Northampton, MA, USA: Edward Elgar Publishing, pp. 99–127.

Knight, G.A. and S.T. Cavusgil (1996), 'The born global firm: a challenge to traditional internationalization theory', in T.K. Madsen (ed.), *Advances in International Marketing* (Vol. 8), Greenwich, CT: JAI Press Inc, pp. 11–26.

Knight, G.A. and S.T. Cavusgil (2004), 'Innovation, organizational capabilities, and the born-global firm', *Journal of International Business Studies*, **35**(2), 124–41.

Knight, G., T.K. Madsen and P. Servais (2004), 'An inquiry into born-global firms in Europe and the USA', *International Marketing Review*, **21**(6), 645–65.

Kocak, A. and T. Abimbola (2009), 'The effects of entrepreneurial marketing on born global performance', *International Marketing Review*, **26**(4), 439–52.

Kohli, A.K. and B.J. Jaworski (1990), 'Market orientation: the construct, research propositions, and managerial implications', *Journal of Marketing*, **54**(2), 1–18.

Kropp, F., N.J. Lindsay and A. Shoham (2006), 'Entrepreneurial, market, and learning orientations and international entrepreneurial business venture performance in South African firms', *International Marketing Review*, **23**(5), 504–23.

Kuivalainen, O., P. Sundqvist and P. Servais (2007), 'Firms' degree of born-globalness, international entrepreneurial orientation and export performance', *Journal of World Business*, **42**(3), 253–67.

Lages, L.F., J.L. Abrantes and C.R. Lages (2008), 'The STRATADAPT scale: a measure of marketing strategy adaptation to international business markets', *International Marketing Review*, **25**(5), 584–600.

Lee, C. and D.A. Griffith (2004), 'The marketing strategy–performance relationship in an export-driven developing economy: a Korean illustration', *International Marketing Review*, **21**(3), 321–34.

Leonidou, L.C. and S. Samiee (2012), 'Born global or simply rapidly internationalizing? Review, critique, and future prospects', in M. Gabrielsson and V.H.M. Kirpalani (eds), *Handbook of Research on Born Globals*, Cheltenham, UK and Northampton, MA, USA: Edward Elgar Publishing, pp. 16–35.

Leonidou, L.C., C.S. Katsikeas and S. Samiee (2002), 'Marketing strategy determinants of export performance: a meta-analysis', *Journal of Business Research*, **55**(1), 51–67.

Madsen, T.K., E. Rasmussen and P. Servais (2000), 'Differences and similarities between born globals and other types of exporters', in S. Zou (ed.), *Advances in International Marketing* (Vol. 10), Greenwich, CT: JAI Press, pp. 247–65.

Mazzarol, T. (2011), *Entrepreneurship and Innovation: Readings and Cases* (2nd edition), Prahran: Tilde University Press.

McDougall, P.P. and B.M. Oviatt (1996), 'New venture internationalization, strategic change, and performance: a follow-up study', *Journal of Business Venturing*, **11**(1), 23–40.

Moen, Ø. (2002), 'The born globals – a new generation of small European exporters', *International Marketing Review*, **19**(2/3), 156–75.

Morgan, N.A., A. Kaleka and C.S. Katsikeas (2004), 'Antecedents of export venture performance: a theoretical model and empirical assessment', *Journal of Marketing*, **68**(1), 90–108.

Navarro, A., F. Losada, E. Ruzo and J.A. Díez (2010), 'Implications of perceived competitive advantages, adaptation of marketing tactics and export commitment on export performance', *Journal of World Business*, **45**(1), 49–58.

O'Cass, A. and C. Julian (2003), 'Examining firm and environmental influences on export marketing mix strategy and export performance of Australian exporters', *European Journal of Marketing*, **37**(3/4), 366–84.

Oviatt, B.M. and P.P. McDougall ([1994] 2005), 'Toward a theory of international new ventures', *Journal of International Business Studies*, **36**(1), 29–41.

Rialp, A., J. Rialp and G.A. Knight (2005), 'The phenomenon of early internationalizing firms: what do we know after a decade (1993–2003) of scientific inquiry?', *International Business Review*, **14**(2), 147–66.

Ryans, J.K. Jr., D. Griffith and D.S. White (2003), 'Standardized/adaptation of international marketing strategy: necessary conditions for the advancement of knowledge', *International Marketing Review*, **20**(6), 588–603.

Samiee, S. and K. Roth (1992), 'The influence of global marketing standardization on performance', *Journal of Marketing*, **56**(2), 1–17.

Schilke, O., M. Reimann and J.S. Thomas (2009), 'When does international marketing standardization matter to firm performance?', *Journal of International Marketing*, **17**(4), 24–46.

Sharma, D.D. and A. Blomstermo (2003), 'The internationalization process of born globals: a network view', *International Business Review*, **12**(6), 739–53.

Shoham, A. (1996), 'Marketing-mix standardization', *Journal of Global Marketing*, **10**(2), 53–73.

Shoham, A. (1999), 'Bounded rationality, planning, standardization of international strategy, and export performance: a structural model examination', *Journal of International Marketing*, **7**(2), 24–50.

Solberg, C.A. (2000), 'Standardization or adaptation of the international marketing mix: the role of the local subsidiary/representative', *Journal of International Marketing*, **8**(1), 78–98.

Svensson, G. (2006), 'A quest for a common terminology: the concept of born glocals', *Management Decision*, **44**(9), 1311–17.

Theodosiou, M. and L.C. Leonidou (2003), 'Standardization versus adaptation of international marketing strategy: an integrative assessment of the empirical research', *International Business Review*, **12**(2), 141–71.

Wang, C.L., G.T.M. Hult, D.J. Ketchen and P.K. Ahmed (2009), 'Knowledge management orientation, market orientation, and firm performance: an integration and empirical examination', *Journal of Strategic Marketing*, **17**(2), 99–122.

Zahra, S.A. (2005), 'A theory of international new ventures: a decade of research', *Journal of International Business Studies*, **36**(1), 20–28.

Zahra, S.A., R.D. Ireland and M.A. Hitt (2000), 'International expansion by new venture firms: international diversity, mode of market entry, technological learning, and performance', *The Academy of Management Journal*, **43**(5), 925–50.

Zhou, L., W.-P. Wu and X. Luo (2007), 'Internationalization and the performance of born-global SMEs: the mediating role of social networks', *Journal of International Business Studies*, **38**(4), 673–90.

Zou, S., D.M. Andrus and D.W. Norvell (1997), 'Standardization of international marketing strategy by firms from a developing country', *International Marketing Review*, **14**(2), 107–23.

Zou, S., C.R. Taylor and G.E. Osland (1998), 'The EXPERF scale: a cross-national generalized export performance measure', *Journal of International Marketing*, **6**(3), 37–58.

4. International entrepreneurial networking strategies: breaking out as a global player

Saara Julkunen, Mika Gabrielsson and Markus Raatikainen

INTRODUCTION

Finland consists of a large region and a population of over 5.5 million people. The GDP is USD250 million and the per capita income is approximately USD38 700. Basically, the domestic market is relatively limited for most products. Therefore production for export as a percentage of GDP is higher than in Western Europe, thus making Finland more vulnerable to global economic trends. The Finnish economy is mainly focused on export-led industries like the metals industry, the forest industry and high technology. However, the service sector has grown rapidly, now comprising the largest sector of the economy.

Finnish entrepreneurship culture is founded in small and medium-sized enterprises (SMEs). As much as 99.8 per cent of firms have fewer than 250 employees (Ministry of Employment and the Economy, 2012; Hyrsky, 2007) and these firms often create new know-how and innovations (Partanen and Servais, 2012). On that account, Finland belongs to the group of small and open economies (SMOPECs). National policy supports a firm foundation for business, which is mainly based on technology-led aspects but, as a local speciality, the Finnish government has a long, successful history of playing an efficient and fruitful role in fostering an energetic video game industry, which is now paying dividends (e.g., Angry Birds).

The influence of globalization and technology development for the business world as well as the importance of SMEs for both local and global economies has led to a major turnaround in Finnish society. During the last five years, many large corporations have moved their businesses abroad, yet many small companies were established. Therefore, know-how has increasingly shifted from big companies to smaller firms. Factors such as constrained domestic markets and increasing competition are pushing growth-oriented firms into global markets (Madsen and Servais, 1997). The number of new international ventures (INVs) and growth-oriented firms is higher in Finland than in Europe in general (Eurofound, 2012).

Based on the earlier research, the international and entrepreneurial processes and strategies can be expected to have an impact on the networking of the firm. International business environments require an effective use of networks and interorganizational relationships in order to safeguard access to necessary resources needed to generate competitive advantage (Sepulveda and Gabrielsson, 2013). The theoretical background is then found in research of the resource-based view (RBV), which separates tangible, intangible and organizational resources that provide sustainability through their specific characteristics: value, uniqueness, non-imitability and non-substitutability (Barney, 1991). The theory exposes different alternatives in the internationalization of SMEs when they try to achieve and secure a sustainable competitive position in the global marketplace. Young INVs often lack Barney's (1991) resources and therefore networks become vital.

With the focus on partnerships, entrepreneurial, international and strategic processes influence the question of how to create benefits for the partners in networks despite asymmetries of power or firms' sizes, or differences in the degree of internationalization. Strong bilateral partnerships between multinational enterprises (MNEs) and SMEs are crucial for creating successful global business in a region such as Finland. Though SME partners have apparent asymmetry between each other, SMEs can achieve a great number of benefits in collaboration with stronger (MNE) partners – a better position on the side of a bigger partner in the market, for example. MNEs can achieve new or different perspectives with smaller partners and can expand their network outside their own business environment.

In this chapter, international strategies of Finnish SMEs are presented as examples of traditional internationalization approaches and INVs. The cases highlight the important role of strong relationship ties as a key source for achieving vital positions in global networks. Relationships with industry leaders were highly emphasized among firms aiming for a better position compared to their main competitors. The practical recommendations relate to how entrepreneurs from different types of internationalizing SMEs should network with larger counterparts and how to succeed in breaking out from the high-dependence relationship into independent global players.

ENTREPRENEURSHIP AND INTERNATIONALIZATION

International entrepreneurship is a theme that has been recently discussed more frequently in Finnish society. More than ever it is asked

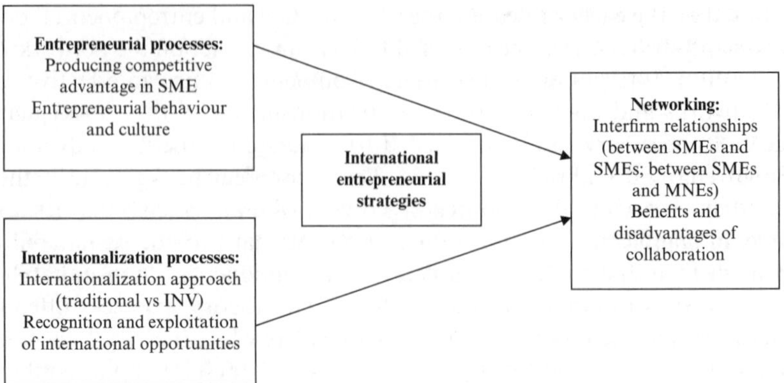

Figure 4.1 Theoretical framework of the chapter

how so-called traditional firms and INVs can create, develop and maintain their international networks. This calls for an understanding of the processes of entrepreneurship and internationalization and the influence they have on networking (Gabrielsson et al., 2008). In Figure 4.1, the entrepreneurial processes are suggested to be composed of competitive advantage as well as entrepreneurial behaviour and culture of SMEs. Internationalization processes include the internationalization approaches of SMEs and recognition and exploitation of international opportunities. These factors influence networking through international entrepreneurial strategies used by traditional internationalizing firms or INVs. Different interfirm relationships as well as benefits and disadvantages of collaboration may result from networking.

Entrepreneurial Processes

The classic literature mainly determines the entrepreneur's role in terms of transaction cost economics, internationalization decisions, theories of the firm and its growth and theories of innovation. In the most current international business literature, the entrepreneur's role has been presented as a participant and main actor in the social environment including different systems and networks between business actors (Jones and Coviello, 2005). The view is dependent on an entrepreneur's identity, values and preferences, and emotions that influence on his or her decision-making and ability to handle risk (Miller, 2007). Freeman (2012), for example, underlines the role of social ties of the international entrepreneur next to recognition and exploitation of international opportunities when building interfirm networks.

Both international business and entrepreneurship literature have shown that firms' knowledge, know-how and competence have an effect on international growth and commitment decisions (Johanson and Vahlne, 1977; Reuber and Fischer, 1997). McDougall and Oviatt (2000, p. 903) write that 'international entrepreneurship is a combination of innovative, proactive, and risk-seeking behavior that crosses national borders and is intended to create value in organizations'. Kuivalainen et al. (2007) add that such an entrepreneurial orientation promotes firms' early, rapid and large-scale internationalization. The competitive advantage of SMEs (Sepulveda and Gabrielsson, 2013) is built on these elements and hence entrepreneurial behaviour (McDougall and Oviatt, 2000) and culture are critical elements for successful networking and firm performance.

Finnish entrepreneurship culture is often described through facility limitations in SMOPEC countries. Lack of economies of scale or poor access to economies of scale (Welch and Luostarinen, 1988; Madsen and Servais, 1997) is a general constraint for specialized firms, especially in business environments like Finland. Environmental (or industry) factors – smallness, saturation and isolation of domestic market with the effects of globalization – push firms overseas (Chetty and Campbell-Hunt, 2004; Knight and Cavusgil, 2004). There are simply not enough domestic customers for the firms' products/services, and in order to safeguard their demand and avoid bankruptcy firms seek buyers from abroad. Furthermore, resource constraints often force firms to adopt a strategy of a few key customers (i.e., niche) with core competency (Knight and Cavusgil, 2004; Partanen and Servais, 2012).

On the side of entrepreneurial and internationalization processes, strategic decisions therefore have a strong influence on firms' network building. Finnish entrepreneurship culture is based on SMEs, which employ over 62 per cent of the entire workforce in Finland and nearly 40 per cent Finnish GDP came from these firms in 2013 (Federation of Finnish Enterprises, 2014). On the other hand, the current global situation is changing all the time and the EU particularly is in a more and more challenging financial state. The last big surprise was when Nokia moved out of Finland due to the Microsoft buyout in 2013. The forthcoming changes have an extensive influence on the whole of Finnish business life. The know-how that has been generated by Nokia is hopefully shifting to Finnish SMEs as a result of former Nokia employees establishing start-ups. Such a development offers new challenges to SMEs but also requires an open mind to benefit from the newly available personnel resources. This could be the right time to create new success stories.

Internationalization Processes

The internationalization of traditional firms has been described as a process of step-by-step expansion. In this model, firms' internationalization activities are first targeted to markets that are psychically close and exploit less committed entry modes such as exporting (Johanson and Vahlne, 1977, 1990). The firms learn and increase their foreign market knowledge over time through international experience. After that, they slowly increase their foreign market commitments, and may later expand their business to more psychically distant markets. Based on historical and geographical circumstances, Finnish SMEs have originally begun their international actions in EU countries or Russia when following that traditional internationalization.

The international business literature (covering management and entrepreneurship) has described SMEs that enter rapidly into foreign markets in terms such as INVs, export/import start-ups, global start-ups, instant internationals and born globals. The INVs are specifically determined by the definition that the management of a firm views the world as their marketplace since inception (Rennie, 1993). Among these firms, the role of entrepreneurs' international experience has specifically been regarded with empathy (Madsen and Servais, 1997; Reuber and Fischer, 1997; Chetty and Campbell-Hunt, 2004). Despite the use of the term INV and its processes, the main attempt of all current studies has been to try to understand these new SMEs whose behaviour deviates from the traditional ones. Nowadays, Finland is one area of the world where the number of SMEs has rapidly increased during the last decade (Gabrielsson et al., 2008).

Previous literature on internationalization of SMEs has indicated in particular that lack of knowledge induces major challenges for the internationalization process (Johanson and Vahlne, 1977). Focusing on entrepreneurs, Westhead et al. (2002) argue that a high degree of risk is a part of internationalization and entrepreneurs of SMEs are less able to manage uncertainty and risk than larger and more financially stable and experienced companies (Freeman et al., 2006). On the other hand, Gleason and Madura (2006) found in their study that risks between globally and geographically operating INVs are not significant. Overall though, the results are not black and white. For example, Kuivalainen et al. (2007) studied 783 Finnish export firms and 185 of those firms were INVs. They analysed firms' levels of rapid internationalization and compared these firms to each other. Surprisingly, the results did not show any support for the higher risk taking of global firms.

As a SMOPEC country, Finland has been relatively successful in creating new firms and innovations in the global market. This can be evidenced by, for example, the mobile game firm Supercell that is globally well known for its *Clash of Clans*, *Hay Day* and *Boom Beach* games. One of the main challenges is actually how to keep these firms connected with Finland and Finnish game developers in the future. It is important to note that these employees are highly dependent on the success of their firms' internationalization. In Holmlund and Kock's (1998) study of 128 Finnish SMEs, findings show that internationalization is highly related to home-based social relationships as well as foreign networks.

International Entrepreneurial Strategies

The success of SMEs' internationalization is highly dependent on the chosen strategy. Among the traditional internationalizing firms, strategic choices are initially based on learning and accumulation of foreign market knowledge over time. The international experience increases as a result of this learning, which leads to specific investments and commitment to the well-known foreign market. Later these firms may expand their investments to more psychically distant markets (Johanson and Vahlne, 1997; Gabrielsson et al., 2008).

In contrast, INVs meet three types of challenges in their inception. First, because of firms' origins, they lack economies of scale (Welch and Luostarinen, 1993; Freeman et al., 2006). Second, they have limited knowledge and financial resources (Karlsen et al., 2003; Freeman et al., 2006; Gabrielsson et al., 2008). Third, risk aversion arises when inexperienced managers take the high-level risk of internationalization (Dimitratos and Plakoyiannaki, 2003; Freeman et al., 2006).

On these accounts however, both Finnish traditional firms and INVs are quite open to building new relationships with strong partners, despite the probability of resulting asymmetry with MNEs. Finnish business agrees with the thoughts of Loane and Bell (2006, p. 474) who write that 'growth takes place through the extension of the firm's network through investment in network positions and development of network relationships'.

Among INVs, a great number of risks are involved in rapid foreign market expansion. These risks can be minimized by successful strategic choices that underline the role of international entrepreneurial strategies (Figure 4.1). Hallbäck and Gabrielsson (2013) suggest that INVs should use entrepreneurial marketing strategies in order to overcome their resource constraints. Bell et al. (2003) proposes a strategy of client followership. Freeman et al. (2006) assume that trusted relationships decrease the level of risk in foreign market entry. Consequently, arrangements with existing partners reduce the risk of INVs entering new markets.

In current research, SMEs have particularly been advised to avoid losing their way in rapid globalization. Therefore, INVs have to plan a breakout strategy that aims at the firm's own development (Gabrielsson et al., 2008). Without a breakout strategy INVs will otherwise become stuck with a global player's strategy that results in development slowdown and finally to consolidation.

Firms that choose the strategy of rapid internationalization and globalization have to utilize both their existing relationships (personal relationships) and create new ones (both personal and interfirm) in order to survive, grow, maintain their independence, and finally to succeed. Because of the varied power balance among interfirm relationships, the acceptance of asymmetrical power is often required between partners. Hence, international entrepreneurial strategies must take a stand on at least the following: (1) how to best leverage the resources of a large partner, and whether this will relate to market access, distribution, branding or R&D resources; (2) the extent that overdependence can be allowed and for how long; (3) how the company breaks out from the relationship as an independent global player.

Networking

Network is a broad concept that consists of different relationships (i.e., bilateral relationships). Three various perspectives can be identified from the previous network research: entrepreneurial network research, social network research and business network research (Slotte-Kock and Coviello, 2010). Literature has also emphasized the importance of personal relationships in the founding process, strategy implementation and rapid internationalization of INVs (Coviello and Munro, 1995, 1997; Rasmussan et al., 2001). The international business environment in Finland is strongly dependent on different networks and business relationships. Environmental, industrial and firm-specific factors in Finland push SMEs towards foreign markets because of the limited market area (Knight and Cavusgil, 2004; Oviatt and McDougall, 2005). Therefore the aim of competitive advantage in entrepreneurial processes includes an impact on well-managed relationships in well-functioning networks right around the world.

The lack of financial resources is one of the main reasons that push firms to create, develop and maintain interfirm relationships. For example, Rovio Entertainment (a firm behind the Angry Birds brand) had to accept all the relationships that paid even a little to secure their turnover in its early days. Therefore we can say in practice that SMEs' performance is produced with different partners that have changing roles in the SME's life cycle. Ritter et al. (2004) propose that more focus is needed on the managerial topics of external, interorganizational and cross-departmental relationships.

MNE–SME relationships

Firms' internationalization is important also for firms that already have a position in foreign networks and these connections can be seen as a bridge to new market areas (Johanson and Mattsson, 1988). Networking between international firms seems to be a very challenging area where firms have a different position in the market. SMEs have to evaluate a balance between relationships that are beneficial and those that are not. That means forecasting about rewards that legitimate some relationship. It is sometimes impossible to predict the future and therefore short-term gains from a certain business network might turn against the firm in the long run. Gabrielsson et al. (2008) mention that SMEs' cooperation with MNEs might become too intensive and therefore SMEs may become overly dependent on a particular relationship.

SMEs are often able to achieve rapid growth from their inception when they are in collaboration with MNEs. Using other networks (and the Internet) the creation of demand usually takes longer (Gabrielsson et al., 2008). Literature indicates that INV firms from the software sector in particular utilize contacts with larger firms. With the help of MNEs, these young firms are able to create networks of informal and formal contacts offering both knowledge and global market entry options that facilitate rapid globalization (Coviello and Munro, 1997; Sharma and Blomstermo, 2003; Gabrielsson et al., 2004; Gabrielsson and Gabrielsson, 2013). For example, Rovio took a big leap towards a successful business life when Apple identified it as an important partner because of its Angry Birds product. Loane and Bell (2006) have, however, written that instead of explaining the rapid internationalization of SMEs, the network approach often provides tools to overcome resource constraints.

The global level of competition pushes SMEs to build networks between each other and with MNEs. Freeman et al. (2006) propose that strategic alliances, licensing and joint ventures with large players should be utilized in overcoming financial risks and developing sourcing, sales and new product development. They state that with client followership new customers will be made and visibility in foreign network will be enhanced. Obviously these are the options that entrepreneurs weigh up, but before any decisions or contracts are concluded it is important to keep in mind that poorly planned cooperation with a large multinational player can be a double-edged sword for a small firm in its internationalization process.

A high level of competition may ensue from highly active relationship building (Ulaga and Eggert, 2010).

Network types

Local and foreign relationships can be divided into three main categories based on their nature. The first category is a formal relationship category that includes all business relationships that firms possess (Coviello and Munro, 1995, 1997). Ritter et al. (2004) have stated that business relationships are embedded internally in departments, units and employees and externally with customers, suppliers and rivals/competitors of a company. The second category belongs to family and friends where personal relationships (i.e., non-business relationships) are informal relationships (Coviello and Munro, 1995, 1997). In line with Coviello and Munro (1995, 1997), entrepreneurs'/CEOs' personal contacts have an influence on a market selection and how actively a firm seeks foreign contacts in their market entry process. However, Ojala (2009) found in his study of eight Finnish software companies that the market initiative for psychically distant market may be a strategic decision and new networks would be actively developed only after a target market and an entry mode selection.

There are also third party actors that constitute our last category, which is that of intermediary relationships. These intermediaries (or agents) connect buyers and sellers so that the relationship works through the third party (Oviatt and McDougall, 2005). This type of situation can also be described as indirect ties, where the intermediary helps otherwise disconnected companies to communicate and forge relationships. In the previous literature these actors have also been called 'brokers' and they are able to provide links between buyers and sellers in various markets (ibid.)

EMPIRICAL RESULTS AMONG FINNISH BUSINESSES

In this chapter, we present a case comparison from Finland consisting of one INV and one traditional firm by describing their development in terms of globalization, strategies and networking approach.

The Case of an INV Firm: Optitec

Optitec (pseudonym) founded in 2012 is an INV, which operates in the industry of high technology and is a good example of business that has started from university research (see Table 4.1). The core business of this academic spin-off is based on mathematical modelling and on providing

Table 4.1 Characteristics, challenges and networking of the case firms

	INV, Optitec (Pseudonym)	Traditional Firm, Powerflute
Characteristics	Founded in 2012	Founded in 1968
	B2B high solutions	B2B low solutions
	Vision of going global from inception	Global vision has emerged step by step
	Previous research and industrial experience	Long-term industrial experience
Challenges	Global strategy, reputation and team building from inception	Limited customer base in the global business. Major paper manufacturing customers exist in few countries
	Finding the first global customers, enabling rapid globalization	Establishing strategic alliance with the main MNEs emerging in the consolidating industry
	Physical presence in later development	
	Dependency on pilot customers	Avoids high dependency with partners
Entrepreneurial strategies	Leveraging of market access, distribution, branding and R&D resources from its MNE partners	Local flexibility in organizing sales distribution to large MNE customers or through other channels to achieve market access to relevant markets
	Avoids over-dependence (business decentralization to three industries; exit plans)	Own independence is highly emphasized. However, dependence on them is enhanced through entrepreneurial support services offered to key MNE customers
	Unique solution and education programme development capabilities to serve MNE partners' needs guarantee INV new customer acquisition and sustain its position as a global player	The strong brand and long-term relationships enable it to expand within its MNE customer base and strengthen the firm's position as an independent global player
Networking	Strategic alliances with MNEs provide distribution, sales and service channels to target global business segments,	The sales organization is selected highly dependent on the country location of the international partner
	Achieving alliances and end customers with pilot customers	Strong relationship ties emphasized and maintained by the regional sales management of Powerflute

measurement system solutions for its customers. It is focused on developing and marketing high-technology sensors that supply high solutions in response to the needs of various processing industries (e.g., food, chemical, oil and paper industry). The INV was established in spring 2012 immediately after a corporate acquisition of the predecessor firm that had been founded four years earlier in 2008 by the CEO and a few other founding members. The current firm uses similar technology to its predecessor, although it operates with a different concept and in a new global business environment. The firm's business vision of rapid globalization was adopted since its inception. The main argument for the global vision was that local Finnish markets were too limited for firms' high-technology products and high solutions. The CEO explains: 'We are having a very harsh economic recession in the EU . . . you don't develop or innovate here'.

Interpersonal and interfirm relationships were utilized especially for finding business know-how during the inception. Governmental intermediaries, local consultancy firms and individuals with industrial experience were found particularly helpful when founding the firm. The CEO sees that the main challenges of INVs often relate to how well known the firm is nationally and globally and where it can find skilful team members. He underlines that lots of media attention during the corporate acquisition benefited them in the firm's establishment. Along with efficient recruiting, the CEO emphasizes strategic management and all employees' understanding and commitment to a firm's strategy. The INV's big challenge was therefore to create an explicit strategy at the beginning of its history.

For the firm's increasing familiarity with global business, coverage in different media has been adapted as a part of the firm's marketing strategy by allocating a lot of resources to marketing. Specifically, the Internet has been an important marketing tool for the company. The marketing team has focused on the firm's home pages: they had to look fresh and innovative from the beginning.

Focusing on successful networking, the marketing strategy has been selected to increase the reliability of the firm. The CEO finds it challenging to convince the firm's network partners in the start-up phase as well as when rapidly expanding to global markets. Despite the challenges of recession in global business, existing interpersonal and interfirm relationships have positively influenced identifying pilot customers for the new firm. Focusing on these positive signs in the market, the CEO believes that market potential can be found in Europe and every other continent, although the areas with the most potential are North and South America and Oceania. Now the global competitors can be identified and the INV needs to provide various solutions for different customer segments. The differentiation of the firm's core in technology and customers' sales and service units will be therefore understood as being crucial to the firm's future. The firm's success in the future will be based on successful development of and maintaining networking. The CEO also mentioned that after a certain stage of growth, service and maintenance would become important and it would be difficult or impossible to control the after-sales from Finland.

Optitec's business requires leveraging of the large resources of its MNE partners in terms of market access, distribution, branding and R&D. The relationships with MNEs strengthen its business through the critical resources it gets from the bigger partners. Along with that, Optitec offers unique solution building and specialized education to its MNE partners. The firm wants to avoid over-dependence on partners but still needs strong relationships with different MNEs. Three of its main partners come from different industries: paper, mining and the chemical industry. The firm has established these strategic alliances to facilitate the challenges of rapid globalization. These partnerships, however, also cause negative impacts in the INV's business. For instance, such a relationship can be seen as a financial risk because the firm does not want to become too dependent on its partners. Therefore the firm wants to achieve position in the business such that the partner can be replaced when necessary. For that reason it needs to generate new reference customers. However, the firm's CEO underlines that: 'Firstly we need to find these innovators and how this happens . . . our answer is by networking . . . strategic alliances are the key question for us and we create the sales channel for this technology entirely with larger companies'.

Finnish entrepreneurial culture is often based on direct contacts between human beings. Such behaviour helps the INV to contact new partners in global business. Along with efficient networking, the firm has identified several lines of businesses that could utilize the firm's core know-how, and the technology could alternatively be sold after it has been certificated. Furthermore, the pilot customers will have a strong effect on the technology valuation. First, the references will significantly increase the value of the certified technology. The CEO estimates that the next growth stage requires global presence, such as sales offices including service and maintenance. The INV has strong confidence in its unique solution provider capability, including the highest level of professional knowledge within the specific field, which should enable the successful acquisition of new customers in the future. Therefore, it has high confidence in achieving a leading position as a global business player.

The Case of the Traditional Firm: Powerflute

The traditional firm (see Table 4.1) was established in 1968 based in a paper mill at Kuopio, in the middle of Finland. It is a leading producer of Nordic semi-chemical fluting for use in the production of high-quality corrugated board. The product is sold and distributed under the brand name Powerflute. The firm highlights that it can offer users exceptional performance and value focusing on the high level of its solution. The mill's certified quality systems include ISO9001, ISO14001 and food safety management certificate ISO 22000. Capacity of the mill is 275 000 t/a (in 2014). The firm meets the strict EU and US requirements for food packaging. It actively promotes environmental sustainability and protection throughout its production processes – from wood handling and manufacturing to product transportation – which is described as its competitive advantage among the customers. Based on that capability, it is well prepared to access new partners when necessary. The firm is listed on the London Stock Exchange's AIM list (Powerflute, 2014).

The firm has increased its market share in the international market step by step. Based on that international strategy, it is seeking access to new partners. It emphasizes the deep understanding of the new market area before its penetration. The sales manager of Powerflute states: 'We have been forced to search for somewhat different solutions [sales channels] for separate [country] markets; we need such sales processes by which the seller really understands its market and its customers. . .what paper it has so far bought and for what type of user applications'.

The different types of sales channels used in the firm depend on the chosen area for sales. At the current time it uses its own sales organizations, local agents, and the sales manager may sell directly by himself as well. The CEO and the sales manager want to decide on the model they will use on the basis of market area in their business. They also underline how important it is to understand the local culture, including customs, practices and the language of the new market area. Therefore they focus on strategic conversations before they penetrate the new market area and decide the sales organizations or models and choose the person who can operate in the new area.

The traditional firm wants to build long-term relationships with its customers, which are often described as partners. The relationships are developed and maintained by the business, but also at appropriate events that support the positive attitude between the partners: 'The golf course and no business talk. And that's enough. And then he buys from us again'.

The firm mainly builds its relationships through personal contacts and meetings. The management also make a lot of phone calls and continually communicate with possible partners. They use references and so-called test runs in business meetings with customers. However, they mention that they avoid the strong dependency between business partners and recommend that to their customers as well: 'I would not buy solely from us. . . I would also buy from competitors. So, buy, for instance, 80 per cent from us, but buy the other 20 per cent from elsewhere. . .because from time to time we have allocation problems'.

The firm therefore wants to build different relationships with different partners, including SMEs and MNEs, all over the world but keep its independence at the same time. It has a highly trusted reputation among its business partners. Through its support services, which it offers to its key MNE partners, it can ensure that the most profitable customers will remain and to some extent even be locked in with the firm. These services include, for instance, the fine-tuning of its customer's production line so that its own pulp will perform well.

The principal markets of the traditional firm are focused on fruit-growing countries in Western and Southern Europe such as Spain, Italy, Turkey and Greece. Powerflute also has a significant share of the developing markets in Asia and South America. The Group supplies many of the world's leading manufacturers of corrugated board and packaging and the use of Powerflute is specified by many end users. When it has successfully entered an MNE customer account it leverages those relations when spreading into the other countries the MNE operates in. Powerflute has a strong brand that strengthens the firm's position as an independent and global player.

CONCLUSIONS

In both cases, the development of the global recession pushes Finnish SMEs into foreign markets. The know-how is shifting from big companies to smaller firms at the same time. The development emphasizes the findings of Madsen and Servais (1997) who have written that factors such as constrained domestic markets and increasing competition are pushing growth-oriented firms into global markets. The current economic situation in Europe has also influenced the plans and finding enough potential customers in Europe was seen as a difficult or almost impossible mission. Finland is located on the fringe of Europe, which decreases realistic challenges to achieve profitable customers in the neighbouring area. Therefore, the most common reason for rapid globalization among Finnish SMEs is the geographical encroachment of customers.

Based on our empirical cases, SMEs' networking can be explained by successful entrepreneurial and internationalization processes (Gabrielsson et al., 2008) and emergence of effective international entrepreneurial networking strategies that are well fitted to the needs of INVs and traditional firms. The competitive advantage of SMEs (Sepulveda and Gabrielsson, 2013), entrepreneurial behaviour (McDougall and Oviatt, 2000) and culture, have strong impacts on successful networking (Ritter et al., 2004). Along with these elements, the networking approach is influenced by the SME's internationalization approach, whether traditional or INV, and by the need to use the network for the recognition and exploitation of opportunities (Gabrielsson et al., 2008; Freeman, 2012).

The entrepreneurship and entrepreneurial processes were more apparent in the INV, but in both cases the firms had a strong commitment to the chosen strategy, including all behaviours, decisions and processes of internationalization. In the case of the INV, a global market segment existed for the firm and therefore this strategy of rapid globalization was exploited. Lack of resources was found challenging in rapid globalization. External financing was needed to cover long research and development periods as well as the expansion to global markets. Particularly, reputation and both professional and commercial evidence played an important role in convincing the investors. The INV has developed a unique solution providing capability in specific high-technology sectors, including a specialized education programme that is built for every partner's needs in the different industries. Varied solutions offer the possibility to avoid overdependence on the relationships with MNEs. Based on its uniqueness and capabilities, the INV can be an appropriate partner for MNEs, current and new, and it can sustain a position as a global player in international business.

In the earlier research, knowledge, know-how and competence have a direct effect on international growth and commitment decisions (Johanson and Vahlne, 1977; Reuber and Fischer, 1997). Rapid internationalization and globalization often negatively relate to a lack of economies of scale, lack of resources and risk aversion (Freeman et al., 2006). Among the empirical cases, the core know-how for the INV was acquired mainly by 'sweat and tears' though existing and new interpersonal relationships provided new know-how for the firm's operations, including rapid decisions during the internationalization. In the case of the traditional firm, the firm's competence is based on long-term experience of the professional employees and a well-known reputation of the firm in the industry. These elements were supporting the step-by-step strategy in its internationalization processes. Moreover, it has enough resources and financial possibilities to build appropriate and flexible country-based sales channels in the varied international markets. It has an entrepreneurial attitude to its international strategies, including a willingness to provide different solutions for the technical problems of its customers. Also, it is able to expand its business in the existing MNE customer markets. During the four decades of its history, it has built a strong positive brand as well as a position as an independent and global player.

Despite rapid or traditional strategy in firms' internationalization, the power of different business relationships and networks are highly emphasized among Finnish SMEs. The SMEs have a need to grow beyond Finnish conditions, which leads to a search for new partners abroad within the targeted global segments. Establishing and developing relationships with MNEs was challenging but also described as strong, active and irreplaceable. Furthermore, these relationships were necessary for the growth of the INV. The firm was very dependent on these partners and this adds to the increasing risk in finding adequate investors. Interpersonal networks particularly became important for the INV because of the power of personal contacts on the side of good reputation and the Internet. The traditional firm emphasized the important role of large customers, including MNEs, which have a strong existing presence in the national markets it endeavoured to enter. At the same time, it underlined its need for autonomy and wanted to avoid a strong dependency on the partners, yet using an interesting entrepreneurial approach of tying its major MNE customer through the support services that it offers.

In the INV's case, the deeper its professional knowledge in high technology and its education, the stronger its competitive position became with its partnering MNEs and this led to an increased commitment from the MNEs. Respectively, the traditional firm's competitive position became stronger and deeper as a result of its local understanding and flexibility in sales distribution with MNEs and other SMEs and this approach led to long-term relationships.

For the managers in charge of entrepreneurially internationalizing firms it becomes essential to understand the market strategy of the firm, so that powerful networking strategies can be designed. In the case of the INV the networks must be built to reach the global segments that it is addressing, whereas for the traditional internationals the country market-based networking approach based on expected business volume drives the networking. Breaking out from over-dependency on an MNE must be the objective of both the INV and the traditional internationalizer, albeit that this is necessarily easier for a traditional firm that has achieved a strong market position than it is for an INV that is in its initial stages of building its market presence. Our contribution and suggestion to researchers and managers alike is that they should apply international entrepreneurial networking strategies in these endeavours. Clearly, more research is needed within this fascinating and important research area, calling for a longitudinal research approach.

REFERENCES

Barney, J. (1991), 'Firm resources and sustained competitive advantage', *Journal of Management*, **17**(1), 99–120.

Bell, J., R. McNaughton, S. Young and D. Crick (2003), 'Towards an integrative model of small firm internationalisation', *Journal of International Entrepreneurship*, **1**(4), 339–62.

Chetty, S. and C. Campbell-Hunt (2004), 'A strategic approach to internationalization: a traditional versus "born global" approach', *Journal of International Marketing*, **12**(1), 57–81.

Coviello, N. and H. Munro (1995), 'Growing the entrepreneurial firm: networking for international market development', *European Journal of Marketing*, **29**(7), 49–61.

Coviello, N. and H. Munro (1997), 'Network relationships and the internationalisation process of small software firms', *International Business Review*, **6**(4), 361–86.

Dimitratos, P. and E. Plakoyiannaki (2003), 'Theoretical foundations of an international entrepreneurial culture', *Journal of International Entrepreneurship*, **1**(2), 187–215.

Eurofound (2012), *Born Global: The Potential of Job Creation in New International Businesses*, accessed 5 May 2014 at www.eurofound.europa.eu/pubdocs/2012/65/en/1/EF1265EN.pdf.

Federation of Finnish Enterprises (2014), website, accessed 23 March 2014 at www.yrittajat.fi/en-gb//.

Freeman, S. (2012), 'Born global firms' use of networks and alliances: a social dynamic perspective', in M. Gabrielsson and V.H.M. Kirpalani, *Handbook of Research on Born Globals*, Cheltenham, UK and Northampton, MA, USA: Edward Elgar Publishing.

Freeman, S., R. Edwards and B. Schroder (2006), 'How smaller born-global firms use networks and alliances to overcome constraints to rapid internationalization', *Journal of International Marketing*, **14**(3), 33–63.

Gabrielsson, M., V. Sasi and J. Darling (2004), 'Finance strategies of rapidly-growing Finnish SMEs: born internationals and born globals', *European Business Review*, **16**(6), 590–604.

Gabrielsson, M., V.H.M. Kirpalani, P. Dimitratos, C.A. Solberg and A. Zucchella (2008), 'Born globals: propositions to help advance the theory', *International Business Review*, **17**(4), 385–401.

Gabrielsson, P. and M. Gabrielsson (2013), 'A dynamic model of growth phases and survival in international business-to-business new ventures: the moderating effect of decision-making logic', *Industrial Marketing Management*, **42**(8), 1357–73.

Gleason, K. and J. Madura (2006), 'Operating characteristics, risk, and performance of born-global firms', *International Journal of Managerial Finance*, **2**(2), 96–120.

Holmlund, M. and S. Kock (1998), 'Relationships and the internationalisation of Finnish small and medium-sized companies', *International Small Business Journal*, **16**(4), 46–63.

Hallbäck, J. and P. Gabrielsson (2013), 'Entrepreneurial marketing strategies during the growth of international new ventures originating in small and open economies', *International Business Review*, **22**(6), 1008–20.

Hyrsky, K. (2007), *Yrittäjyyskatsaus 2007* [Entrepreneurship Survey 2007], Finnish Ministry of Economy, KTM julkaisuja 32/2007, Elinkeino-osasto, accessed 1 June 2015 at julkaisurekisteri.ktm.fi/ktm_jur/ktmjur.nsf/All/B348AFBDAA15B434C22573AD00276B9F/$file/jul32elo_2007_netti.pdf, accessed 1 June 2015.

Johanson, J. and L.-G. Mattsson (1988), 'Internationalisation in industrial systems – a network approach', in N. Hood and J.-E. Vahlne, *Strategies in Global Competition*, New York: Croom Helm.

Johanson, J. and J.-E. Vahlne (1977), 'The internationalization process of the firm – a model of knowledge development and increasing foreign market commitments', *Journal of International Business Studies*, **8**(1), 23–32.

Johanson, J. and J.-E. Vahlne (1990), 'The mechanism of internationalization', *International Marketing Review*, **7**(4), 11–12.

Jones, M.V. and N.E. Coviello (2005), 'Internationalisation: conceptualising an entrepreneurial process of behaviour in time', *Journal of International Business Studies*, **36**(3), 284–303.

Karlsen, T., P. Silseth, G. Benito and L. Welch (2003), 'Knowledge, internationalization of the firm, and inward-outward connections', *Industrial Marketing Management*, **32**(5), 385–96.

Knight, G. and S.T. Cavusgil (2004), 'Innovation, organizational capabilities, and the born-global firm', *Journal of International Business Studies*, **35**(2), 124–41.

Kuivalainen, O., S. Sundqvist and P. Servais (2007), 'Firms' degree of born-globalness, international entrepreneurial orientation and export performance', *Journal of World Business*, **42**(3), 253–67.

Loane, S. and J. Bell (2006), 'Rapid internationalisation among entrepreneurial firms in Australia, Canada, Ireland and New Zealand: an extension to the network approach', *International Marketing Review*, **23**(5), 467–85.

Madsen, T. and P. Servais (1997), 'The internationalism of born globals: an evolutionary process?', *International Business Review*, **6**(6), 561–83.

McDougall, P.P. and B.M. Oviatt (2000), 'International entrepreneurship: the intersection of two research paths', *Academy of Management Journal*, **43**(5), 902–8.

Miller, K.D. (2007), 'Risk and rationality in entrepreneurial processes', *Strategic Entrepreneurship Journal*, **1**(1–2), 57–74.

Ministry of Employment and the Economy (2012), *Työ ja elinkeinoministeriöön julkaisuja. Työ ja yrittäjyys, 46/2012* [Work and the Economy Publications: Work and Entrepreneurship, accessed 1 June 2015 at www.tem.fi/files/35080/TEMjul_46_2012_web.pdf.

Ojala, A. (2009), 'Internationalization of knowledge-intensive SMEs: the role of network relationships in the entry to a psychically distant market', *International Business Review*, **18**(1), 50–59.

Oviatt, B. and P. McDougall (2005), 'Defining international entrepreneurship and modeling the speed of internationalization', *Entrepreneurship Theory and Practice*, **29**(5), 537–53.

Partanen, J. and P. Servais (2012), 'Sourcing networks of born global firms', in M. Gabrielsson and V.H. Kirpalani (eds), *Handbook of Research on Born Globals*, Cheltenham, UK and Northampton, MA, USA: Edward Elgar Publishing.

Powerflute (2014), website, accessed 12 May 2014 at www.powerflute.fi.

Rasmussan, E., T. Madsen and F. Evangelista (2001), 'The founding of the born global company in Denmark and Australia: sensemaking and networking', *Asia Pacific Journal of Marketing and Logistics*, **13**(3), 75–107.

Rennie, M. (1993), 'Global competitiveness: born global', *The McKinsey Quarterly*, No. 4, 45–52.

Reuber, R. and E. Fischer (1997), 'The influence of the management team's international experience on the internationalization behaviors of SMEs', *Journal of International Business Studies*, **28**(4), 807–25.

Ritter, T., I. Wilkinson and W. Johnston (2004), 'Managing in complex business networks', *Industrial Marketing Management*, **33**(3), 175–83.

Sepulveda, F. and M. Gabrielsson (2013), 'Network development and firm growth: a resource-based study of B2B born globals', *Industrial Marketing Management*, **42**(5), 792–804.

Sharma, D. and A. Blomstermo (2003), 'The internationalization process of born globals: a network view', *International Business Review*, **12**(6), 739–53.

Slotte-Kock, S. and N. Coviello (2010), 'Entrepreneurship research on network processes: a review and ways forward', *Entrepreneurship Theory and Practice*, **34**(1), 31–57.

Ulaga, W. and A. Eggert (2010), 'Relationship value in business markets: the construct and its dimensions', *Journal of Business-to-Business Marketing*, **12**(1), 73–97.
Welch, L.S. and R. Luostarinen (1988), 'Internationalization: evolution of a concept', in P.J. Buckley and P.N. Ghauri (eds), *The Internationalization of the Firm*, London: Thomson Learning, pp. 83–98.
Welch, L. and R. Luostarinen (1993), 'Inward and outward connections in internationalization', *Journal of International Marketing*, **1**(1), 46–58.
Westhead, P., M. Wright and D. Ucbasaran (2002), 'International market selection strategies selected by "micro" and "small" firms', *Omega*, **30**(1), 51–68.

5. Market strategy of international new ventures originating from a small and open economy

Salman Kimiagari, Peter Gabrielsson, Mika Gabrielsson and Benoit Montreuil*

INTRODUCTION

Although the importance of international new venture (INV) firms has increased in today's fast-moving global economy, their market strategies have been studied to a very limited extent despite their importance to firms with a global vision from inception (Oviatt and McDougall, 1994). We define INVs in keeping with Oviatt and McDougall (ibid., p. 49); according to their original definition, an INV is a 'business organization that, from inception, seeks to derive significant competitive advantage from the use of resources and the sale of outputs in multiple countries'.

INV firms have a tendency to view the world as a potential market. To serve that world market, economies of scale are gained by selling products in multiple foreign markets, which is also referred to as market scope (Leonidou and Samiee, 2012). Although it is obvious that INVs sell their products in several countries, there are no clear definitions in the existing literature as to the number of countries and the geographical locations in which they are expected to sell. The other dimension in INV growth is time. The time that passes between the formation of the firm and its initial entry into the international market can be called the starting time. According to earlier studies, starting times range from two years (Rennie, 1993; Moen and Servais, 2002) to eight years (McDougall et al., 1994). Speed is yet another dimension and refers to market expansion time or penetration swiftness. This dimension usually depends on the company's ability to tackle the problems and complexities of foreign markets (Vermeulen and Barkema, 2002). Moreover, research has focused mainly on country market strategy (Laanti et al., 2007; Hashai, 2011), but either neglected the customer strategy dimension or made simple assumptions according to which firms choose between international concentration and global diversity. We suggest that the customer aspects should be included in the examination. On the basis of the above discussion, we may conclude that INV literature lacks an in-depth and comprehensive understanding of international market strategy selection and market expansion of INVs. Hence the research questions can be postulated as follows: (1) What are the essential theories that explain the market strategy of INVs? (2) How can we develop an integrated approach to understand market strategy selection and development of INVs?

The next section examines the market strategy concept and related approaches in greater detail, followed by an empirical investigation. The final part discusses the results and presents the conclusion.

MARKET STRATEGY FOR INVs

International new ventures (INVs) have received increasing attention from a number of researchers. INVs face a tremendous challenge given their resource constraints and typically rapid market expansion plan. For INVs, it is not only important to decide which market to enter but also how to expand to the target market with a suitable market strategy. Oviatt and McDougall (1994) touch upon market strategies in their classification of the different typologies of INV firms. This classification includes the following: (1) export–import start-ups, operating in few international markets, with few activities coordinated abroad; (2) multinational traders, which have a high degree of international diversification and few coordinated activities; (3) geographically focused start-ups, which are internationally concentrated, but coordinate plenty of operations abroad; and (4) global start-ups, which are characterized by a huge number of foreign markets and many coordinated activities. Oviatt and McDougall (1994), however, treat these four alternatives as rather static and do not examine the possible dynamism created by movement from one group to another.

Market expansion plans have two substeps, the first of which is the actual market strategy, which refers to the act of choosing the appropriate market strategy on the basis of firm and customer characteristics. The second is market expansion, which consists of entering, adding, eliminating, or maintaining markets. Market growth often occurs as a series of market deployment stages (Slotegraaf et al., 2003; Luostarinen and Gabrielsson, 2006). In the context of this research, market strategy is defined as a process of selecting and expanding foreign target markets over time and covering the country and customer market dimensions.

According to Ayal and Zif (1979) there are two types of generic foreign market strategies for international firms: market concentration and market diversification. The comparison between the different characteristics of these strategies is presented in Table 5.1 and covers the essential aspects

Table 5.1 The different characteristics of generic foreign market strategies

Generic market strategies	Geographic scope	Objective	Flexibility	Entry mode	Risk	Product and services	Speed
Diversification strategy	Large number of markets (Kuivalainen et al., 2012)	Obtain a high rate of return while maintaining a low level of resource commitment	More flexible	Exporting or licensing (Bradley, 2005; Madsen, 2012)	Risk of underinvestment in each market (Madsen, 2012)	Standardize the product offering (Gabrielsson and Gabrielsson, 2003)	Rapidly enter many foreign markets (Bradley, 2005; Madsen, 2012)
Concentration strategy	Small number of markets (Madsen, 2012)	Specialization and scale economies, long-term profit (Bradley, 2005)	Less flexible	Higher commitment entry modes (Madsen, 2012)	Leaving important markets to competitors (Daniels et al., 2009)	Adaptation is required (Daniels et al., 2009; Madsen, 2012)	Gradual and often intensive penetration (Madsen, 2012)

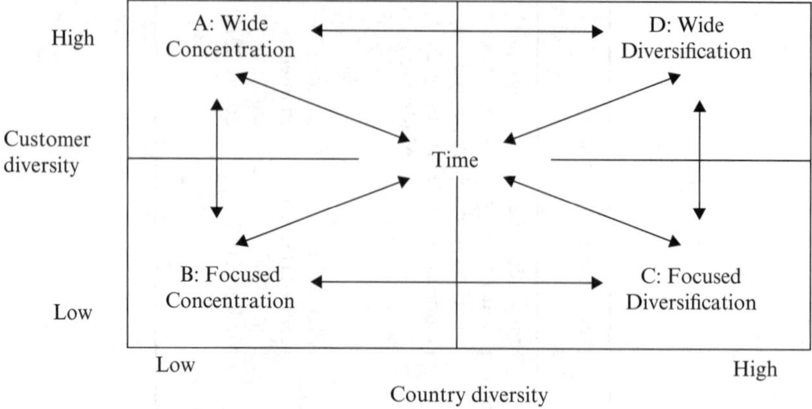

Figure 5.1 Foreign market strategy based on country and customer diversity

of market expansion, including scope, flexibility, risk and speed. The main objective of diversification strategy is to reach a wide market presence by typically applying low commitment entry modes with limited risk (McDougall et al., 1994; Coviello and Munro, 1997; Burgel and Murray, 2000; Crick and Jones, 2000; Gabrielsson and Kirpalani, 2004). In contrast, concentration strategy provides a more modest expansion speed but intensive penetration typically uses high commitment entry modes involving a higher risk for the markets entered. Also, due to a lower expansion speed, the risk of leaving markets to competitors is inevitable (Tjosevik and Refsland, 2012). Both market expansion strategies may force the firm to establish a new entity to serve new markets (Gilbert et al., 2006).

In addition to these two strategies, firms may also prefer hybrids of these two (Aspelund et al., 2007; Daniels et al., 2009; Moghadam, 2013). As illustrated in Figure 5.1, when the customer dimension is added we can actually depict four different strategies: focused concentration, wide concentration, focused diversification and wide diversification. Two last ones include hybrid elements with a combination of low and high strategy. The most extreme hybrid market strategy is the one that builds on simultaneously addressing both high country and customer diversity.

Earlier research results seem to indicate that a diversified country scope is characteristic of many INVs (Oviatt and McDougall, 1994; Crick and Jones, 2000; Knight and Cavusgil, 2004; Gabrielsson and Kirpalani, 2012). INVs seem to be rather early adopters of internationalization activities; they deploy on many markets rather than concentrate efforts in a few key markets. On the basis of their research, Luostarinen and Gabrielsson

(2006) found that some of the mature INVs 'proceed faster into new markets, jump over, or even proceed in reverse order compared with what the business distance would indicate for conventional companies' (p. 798). In general, however, the market strategy followed the conventional stages approach, although the process was implemented faster. They found that Europe was often entered first and North American or Asian markets were entered within the first to fourth year after establishment of the company (Luostarinen and Gabrielsson, 2006, p. 785). According to Laanti et al. (2007), the resources and capabilities of INVs and networks have a key role in operation strategies and achievement of global market presence. Also, business networks have been found be crucial for rapid market expansion (Sepulveda and Gabrielsson, 2013). INVs have been found to particularly cooperate with channel members and suppliers to leverage their resources in marketing during foreign expansion (Gabrielsson and Kirpalani, 2004; Hallbäck and Gabrielsson, 2013). In addition, Hashai (2011) studied the expansion of the geographic scope and foreign operations sequence of INVs and concluded that simultaneous expansion of geographic scope and commitment of value chain activities to foreign markets are not possible. From the risk and cost perspective, INVs use the capabilities of an existing internationalization path until further expansion along this path is no longer possible. Hence it seems important for INVs to take a dynamic approach to market expansion. Theoretical approaches explaining the market strategy choice and expansion of INVs will be reviewed in the next section.

THEORETICAL FRAMEWORK

This research briefly presents five theoretical approaches for explaining the market deployment of INVs. These approaches are (1) psychic distance, (2) the learning advantages of newness, (3) international management orientation, (4) consumer segmentation theory and (5) effectuation theory. These approaches have been selected for their ability to explain dynamism, longitudinal development and transitions in INV global market strategy.

Psychic Distance

Johanson and Vahlne (1977) and Luostarinen (1979) describe a mainstream pattern by which companies gradually increase their commitment in international markets. This depicts a risk-averse and learning-based market expansion strategy based on advancement first to countries with low geographic, economic and cultural distance and then to more distant countries only as learning occurs.

As Ellis (2007) explained, the uncertainty involved in entering international markets due to psychic distance is a central theme of internationalization research. Examination of the psychic distance concept for INVs has shown that the importance of geographical distance for market strategies has diminished and INVs enter lead markets rapidly (Madsen and Servais, 1997; Majkgård and Sharma, 1999; Burgel and Murray, 2000; Crick and Jones, 2000; Ellis, 2000; Laanti et al., 2007). However, cultural, language and time differences still have a role to play (Laanti et al., 2007). According to Dikova (2009), psychic distance stems from alterations in local consumer preferences and culture and business systems between the home and foreign country.

Learning Advantages of Newness

In dynamic environments the learning advantages of newness – or how quickly firms learn to adapt – is more important than prior acquired knowledge (Autio et al., 2000; Bals et al., 2013). Examination of the learning advantages of newness for INVs has shown that it is crucial to understand the opportunities driving growth (Alvarez and Barney, 2007) and the importance of learning for survival (March, 1991). Rapid learning during globalization (Autio et al., 2000), or in some cases unlearning and overcoming rigidity in decision-making, is critical for INV market expansion (Gabrielsson and Gabrielsson, 2013).

Enabled by faster learning capabilities (Autio et al., 2000), INVs have been found to expand rapidly into foreign markets. As they have not developed routines and other impediments that may hinder their decision-making, they learn from both their successes and their failures and take rapid advantage of the opportunities that open up. Hohenthal et al. (2003) highlighted that an unpredicted market discovery (Kirzner, 1997) can be exploited by chance (Mainela et al., 2014). The firm's current knowledge and its willingness to search for new directions are critical for market expansion (ibid.).

International Management Orientation

International managerial orientation is another significant factor that helps to explain market strategy selection and expansion. This is the orientation of management towards foreigners, ideas and resources at virtually all levels of management and that can range through a number of profiles, from the ethnocentric (home country oriented), to the polycentric (target country oriented), regiocentric (region oriented) and finally the geocentric (globally oriented) (Perlmutter, 1969).

Central in the international management orientation is the distinction between global integration and local responsiveness (Doz, 1986; Hedlund, 1986; Bartlett and Ghoshal, 1989). Harveston et al. (2000) found that managers in INVs are typically more globally oriented than their counterparts in more conventional firms that develop step by step during the internationalization process.

Consumer Segmentation

The primary objective of segmentation theory literature is to refine marketing strategies to match customer expectations and help firms to maximize earnings and minimize losses. Earlier marketing literature can educate us with regard to suitable criteria for segmenting markets (Wind, 1978). These characteristics can be divided into the general such as demographics and the situation specific such as product or purchase patterns.

Homogeneous consumer needs, tastes and values and globally standardized products steer INVs towards global market segments and country-specific tactical issues follow this segmentation (Laanti et al., 2007). However, local clustering of economic activity inhibits international opportunity recognition (Zander, 2004) and therefore an understanding of differences in foreign markets expands the cognitive capacity of the managers and enables them to make decisions on the customer segments to which they should target their products (Miocevic and Crnjak-Karanovic, 2012).

Effectuation Theory

Effectuation theory explains entrepreneurial decision-making (Sarasvathy, 2001) and is therefore also important for examination of foreign market strategy. The impact of entrepreneurial decision-making logic on market strategy selection is different if entrepreneurial actions are based on discovery or creation theories (Alvarez and Barney, 2007). When the growth opportunities are predictable and an analysis of market opportunities is possible, then planning can be based on causation. In the causation process a particular effect is given and the focus is on choosing between the means that create that effect (Sarasvathy, 2001). In contrast, if the possible outcomes and their probabilities are unknown, effectuation-based decision-making logic is more probable. Less planning is involved in this process and entrepreneurs seek to utilize their existing contacts and resources when selecting foreign markets. Hence, effectuation is seen

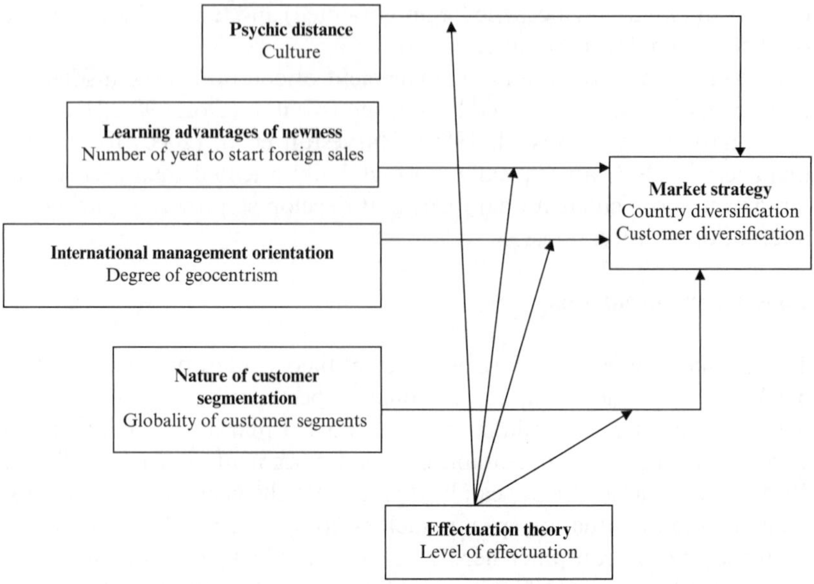

Figure 5.2 Framework for the market strategy of INVs

to moderate the effect of the previously discussed constructs (see also Gabrielsson and Gabrielsson, 2013).

Based on the above review of five major theoretical approaches, a framework for guiding the empirical study was postulated as in Figure 5.2.

RESEARCH METHODOLOGY

Case study research is especially appropriate for answering 'how' and 'why' questions (Yin, 2009, p. 9) and provides a detailed understanding of the behaviour of a complex phenomenon such as the market strategy formulation of INVs. The strength of the case method is the likelihood that it will result in theory development (Eisenhardt, 1989, p. 17). For this kind of complex and multidimensional decision a single case study method was considered appropriate. According to Yin (2009, p. 38):

> [T]he single-case study is an appropriate design under several circumstances. One rationale for a single case is when it represents the critical case in testing a well-formulated theory . . . a single case, meeting all of the conditions for testing the theory. The single case can then be used to determine whether a theory's propositions are correct or whether some alternative set of explanations might be more relevant.

We focused on a company founded in Finland for several reasons. First, the population of the country is approximately five million and its small market pushes companies to internationalize from inception. Moreover, it has very few trade restrictions, particularly in the high-technology field (Gabrielsson and Gabrielsson, 2013). We sought an SME with a high degree of globalization. Based on these considerations, we selected SSH Communications Security Corp for our case analysis. We interviewed both the founder and the president of the firm and also used press releases and secondary material from the company (www.ssh.com; see also Hashimoto, 2011). Validity and reliability were maintained by careful data collection and formation of a case database and by having key informants review the draft case report.

EMPIRICAL RESULTS, CASE STUDY ANALYSIS AND DEVELOPMENT OF PROPOSITIONS

Background of the Case Firm

In 1995, SSH Communications Security (SSH) was established by Tatu Ylönen, a university student who had invented the Secure Shell protocol, which soon became an important standard for data-in-transit security. SSH has grown to serve over 3000 customers around the globe.

According to Gabrielson and Gabrielson (2013), international new ventures can develop via four growth phases: (1) INV creation, (2) commercialization and foreign entries, (3) rapid growth and foreign market expansion and (4) rationalization and foreign maturity. SSH started to sell software directly after its founding through multinational firms in its home country. The company commercialized by selling products in large volumes through an MNC customer and other original equipment manufacturer (OEM) customers in 1997–98 and entered the US market by establishing a sales office in 1998. In the initial phase it sold to technology enthusisasts and increasingly also to other customers, including universities, laboratories and some major corporations with a focused diversification strategy. Rapid growth was achieved in 2000–02 by expansion in the markets of the USA, Asia and Europe, which increased the level of customer and country diversity. Within this wide diversification approach, products, services, consulting and systems were addressed to all customer groups, including operators, large enterprises, SMEs and even individuals. In addition, OEM customers were addressed with separate products. Global maturity was achieved during these years, but the lack of a systematic approach to expansion and the financial crisis forced the firm to decrease its customer diversity, hence leading into a focused diversification strategy in which systems products were divested and focus was on servicing the corporate customers well. See Table 5.2 for information on SSH market expansion.

Examination of the Factors Influencing Market Strategy

Psychic distance

First, the impact of psychic distance will be examined. It apparently plays a specific role when the country market strategy is selected. Psychic distance may reduce the willingness of INVs to increase country diversification, particularly to countries located in unfamiliar cultural settings.

For target markets in Europe Asia and USA, the geographical location of the home country (in the case of SSH, Finland) can obviously be an issue due to substantial differences in time and physical distance between the countries. In addition, climate, language and taxation can be understood as barriers to global expansion and international business. The founder of the company addressed the main problems as follows:

> And we have a number of disadvantages, including geographic location. We are far from anywhere, from the centers of the world. And there's a distance, there's a time zone difference to the US. Of course it's much easier if your primary market is in Europe, but if your primary market is in the US or in Asia, then this is not a very good location . . . The language issue, though almost everybody speaks English, but still, the language barrier is a difficult one.

Regardless of these barriers, the company selected the USA for foreign entry and then in the global expansion phase, other parts of the USA, Asia including Japan, South Korea and Taiwan and Europe (Germany and the UK). Hence, psychic distance does not seem to prevent INV firms from diversifying to countries with high business distance. Thus, Proposition 1 is postulated as follows:

P1: High psychic distance does not have a negative impact on country diversification as a market strategy for INVs.

Learning advantages of newness

Earlier research has contended that as firms get older, it is much more difficult for them to learn and this decreases their ability to grow successfully in new environments, whereas newer firms are more flexible and learn the competencies needed to grow in foreign markets more rapidly (Autio et al., 2000). As a result, it can be expected that a country diversification

Table 5.2 Background of foreign market expansion of SSH

#th Year	Year	Number of employees	Internationalization degree (%)	Globalization degree (%)	Market strategy	Details
3	4/98–3/99	28	56.25	37.50	Focused diversification	Of net sales, 43.75% was from Finland, 18.75% from other European countries, and 37.50% from outside of Europe. Products sold mainly to technology enthusiasts
6	2001	181	78.40	62.50	Wide diversification	Of net sales, 21.6% was from Finland, 15.9% from other European countries, 49.7% from North America, and 12.8% from other markets. Products sold to many customer groups
14	2009	64	95.46	71.90	Focused diversification	Of net sales, 28.1% was from Europe and the rest of the world, 62.8% from Americas, and 9.1% from Asia Pacific. Focus on large enterprise customers

strategy will be used by firms that made their first foreign entries soon after foundation.

Soon after its establishment, SSH started with its home country, certain European countries and the USA with a 37 per cent degree of globalization. The introductory phase at SSH took only two to three years and during the rapid growth and foreign expansion phase the company raised its degree of globalization to 62.5 per cent. Despite the risks involved, it began by opening a sales office in the USA, because half of its potential business was located in Silicon Valley. The founder of SSH commented on the associated risk: 'It was a big risk and everybody was saying how difficult it is to do business in the US and how big the legal risks are and so on. I, by the way, found that the US is a very easy place to do business'.

The role of Japanese firms in the software business led the company to expand to Japan. This was followed by opening a sales office in Germany in 2001 and the UK in 2002 to serve its existing customers, as they were major markets in Europe for technology. In 2001, representative offices in South Korea and Taiwan were also opened. We can conclude that SSH entered rapidly into foreign markets after its foundation and was able to achieve a wide variety of foreign markets within only six years of its foundation. It seems that the firm benefited from 'learning advantages of newness' characteristics such as flexibility, an international identity and a strong aptitude for growth that led to a country diversification strategy. Hence, Proposition 2 is suggested as follows:

P2: The shorter the period of operation in the domestic market before foreign markets are served, the greater the use of country diversification as a market strategy by INVs.

International management orientation

The international management orientation (e.g., Perlmutter, 1969) literature examines the locus of decision-making and suggests that an important aspect affecting market strategy decisions is the predisposition of the firms towards either global integration or local responsiveness. According to the management orientation literature, the geocentric approach considers the entire world a unique market and follows integrated marketing strategies. In this orientation, similarities between different markets are identified and a unified marketing strategy is formulated. Business ventures with this approach analyse and manage marketing strategy with integrated marketing packages. The market strategy in the rapid growth and foreign expansion phase of the company was to sell the products in large volumes to many different target markets and countries. The firms used a geocentric approach when penetrating the US market and expanded and penetrated new countries and regions including Europe, Asia and North America. Although a lack of global processes and inefficiencies led to a financial crisis in 2001–02, entering global markets from the very beginning to seek growth and become a reputed company in the software business was the global vision of SSH. The founder and president of the case company commented on the global vision:

> Finland is a typical small market for software, so the markets are global and you have to go global from the very beginning if you want to do something bigger in software . . . The software business can be global immediately as it doesn't need physical channels and it can be distributed rapidly.

Hence, Proposition 3 is suggested as follows:

P3: The higher the geocentric orientation, the higher the country diversification of INVs and the lower the customer diversification.

Customer segmentation

Clustering the target markets on the basis of potential groups of customers can provide insight for INVs in choosing a market strategy. In addition, the nature of the business (business-to-business or business-to-customer) can determine the market size, phasing and market strategy. For digital or otherwise standardized products, global diversity (high country diversification) can be the choice of market strategy (Zaheer and Manrakhan, 2001; Moen and Servais, 2002). For business-to-business INVs, considering complexity and high assets, customer diversification may sometimes be appropriate. In these cases, the number of industrial customers is smaller than in business-to-consumer firms (Loane and Bell, 2006). However, due to the often limited resources of SMEs this may be difficult. The founder and president of the case company commented on customer diversification:

> We lost the customer focus. We were no longer focusing on a single customer or a single group of customers. We were doing a number of technologies that were all somehow related to security, but that were quite different technologically and were targeting somewhat different customers. Some were targeted to operators, some were targeted to large enterprises, others were targeted more to small companies or even individuals . . . the element included there was that we are not only trying to target the US market segment but also Europe and Asia Pacific because global means global. It doesn't mean the US.

Our case firm initially was expanding almost out of control along both country and customer dimensions, which is called wide diversification in Figure 5.1. However, it seems that trying to achieve a hybrid strategy with both country and customer diversification simultaneously is very challenging for INVs. We propose the following:

P4: INVs strive for both high customer and country diversification. However, this is challenging and may endanger survival.

Effectuation theory

According to Sarasvathy (2001), when the growth opportunities are conventional and market research can be conducted, then causation is most probably used. Moreover, she argues that in the causation process a particular effect is given and the focus is on selecting between the means that generate that effect. In these conditions market strategy planning is emphasized. However, if the future is unpredictable, planning is not possible and INVs presumably adopt the effectuation decision-making logic, which does not rely on the use of formal market planning. In the effectuation process a set of means is taken as given and the focus is on selecting between the effects that can be created with that set of means (ibid.). INVs make effective use of contingencies in the environment and try to create new opportunities from them. In this approach the entrepreneur also selects actions that have an affordable loss, if the risk realizes. The founder commented on this: 'Of course the loss has to be affordable, at least if it's very risky'. Entrepreneurs build relationships with other companies in order to mitigate business risks and reduce uncertainty. SSH signed strategic cooperation agreements with many firms. Many of these partnerships helped the company become more credible.

However, the use of effectuation led the SSH to a rapid growth that resulted in a financial crisis. Its crisis was created by overly rapid growth in size and product variation and by a failure to focus on a few customers, international management and control mechanisms. It responded to the crisis by adopting a systematic approach to growth management in the maturity phase and by focusing its activities by reducing the number of products and customers served. The case evidence suggests that in the early phase of firm development an effectuation-based approach meant pursuit of a market strategy involving less planning. However, effectuation eventually gave way to greater emphasis on causation logic. The use of effectuation logic in the beginning seemed to diminish the influence of psychic distance on country diversification and enhance the full use of the learning advantages of newness in exploring a number of country and customer alternatives. As evidenced in the case, effectuation may lead to use of a hybrid market strategy with both high customer and country diversification. Such an approach may even be harmful for the profitability and survivability of the firm. The use of causation in the later phase of development seemed to stress the importance of considering the psychic distance, international management orientation and need for careful selection of customer segments. Earlier research has argued that the use of an effectuation decision-making logic may mitigate the need of resources for achieving foreign growth, while causation logic requires careful consideration that the required means are available to reach its goals (Gabrielsson and Gabrielsson, 2013). Hence, Proposition 5 is suggested as follows:

P5: Decision-making logic moderates the relationship between the antecedents and foreign market strategy of INVs. When using effectuation logic the market strategy is less planned and the influence of psychic distance on country diversification decreases, while the influence of the learning advantages of newness on country and customer diversification increases. When using causation logic the market strategy is more planned and the influence of psychic distance, international management orientation and focus on segmentation increases.

CONCLUSION

The contribution of this study is its in-depth investigation of the foreign market strategy of INVs and particularly of high-technology firms originating in small and open economies. From the perspective of international entreprenership and business, it provides knowledge of the behaviour of INVs in choosing target markets during growth. Very few studies address the foreign market strategy of INVs. Hence, this study offers insight into how INVs select and approach global markets. We contribute by developing a model that illustrates the relationships between influential factors of market strategy and three patterns of market strategy: country diversification, customer diversification and a hybrid alternative that combines both. Normally psychic distance in terms of the cultural distance between the home country and the target countries decreases country diversification. However, our case analysis shows that for high-tech INVs originating in small and open economies, this factor seems less important. The learning advantage of newness leads to early use of country diversification. Hence, the shortness of the period before foreign markets are served stimulates INVs to achieve a higher degree of globalization. International market orientation is another factor that influences the behaviour of INVs in market strategy. A higher country diversification is the result of a geocentric orientation. As the geocentric approach considers the entire world market as target market and thus tries to take integrated marketing strategies further, a higher country diversification is more plausible in this market orientation.

There was preliminary evidence that decision-making logic may be an important consideration in the selection of foreign market strategies by INVs, thus giving support to some earlier studies (Gabrielsson and Gabrielsson, 2013). Effectuation logic seems to lead to less planning of market strategies; the influence of psychic distance decreases, while the flexibility achieved from the learning advantages of newness increases. While causation led to more planned market strategies with conventional considerations regarding the influence of psychic distance, management orientation and sufficiency of resources. We found that as a result of effectuation logic the case firm expanded rapidly with both customer and country diversification, which was not sustainable in terms of performance. It subsequently adopted causation logic and selected a low customer diversity and high country diversification as its market strategy. Striving for both customer and country diversification simultanously proved to be challenging. The novel contribution to INVs is that effectuation logic can facilitate fast diversification to a number of customers and countries by leveraging the resources of business partners in distribution and marketing in an uncertain environment. But, as seen, this can lead to enhanced business risk, which may endanger survival and call for a more causation-based approach.

Generalization based on case study research is often considered challenging. If, however, readers identify important similarities to cases of interest to them, they can apply the results in their own operations. The results of this study can be applied in the case of high-tech INVs – particularly those initiated in open economies. A survey methodology approach could ascertain whether these results are generalizable to a wider population. More research is also needed on the effect of effectuation on market strategy selection. Studying the market strategy of INVs in different countries and different industries and comparing the results would be an interesting approach in future research.

NOTE

* This chapter is based on part of this author's PhD thesis.

REFERENCES

Alvarez, S.A. and J.B. Barney (2007), 'Discovery and creation: alternative theories of entrepreneurial action', *Strategic Entrepreneurship Journal*, **1**(1–2), 11–26.

Aspelund, A., T.K. Madsen and Ø. Moen (2007), 'A review of the foundation, international marketing strategies and performance of international new ventures', *European Journal of Marketing*, **41**(11/12), 1423–48.

Autio, E., H.J. Sapienza and J.G. Almeida (2000), 'Effects of age at entry, knowledge intensity and imitability on international growth', *Academy of Management Journal*, **43**(5), 909–24.

Ayal, I. and J. Zif (1979), 'Market expansion strategies in multinational marketing', *Journal of Marketing*, **43**(2), 84–94.

Bals, L., H. Berry, E. Hartmann and G. Raettich (2013), 'What do we know about going global early? Liabilities of foreignness and early internationalizing firms', in T. Devinney, R. Pedersen and L. Tihany (eds), *Advances in International Management* (Vol. 26), Greenwich, CT: JAI Press, pp. 397–433.

Bartlett, C.A. and S. Ghoshal (1989), *Managing Across Borders: The Transnational Solution*, Boston, MA: Harvard Business School Press.

Bradley, F. (2005), *International Marketing Strategy*, Harlow, UK: Pearson Education Limited.

Burgel, O. and G.C. Murray (2000), 'The international market entry choices of start-up companies in high-technology industries', *Journal of International Marketing*, **8**(2), 33–62.

Coviello, N. and H. Munro (1997), 'Network relationships and the internationalization process of small software firms', *International Business Review*, **6**(4), 361–86.

Crick, D. and M. Jones (2000), 'Small high-technology firms and international high-technology markets', *Journal of International Marketing*, **8**(2), 63–85.

Daniels, J., L. Radebaugh and D. Sullivan (2009), *International Business – Environments and Operations*, Upper Saddle River, NJ: Pearson Education Inc.

Dikova, D. (2009), 'Performance of foreign subsidiaries: does psychic distance matter?', *International Business Review*, **18**(1), 38–49.

Doz, Y.L. (1986), *Strategic Management in Multinational Companies*, Oxford: Pergamon Press.

Eisenhardt, K.M. (1989), 'Making fast strategic decisions in high-velocity environments', *Academy of Management Journal*, **32**(3), 543–76.

Ellis, P. (2000), 'Social ties and foreign market entry', *Journal of International Business Studies*, **31**(3), 443–69.

Ellis, P.D. (2007), 'Paths to foreign markets: does distance to market affect firm internationalisation?', *International Business Review*, **16**(5), 573–93.

Gabrielsson, M. and P. Gabrielsson (2003), 'Global marketing strategies of born globals and globalising internationals in the ICT field', *Journal of Euromarketing*, **12**(3–4), 123–45.

Gabrielsson, M. and V.H.M. Kirpalani (2004), 'Born globals: how to reach new business space rapidly', *International Business Review*, **13**(5), 555–71.

Gabrielsson, M. and V.H.M. Kirpalani (eds) (2012), *Handbook of Research on Born Globals*, Cheltenham, UK and Northampton, MA, USA: Edward Elgar Publishing.

Gabrielsson, P. and M. Gabrielsson (2013), 'A dynamic model of growth phases and survival in international business-to-business new ventures: the moderating effect of decision-making logic', *Industrial Marketing Management*, **42**(8), 1357–73.

Gilbert, B.A., P.P. McDougall and D.B. Audretsch (2006), 'New venture growth: a review and extension', *Journal of Management*, **32**(6), 926–50.

Hallbäck, J. and P. Gabrielsson (2013), 'Entrepreneurial marketing strategies during the growth of international new ventures originating in small and open economies', *International Business Review*, **22**(6), 1008–20.

Harveston, P.D., B.L. Kedia and P.S. Davis (2000), 'Internationalization of born global and gradual globalizing firms: the impact of the manager', *Advances in Competitiveness Research*, **8**(1), 92–9.

Hashai, N. (2011), 'Sequencing the expansion of geographic scope and foreign operations by "born global" firms', *Journal of International Business Studies*, **42**(8), 995–1015.

Hashimoto, S. (2011), 'Growth phases and survival of born globals – case: Finnish software firms', unpublished Master's thesis, Aalto, Finland: Aalto University School of Economics.

Hedlund, G. (1986), 'The hypermodern MNC: a heterarchy?', *Human Resource Management*, **25**(1), 9–35.

Hohenthal, J., J. Johanson and M. Johanson (2003), 'Market discovery and the international expansion of the firm', *International Business Review*, **12**(6), 659–72.

Johanson, J. and J.-E. Vahlne (1977), 'The internationalization process of the firm: a model of knowledge development and increasing foreign commitments', *Journal of International Business Studies*, **8**(1), 23–32.

Kirzner, I. (1997), 'Entrepreneurial discovery and the competitive market process: an Austrian approach', *Journal of Economic Literature*, **35**(1), 60–85.

Knight, G.A. and S.T. Cavusgil (2004), 'Innovation, organizational capabilities and the born-global firm', *Journal of International Business Studies*, **35**(2), 124–42.

Kuivalainen, O., S. Saarenketo and K. Puumalainen (2012), 'Start-up patterns of internationalization: a framework and its application in the context of knowledge-intensive SMEs', *European Management Journal*, **30**(4), 372–85.

Laanti, R., M. Gabrielsson and P. Gabrielsson (2007), 'The globalization strategies of business-to-business born global firms in the wireless technology industry', *Industrial Marketing Management*, **36**(8), 1104–17.

Leonidou, L.C. and S. Samiee (2012), 'Born global or simply rapidly internationalization? Review, critique and future prospects', in P. Gabrielsson and V.H.M. Kirpalani (eds), *Handbook of Research on Born Globals*, Cheltenham, UK and Northampton, MA, USA: Edward Elgar Publishing.

Loane, S. and J. Bell (2006), 'Rapid internationalisation among entrepreneurial firms in Australia, Canada, Ireland and New Zealand: an extension to the network approach', *International Marketing Review*, **23**(5), 467–85.

Luostarinen, R. (1979), 'Internationalization of the firm: an empirical study of the internationalization of firms with small and open domestic markets with special emphasis on lateral rigidity as a behavioral characteristic in strategic decision-making', doctoral dissertation, Helskinki: Helsinki School of Economics.

Luostarinen, R. and M. Gabrielsson (2006), 'Globalization and marketing strategies of born globals in SMOPECs', *Thunderbird International Business Review*, **48**(6), 773–801.

Madsen, T.K. (2012), 'Entry strategies – foreign markets' [lecture], in R. Tjosevik and B. Refsland (2012), 'Factors influencing international entry strategies: a born global approach', Master's thesis, Trondheim: Norwegian University of Science and Technology.

Madsen, T.K. and P. Servais (1997), 'The internationalization of born globals: an evolutionary process?', *International Business Review*, **6**(6), 561–83.

Mainela, T., V. Puhakka and P. Servais (2014), 'The concept of international opportunity in international entrepreneurship: a review and a research agenda', *International Journal of Management Reviews*, **16**(1), 105–29.

Majkgård, A. and D. Sharma (1999), 'The born internationals', paper for the 5th Workshop in International Business and Nordic Workshop on Interorganizational Research, Vaasa, Finland: University of Vaasa.

March, J.G. (1991), 'Exploration and exploitation in organizational learning', *Organization Science*, **2**(1), 71–87.

McDougall, P.P., S. Shane and B.M. Oviatt (1994), 'Explaining the formation of international new ventures: the limits of theories from international business research', *Journal of Business Venturing*, **9**(6), 469–87.

Miocevic, D. and B. Crnjak-Karanovic (2012), 'Global mindset – a cognitive driver of small and medium-sized enterprise internationalization: the case of Croatian exporters', *EuroMed Journal of Business*, **7**(2), 142–60.

Moen, Ø. and P. Servais (2002), 'Born global or gradual global? Examining the export behavior of small and medium-sized enterprises', *Journal of International Marketing*, **10**(3), 49–72.

Moghadam, K. (2013), 'Two decades of born global research: an analytical framework', in *Proceedings of the Academy of International Business–US Midwest Annual Meeting*, Illinois, 27 February–1 March.

Nordstrom, K. and P.P. McDougall (1994), 'Toward a theory of international new ventures', *Journal of International Business Studies*, **25**, 45–64.

Perlmutter, H.V. (1969), 'The tortuous evolution of the multinational corporation', *Columbia Journal of World Business*, **4**(1), 9–18.

Rennie, M.W. (1993), 'Born global', *McKinsey Quarterly*, No. 4, 45–52.

Sarasvathy, S.D. (2001), 'Causation and effectuation: toward a theoretical shift from economic inevitability to entrepreneurial contingency', *Academy of Management Review*, **26**(2), 243–63.

Sepulveda, F. and M. Gabrielsson (2013), 'Network development and firm growth: a resource-based study of b2b born globals', *Industrial Marketing Management*, **42**(5), 792–804.

Slotegraaf, R.J., C. Moorman and J.J. Inman (2003), 'The role of firm resources in returns to market deployment', *Journal of Marketing Research*, **40**(3), 295–309.

Tjosevik, R. and B. Refsland (2012), 'Factors influencing international entry strategies: a born global approach', Master's dissertation, Trondheim: Norwegian University of Science and Technology.

Vermeulen, F. and H. Barkema (2002), 'Pace, rhythm and scope: process dependence in building a profitable multinational corporation', *Strategic Management Journal*, **23**(7), 637–53.

Wind, Y. (1978), 'Issues and advances in segmentation research', *Journal of Marketing Research*, **15**(3), 317–37.

Yin, R.K. (2009), *Case Study Research: Design and Methods* (4th edition), Thousand Oaks, CA: Sage Publications, Inc.

Zaheer, S. and S. Manrakhan (2001), 'Concentration and dispersion in global industries: remote electronic access and the location of economic activities', *Journal of International Business Studies*, **32**(4), 667–86.

Zander, I. (2004), 'The micro foundations of cluster stickiness – walking in the shoes of the entrepreneur', *Journal of International Management*, **10**(2), 151–75.

6. Where and when? A longitudinal study of export behaviour of new ventures

Geir Gripsrud, Auke Hunneman and Carl Arthur Solberg

INTRODUCTION

The internationalization of companies is a complicated process with many variables involved. A seminal contribution to understanding and explaining this process is usually referred to as the Uppsala model (Johanson and Wiedersheim-Paul, 1975; Johanson and Vahlne, 1977). The basic assumption of the model is that the decision-makers in companies are characterized by bounded rationality and uncertainty. Initially, a firm has limited knowledge of foreign markets. It learns from current activities abroad and from the commitments it makes, but the only sensible way to proceed is to expand in a careful and gradual way, since the risks and costs involved are lower. The expansion takes place in two main dimensions: entry mode and choice of foreign markets. In both cases, the perceived risk involved causes the firm to make commitments that correspond to its present state of knowledge. Initially, this implies that the typical entry mode is exporting and the first export market is close in terms of geographical and cultural distance. The latter is captured by saying that internationalization frequently starts in foreign markets that are 'close to the domestic market in terms of *psychic distance*, defined as factors that make it difficult to understand foreign environments' (Johanson and Vahlne, 2009, p. 1412; original emphasis).

While previous studies have found empirical support for the Uppsala model (Aaby and Slater, 1989; Johanson and Vahlne, 1990; Andersen, 1993), the question is whether the assumptions underlying the model are still valid in today's globalized and connected business environment. In particular, the environment now typically consists of a web of relationships among companies and not of independent companies. This means that psychic distance is no longer the most important cause of uncertainty; rather, it is being an *outsider* relative to the important networks that creates uncertainty. If this is the case, firms may no longer start by exporting to countries that are close in terms of geography and/or culture. The network a new venture belongs to may encompass members from many distant countries; hence the first export may be to one of these countries rather than to a close market in terms of psychic distance.

The first markets entered, and the sequence of market entries in general, concerns the *path* of internationalization. A related question is the *speed* of internationalization, which has attracted a great deal of attention recently as documented in the literature review conducted by Chetty et al. (2014). While the time construct in firm internationalization has many dimensions, most studies focus on the early start of international activities (Zucchella et al., 2007). It has been found that managers with an international orientation perceive a lower risk in entering foreign markets, which results in a higher speed of internationalization (Acedo and Jones, 2007). The early start of internationalization is also one of the defining criteria of the so-called born globals.

This chapter deals with issues related to the path as well as the speed of export behaviour. In contrast to most previous studies that typically use small samples of more or less successful exporters, we utilize a database comprising all companies exporting goods from Norway in the time period 2003–11. We will explore the following two research questions: (1) Do new ventures still start to export to countries that are close in terms of psychic distance from the domestic market? (2) Does the speed of export start-up matter for the firms' future export success and expansion? To investigate these issues we have used – as part of a larger project financed by Innovation Norway – a database from Statistics Norway containing two datasets: Structural Business Statistics and the National Register of Establishments and Enterprises. The former describes the economy through all units engaged in economic activities, including external trade of goods and services. The National Register comprises variables describing for each Norwegian enterprise contact details, legal form, people involved and their managerial roles, main economic activities, number of employees, and so on. In the present study, we focus on all 2390 goods-exporting companies that were established in 2003. These companies represent 4 per cent of all the 54472 companies exporting in the period 2003–11, included in the database. The reason for this is that focusing on the 2003 cohort of companies allows for studying the export behaviour of these companies from their inception for as long a period as possible (given the export data included in the database).

CHOICE OF FIRST EXPORT MARKET

Figure 6.1 shows the distribution of the most popular first entry markets in the 2003–11 period, regardless of when the company was established.

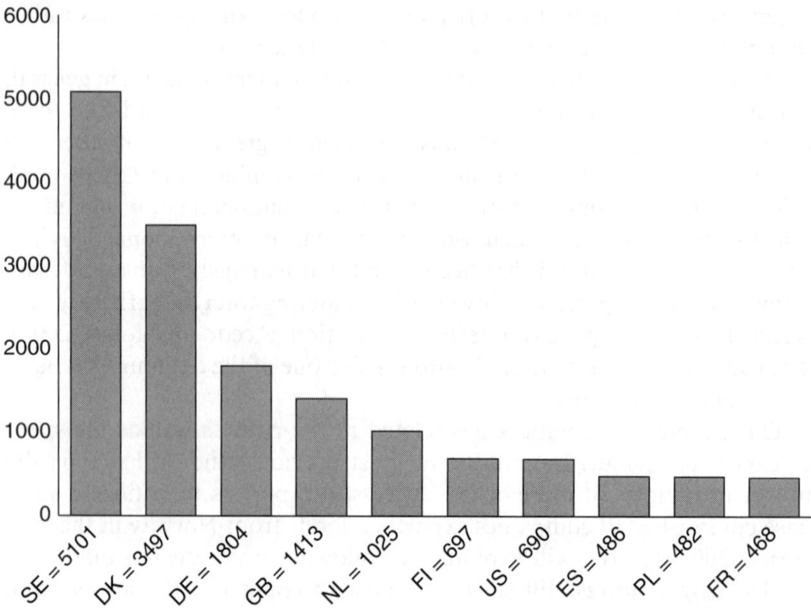

Figure 6.1 First country market entry of Norwegian exporters: 2003–11

It is evident that Norway's neighbours are the favourites of Norwegian firms when they start exporting. Almost a quarter of the exporters start venturing into Sweden as their first export project, whereas 16 per cent start in Denmark. These two countries share not only cultural and linguistic heritage with Norway, they are also the geographically closest markets and are also located in the same cultural cluster in the Hofstede (1980) framework. In other words, easy communication (low language barriers), less cultural shocks, and limited transport/travel distance – briefly low risk and low cost – characterize the first export endeavour of Norwegian start-ups in the beginning of the twenty-first century.

Next in the list of export destinations are also – if not direct neighbours, at least pretty close neighbours both geographically and culturally (but not linguistically, although all countries except one belong to the Anglo-Saxon language family) – Germany, Britain, the Netherlands and Finland. These first six countries in the list represent 63 per cent of Norwegian start-up exporters. This indicates that countries that are close in terms of psychic distance are still the most popular for new exporters, in line with the original Uppsala hypothesis. Of course other and more distant countries are on this list as well – in fact as many as 177 countries are represented on the list of first export markets. We believe (but cannot support empirically) that firms starting to export to many of these countries do so indirectly, for instance as part of a subcontract of another well-established exporter or partner (thus considerably reducing the risks and the costs). Many of these countries are still to be found in Europe – the 'home continent' of Norwegian exporters: for instance 16 out of the 17 first market entries are in European countries, so the geographic aspect is still prevalent. The much mentioned BRICS (Brazil, Russia, India, China and South Africa) countries, for instance, represent only 2.6 per cent of all first market entries.

The next question is then: where do they go next? Which country is export market number 2? Again the gradual expansion hypothesis seems to receive support. In fact, firms that start in Sweden continue to Denmark, Germany, Britain, Finland and the Netherlands as their second market entry. Figure 6.2 gives the numbers.[1] Firms starting in Denmark go mainly to Sweden, Germany, Britain, Finland and the Netherlands; and if they start in Germany they end up in these same markets as their second entry in their internationalization process. For all practical purposes, our analyses seem to support the Uppsala pattern of gradual expansion. Interestingly, this is in opposition to the findings of Benito and Gripsrud

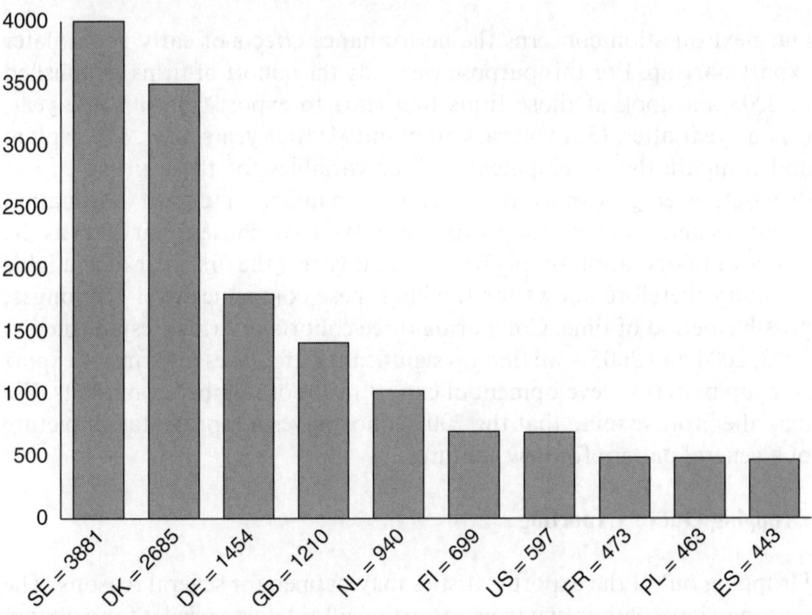

Figure 6.2 Second country market entry of Norwegian exporters after Sweden: 2003–11

(1992) who study foreign direct investment (FDI) patterns of Norwegian firms. They found no evidence of gradual geographic expansion in the 'Uppsala' way concerning FDI. However, firms already established in exporting normally undertake FDI and they thus have climbed the 'internationalization ladder' higher, or for reasons other than market seeking only (for instance, sourcing). First-time exporters, on the other hand, have no previous international business experience and will therefore naturally seek safer waters when they set sail for the first time.

Is this then irrefutable proof of the Uppsala hypothesis of gradual geographic expansion? Our answer is a qualified yes. The expansion pattern seems to a convincing degree to comply with the premise of a gradual geographic expansion of exporters in their internationalization process. On the other hand, even though this is the prevalent trajectory to international markets, nothing is said about the extent to which this stepwise initial approach to exporting is the optimal route. This question has to our knowledge not really been asked in the literature. In fact, the Uppsala model is a descriptive model rather than a normative one.

SPEED OF EXPORT START-UP

Our next question concerns the performance effects of early versus later export start-up. For this purpose we study the cohort of firms established in 2003 and look at those firms that start to export (1) the same year, (2) one year after, (3) two years after and (4) four years after. We explore and compare the development in four variables for these firms: export dropout, average export ratio, average number of export destination countries and average firm profitability. We have chosen year 2003 as the first year of operation simply because that year is the first year of available data and therefore allows for tracking these companies over the longest possible period of time. Comparing three cohorts of firms – established in 2003, 2004 and 2005 – we find no significant differences in terms of export start-up patterns, development of export ratios or number of markets. We may therefore assume that the 2003 cohort gives a representative picture of a general pattern for new ventures.

Dropping Out of Exporting

Dropping out of the export statistics may happen for several reasons. The firm may have withdrawn from exporting after having tried it for a certain period of time – one, two or three years; it may have stopped exporting one year only to reoccur after some years as exporter in the statistics; it may have gone bankrupt and therefore vanished from the statistics; it may have been acquired by or merged with another firm, changing its organizational number and then disappearing from our database. We unfortunately do not have any data to substantiate the reasons for the drop-out, but assume for the subsequent exercise that these four explanations do not systematically affect the results of our analyses.[2] We also assume that remaining in the database as exporters is an indication of a firm's viability.

We may expect lower export dropout rates if a firm starts exporting later and thus not immediately after its inception. The argument will in this case be that exporting requires resources both in terms of capital, experience and otherwise, and since the eventual exporter waits a number of years before starting to export, it will have had time to build such resources. On the other hand, one may also – in line with born global (BG) literature (see, for instance, Oviatt and McDougall, 1994; Knight and Cavusgil, 1996; Coviello and McAuley, 1999) – argue in the opposite direction: entrepreneurs starting to export already in the first year may do so because they (1) have an internationally marketable product at the outset, (2) have a network of potential and relevant partners abroad and (3) are more gregarious and entrepreneurial and therefore are more committed to the export venture (Oviatt and McDougall, 1994; Knight and Cavusgil, 1996; Madsen and Servais, 1997; Gabrielsson and Kirpalani, 2012). It has also been found that late export start-ups will encounter more problems because management is mostly concerned with their ongoing domestic business operations, and will therefore not dedicate the same amount of attention toward the new export venture (Korth, 1991; Shoham and Albaum, 1995). Figure 6.3 displays the development in retention rates for exporters from the 2003 cohort for companies starting to export in years 2003, 2004, 2005 and 2006. The number of new ventures founded in 2003 starting to export in these years is 318, 564, 403 and 288, respectively.

The columns indicate remaining firms; the curved line indicates the dropout level of firms starting to export in year 1 (2003). Based on this figure we conclude that (1) the earlier a firm starts to export the lower the dropout rate, and (2) the dropout rate is the highest early in the firms' export life (particularly in year 2). Interestingly these dropout rates parallel those of the total population of firms established in 2003 (Statistics Norway, 2010). Of the 38 747 firms that were established in 2003 53 per cent survived in 2004, 48 per cent in 2005, 40 per cent in 2006, 35 per cent in 2007 and 32 per cent in 2008. This could indicate that firms disappear from the export statistics just because of bankruptcies, although this is unlikely to be the full story.

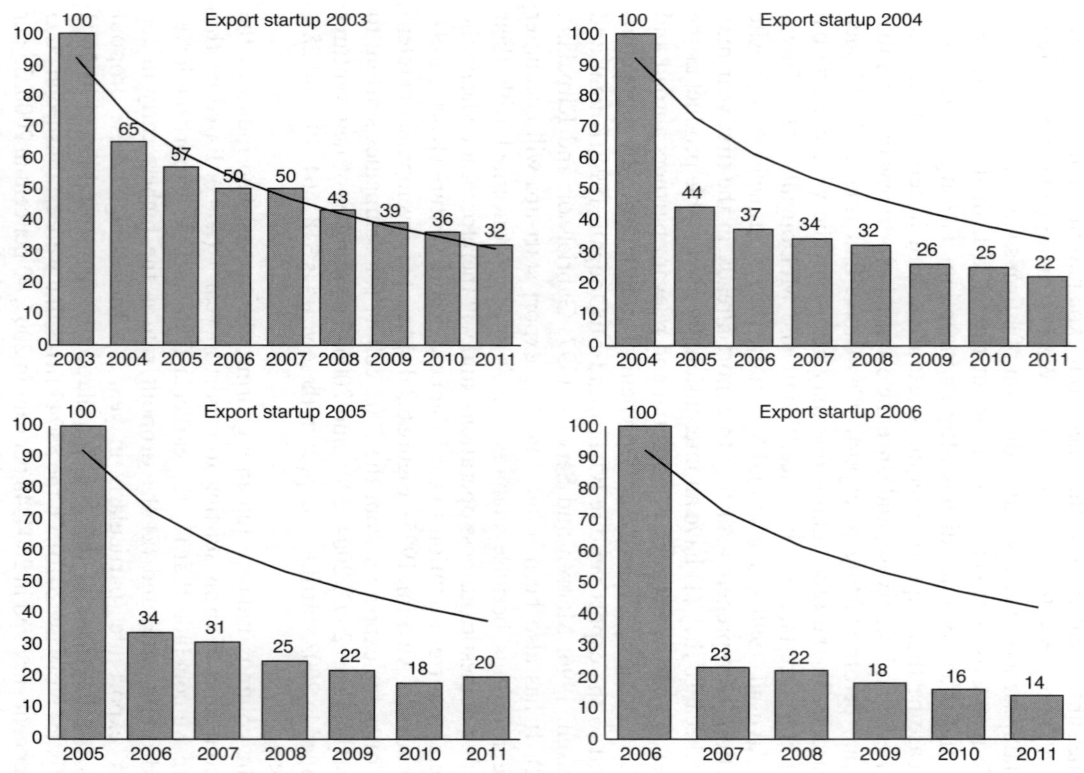

Figure 6.3 Exporter drop-out per year of export start-up of firms established in 2003

Table 6.1 Average export ratios of new ventures starting to export in years 1, 2, 3 and 4 (%)

Year	Export Start 2003	Export Start 2004	Export Start 2005	Export Start 2006
	Export Ratios	Export Ratios	Export Ratios	Export Ratios
2003	12	–	–	–
2004	15	8	–	–
2005	15	10	5	–
2006	15	9	6	4
2007	15	8	4	4
2008	15	7	7	5
2009	14	8	5	5
2010	15	7	4	3
2011	15	8	9	3

Export Ratio

The export ratio, defined as the total export amount divided by sales, has been used as a proxy for export success (Cavusgil and Zou, 1994). Even though this definition has its limits and should be accompanied by other indicators of success (market share, growth rate, profitability etc. – cf. for instance, Shoham, 1998), it translates the commitment and readiness of firms to engage in exporting. In any event we deem that export ratio is an appropriate expression of the firm's internationalization process that is our focus here. Table 6.1 exhibits the development of export ratios of firms starting to export in the same year as they were established and years 2, 3 and 4.

The table clearly shows that first-year export start-ups not only achieve a higher export ratio (12 per cent) the first year, but the following years these exporters also increase the ratio to around 15 per cent and then hold on to that level over the remaining years. Firms starting to export in year 2 attain an export ratio of only 10 per cent, and those starting in years 3 and 4 even lower with export ratios of respectively 5 and 4 per cent. In addition, those firms starting later than year 1 display a much more erratic development of their exports.

Number of Markets

The number of markets the firm is involved in through exports may be another indication of successful exporting. We also find the same pattern

Table 6.2 Average number of markets of firms per year of export start-up

Year	Export Start 2003	Export Start 2004	Export Start 2005	Export Start 2006
	Number of Markets	Number of Markets	Number of Markets	Number of Markets
2003	2.0	–	–	–
2004	4.0	1.7	–	–
2005	4.8	2.7	1.2	–
2006	5.1	3.0	1.6	1.1
2007	5.2	3.2	1.8	1.6
2008	5.7	3.3	2.1	1.7
2009	5.8	3.4	2.1	1.8
2010	6.5	3.1	2.2	1.7
2011	6.6	3.2	2.2	1.6

here: first-year exporters export to more markets than 'latecomers'. Table 6.2 shows the numbers.

Firms that start exporting the same year they are established sell their products on average to two countries, increasing to four in year 2, and ending up with six different markets after six years, slowly increasing thereafter. This is in stark contrast to firms that start exporting only after four years. They sell to only one foreign market the first year of exporting, and after six years they export to 1.6 markets on average. The two other groups of exporters – with start-ups two and three years after foundation – are somewhere in between. The general pattern is quite astounding: the later the firm starts exporting, the fewer markets it will end up with.

Profitability

Finally we ask the question if the profitability of firms varies according to year of export start-up (Table 6.3).

We notice that the profitability in general is quite low for new start-ups the first six to nine years after starting to export, with operating margins oscillating around zero. One exception occurs in 2009 for all firms, and is explained by a new tax regime being introduced that year. However, first-year start-ups display a smoother development of their profitability, fluctuating around zero the first six years of operation, and then picking up (after the extraordinary year 2009). Those firms starting exporting in year 2 seem to fare moderately better (after two initial negative years) with operating margins between 1 and 4 per cent, but do not attain higher rates

Table 6.3 Average profitability of firms per year of export start-up – % return on sales

Year	Export Start 2003	Export Start 2004	Export Start 2005	Export Start 2006
	Profitability	Profitability	Profitability	Profitability
2003	–0.02	–	–	–
2004	0.0	–0.16	–	–
2005	–0.01	–0.01	–0.01	–
2006	0.03	0.04	–0.06	0.03
2007	–0.01	0.02	0.01	–0.02
2008	0.02	0.04	–0.07	–0.16
2009	0.53	0.36	0.26	0.16
2010	0.04	0.01	0.0	0.02
2011	0.06	0.02	–0.13	0.03

after the extraordinary year 2009. The other two groups display a more negative picture. The pattern is not as distinct concerning profitability as with the indicators directly linked to internationalization, although we discern a tendency of first-year export start-ups to be slightly more profitable in the longer run. One reason for this more deviating pattern is possibly the fact that operating margins concern total sales, and not exports in particular.

DISCUSSION

Based on our findings we claim that early internationalization is not only possible, but it seems to be desirable. It is related to lower dropout rates, higher export ratios, more diversity in terms of market destination (spreading risks), and also a smoother development of operating margins. Interestingly, the exit rate of first-year export starters is lower than the general dropout rate of new ventures in Norway (58 vs 68 per cent), whereas the latecomers – starting to export the second, third and fourth year of operation – drop out more rapidly (68, 75 and 78 per cent respectively). Indeed, this suggests that there is something about first-year export start-ups. The null hypothesis would be that indifferent of year of export start-up these figures would be more or less the same. Given the high degree of uncertainty related to new ventures, compounded by the uncertainty of expanding internationally (Johanson and Vahlne, 1977, 2009) it is a fair assumption that experience gained at home before export start-up would be beneficial for a late start-up of international expansion. It is therefore thought provoking that our findings go in the opposite direction. The hypothesis would then be that firms that have operated a certain number of years at home will have had time to test the product or service in the home market, and to build resources and experience, thereby enabling them to more effectively meet the challenges of export initiation and further internationalization. Since we find otherwise, we have to investigate the reasons for the relative success of early export start-up.

The question then is whether early export start-up leads to success or the other way around: whether success leads to exporting. Unfortunately, we do not have access to data concerning, for instance, the background and commitment of the founders of the firm, its shareholders, or equity, access to networks and so forth – factors that may explain early successful start-up and that have been put forward in the BG literature (Oviatt and McDougall, 1994; Knight and Cavusgil, 1996; Madsen and Servais, 1997; Gabrielsson and Kirpalani, 2012). Therefore, for this particular chapter, we can only speculate around possible explanations for the patterns found. These characteristics have been mentioned as typical of BGs and may therefore also describe early export start-up firms. We consequently find it reasonable to tentatively conclude that exporters starting their internationalization already in their first year of operation are endowed with superior resources compared to those starting to export in later years. These resources may be in the form of superior products with a global market potential, a management and founder that have previous international experience – and perhaps also an existing network of potential partners and customers, financial resources from investors (that are easier to attract if the two previous resources – product and management/network – are in place).

In order to cast light on the causality we are inclined to believe that the arrow goes in the direction of some factors (founder, network, resources, product) being in place at the outset and then success (export start and subsequent growth). Firms endowed with these resources will then start exporting already in the first year of operation. They will much more rapidly than other firms achieve higher export ratios, sell to more markets and not drop out of business as severely as export latecomers. However, the financial rewards of early exporters seem to come only after a number of years – in our case after five to six years of export operations. We may speculate that this has to do with two factors: (1) rapid export development involving higher than 'normal' financial disbursements and thereby reducing the returns, and (2) the time required to learn the 'game of exporting' (Eriksson et al., 1997), including the intricate interplay between players in the market (customers, partners, competitors), building trust with partners (Hohenthal, 2001) and understanding the market and how to cost efficiently adapt the product. If this is the correct interpretation of our data, we may still say that we find support of the Uppsala model in that exporting is a *learning process* (Johanson and Vahlne, 1977, 1990, 2009). We maintain that the incremental internationalization process should be assessed in terms of 'learning to master the game' rather than measured by the pace of growth in export ratio or number of countries. Our data also reveal that for early exporters – after a build up of international sales over the first three to four years of exporting – the operations are consolidated (export ratio and the number of markets do not increase markedly any more).

The reason for late start-ups' much poorer performance – both in terms of export growth and dropout, but also in terms of profitability – may then simply reside in something quite provincial and unworldly: at foundation they have fewer competitive advantages in terms of founder characteristics, resources, access to networks or product features. Those that survive (between 25 and 14 per cent after six years of operation depending on year of export start-up) need time to assert themselves in the home market before venturing abroad. And when venturing abroad they encounter harsher challenges than early exporters, supposedly because of their shortcomings.

However we are not in a position to state that a firm that starts exporting in year 3 or 4 has fewer resources than those the year before. We speculate that other mechanisms come into play: the more a firm is operating in its home market the more its resources are committed to this market and the more the learning about idiosyncratic features about this market are being embedded in the organization – including routines and ways of thinking. As a consequence, the less prepared the firm will be in meeting the challenges of operating in international markets. The words of Johanson and Vahlne (1977, p. 28) of the importance of experiential knowledge providing 'the framework for perceiving and formulating opportunities' are also valid in the domestic market – in this case constraining the range of opportunities in international markets.

CONCLUSIONS AND IMPLICATIONS

Reviewing the export development of Norwegian new ventures since 2003 reveals interesting patterns. Although our findings show that the geographic dimension of the Uppsala school is followed by the large majority of new ventures, it is not clear whether this is the most effective strategy.

Our results suggest that the earlier the new venture starts exporting, the higher the export ratio, the lower the dropout rate, the more markets it gets involved in, and the smoother the development of operating margins. Consistently, our data reveal that firms starting to export a year later risk failing (drop out) or take a less proactive stance to exporting (lower export ratio and fewer markets) compared to those starting the previous year. These are not explicitly discussed by the Uppsala scholars, not in their original works (Johanson and Wiedersheim-Paul, 1975; Johanson and Vahlne, 1977 and 1990) nor in the revised version (Johanson and Vahlne, 2009), although – implicitly – some notion of success looms between the lines as the cases studied in 1975 by and large exhibit a trajectory of successful international expansion. Our findings suggest that different export start-up years indeed lead to different performance outcomes, begging the questions of why and how. We suggest two mechanisms.

First, early exporters are endowed with better resources, networks and products, and have founders that are more committed, and therefore start exporting already in the year of foundation. In particular, we suggest that the success of the early exporters is achieved because they do not suffer from the same 'liability of outsidership' as many of the others. We believe – in line with the arguments put forward by Johanson and Vahlne (2009) – that access to relevant networks is the key to success in international markets. This has also been found in other research from Norway (Solberg and Durrieu, 2006; Solberg et al., 2014). When the export venture is well entrenched – after say five to six years – then the causality may go in the other direction: the more the firm exports the more successful it will be. At this point the now not so new venture has achieved an entrenched position in a number of international markets, and is in a position to capitalize on the learning of previous years of international operations. We also conjecture that latecomers to export markets are latecomers because of shortcomings in their resource base and lack of commitment by the founders.

The later the new venture starts exporting, the more it is disadvantaged in meeting challenges in international markets, and less successful it will be. Exporting for these firms may be prompted by some success at home or other triggers such as competition, global pressures and opportunities. However, the experiential knowledge acquired in the home market restrains its search for opportunities abroad and makes them less prepared to engage in exporting.

This study has several implications, both for managers, policy-makers and researchers. New ventures endowed with the advantages described above should take a proactive stance towards internationalization. Doing so increases the chances of a positive spiral of market development. Those not so convinced of their resources and competitive advantages should possibly take a more modest posture to getting involved in international markets. They should spend time building resources, understanding and developing their business model relative to customer needs and competitor positions – also in an international context, and then – eventually – start their export ventures.

For policy-makers our findings are most relevant concerning government export promotion (GEP). Even though research on GEP mostly finds positive relationships between export assistance programmes and different performance measures (Bloodgood et al., 1996; Shamsuddoha and Ali, 2006; Wilkinson and Brouthers, 2006) other studies conclude more ambiguously (Westhead et al., 2001; Francis and Collins-Dodd, 2004; Solberg et al., 2013). Our general impression is that the mechanisms of export assistance leading to export behaviour and eventually improved performance are complex and not well understood. Solberg et al. (2013) suggest that promotional programmes should aim at fostering the commitment and dedication of exporters. Whereas early exporters hardly need any encouragement from GEP agencies to that effect, latecomers may benefit from such backing. Also, access to networks is facilitated by many GEP programmes. This kind of GEP assistance may alleviate the shortcomings of many latecomers, and give these new ventures a better starting point for early export.

We speculate about the differences of early exporters and latecomers, and about the direction of causality between firm performance and different export patterns. Future research should delve more deeply into the underlying hypotheses of these speculations. Is it really so that important success factors are already in place in early exporters whereas latecomers are more scantily bestowed with such favours? And does two or three years of operating in domestic markets really create inhibitors to exports? Future research should aim at finding out.

NOTES

1. These numbers exceed the number of firms exporting to Sweden as the first market entry, because they enter more than one market during the year of registration. In this case we cannot read from our data what market is number 2, 3 or 4, only what markets they entered in the same year. Also, Sweden is registered as market number 2 for 3881 firms only because this is the number of firms that *continue* exporting to Sweden.
2. One may claim that these explanations differ over time: for instance, first-year export starter dropouts may be more prone to bankruptcy or acquisition since their resources have not had time to build. On the other hand this is pure speculation so *ceteris paribus* we assume equal distribution over the years.

REFERENCES

Aaby, N.-E. and S.F. Slater (1989), 'Management influences on export performance: a review of the empirical literature 1976–88', *International Marketing Review*, **6**(4), 7–26.

Acedo, F.J. and M.V. Jones (2007), 'Speed of internationalization and entrepreneurial cognition: insights and a comparison between international new ventures, exporters and domestic firms', *Journal of World Business*, **42**(3), 236–52.

Andersen, O. (1993), 'On the internationalization process of firms: a critical analysis', *Journal of International Business Studies*, **24**(2) 209–31.

Benito, G.R.G. and G. Gripsrud (1992), 'Expansion of foreign direct investments: discrete rational location choice or a cultural learning process?', *Journal of International Business Studies*, **23**(3), 461–76.

Bloodgood, J.M., H.J. Sapienza and J.G. Almeida (1996), 'The internationalization of new high-potential US ventures: antecedents and outcomes', *Entrepreneurship Theory and Practice*, **20**(4), 61–76.

Cavusgil, S.T. and S. Zou (1994), 'Marketing strategy–performance relationship: an investigation of the empirical link in export market ventures', *Journal of Marketing*, **58**(1), 1–21.

Chetty, S., M. Johanson and O.M. Martín (2014), 'Speed of internationalization: conceptualization, measurement and validation', *Journal of World Business*, **49**(4), 633–50.

Coviello, N.E. and A. McAuley (1999), 'Internationalisation and the smaller firm: a review of contemporary empirical research', *Management International Review*, **39**(3), 223–56.

Eriksson, K., J. Johanson, A. Majkgård and D.D. Sharma (1997), 'Experiential knowledge and cost in the internationalization process', *Journal of International Business Studies*, **28**(2), 337–60.

Francis, J. and C. Collins-Dodd (2004), 'Impact of export promotion programs on firm competencies, strategies and performance: the case of Canadian high-technology SMEs', *International Marketing Review*, **21**(4/5), 474–96.

Gabrielsson, M. and V.H.M. Kirpalani (2012), 'Overview, background and historical origin of born globals: development of theoretical and empirical research', in M. Gabrielsson and V.H.M. Kirpalani (eds), *Handbook of Research on Born Globals*, Cheltenham, UK and Northampton, MA, USA: Edward Elgar Publishing, pp. 3–15.

Hofstede, G. (1980), *Culture Consequences: International Differences in Work Related Values*, Beverly Hills, CA: Sage.

Hohenthal, J. (2001), 'The creation of international business relationships: experience and performance in the internationalization process', PhD thesis, Uppsala, Sweden: Department of Business Studies, Uppsala University.

Johanson, J. and J.E. Vahlne (1977), 'The internationalization process of the firm: a model of knowledge development and increasing foreign market commitment', *Journal of International Business Studies*, **8**(1), 23–32.

Johanson, J. and J.E. Vahlne (1990), 'The mechanisms of internationalization', *International Marketing Review*, **7**(4), 11–24.

Johanson, J. and J.-E. Vahlne (2009), 'The Uppsala internationalization process model revisited: from liability of foreignness to liability of outsidership', *Journal of International Business Studies*, **40**(9), 1411–31.

Johanson, J. and F. Wiedersheim-Paul (1975), 'The internationalization of the firm – four Swedish cases', *Journal of Management Studies*, **12**(3), 305–22.

Knight, G.A. and S.T. Cavusgil (1996), 'The born global firm: a challenge to traditional internationalization theory', in S.T. Cavusgil and T. Madsen (ed.), *Advances in International Marketing* (Vol. 8), London: JAI Press, pp. 11–26.

Korth, C.M. (1991), 'Managerial barriers to US exports', *Business Horizon*, **32**(2), 18–26.

Madsen, T.K. and P. Servais (1997), 'The internationalization of born globals: an evolutionary perspective', *International Business Review*, **6**(6), 561–83.

Oviatt, B.M. and P.P. McDougall (1994), 'Towards a theory of international new ventures', *Journal of International Business Studies*, **25**(1), 45–64.

Shamsuddoha, A.K. and M.Y. Ali (2006), 'Mediated effects of export promotion programs on firm export performance', *Asia Pacific Journal of Marketing and Logistics*, **18**(2), 93–110.

Shoham, A. (1998), 'Export performance: a conceptualization and empirical assessment', *Journal of International Marketing*, **6**(3), 59–81.

Shoham, A. and G.S. Albaum (1995), 'Reducing the impact of barriers to exporting: a managerial perspective', *Journal of International Marketing*, **3**(4), 85–105.

Solberg, C.A. and F. Durrieu (2006), 'Access to networks and commitment to internationalisation as precursors to marketing strategies in international markets', *Management International Review*, **46**(1), 57–83.

Solberg, C.A., G. Gripsrud and A. Hunneman (2014), *Mapping and Analysing Norway's Export Patterns and Strategies of Norwegian Exporters*, Research Report, Oslo: BI Norwegian Business School.

Solberg, C.A., E. Helseth and L. Piitulainen (2013), 'Does government export promotion boost export performance?', conference paper, EIBA Conference, Brehmen, Germany.

Statistics Norway (2010), 'Nyetablerte foretaks overlevelse og vekst, 2003–2008' [Newly established enterprise survival and growth, 2003–2008], 22 October 2010, accessed 29 May 2015 at https://www.ssb.no/virksomheter-foretak-og-regnskap/statistikker/fordem/aar/2010-10-22.

Westhead P., M. Wright and D. Ucbasaran (2001), 'The internationalization of new and small firms: a resource-based view', *Journal of Business Venturing*, **16**(4), 333–58.

Wilkinson, T.J. and L.E. Brouthers (2006), 'Trade promotion and SME export performance', *International Business Review*, **15**(3), 233–52.

Zucchella, A., S. Denicolai and G. Palamara (2007), 'The drivers of the early internationalisation of the firm', *Journal of World Business*, **42**(3), 268–80.

7. Simultaneous effects between innovativeness and export behavior in small firms: evidence from Spain

Izaias Martins, Alex Rialp-Criado and Yancy Vaillant

INTRODUCTION

It is generally agreed that export activities are an important issue at the micro-level for the growth and expansion of a business (Knight and Cavusgil, 2004; Leonidou and Katsikeas, 1996), as well as at the macro-level for the generation of wealth for the nation (Da Rocha et al., 2009; Roper and Love, 2002). Unsurprisingly, it is one of the most popular topics in business management and international entrepreneurship (IE) literatures (e.g., Cassiman and Golovko, 2011; Golovko and Valentine, 2011; Kirbach and Schmiedeberg, 2008; Lages et al., 2009). In turn, there is a consensus in strategic management and IE that one of the keys to generate a competitive advantage in a global economy is through innovativeness (Alpay et al., 2012; Filipescu et al., 2013; Flor and Oltra, 2005; Hagen et al., 2014; Prasad, 2004; Rhee et al., 2010; Tajeddini et al., 2006). Innovativeness reflects the propensity of a firm to actively support new ideas, novelty, experimentation and creative solutions in pursuit of a competitive advantage (Hult et al., 2004; Lumpkin and Dess, 1996). Nowadays most small firms seem to get into the international market more rapidly than before (Andersson et al., 2004), and they are more concerned with adopting strategies that involve activities in the foreign marketplace (McDougall and Oviatt, 2000; Rialp et al., 2005).

In the European business context, usually characterized by small domestic markets associated with the situational uncertainty due the current economic crisis, several economies are facing difficulties due to recessions in their domestic markets. Thus, one of the avenues for small firms to gain market share and ensure their survival may be in operating abroad (Dejo-Oricain and Ramírez-Alesón, 2009). In this sense, a study of Spanish small firms could help to extend the knowledge in this research field. Spain is among the European Union's largest economies; however, it is one of the countries most affected by the current crisis. In addition, its international presence through exports is relatively weak, perhaps caused by the low levels of innovativeness culture (Monreal-Pérez et al., 2012).

Especially nowadays, firms must explore the interaction between innovativeness and export activities. Many scholars examined the relationship between innovativeness and export behavior (e.g., Caldera, 2010; Cassiman and Golovko, 2011; Kirbach and Schmiedeberg, 2008; Lachenmaier and Wobmann, 2006), or even, the complementarity between innovativeness and export for SMEs' growth (Golovko and Valentine, 2011). However, most prior research on this topic focuses on specific aspects of innovation rather than the innovativeness culture, or even present an interchangeable use of the constructs 'innovation' and 'innovativeness' (Garcia and Calantone, 2002), resulting in a lack of consistency in operationalizing these constructs.

Thus, this study contributes, extends, confirms and/or contradicts the current debate around this research topic. We also highlight the more ample existence of single-sided rather than double-sided research looking at the innovativeness–export relationship. The former is often limited to cross-sectional studies (considering only a year). Furthermore, there are few studies examining separately each dimension of innovativeness and their impacts on firms' exports. In addition, while it is generally agreed that innovativeness contributes to business performance, relatively little is known about the drivers of innovativeness (Hult et al., 2004).

Consistent with the resource- and learning-based views, we focus on the relationship between innovativeness and export activity. Thus, this allows us to contribute to the literature by examining the impact of small firms' innovativeness on the decision to operate abroad, as well as on their export performance. At the same time, and equally as important, we draw on learning-by-exporting (Salomon and Shaver, 2005). Hence, our study responds to calls by scholars who have encouraged more research on the role of export propensity on firm innovativeness (e.g., Damijan et al., 2010; Salomon and Shaver, 2005). Furthermore, we theoretically contribute to the discussion on the differences between innovation and innovativeness that generate confusion and sometimes an interchangeable use of these constructs.

The remainder of this chapter is organized as follows: Section 2 provides the theoretical framework, a brief overview of previous studies and the hypotheses proposed; Section 3 specifies the research design and describes the main data sources; Section 4 presents the estimation results; and Section 5 provides a discussion and concluding remarks.

THEORETICAL FRAMEWORK, PREVIOUS RESEARCH AND HYPOTHESES

Clarifying Innovation and Innovativeness Concepts

As we mentioned above, the plethora of definitions for innovation types is confusing and has resulted in an ambiguity in the way the terms innovation and innovativeness are used. The result is an interchangeable use of these constructs to define innovation types (Adams et al., 2006; Garcia and Calantone, 2002; Kamaruddeen et al., 2009). In order to achieve distinctions between innovation and innovativeness we reflected on different aspects such as the stages of the innovation process – initiation and implementation suggested by Zaltman et al. (1973), the degree of newness of an innovation (Freel, 2005; Roehrich, 2004), or even, the time and degree of adoption of the current technology (Fell et al., 2003).

Although a certain degree of overlap between those concepts may exist (Damanpour, 1991) it is possible to point out some distinctions. Moreover, while the concept of innovation is widely dealt with in research, the definition of innovativeness is rarely discussed (Tajeddini et al., 2006). It happens perhaps because while the definition of innovation is less problematic for research that examines a single innovation such as product or service (where the objective is simply to demonstrate that the phenomenon being studied is an innovation), it becomes more problematic when examining the concept of innovativeness because it is concerned with the full range of innovations developed (Emsley, 2005). Thus, in order to understand innovativeness, it is necessary to discuss the concept of innovation first.

From an overall perspective, the term 'innovation' can be defined as an iterative process initiated by the perception of a new market opportunity for a product or service created through a technology-based process, which leads to development, production and marketing tasks (OECD, 1991). In a complementary way, innovation is the generation, acceptance and implementation of creative ideas within an organization (Hurley and Hult, 1998). In this sense, Garcia and Calantone (2002) pointed out that this iterative character implies varying degrees of innovations and thus it is important to elucidate that an innovation does not necessarily imply the creation of something unique. Furthermore, many companies have taken an innovation strategy of improving upon existing products or technologies, called incremental innovation. Therefore, the implementation of an innovative product or service does not automatically imply highly innovative firms (Garcia and Calantone, p. 117).

On the other hand, an important part of the initiation stage is 'openness to the innovation' (Zaltman et al., 1973, p. 64), which is determined by whether the different actors within an organization are committed to considering the adoption of or are resistant to innovation. In this sense, innovativeness is the notion of openness to new ideas as an aspect of a firm's culture (Hurley and Hult, 1998). However, according to Tajeddini et al. (2006), there is no real consensus on the meaning of innovativeness, because it is a multidimensional, composite variable made up of perceptual measures such as 'radicalness', or operational measures like 'innovations adopted' (Roehrich, 2004). Additionally, innovativeness also might be related to the time of adoption, namely, the degree to which an individual or other unit of adoption is relatively earlier in adopting new ideas, concepts, systems and products than any other competitor (Rogers, 2003; Subramanian and Nilakanta, 1996).

Innovativeness is most frequently used as a measure of the degree of newness of an innovation. Innovativeness is 'possession of newness' (Roehrich, 2004), or the degree of newness of a product (Freel, 2005; Gatignon and Xuereb, 1997). Highly innovative products or services and innovative processes are seen as having a 'high degree of newness' (Garcia and Calantone, 2002, p. 112).

In sum, the innovativeness concept gives a more complete reflection and embraces a range of innovations adopted in a given time period (Damanpour, 1991; Tajeddini et al., 2006). By considering these arguments, for the purposes of this research, the term innovativeness is seen as the creation and possession of newness, thus depicting a firm's skill to create and launch new products, its ability to develop new process innovations and the possession of products and services that are either totally new or radically different from existing products (uniqueness).

Innovative Capability as a Resource: From Innovativeness to Foreign Markets

In the resource-based view (RBV) perspective, the capacity of firms to generate sustained competitive advantages – which means advantages that derive from the resources and capabilities that are valuable, scarce, inimitable and non-substitutable (Barney, 1991) – depends on their particular set of resources. These resources and capabilities can be viewed as bundles of tangible and intangible assets, including business skills and knowledge (Barney et al., 2001). Thus, the best way to understand a firm is by considering it as a collection of productive resources specific to each firm, which allows it to compete successfully against other firms (Penrose, 1959). Considering that SMEs suffer from the structural phenomenon labelled 'liability of smallness' (Gassmann and Keupp, 2007) they cannot be presumed to be well endowed with tangible assets. Thus, the crucial resources of SMEs, such as knowledge, are essentially intangible. In the context of innovativeness, RBV helps to explain how knowledge and the resultant organizational capabilities are developed and leveraged by firms (Knight and Cavusgil, 2004). The knowledge-based view (KBV) has emerged from the RBV by focusing on intangible resources, rather than on physical assets (Gassmann and Keupp, 2007, p. 353). The differential endowment of resources is an important determinant of organizational capabilities and performance (Barney, 1991; Teece et al., 1997). Indeed, organizational capability is the outcome of knowledge integration (Grant, 1996). It points out that innovative capability does not come from exploiting external technologies, which are easily accessible for competitors and therefore insufficient for sustaining a competitive advantage but rather it comes from the generation of internal innovation by generating new resources and building basic technological competences (Barney, 1991), as well as accumulating intangible resources, namely, knowledge (Prashantham, 2005). In addition, technological resources can generate a double competitive advantage for a firm, in lowering costs by creating new and more efficient production processes, and in differentiation by means of product innovations (López Rodríguez and García Rodríguez, 2005).

In international business, knowledge provides particular advantages that facilitate foreign-market entry and operations (Johanson and Vahlne, 1991; Knight and Cavusgil, 2004). Namely, knowledge about international markets, as well as the efficiency by which such knowledge is learned and used to achieve intended ends is an important determinant of success in entrepreneurial firms (Autio et al., 2000). In this vein, innovating firms develop their own unique knowledge and dynamic capabilities that engender organizational performance in fast-moving global environments (Al-Aali and Teece, 2014) and, therefore, new product market development in innovative firms is fluid and dynamic, with ongoing market expansion (Eiriz et al., 2013). Likewise, firms leverage technology to innovate in the creation and improvement of products, as well as the adaptation of products for foreign markets which can also drive the global market entry (López Rodríguez and García Rodríguez, 2005). Moreover, as emphasized by Rialp et al. (2005, p. 160), one of the factors that appear to engender or facilitate a firm's early internationalization is precisely 'high value creation through product differentiation, leading-edge technology products, and technological innovativeness'.

When firms begin their internationalization process, they typically move through different stages, such as exporting operations, joint venturing or foreign direct investment, among others. In this study, we concentrate our analysis only on export activities (i.e., when we talk about international activities, we are referring exclusively to exports, export propensity referring to the act of engaging in exporting and export intensity referring to the proportion of overall sales destined abroad). Particularly for small firms, export activity is the most important strategy for internationalization (Knight and Cavusgil, 2004; Leonidou and Katsikeas, 1996). In turn, the innovativeness might be an important factor in explaining the entry into the export market (Basile, 2001; Cassiman and Golovko, 2011).

Conceptually, an innovative strategic posture is thought to be linked to firm performance (Alpay et al., 2012; Eiriz et al., 2013) because it increases the chances that a firm will realize first-mover advantages and capitalize on emerging market opportunities (Wiklund, 1999). Innovative firms, through the creation and introduction of new products and technologies, develop a market niche with new products/services, differentiate themselves and/or substitute incumbents with better quality, cheaper prices or other means that customers value (Richard et al., 2009; Wiklund and Shepherd, 2005). Innovativeness could be recognized as a key success factor in an increasingly competitive, global economy (Akman and Yilmaz, 2008; Prasad, 2004). In this way, there is a large volume of empirical literature testing the effect of innovative activity on international business (e.g., Cassiman and Martínez-Ros, 2007; Kirbach and Schmiedeberg, 2008; Lachenmaier and Wobmann, 2006; Podmetina et al., 2009; Roper and Love, 2002; Wakelin, 1998).

For instance, Podmetina et al. (2009) highlighted the importance and the significant impact of innovativeness, competition and new products development on the internationalization, as well as on export intensity, of companies in Russia. In the same way, Kirbach and Schmiedeberg (2008) have offered an interesting analysis of export behavior, when comparing firms in West and East Germany. Their estimations confirmed a strong relationship between innovativeness and international operations, as well as structural differences, between West and East German firms.

In the context of Southern Europe, studies have mostly focused on innovation, defined as a result, rather than the more behaviorally defined concept of innovativeness. In fact, the last ten years have seen a proliferation of studies attempting to explain the innovation–export relationship. For example, Caldera (2010), using compiled data from the Encuesta sobre Estrategias Empresariales (ESEE)–Spain, stressed a positive effect of firm innovation on the probability of participation in export markets. In turn, using Spanish manufacturing data, López Rodríguez and García Rodríguez (2005) stated that product innovations, patents and process innovations have positive and significant effects on both the decision to export and international business intensity. Likewise, Cassiman and Martínez-Ros (2007) stressed the importance of innovation on exports and pointed out that product innovations are a more important determinant of export growth, while process innovations are a more important driver of export propensity. More recently, Cassiman and Golovko (2011) emphasize that product innovation improves productivity levels, which pushes firms to enter the export markets, as well as being directly related to the probability of export in a firm's operations. According to these findings, it can be posited that the link between innovation and exports begins with innovativeness, described as the firm's proactive behavior from which innovation may result. The following hypotheses are therefore formulated:

H1a: The greater innovativeness of the firm, the more likely its export propensity.

H1b: The greater innovativeness of the firm, the higher its export intensity.

Learning-by-exporting: From Export Activities Toward Innovativeness

There is growing recognition about the relationship between innovativeness and export activities. Likewise, recent literature on IE has followed this line of research, but analyzes the reverse relationship or even the reciprocity between both innovativeness and export activities. Hence, at the same time, the effects of export activity on firms' innovativeness might be investigated from the perspective on learning-by-exporting. It is acknowledged that the ability of a firm to recognize the value of new and external knowledge with an absorptive capacity (Cohen and Levinthal, 1990; Lane and Lubatkin, 1998; Zahra and George, 2002) is a critical component to learning and innovativeness. Moreover, the knowledge-based view of the firm states that innovativeness is an information- and knowledge-intensive process. Thus, in order to be creative and make the difference, firms need to access and retrieve information from as many sources as possible, including different countries (Kafouros et al., 2008).

In this research, we try to be consistent with prior studies (Eriksson et al., 1997; Monreal-Pérez et al., 2012; Sapienza et al., 2005) assuming that firms can increase their innovativeness by improving the process of knowledge accumulation and by increasing organizational learning (Kafouros et al., 2008). Thus, companies may learn directly from foreign-market experience and indirectly via observation of foreign companies (Johanson and Vahlne, 1991). External contacts can help firms learn new capabilities and may provide access to resources and knowledge (Anand and Khanna, 2000; Chetty and Wilson, 2003; Stoian et al., 2011). That is, firms could learn from foreign markets and their foreign presence (Sapienza et al., 2005).

However, to which extent does export activity make companies more innovative? Specifically, is it possible to have or achieve a positive effect of export intensity on a firm's innovativeness? Consistent with the learning-based view, obviously this is a potential option. Despite not having extensive literature examining the reverse relationship, some authors stress that international trade makes firms more innovative (e.g., Filipescu et al., 2009; Podmetina et al., 2009; Salomon and Shaver, 2005), perhaps because these companies must innovate to remain in foreign markets (Hitt et al., 1997). Furthermore, international firms can leverage their networks around the world to hire better technologists and access skilled technical expertise (Kafouros et al., 2008). Likewise, internationalized firms tend to transfer their experience from international operations into increased innovativeness in the domestic market (Filipescu et al., 2009; Molero, 1998). In this way, several authors agree with the statement that 'the fact of developing international activities has influenced, in a positive way, technological innovation' (Filipescu et al., 2009, p. 147). Furthermore, these two features (internationalization and the innovativeness) reinforce each other to the extent that today's economic analysis has to consider both of them simultaneously when trying to account for any new dynamic of the firms operating at the international level (Molero, 1998).

Therefore, consistent with the learning-by-exporting view, and in accordance with previous research, the following hypothesis can be addressed:

H2: Export propensity positively affects a firm's innovativeness.

RESEARCH DESIGN

Database

In this study, we use data from the Global Entrepreneurship Monitor (GEM) adult population survey (APS) collected for the years 2007 and 2008 in Spain. The GEM research program is an annual assessment of the national levels of entrepreneurial and business activity. Initiated in 1999 it is the single largest study of entrepreneurial activity in the world cumulating nearly 100 national research teams as of 2014. The main advantage of the GEM database is the fairly large sample size, in addition to consistency in definition and measures across multiple contexts. Thus, besides its external validity, the use of the GEM dataset allows understanding of business and entrepreneurial activity across time and space.

The main research instrument of GEM data collection methodology is the adult population survey (APS); the same used in this study. The GEM APS dataset satisfies the definitional requirements of this study. It uses a consistent set of factors and definitions across multiple contexts that can be used to establish external validity of findings. The GEM APS questionnaire has been developed taking into consideration theoretical perspectives and previous empirical findings as well as practical considerations (Reynolds et al., 2005; Levie and Autio, 2008). The countries that participate in the GEM research project have a national team of researchers that oversee the work in their respective countries. This database has been extensively used by researchers across the world (see Amoros et al., 2013; Bosma, 2013).

The sample was selected through multiple sampling. In the first stage, a random sample of municipalities divided according to population quota was selected. This was followed by the selection of a random sample using the random digit dialing (RDD) technique of both fixed and mobile telephone number from the telephone directory (annually updated 'Espana Office v5.2' database). In the third stage individuals in the age group between 18 and 64 years were randomly selected using the birth method to select the within-household respondents. The selected respondent is asked four screening questions and depending on their response to these four questions, the respondents are further asked questions about their involvement in the type and nature of business activities. Finally, information on some profile variables is collected from all respondents. In case of nonresponse, the same telephone number is contacted again and this process is repeated until the suitable respondent is contacted. Once the data from the target number of selected respondents are obtained, the dataset is weighted by gender, age group and habitat (rural–urban). The third party marketing research agency selected by the Global Entrepreneurship Research Association (GERA) (the technical committee of GEM overseeing the Global GEM project), collects the data, normally during May–July of each year as per the GEM guidelines.

The GEM database is considered suitable for this study because it contains all the variables relevant for analyzing the hypothesized relationships. From the original survey we identify the subset of those who are classified as firm owner-manager/s (corresponding to people who declared owning and managing a business). Thus, the final sample included usable responses from 977 (2007) and 1449 (2008) firms. The characteristics of the sample are similar for both years. The reporting companies had a mean of 5.66 employees (2007) and 4.72 employees (2008), and about two-thirds of the companies operated only on the domestic market, while the remaining third had at least 1 percent of their total sales from exports. Full sample characteristics are depicted in Table 7.1.

Table 7.1 Firm characteristics

		2007		2008	
		N	%	N	%
Export					
Export propensity	Export	391	40.02	544	37.54
	No export	586	59.98	905	62.46
Export intensity	Low	244	62.40	349	64.15
	Medium	62	15.86	75	13.79
	High	85	21.74	120	22.06
Innovativeness					
Products or services	New to all or some	398	40.74	580	40.03
Innovativeness	Not new	579	59.26	869	59.97
Process	Less than 5 years	333	34.08	471	32.51
Innovativeness	More than 5 years	644	65.92	978	67.49
Uniqueness of product or service	Product's distinctiveness	295	30.19	413	28.50
	No distinctiveness	682	69.81	1036	71.50
Firm-specific characteristics					
Size	1–9 employees	842	86.18	1266	87.37
	10–49 employees	135	13.82	183	12.63
Age	Less than 10 years	376	38.49	568	39.20
	More than 10 years	601	61.51	881	60.80
Industry	Extractive	89	9.11	155	10.70
	Manufacturing	331	33.88	481	33.20
	Service	167	17.09	222	15.32
	Consumer-oriented	390	39.92	591	40.79

Variables

Export propensity

A dichotomous variable was used with the aim of identifying the companies with some experience selling in foreign markets. Thus, the variable measures whether the firm has an export-oriented behavior or not. If 1 percent or more of the sales goes abroad, this variable assumes the value of 1. Otherwise, if the firm does not sell abroad, this variable assumes the value of 0. Several authors have used a similar measurement (e.g., Calof, 1994; Estrin et al., 2008; Gonzalez-Pernía and Peña-Legazkue, 2011; Zhao and Zou, 2002).

Export intensity

It is the dependent variable in the first part of our analysis. This variable corresponds to the foreign sales rate divided by the total sales in a given period (Pan and Chi, 1999). In fact, according to Katsikeas et al. (2000), this is the main criterion to measure export performance. Thus, we create a categorical variable that assumes the value of 1 if the company does not export (null export propensity), a value of 2 if the rates of exports are between 1 percent and 25 percent (low), value 3 if the rates of exports are between 26 percent and 50 percent (medium), and a value of 4 if the rates of exports are 51 percent or more (high). Our classification is supported in Acs and Amorós (2008), who capture the importance of 'entrepreneurial export orientation' considering as a 'relatively high foreign market rate' more than 50 percent of customers in other countries. The purpose is to generate an ordinal classification attempting to identify firms that do not export, and firms with an increasingly significant proportion of their revenues derived from foreign sales.

Innovativeness

There are several methods by which to classify innovation, and the research by Downs and Mohr (1976) could be a good example; however, innovativeness is more accurately represented when multiple, rather than single, innovations are considered (Damanpour, 1991). It examines the whole range of innovations developed (Emsley, 2005; Tajeddini, 2006). The most useful classification of innovativeness is through product market innovation and technological innovation (Lumpkin and Dess, 1996). In other words, innovativeness is the predisposition to engage in creativity through the introduction of new products or services as well as technological leadership via R&D in new processes.

The innovativeness construct is part of the GEM-available information and its dimensions refer to the poise of an organization to develop creative or novel internal solutions or external offerings (see Reynolds et al., 2005). The questions concerning firm innovativeness indicate: (i) the level of effort made by a firm in an attempt for all, some or none of its current and potential customers to perceive its products and/or services as being more or less innovative (i.e. the degree of effort put by the firm in achieving product/service novelty according to its customers' perceptions); (ii) the extent to which the firm's processes – technologies and/or procedures – required by these products or services become generally available in the market sooner or later; and (iii) the uniqueness or distinctiveness of products or services, namely, the firm's capability of offering products and services that are either 'totally new' or 'radically different' from already existing competitors' products or not (Sharma and Blomstermo, 2003).

Considering the available information in the GEM database, we used this innovativeness concept in two different steps: First, innovativeness was treated as an independent variable. Therefore, in order to assess the level of innovative behavior shown by every firm in the sample, a categorical variable for each innovativeness item was created. We measured the variable *product or service innovativeness* in terms of a firm's level of effort (assuming the value of 1 for high effort, 2 for low effort, and 3 for non effort) in order to achieve that its products and/or services were actually perceived as mostly new and unfamiliar by all, at least some or none of its customers, respectively. Likewise, the variable *process innovativeness* assumes a value of 1 for companies which apply emerging technologies available less than one year ago (extremely new), a value of 2 for companies using technologies available between one and five years ago (new), and a value of 3 for companies using older technologies generally available in the market more than five years ago (not new). Regarding the *uniqueness of products or services*, we used a dichotomous variable to measure the distinctiveness of a firm's offer. It assumes a value of 1 when there are not other businesses – or only very few – offering the same or very similar product or service to their potential customers, and a value equal to 0 if there are many other businesses offering essentially the same product or service to them.

Second, innovativeness was also used as a dependent variable. In this case, *product or service innovativeness* and *process innovativeness* were re-labeled, and a dichotomous variable was created for each innovativeness item. Thus, *product or service innovativeness* assumes the value of 1 for those firms showing a certain level of innovative effort (either high or low) in their attempt to generate products or services seen as rather new and unfamiliar by all or at least some of their customers; otherwise, they assume the value of 0. Likewise, *process innovativeness* assumes the value of 1 for firms using emerging (extremely new) or new technologies available in the market for less than five years; otherwise, they assume the value of 0.

Control variables

Firm size We first include a variable to capture size as an internal resource, considering that firm-specific factors might provide firms with a competitive advantage (Barney, 1991). Thus, firm size is expected to have a positive relationship to exports because larger firms have more resources with which to enter foreign markets (Fariñas and Martín-Marcos, 2007; Wakelin, 1998). In the same way, firm size is expected to have a positive relationship to firm innovativeness. Firms might have an excess workforce capacity with which to produce new products (Salomon and Shaver, 2005). Furthermore, innovative exporters tend to be larger than non-innovative ones (Damijan et al., 2010). Size was measured by the natural log of the number of employees (Andersson et al., 2004; Cassiman and Golovko, 2011) reported in the year of the GEM survey.

Firm age We measured firm age as the number of years that the firm has been operating (Caldera, 2010; Monreal-Pérez et al., 2012). Firm age is an additional characteristic that may differ between exporters and non-exporters. Exporters are usually older than non-exporters (Fariñas and Martín-Marcos, 2007). Age has been introduced to the model in logarithmic form.

Industry We control for industry sector because firms in specific industries may be more inclined to exporting or innovativeness. Likewise, firms in more knowledge-intense industries may be more inclined to exert learning effort (Sapienza et al., 2005). For instance, we expected consumer product-oriented firms to develop more new products (Salomon and Shaver, 2005) and bet on new technologies. The dataset assigned four standard categories that are derived from the standard industrial classification – SIC code (extractive, manufacturing, business service and consumer oriented). The industry variable was coded with categorical variables, and extractive is the omitted category serving as the base case in regression analyses.

ANALYSIS AND RESULTS

The Choice of Specification

The overall aim of the study is to examine whether a firm's innovativeness affects its export activity (in terms of export propensity and export intensity), and whether its export propensity affects innovativeness. In order to meet this overall aim, we address two main research issues. First, we investigate the influence of innovativeness on the internationalization of small firms through export activities, and how innovativeness and uniqueness in products or services as well as process innovativeness affects the proportion of foreign sales (export intensity). The second research issue is to investigate whether firms with export propensity (those which have a positive proportion of foreign sales) show higher innovativeness in products or services, as well as in processes (more recent availability of new technology or procedures necessary to develop their activities). As stated in Section 3, by using data from two years, we have provided some evidence from cross-sectional analyses of 2007 and 2008.

Tables 7.2 and 7.3 show means, standard deviation and correlation between the variables. As can be observed, the magnitude of the correlation between independent variables in both ordinal and logit regression models do not represent problems of multi-collinearity. In fact, the correlation between innovativeness in products or services and process innovativeness was expected, the correlation value being significant but not too high.

Innovativeness and Exports

In order to test Hypotheses H1a and H1b, we applied an ordinal logistic model (OLM). Given that the multinomial regression model ignores any ordering of the values of the dependent variable, and our dependent variable presents a clear ordering of the values, we apply a model that incorporates the ordinal nature of the dependent variable. In the ordinal logistic model, the event of interest is observing a particular score. For example:

$$rating_1 = prob(score\ of\ 1)/prob(score\ greater\ than\ 1)$$
$$rating_2 = prob(score\ of\ 1\ or\ 2)/prob(score\ greater\ than\ 2)$$
$$rating_3 = prob(score\ of\ 1,\ 2\ or\ 3)/prob(score\ greater\ than\ 3).$$

The last category does not have an odds associated with it since the probability of scoring up to, including the last score, is 1. Thus, defining the event, we can write the equation as:

$$\text{Ø}_j = prob(score \leq j)/prob(score > j).$$

Table 7.4 presents the estimated coefficients for the model. The estimates labelled *rating* are the threshold (the intercept equivalent terms), and it is possible to observe an increasing estimated coefficient according to increasing the scale.

As for the control variables, it is observed that firm size is significant with a positive sign in every test. With respect to the firm age, findings confirm that age is positively related to export activity only in 2008. For a continuous variable, a positive coefficient means that as the values of the variable increase, the likelihood of larger scores increases as well.

As expected, especially the size of the company increases the probability of having higher export activities. These results are consistent with previous research (e.g., Monreal-Pérez et al., 2012), 'exporters tend to be larger than non-exporters' (Salomon and Shaver, 2005, p. 440). In regard to the industrial sector, however, only a marginally significant difference has been observed among these four standard categories.

Table 7.2 Summary statistics and correlation for key variables: ordinal regression 2007 and 2008

Variables	2007								
	Mean	SD	(1)	(2)	(3)	(4)	(5)	(6)	(7)
(1) i.prod/serv.	1.637	0.9385	1.00						
(2) proc.innov.	1.543	0.7217	0.124***	1.00					
(3) exp.inten.	1.446	0.6694	0.096**	0.114**	1.00				
(4) uniqueness	0.301	0.4593	0.073**	0.135***	0.031	1.00			
(5) employeesln	1.098	0.9797	0.081**	0.080**	0.039	–0.036	1.00		
(6) ageln	2.482	0.6637	–0.045	–0.058*	–0.037	0.004	–0.008	1.00	
(7) industry	2.878	1.043	0.060*	0.062*	–0.002	–0.001	–0.010	–0.075**	1.00

Note: $*p < 0.05$; $**p < 0.01$. [ln] logarithmic form.

By observing the innovativeness variables, in each relationship we can verify that there is a significant positive influence on export intensity. Thus, the results for many of the variables are as expected. Considering the role of the product/service innovativeness, our findings show that firms which make some innovative efforts – either higher or lower – to convince more customers to recognize the company's output as new and unfamiliar to all or at least some of them (product/service novelty), as compared to those which do not apply any significant effort (omitted category), raise their probability of exporting (export propensity) and mostly increase their export intensity. Looking at the findings in 2007 and 2008, the coefficients are very similar and in both years confirm a positive relationship. For instance (2007: high effort = 1.611 $p < .01$; low effort 1.447 $p < .05$ and 2008: high effort = 1.660 $p < .01$; low effort 1.512 $p < .01$). Regarding the use of more or less up-dated technology (*process innovativeness*), we also found a positive influence on export activities. Namely in small firms whose technologies or procedures to perform their activities were more recently available, especially less than a year ago, the result was as expected. For instance, looking at the result in 2007 (extremely new = 1.451 $p < 0.05$). Equally as important, there are statistical differences between businesses with process technology generally available less than five years ago versus more than five years ago (older available technologies taken as the omitted category) in regard to exporting. For instance, looking at the result in 2008 (new = 1.197 $p < 0.10$). The next specification uses an alternative measure of perceived strategic innovativeness. As mentioned above, the uniqueness of products or services is present if the firm has no (or very few) competitors offering the same product or service to their current or potential customers. The results are

				2008				
Mean	SD	(1)	(2)	(3)	(4)	(5)	(6)	(7)
1.539	0.7263	1.00						
1.386	0.6001	0.143***	1.00					
1.592	0.9178	0.055**	0.145***	1.00				
0.503	0.2188	0.076**	0.116***	0.029	1.00			
1.065	0.9215	0.066**	0.092**	–0.015	–0.027	1.00		
2.497	0.6763	–0.043	–0.064**	–0.064**	–0.043*	0.033	1.00	
2.861	1.072	0.036	–0.042	–0.020	–0.025	–0.063*	–0.048*	1.00

in accordance with those expected, that is, a small firm seemingly without competitors offering the same product or service as compared to another selling non-distinctive or standardized products (omitted category) significantly increases its likelihood of being more intensively export-oriented (*product's distinctiveness* 2007: 1.309 $p < 0.05$, and 2008: 1.283 $p < 0.05$).

As mentioned earlier, an analysis using OLM incorporates an ordinal nature of the dependent variable and generally showed a positive relationship between innovativeness (either in terms of product/service and process) and a firm's export propensity, as well as increasing its export intensity. Hence, Hypotheses H1a and H1b receive support.

Export Propensity and Innovativeness

In order to explore whether export propensity can help explain company innovativeness, we need to deploy a procedure that can estimate the probability of the expected event (i.e., innovativeness). Given that we have binary-dependent variables, logistic regression is more appropriate. Logistic regression is a statistical analysis aimed at predicting and exploring a binary categorical variable (Andersson et al., 2004). Logistic regression differs from multiple regression analysis in that it directly predicts the probability of an event occurring (Hair et al., 1998), and hence enables us to identify whether export propensity is relevant in categorizing firms as innovative or not. Table 7.5 displays the results of the logistic regression.

The chi-square test of both the *product/service innovativeness* and *process innovativeness* complete models was significant and indicates that a significant relationship exists between the entire set of independent variables and dependent variables. Table 7.5 displays the odds ratio, the significance at the corresponding level, and the standard deviation. The predicted values of dependent variables concern the 'log odds' that an event will occur, and

Table 7.3 Summary statistics and correlation for key variables: logit regression 2007 and 2008

Variables	2007								2008							
	Mean	SD	(1)	(2)	(3)	(4)	(5)	(6)	Mean	SD	(1)	(2)	(3)	(4)	(5)	(6)
(1) i.prod/serv.	0.4073	0.4915	1.00						0.4002	0.4901	1.00					
(2) proc.innov.	0.3408	0.4742	0.137**	1.00					0.3250	0.4685	0.112**	1.00				
(3) exp.prop.	0.4002	0.4901	0.134**	0.113	1.00				0.3754	0.4844	0.105**	0.058**	1.00			
(4) employeesln	1.098	0.9797	0.070*	0.048	0.075**	1.00			1.065	0.9215	0.070*	–0.008	0.044*	1.00		
(5) ageln	2.482	0.6637	–0.072*	–0.046	–0.055*	–0.008	1.00		2.497	0.6763	–0.075**	–0.081**	–0.059**	0.033	1.00	
(6) industry	2.878	1.043	0.074*	0.017	0.052*	–0.010	–0075*	1.00	2.861	1.072	0.034	–0.031	0.049*	–0.063**	–0.048*	1.00

Note: *$p < 0.05$; **$p < 0.01$. [ln] logarithmic form.

Table 7.4 Ordinal logistic regression to export intensity: a cross-sectional analysis for the years 2007 and 2008

		2007				2008			
		Model 1		Model 2		Model 1		Model 2	
Rating									
= 1		0.551	(0.345)	0.945	(0.356)	0.179	(0.267)	0.556	(0.280)
= 2		1.897	(0.352)	2.325	(0.364)	1.542	(0.271)	1.941	(0.285)
= 3		2.521	(0.359)	2.957	(0.371)	2.088	(0.276)	2.495	(0.291)
Control									
Size	Log_empl.	1.180**	(0.076)	1.175**	(0.076)	0.145**	(0.066)	1.135**	(0.066)
Age	Log_age	0.866	(0.083)	0.890	(0.085)	0.841**	(0.066)	0.874*	(0.070)
	Manufacturing	1.245	(0.318)	1.140	(0.294)	0.792	(0.148)	0.759	(0.143)
Industry	Service	1.145	(0.320)	1.045	(0.296)	0.950	(0.200)	0.911	(0.193)
	Consumer-oriented	1.710**	(0.427)	1.574*	(0.396)	1.090	(0.196)	1.054	(0.191)
	Extractive[o.c.]	o.c.		o.c.		o.c.		o.c.	
Hypothesis	*Innovativeness*								
	All			1.611***	(0.237)			1.660***	(0.263)
iProd/Serv.	Some			1.447**	(0.283)			1.512***	(0.114)
	No			o.c.				o.c.	
	Extremely new			1.451**	(0.220)			1.255*	(0.154)
Proc.innov.	New			1.591**	(0.325)			1.197*	(0.259)
	No new[o.c.]			o.c.				o.c.	
Uniqueness	Product's distinctiveness			1.309**	(0.182)			1.283**	(0.150)
								o.c.	
Model fit									
	N	977		977		1449		1449	
	Chi² (df)	18.01(5)		47.46 (10)		15.55 (5)		45.49 (10)	
	Prob > Chi²	0.0029		0.0000		0.0082		0.0000	
	Pseudo R^2 (Nagelkerke)	0.0089		0.0233		0.0054		0.0158	

Note: $*p < 0.10$; $**p < 0.05$; $***p < 0.01$. The numbers in brackets are standard errors. o.c. omitted category and the parameter is zero because it is redundant.

Table 7.5 Logit regression to innovativeness: a cross-sectional analysis for the years 2007 and 2008

Control		2007				2008			
		i.prod/serv		*Proc.innov.*		*i.prod/serv*		*Proc.innov.*	
		Model 1	Model 2	Model 1	Model 2	Model 1	Model 2	Model 1	Model 2
Size	*Log_empl.*	1.147**	1.128*	1.102	1.084	1.173**	1.162**	0.976	.969
		(0.076)	(0.076)	(0.075)	(0.074)	(0.068)	(0.068)	(0.060)	(0.059)
Age	*Log_age*	0.824*	0.838*	0.874	0.889	0.800**	0.813**	0.767**	0.775**
		(0.082)	(0.084)	(0.090)	(0.092)	(0.64)	(0.066)	(0.064)	(0.065)
	Manufacturing	1.788**	1.755**	1.284	1.256	1.533**	1.583**	1.163	1.182
		(0.480)	(0.474)	(0.339)	(0.333)	(0.305)	(0.317)	(0.230)	(0.235)
Industry	*Service*	2.195**	2.175**	1.417	1.396	1.678**	1.699**	0.931	0.934
		(0.637)	(0.635)	(0.407)	(0.403)	(0.374)	(0.381)	(0.211)	(0.212)
	Consumer-oriented	2.036**	1.908**	1.257	1.177	1.519**	1.516**	0.920	0.915
		(0.538)	(0.509)	(0.327)	(0.309)	(0.296)	(0.297)	(0.179)	(0.179)
	Extractive o.c.	o.c.	o.c.	o.c.	o.c.	o.c.	o.c.	o.c.	o.c.
Hypothesis	*Export propensity*		1.675***		1.596***		1.525***		1.288**
			(0.226)		(0.221)		(0.170)		(0.149)
Model fit									
	N	977	977	977	977	1449	1449	1449	1449
	LR Chi^2 (df)	18.98(5)	33.60(6)	5.88(5)	17.25(6)	22.33(5)	36.63(6)	13.30(5)	18.06(6)
	Prob > Chi^2	0.0019	0.0000	0.3185	0.0084	0.0005	0.0000	0.0208	0.0061
	Pseudo R^2	0.0144	0.0254	0.0047	0.0138	0.0114	0.0188	0.0073	0.0099
	Correctly classified	59.06%	59.37%	65.92%	65.92%	60.04%	61.35%	67.43%	67.49%

Note: $*p < 0.10$; $* p < 0.05$; $***p < 0.01$. The numbers in brackets are standard errors. o.c. omitted category and the parameter is zero because it is redundant.

the interpretation is thus analogous to that of linear regression (Hair et al., 1998). A positive coefficient implies that an increase in those variables represents a higher likelihood of innovativeness.

The results for the control variables are as expected. Size clearly plays an important role in increasing a firm's product or service innovativeness. We found that larger firms tend to be more innovative in product or service; however, there is no statistical difference concerning the process innovativeness. With respect to age, by observing the odds ratio (smaller than one) this finding might be considered as a negative coefficient. Thus, age seems to have an inverse relationship with innovativeness. In regard to the industrial sector, unsurprisingly firms in an extractive industry (omitted category) tend to be less innovative than firms in other industries. Furthermore, these differences between industries are more evident in products or service innovativeness than in process innovativeness.

Concerning H2, we assessed if the change in the independent binary variable (i.e., export propensity yes/no) increased the likelihood of achieving product or service innovativeness and process innovativeness (dependent variables). The results in Table 7.5 report that export propensity has a positive and significant effect on a firm's innovativeness propensity. In both cases, product/service innovativeness and process innovativeness, the probability that the event will occur is higher in exporters than in non-exporters. Moreover, our results confirm that export propensity has high explanatory power in both consecutive years, 2007 and 2008 (findings 2007: export propensity = 1.675 $p < 0.01$ for product/service innovativeness and export propensity = 1.596 $p < 0.01$ for process innovativeness; findings 2008: export propensity 1.525 $p < 0.01$ for product/service innovativeness and export propensity = 1.288 $p < 0.05$ for process innovativeness). Therefore, Hypothesis H2 is also supported.

DISCUSSION AND CONCLUSIONS

The purpose of this research was to investigate the role of innovativeness on firm export behavior (propensity and intensity) as well as a reverse effect of export propensity on innovation activities. Particular emphasis has been placed on innovativeness in product or service, process innovativeness, uniqueness of products or services and foreign sales. Consistent with calls to examine not only the antecedents of export activity but also its consequences (Salomon and Shaver, 2005), our study shows that, by examining the mutual role of one upon the other, there are simultaneous effects between innovativeness and export behavior.

Overall, our results seem to suggest that there is a double causality chain between innovativeness and exports in both 2007 and 2008, through cross-sectional analyses conducted in these two consecutive years. Our findings provide evidence from two years' analysis, which may indicate a tendency that innovativeness, on the one hand, and exports, on the other hand, may influence each other. We also provide conceptual clarity on the difference between innovation and innovativeness by focusing on the definition of innovativeness which is rarely discussed.

By considering the relationship between innovativeness and export activity, our research has found a positive influence of all proposed variables on export intensity. The capacity of a business to cultivate and appropriate culture required to develop innovative and unique products relative to its competitors is vital for achieving and maintaining foreign sales. This implies that innovativeness could change the behavior of small firms; that is, when small businesses are committed to innovativeness, this significantly increases the likelihood of selling to foreign markets, and especially the level of their foreign sales ratio. In this vein, our findings support the view held by Wakelin (1998), who found considerable differences in the reaction of innovating and non-innovating companies, stressing that they behave differently in terms of export. Indeed, across our analysis, we confirmed the importance of small firms selling products and services that are either totally new or quite different from other existing products or services. Thus, we can state that the uniqueness of products and services is another important basis for internationalization.

The innovativeness culture can generate competitive advantages through product or service innovativeness, process innovativeness and the uniqueness of products and services. It provides firms with the possibility of initiating and/or increasing exports and becoming more entrepreneurial-oriented in different markets. Therefore, in line with other researchers (e.g. Denicolai et al., 2014; Filipescu et al., 2013; López Rodríguez and García Rodríguez, 2005), it can be stated that innovativeness matters for export behavior. Furthermore, from the perspective of the resource-based view, innovativeness represents an original combination of the organization's resources and is developed over the lifetime of the firm (Monreal-Pérez et al., 2012).

Moreover, our empirical results provide support for the direction of a number of recent arguments. For instance, Cassiman and Golovko (2011) argued that product innovativeness has an important moderating effect on the positive association between exports and productivity. Also, analyzing German manufacturers, Kirbach and Schmiedeberg (2008) found a strong impact of product innovativeness on the decision to export, and they suggested that innovating firms are more likely to export and tend to realize a larger share of revenue from the international market.

In turn, the learning-by-exporting hypothesis predicts that organizational innovativeness will increase if the company has export activities and may learn from them accordingly. Our findings corroborate this argument. The positive association between export propensity and a firm's innovativeness observed in the second part of the empirical analysis confirms that firms do increase product/service and process (technology) innovativeness if they are export oriented. This observed superior innovativeness may be related to the firm's ability to get new knowledge in its exports markets, namely, exporting firms tend to increase their innovativeness by absorbing knowledge and ideas from several sources and/or countries (absorptive capacity). Thus, our findings might be consistent with the existence of learning-by-exporting as emphasized in recent literature (Kafouros et al., 2008; Salomon and Jin, 2008; Salomon and Shaver, 2005).

However, we must interpret the results on this learning-by-exporting effect with caution because some previous studies on this issue have found limited evidence and suggested that firms should export to a large number of markets in order to achieve advantages from the potential learning generated by their export activity (Fariñas and Martín-Marcos, 2007; Monreal-Pérez et al., 2012). Nonetheless, when companies not only learn about foreign markets but also use their resources and capabilities to solve potential problems abroad, they can succeed in reaching the learning-by-export effect. In this sense, some abilities such as managerial foreign languages skills and international business knowledge are crucial for improving the course of actions followed by a company abroad (Stoian et al., 2011).

In addition, by observing two consecutive years, the findings may indicate a tendency about the relationships proposed in the study. Hence, we can state that our study contributes to the literature and also presents some implications for research and practice.

For academics, this study adds to the stream of research that explains the antecedents of the decision to export and in which degree. We take a different perspective, providing evidence from each innovativeness dimension, namely considering the influence of innovativeness and uniqueness in product and/or service as well as in process/technology. In summary, the firm's ability to innovate in product or service in a certain degree – the more, the better – constitutes an essential driver to face international challenges, and associated with technological innovativeness impels small firms to operate abroad by exporting with even more intensity. Equally as important, the level of uniqueness concerning the product–market relationship should be interpreted as further evidence of the relevance of firm innovativeness at the moment of entering and expanding the firm's international market share because the fewer the number of other businesses offering the same product or service to customers, the more innovative the firm's outputs are. Moreover, we contribute to research in another particular dimension (i.e., the effect of export propensity on a firm's innovativeness). Hence, the theoretical contributions of this study lie in the extension of innovativeness research with an emphasis on export propensity and intensity.

Our findings also contribute to the literature by offering further evidence on the controversial relationship between innovativeness and internationalization. In particular, our study contributes to a better understanding of the SME internationalization–innovativeness relationship, as well as to theoretical literature on resource capabilities and learning-by-exporting. The theoretical contribution shows that innovativeness, seen as an essential firm capability, might have a positive influence on the probability and intensity of participation in export markets. Equally important, our study contributes to the extant literature by investigating the learning effect associated with export behavior on the likelihood of innovation commitment in small firms. Finally, unlike most studies that limit their focus to innovative and high-technology firms and often only consider innovation in products and/or technology available but not both at the same time, our study is based on evidence from small firms in different types of industries (both high- and low-tech). We also adopt the construct of innovativeness which gives a more complete reflection and embraces a wider range of innovations adopted in a given time period. This helps us provide clarity on the difference between innovation and innovativeness as mentioned above.

For business managers, it is important to know that firms aiming at innovating in products or services and/or technological resources will have a superior capacity to gain access to international markets as well as to increase their sales abroad. Our results suggest that exporting is more than just a decision to increase sales and reach other markets. Knowledge and learning obtained by means of gaining experience in foreign markets may also help firms increase their capacity to innovate. Thus, if globalization pushes companies to enter foreign markets and acquire specific knowledge in order to implement technology and business innovation (Podmetina et al., 2009), the ability of a firm to assimilate, learn and apply their export-related experience to commercial ends is critical to developing their innovative capabilities.

There are several other possibilities for future research in line with our results. The main issue is the need to understand the causal relationship between innovativeness and export behavior/activities. We observed that there seem to be mutual effects between them. Nonetheless, this chapter is subject to several limitations and we suggest caution in interpreting its findings. First, export behavior may be affected by many factors that cannot be easily controlled (Monreal-Pérez et al., 2012). Second, our sample consists only of business owner-managers surveyed by the GEM research programme. Despite the fact that self-reported data from the owner-managers of small firms were highly correlated with accounting information, supporting the accuracy and reliability of the data (Chandler and Hanks, 1993), future research utilizing other more objective measures on export performance will be welcome. Third, the cross-sectional design of the study cannot guarantee the direction of causality among variables. Future research could examine, using refined panel data, whether a firm's innovativeness enhances its probability of exporting or even increases its sales abroad across time (e.g., Cassiman and Golovko, 2011; Filipescu et al., 2013; Monreal-Pérez et al., 2012). Moreover, it is acknowledged that firms learn more when they exert significant effort in processing new external knowledge (Sapienza et al., 2005). In this sense, future studies should include a longitudinal perspective observing the effects of learning-by-exporting on a firm's innovativeness (e.g. Damijan et al., 2010; Salomon and Shaver, 2005). Furthermore, time-series analysis and some exploratory qualitative research could provide more insight on the direction of causality between innovativeness and export activities and could be another interesting avenue for future work in order to clarify such relationships.

Finally, regarding the models being used in this study, we controlled the main potential variables that may have influence on export, such as a firm's size, firm's age and industry. However, another potential limitation of this study is that we have not considered the possible foreign ownership of the firms which, as stressed in previous studies, can make entry abroad easier (Basile, 2001), and share of foreign capital can moderate the effects of innovativeness dimensions on overall firm performance (Alpay et al., 2012).

REFERENCES

Acs, Z.J. and J.E. Amorós (2008), 'Entrepreneurship and competitiveness dynamics in Latin America', *Small Business Economics*, **31**(3), 305–22.

Adams, R., J. Bessant and R. Phelps (2006), 'Innovation management measurement: a review', *International Journal of Management Reviews*, **8**(1), 21–47.

Akman, G. and C. Yilmaz (2008), 'Innovative capability, innovation strategy and market orientation: an empirical analysis in Turkish software industry', *International Journal of Innovation Management*, **12**(1), 69–111.

Al-Aaly, A. and D.J. Teece (2014), 'International entrepreneurship and the theory of the (long-lived) international firm: a capabilities perspective', *Entrepreneurship Theory and Practice*, **38**(1), 95–116.

Alpay, G., M. Bodur, C. Yilmaz and P. Buyukbalci (2012), 'How does innovativeness yield superior firm performance? The role of marketing effectiveness', *Innovation: Management, Policy & Practice*, **14**(1), 107–28.

Amoros, J.E., N. Bosma and J. Levie (2013), 'Ten years of Global Entrepreneurship Monitor: accomplishments and prospects', *International Journal of Entrepreneurial Venturing*, **5**, 120–52.

Anand, B.N. and T. Khanna (2000), 'Do firms learn to create value? The case of alliances', *Strategic Management Journal*, **21**(3), 295–315.

Andersson, S., J. Gabrielsson and I. Wictor (2004), 'International activities in small firms: examining factors influencing the internationalization and export growth of small firms', *Canadian Journal of Administrative Sciences*, **21**(1), 22–34.

Autio, E., H.J. Sapienza and J.G. Almeida (2000), 'Effects of age at entry, knowledge intensity, and imitability on international growth', *Academy of Management Journal*, **43**(5), 909–24.

Barney, J. (1991), 'Firm resources and sustained competitive advantage', *Journal of Management*, **17**(1), 99–120.

Barney, J., M. Wright and D.J. Ketchen (2001), 'The resource-based view of the firm: ten years after 1991', *Journal of Management*, **27**, 625–41.

Basile, R. (2001), 'Export behaviour of Italian manufacturing firms over the nineties: the role of innovation', *Research Policy*, **30**(8), 1185–201.

Bosma, N. (2013), *The Global Entrepreneurship Monitor (GEM) and its Impact on Entrepreneurship Research*, Foundations and Trends in Entrepreneurship, London: NOW Publishers.

Caldera, A. (2010), 'Innovation and exporting: evidence from Spanish manufacturing firms', *Review of World Economics*, **146**(4), 657–89.

Calof, J.L. (1994), 'The relationship between firm size and export behavior revisited', *Journal of International Business Studies*, **25**(2), 367–87.

Cassiman, B. and E. Golovko (2011), 'Innovation and internationalization through exports', *Journal of International Business Studies*, **42**(3), 1–20.

Cassiman, B. and E. Martínez-Ros (2007), 'Product innovation and exports. Evidence from Spanish manufacturing', mimeo, Barcelona: IESE Business School, 1–36.

Chandler, G.N. and S.H. Hanks (1993), 'Measuring performance of emerging business: a validation study', *Journal of Business Venturing*, **8**(5), 391–408.

Chetty, S.K. and H. Wilson (2003), 'Collaborating with competitors to acquire resources', *International Business Review*, **12**(1), 61–81.

Cohen, W.M. and D.A. Levinthal (1990), 'Absorptive capacity: a new perspective on learning and innovation', *Administrative Science Quarterly*, **35**(1), 128–52.

Damanpour, F. (1991), 'Organizational innovation: a meta-analysis of effects of determinants and moderators', *Academy of Management Journal*, **34**(3), 555–90.

Damijan, J.P., C. Kostevc and S. Polanec (2010), 'From innovation to exporting or vice versa?', *The World Economy*, **33**(3), 374–98.

Da Rocha, A., B. Kury and J. Monteiro (2009), 'The diffusion of exporting in Brazilian industrial clusters', *Entrepreneurship and Regional Development*, **21**(5–6), 529–52.

Dejo-Oricain, N. and M. Ramírez-Alesón (2009), 'Export behaviour: a study of Spanish SMEs', *GCG: Revista de Globalización, Competitividad y Gobernabilidad*, **3**(2), 52–67.

Denicolai, S., A. Zucchella and R. Strange (2014), 'Knowledge assets and firm international performance', *International Business Review*, **23**, 55–62.

Downs, R.D. and L.B. Mohr (1976), 'Conceptual issues in the study of innovation', *Administrative Science Quarterly*, **21**(3), 700–714.

Eiriz, V., A. Faria and N. Barbosa (2013), 'Firm growth and innovation: toward a typology of innovation strategy', *Innovation: Management, Policy & Practice*, **15**(1), 97–111.

Emsley, D. (2005), 'Restructuring the management accounting function: a note on the effect of role involvement on innovativeness', *Management Accounting Research*, **16**(2), 157–77.

Eriksson, K., J. Johanson, A. Majkgård and D. Sharma (1997), 'Experiential knowledge and cost in the internationalization process', *Journal of International Business Studies*, **28**(2), 337–60.

Estrin, S., K.E. Meyer, M. Wright and F. Foliano (2008), 'Export propensity and intensity of subsidiaries in emerging economies', *International Business Review*, **17**(5), 574–86.

Fariñas, J.C. and A. Martín-Marcos (2007), 'Exporting and economic performance: firm-level evidence of Spanish manufacturing', *The World Economy*, **30**(4), 618–46.

Fell, D.R., E.N. Hansen and B.W. Becker (2003), 'Measuring innovativeness for the adoption of industrial products', *Industrial Marketing Management*, **32**(4), 347–53.

Filipescu, D.A., A. Rialp and J. Rialp (2009), 'Internationalization and technological innovation: empirical evidence on their mutual relationship', in S. Zou (ed.), *Advances in International Marketing* (Vol. 20), Greenwich, CT: JAI Press, pp. 125–54.

Filipescu, D.A., S. Prashantham, A. Rialp and J. Rialp (2013), 'Technological innovation and exports: unpacking their reciprocal causality', *Journal of International Marketing*, **21**(1), 23–38.

Flor, M. and M. Oltra (2005), 'The influence of firms' technological capabilities on export performance in supplier-dominated industries: the case of ceramic tiles firms', *R&D Management*, **35**(3), 333–47.

Freel, M.S. (2005), 'Patterns of innovation and skills in small firms', *Technovation*, **25**(2), 123–34.

Garcia, R. and R. Calantone (2002), 'A critical look at technological innovation typology and innovativeness terminology: a literature review', *Journal of Product Innovation Management*, **19**(2), 110–32.

Gassmann, O. and M.M. Keupp (2007), 'The competitive advantage of early and rapidly internationalising SMEs in the biotechnology industry: a knowledge-based view', *Journal of World Business*, **42**(3), 350–66.

Gatignon, H. and J.M. Xuereb (1997), 'Strategic orientation of the firm and new product performance', *Journal of Marketing Research*, **34**(1), 77–90.

Golovko, E. and G. Valentine (2011), 'Exploring the complementarity between innovation and export for SMEs' growth', *Journal of International Business Studies*, **42**(3), 362–80.

Gonzales-Pernía, J. and I. Peña-Legazkue (2011), 'FDI, external knowledge and the export-oriented behaviour of Spanish early-stage entrepreneurs', paper presented at 5th Global Entrepreneurship Research Conference, 6–8 October, Cartagena de Indias (Colombia).

Grant, R.M. (1996), 'Prospering in dynamically-competitive environments: organizational capability as knowledge integration', *Organization Science*, **7**(4), 375–87.

Hagen, B., S. Denicolai and A. Zucchella (2014), 'International entrepreneurship at the crossroads between innovation and internationalization?', *Journal of International Entrepreneurship*, **12**, 111–14.

Hair, J.F., R.E. Anderson, R.L. Tatham and W.C. Black (eds) (1998), *Multivariate Data Analysis* (5th edition), London: Prentice-Hall International Corp.

Hitt, M.A., R.E. Hoskisson and H. Kim (1997), 'International diversification: effects on innovation and firm performance in product diversified firms', *Academy of Management Journal*, **40**(4), 467–98.

Hult, G.T.M., R.F. Hurley and G.A. Knight (2004), 'Innovativeness: its antecedents and impact on business performance', *Industrial Marketing Management*, **33**(5), 429–38.

Hurley, R.F. and G.T.M. Hult (1998), 'Innovation, market orientation, and organizational learning: an integration and empirical examination', *The Journal of Marketing*, **62**(3), 42–54.

Johanson, J. and J.E. Vahlne (1991), 'The mechanism of internationalization', *International Marketing Review*, **7**(4), 11–24.

Kafouros, M.I., P.J. Buckley, J.A. Sharp and C. Wang (2008), 'The role of internationalization in explaining innovation performance', *Technovation*, **28**(1–2), 63–74.

Kamaruddeen, A., N. Yusof and I. Said (2009), 'A proposed framework for measuring firm innovativeness in the housing industry', *International Journal of Organizational Innovation*, **2**(2), 101–32.

Katsikeas, C.S., L.C. Leonidou and N.A. Morgan (2000), 'Firm-level export performance assessment: review, evaluation, and development', *Journal of the Academy of Marketing Science*, **28**(4), 493–511.

Kirbach, M. and C. Schmiedeberg (2008), 'Innovation and export performance: adjustment and remaining differences in East and West German manufacturing', *Economics of Innovation and New Technology*, **17**(5) 435–57.

Knight, G.A. and S.T. Cavusgil (2004), 'Innovation, organizational capabilities, and the born-global firm', *Journal of International Business Studies*, **35**(2), 124–41.

Lachenmaier, S. and L. Wobmann (2006), 'Does innovation cause exports? Evidence from exogenous innovation impulses and obstacles using German micro data', *Oxford Economic Papers*, **58**(2), 317–50.

Lages, L.F., G. Silva and C. Styles (2009), 'Relationship capabilities, quality, and innovation as determinants of export performance', *Journal of International Marketing*, **17**(4), 47–70.

Lane, P.J. and M. Lubatkin (1998), 'Relative absorptive capacity and interorganizational learning', *Strategic Management Journal*, **9**(5), 461–77.

Leonidou, L. and C. Katsikeas (1996), 'The export development process: an integrative review of empirical models', *Journal of International Business Studies*, **27**(3), 517–51.

Levie, J. and E. Autio (2008), 'A theoretical grounding and test of the GEM model', *Small Business Economics*, **31**, 235–63.

López Rodríguez, J. and R. García Rodríguez (2005), 'Technology and export behaviour: a resource-based view approach', *International Business Review*, **14**(5), 539–57.

Lumpkin, G.T. and G.C. Dess (1996), 'Clarifying the entrepreneurial orientation construct and linking it to performance', *Academy of Management Review*, **21**(1), 135–72.

McDougall, P.P. and B.M. Oviatt (2000), 'International entrepreneurship: the intersection of two research paths', *Academy of Management Journal*, **43**(5), 902–8.

Molero, J. (1998), 'Patterns of internationalization of Spanish innovatory firms', *Research Policy*, **27**(5), 541–58.

Monreal-Pérez, J., A. Aragón-Sánchez and G. Sánchez-Marín (2012), 'A longitudinal study of the relationship between export activity and innovation in the Spanish firms: the moderating role of productivity', *International Business Review*, **21**(3), 862–77.

Organisation for Economic Co-operation and Development (1991), *The Nature of Innovation and the Evolution of the Productive System, Technology and Productivity: The Challenge for Economic Policy*, Paris: OECD, pp. 303–14.

Pan, Y. and P.S.K. Chi (1999), 'Financial performance and survival of multinational corporations in China', *Strategic Management Journal*, **20**(4), 359–74.

Penrose, E. (1959), *Theory of the Growth of the Firm*, Oxford: Basil Blackwell.

Podmetina, D., M. Smirnova, J. Vaatanen and M. Torkkeli (2009), 'Innovativeness and international operations: cause of Russian R&D companies', *International Journal of Innovation Management*, **13**(2), 295–317.

Prasad, R. (2004), 'Transformation of national innovations systems towards the knowledge economy in a globalised world, with special reference to key industrial sector in India', *Innovation: Management, Policy & Practice*, **6**(3), 392–403.

Prashantham, S. (2005), 'Toward a knowledge-based conceptualization of internationalization', *Journal of International Entrepreneurship*, **3**(1), 37–53.

Reynolds, P., N. Bosma, E. Autio, S. Hunt, N. De Bono and I. Servais et al. (2005), 'Global entrepreneurship monitor: data collection design and implementation 1998–2003', *Small Business Economics*, **24**(3), 205–31.

Rhee, J., T. Park and D.H. Lee (2010), 'Drivers of innovativeness and performance for innovative SMEs in South Korea: mediation of learning orientation', *Technovation*, **30**(1), 65–75.

Rialp, A., J. Rialp and G.A. Knight (2005), 'The phenomenon of early internationalizing firms: what do you know after a decade (1993–2003) of scientific inquiry?', *International Business Review*, **14**(2), 147–66.

Richard, O.C., P. Wu and K. Chadwick (2009), 'The impact of entrepreneurial orientation on firm performance: the role of CEO position tenure and industry tenure', *The International Journal of Human Resource Management*, **20**(5), 1078–95.

Roehrich, G. (2004), 'Consumer innovativeness concepts and measurements', *Journal of Business Research*, **57**(2), 671–7.

Rogers, E.M. (2003), *Diffusion of Innovations* (5th edition), New York: The Free Press.

Roper, S. and J.H. Love (2002), 'Innovation and export performance: evidence from the UK and German manufacturing plants', *Research Policy*, **31**(7), 1087–102.

Sapienza, H.J., D. De Clercq and W.R. Sandberg (2005), 'Antecedents of international and domestic learning effort', *Journal of Business Venturing*, **20**(4), 437–57.

Salomon, R. and B. Jin (2008), 'Does knowledge spill to leaders or laggards? Exploring industry heterogeneity in learning by exporting', *Journal of International Business Studies*, **39**(1), 132–50.

Salomon, R. and J. Shaver (2005), 'Learning-by-exporting: new insights from examining firm innovation', *Journal of Economics and Management Strategy*, **14**(2), 431–61.

Sharma, D.D. and A. Blomstermo (2003), 'The internationalization process of born globals: a network view', *International Business Review*, **12**(6), 739–53.

Stoian, M.C., A. Rialp and J. Rialp (2011), 'Export performance under the microscope: a glance through Spanish lenses', *International Business Review*, **20**(2), 117–35.

Subramanian, A. and S. Nilakanta (1996), 'Organizational innovativeness: exploring the relationship between organizational determinants of innovation, types of innovations, and measures of organizational performance', *Omega*, **24**(6), 631–47.

Tajeddini, K., M. Trueman and G. Larsen (2006), 'Examining the effect of marketing orientation on innovativeness', *Journal of Marketing Management*, **22**(4) 529–51.

Teece, D.J., G. Pisano and A. Shuen (1997), 'Dynamic capabilities and strategic management', *Strategic Management Journal*, **18**(7), 509–33.

Wakelin, K. (1998), 'Innovation and export behavior at the firm level', *Research Policy*, **26**(7/8), 829–41.

Wiklund, J. (1999), 'The sustainability of the entrepreneurial orientation–performance relationship', *Entrepreneurship Theory and Practice*, **24**(1), 37–48.

Wiklund, J. and D. Shepherd (2005), 'Entrepreneurial orientation, and small business performance: a configurational approach', *Journal of Business Venturing*, **20**(1), 71–91.

Zahra, S.A. and G. George (2002), 'Absorptive capacity: a review, reconceptualization, and extension', *Academy of Management Review*, **27**(2), 185–203.

Zaltman, G., R. Duncan and J. Holbek (1973), *Innovations and Organizations*, New York: John Wiley & Sons.

Zhao, H. and S. Zou (2002), 'The impact of industry concentration and firm location on export propensity and intensity: an empirical analysis of Chinese manufacturing firms', *Journal of International Marketing*, **10**(1), 52–71.

8. Managerial attitude as antecedent of network development for SME internationalization

M. Cristina Stoian and Pervez N. Ghauri

INTRODUCTION

Scholars and practitioners have widely recognized the importance of networks for organizations' behaviour and performance outcomes as well as for governing interorganizational relationships (see reviews by Borgatti and Foster, 2003; Brass et al., 2004; Provan et al., 2007; Zaheer et al., 2010). Network research has increasingly gained momentum over a wide variety of disciplines ranging from organizational theory and behaviour to sociology and health care services, from strategic management and business studies to communications and computer science (Provan et al., 2007).

The international business field clearly acknowledges networks as a vital driver of international expansion (Johanson and Mattsson, 1988; Blankenburg-Holm et al., 1996; Johanson and Vahlne, 2009; Vahlne and Johanson, 2013). For example, the revisited Uppsala network internationalization process model (Johanson and Vahlne, 2009) suggests that foreign market and mode selection are driven by business relationships. Becoming a partner in a business network should be seen as an asset, as new knowledge about foreign markets can be developed by interacting with other actors in the network. Learning and knowledge creation take place through dynamic interactions with business partners, governed by trust. If network partners commit to the relationship, the firm can gain access not only to knowledge and other resources, but also to the network of contacts of other actors. New international opportunities may be recognized in consequence of the dynamic interplay between the actors involved.

Networks gain even greater importance for fostering the internationalization strategies of small and medium-sized enterprises (SMEs) given their role for overcoming their innate dearth of resources that may prevent their international expansion (Freeman et al., 2006; Laanti et al., 2007). The SME internationalization and international entrepreneurship literature has repeatedly highlighted the crucial role played by networks for international new ventures/born globals/internationalized SMEs' international propensity, the selection of foreign markets and entry modes and performance results (Oviatt and McDougall, 1994; Coviello and Munro, 1995, 1997; Chetty and Blankenburg-Holm, 2000; Sullivan-Mort and Weerawardena, 2006; Ojala, 2009; Manolova et al., 2010; Fernhaber and Li, 2013; Sepulveda and Gabrielsson, 2013).

Considering the increased legitimacy gained by networks for internationalization, network causes/development have been relatively under-researched so far, with a few notable exceptions (e.g., Harris and Wheeler, 2005; Coviello, 2006; Freeman et al., 2006; Agndal and Chetty, 2007; Agndal et al., 2008; Ciravegna et al., 2014). The main entrepreneur/founder/owner/manager[1] is likely to be key for (international) network development (Lloyd-Reason and Mughan, 2002; Sullivan-Mort and Weerawardena, 2006; Sepulveda and Gabrielsson, 2013) as her/his attitudes are expected to influence a broad range of performance outcomes (Caligiuri et al., 2004). Eberhard and Craig (2013) suggest the internationalization outcomes will vary across firms whose managers purposely form networks for expanding internationally, as opposed to firms that do not do so.

This study therefore examines the role of managerial attitude for network development for international expansion. Consequently, the research question addressed by this investigation is: how does the managerial attitude affect the development of networks for internationalization? Underpinnings from network theory in the broader management field (e.g., Zaheer et al., 1998; Borgatti and Foster, 2003; Brass et al., 2004; Provan et al., 2007) as well as key contributions to the network approach in entrepreneurship (Hoang and Antoncic, 2003) and international business literature (Coviello, 2006; Johanson and Vahlne, 2009; Hilmersson and Jansson, 2012; Vahlne and Johanson, 2013) are considered for elaborating the research background of this chapter. This research contributes to the international business literature and to the egocentric network perspective by examining network development through a multidimensional perspective considering network structure, content and governance (Hoang and Antoncic, 2003) simultaneously.

The remainder of this chapter is structured as follows. First the research background related to network development is provided. Thereafter, the research method is described. The empirical findings derived from the UK context are then presented. Next, these findings are discussed in light of the relevant literature. This section also highlights pertinent managerial implications, limitations and future research avenues.

NETWORK DEVELOPMENT

Considering their innate limited resource, SMEs typically are subject to liablities of smallness (Aldrich and Auster, 1986) and foreigness (Hymer, 1976), which may constrict their strategic growth options. SME decision-makers will solely and intentionally focus their attention on issues and activities deemed as relevant for their firm's growth. Fernhaber and Li (2013) suggest that decision-makers may purposely seek opportunities to expand internationally, in order to maintain firm competitiveness. Entrepreneurs would frequently take a proactive attitude towards network building for the benefit of internationalization (Sullivan-Mort and Weerawardena, 2006; Sepulveda and Gabrielsson, 2013).

By and large, the management and mainstream entrepreneurship fields conceptualize networks along three dimensions: network structure (the pattern of direct and indirect ties between actors, both interpersonal and interorganizational), network content (the resources exchanged between actors) and network governance (the mechanisms that underpin an exchange to coordinate and manage the relationship) (Hoang and Antoncic, 2003). In the same vein, the SME internationalization and international entrepreneurship studies also discuss these three dimensions in relationship to network development for international expansion. Yet, studies in the international business area frequently focus on one element only, as networking tends to be examined from a unidimensional perspective, potentially leading to overlooking specific attributes of networks (Eberhard and Craig, 2013). With a view to providing a more comprehensive approach to network development for international expansion, this study investigates the influence of managerial attitude on elements pertaining to these three dimensions: structure, content and governance.

Network Structure

Similar to core contributions to network theory (Burt, 1992, 2000; Borgatti and Foster, 2003; Provan et al., 2007) as well as network-based research in (international) entrepreneurship (Hoang and Antoncic, 2003; Coviello, 2006), this study examines, within the network structure, the size of the network and the mix of direct/indirect ties. According to Borgatti et al. (1998), the more regions of the network the actor connects with, the greater are the potential information and control benefits. The size of the network is reported to increase as international new ventures evolve from conception through to internationalization and growth (Coviello, 2006). Increasing the size of the network is critical for the SME obtaining leverage effects in international activity (Hilmersson and Jansson, 2012).

The increase in network size generally supposes an increase in direct as well as indirect ties. While the importance of both these types of network ties for the international success of SMEs is recognized, findings so far are rather mixed. For example, Agndal et al. (2008) found that although both direct and indirect relationships are significant for foreign market entry for their whole empirical sample, composed of SMEs from Sweden and New Zealand, direct relationships, however, are prevalent in the early internationalization phase, whereas indirect ties become gradually important in later phases for the Swedish subsample. Moreover, more changes in the entry mode and foreign markets can be attributed to direct relationship influences than indirect third party influences (Agndal and Chetty, 2007).

Network Content

Studies increasingly confirm the significance of networks for diminishing liabilities of smallness or foreignness that may impede SME internationalization such as the lack of financial resources, capabilities and knowledge (Freeman et al., 2006; Laanti et al., 2007; Lindstrand et al., 2011). Networks are considered key for the internationalization strategies of SMEs involved in high commitment foreign market entry modes, as resources may exist within the networks rather than be owned by individual SMEs (Dimitratos et al., 2003). In addition to information and/or knowledge sharing, by interacting among partners, learning and new knowledge building occur through dynamic interactions between business partners (Sullivan-Mort and Weerawardena, 2006; Johanson and Vahlne, 2009; Dimitratos et al., 2010). According to Sepulveda and Gabrielsson (2013), as a result of firm growth and the corresponding development of resources, the network content of born global firms became progressively more strategic. Once legitimacy has been established, these firms aimed at engaging in business relationships with large and more influential firms, strengthened their brand and reputation, increased the firm's influence on the industry and public policy, positioned the company closer to the clients and acquired collective market intelligence. Conversely, a smaller part of their sample experienced limited change in terms of network content over time and internal resource accumulation.

Network Governance

Trust has been commonly acknowledged as the main mechanism governing the exchange in network relationships and enhancing the quality of resource flow of entrepreneurial ventures (Hoang and Antoncic, 2003; Brass et al., 2004). Zaheer et al. (1998) distinguish between interpersonal and interorganizational trust while highlighting the importance of both for the exchange flow within the dyad. Trust is built on expectations that the business partner 'will perform a particular action important to the trustor, irrespective of the ability to monitor or control that other party' and it relates to three key elements: 'ability', 'benevolence' and 'integrity' (Mayer et al., 1995, p. 712). The international business literature acknowledges that trust is vital for relationship development internationally, while recognizing that trust building is time and resource consuming (Madhok, 2006; Johanson and Vahlne, 2009; Vahlne and Johanson, 2013). Trust is indispensable in order for the knowledge transfer to take place effectively (Loane and Bell, 2006; Johanson and Vahlne, 2009). Good reputation establishes the basis for mutual trust in international business relationships (Agndal and Chetty, 2007). Chetty and Agndal's (2007) study emphasizes the relevance of trust, mutual commitment, control and power balance in international entrepreneurship relationships. Nonetheless, they also note that partners may also act opportunistically, for example, by forming a relationship specifically for the acquisition of knowledge, and then turning to competitors.

Conceptual Model

Based on the arguments presented to this point, the conceptual model presented in Figure 8.1 was developed drawing on theoretical underpinnings provided by the network theory in the international business context. In short, this model proposes that managerial attitude will influence network development for internationalization purposes. Specifically, this model sets to explore how will purposive network building, expressed by

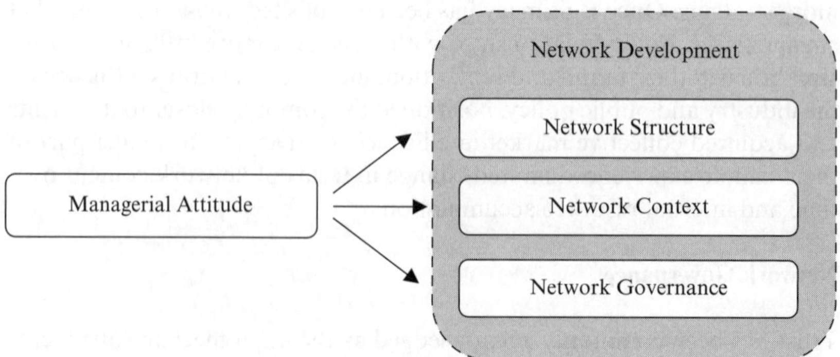

Figure 8.1 Conceptual model: the impact of managerial attitude on network development

a proactive managerial attitude as opposed to a reactive attitude, influence network structure, content and governance. In line with previous literature (e.g., Hoang and Antoncic, 2003) this study considers under network structure the mix of direct/indirect ties, as well as the overall size of the network that is instrumental for the internationalization of the firm. Network content is related to the exchange of resources between the focal SME and other actors. Network governance refers to the mechanisms that underpin the exchange of resources, and are responsible for coordinating and managing the relationship. The conceptual model is investigated with empirical evidence deriving from a sample of UK SMEs as explained in the following sections.

METHOD

In line with earlier research in the SME internationalization and international entrepreneurship literature, which specifically focuses on understanding and examining networks and/or the role of the decision-maker for SME internationalization (e.g., Sullivan-Mort and Weerawardena, 2006; Freeman and Cavusgil, 2007) this study adopted a multiple case study methodology. This research method was considered the most appropriate approach for providing a comprehensive perspective on the influence of managerial attitude on the subsequent network development evaluated across multiple dimensions. Case studies are best positioned to answer 'how' (and 'why') questions (Yin, 2014), as is the case with the research question addressed by this study. Furthermore, multiple case studies are particularly suitable as a methodology as they enable comparison in a systematic way across cases of the influence of managerial attitude on network development for international expansion. Thus, it is possible to verify whether the findings are specific to a single case, or consistently replicated in different cases (Eisenhardt, 1991; Ghauri, 2004). Adopting this research design also enabled the development of a historically retrospective approach (Chetty and Stangl, 2010).

The main information source comprised of in-depth interviews with the main decision-makers in three internationalized UK SMEs. A purposeful sampling technique was selected for collecting the empirical data from particular participants in order to ensure they represented relevant cases for this study (Patton, 2002; Ghauri, 2004; Piekkari et al., 2010). The following criteria were employed for selecting the firms to be included in the empirical analysis: (1) they must be independent UK-based firms; (2) be SMEs as defined by the European Commission (2003)[2]; (3) be active internationally for at least ten years; (4) derive at least 25 per cent of their turnover from international activity; (5) be business-to-business firms, as these companies offer a more observable opportunity for examining network relationships leading to empirical findings and managerial insights difficult to attain in a business-to-consumer network (Sepulveda and Gabrielsson, 2013); (6) belong to distinct industries in order to assure variation within the sample. Data confidentiality and anonymity were assured by using coded names for the companies investigated: Messier, Omega and Triangulum. Table 8.1 presents information concerning the profile of the three SMEs investigated: industrial sector, number of employees, age of the firm, years of international experience, foreign market entry modes and total number of foreign countries and continents serviced.

In-depth interviews were selected to be the main data source for this project as they have been recognized as a particularly efficient way of gathering rich empirical data (Eisenhardt, 1989; Eisenhardt and Graebner, 2007). All interviews were held with the main decision-maker in the firms. The interviews were divided into two main stages, with different sets of questions in each. The first stage of the interview process involved a discussion about the general profile of the SME as well as managerial vision and business objectives. In the second stage, open-ended questions were discussed in relation to the perceived usefulness of network development for SME internationalization; the attention dedicated by the decision-maker to the development of networks during the early and later stages of internationalization; and network development in terms of structure, content and governance. In this stage, the interviewees were asked to describe the reasoning and thoughts behind their answers. The same interview protocol was used for each interview (Harris and Ghauri, 2000) in order to ensure reliability as well as for facilitating comparison across cases.

The interviews, which lasted between 60 and 90 minutes, were conducted face to face and audio recorded, in July–September 2013. Next, they were transcribed verbatim and a complete database was created before conducting the analysis. In line with guidelines by Eisenhardt (1989) and Ghauri (2004), archives and direct observation were used to assure data triangulation. Thus, a more comprehensive and contextual representation of the research theme analysed (Ghauri, 2004) was elaborated. Prior to arranging the interviews, secondary data sources such as websites and enterprise documents for each firm were carefully consulted in order to facilitate purposeful sampling and become familiarized with the particular context and idiosyncrasies of each case selected (Poulis et al., 2013).

Data analysis was conducted in accord with well-established guidelines in qualitative research (Eisenhardt, 1989; Miles and Huberman, 1994;

Table 8.1 Profile of the investigated SMEs

	Industrial sector	Number of employees	Firm age	Years abroad	Foreign market entry modes	Total number of foreign countries serviced	Total number of continents served
Messier	Computer industry	87	16	15	Direct export International licence Foreign subsidiary International joint venture International strategic alliances	60+	5
Omega	Machinery manufacture and design	60	22	20	Direct/indirect export Subcontracting manufacturing abroad	12	1
Triangulum	Furniture manufacture	57	28	23	Direct/indirect export Foreign subsidiary International strategic alliances	30	2

Ghauri and Grønhaug, 2010). Data coding and management were carried out in NVivo 10, which was particularly helpful for shifting between different sources of evidence for each case and retrieving relevant phrases and paragraphs according to the main aspects of the research theme investigated. NVivo enabled the storage of empirical data under nodes corresponding to generic categories and subnodes representing items included under the same main category, thus facilitating data interpretation and analysis. The following four fundamental tasks, specific for qualitative analysis, were carried out: categorization, abstraction, comparison and integration (Spiggle, 1994).

FINDINGS

The empirical evidence, related to the impact of managerial attitude on network development for internationalization for each individual firm case is presented below.

Case 1 – Messier

The managing director of Messier had consistently dedicated attention to international expansion based on interorganizational networks. Time and financial resources were allocated to building the network by participation at numerous trade fairs, trade missions, creating links with multinational companies and international institutions. Market research campaigns and professional seminars were conducted to identify suitable foreign business partners. Network development for international expansion started soon after company start-up. Networks for internationalization were built consistently in a calculative and sustained manner. As explained by the managing director:

> In our industry there are business opportunities worldwide waiting to be explored . . . The best way to do that is by building a trustworthy network . . . Each year we designed a specific budget and time to make international contacts . . . a few members of our staff spend probably half of their time attending relevant trade events abroad . . . visiting foreign markets, existing business partners and possible future customers. (Managing director, Messier)

Consequently, network size has trebled over time. Both direct and indirect ties are present, with indirect networks increasing frequency in later stages. Limited centrality existed at inception; however, there has been a slight gradual improvement. The managing director initially sought interorganizational networks for obtaining financial resources to rapidly expand internationally; later on, information, knowledge and tangible resources were exchanged with network partners. As a result of the ongoing communication and increase in centrality, joint identification of business opportunities occurred. Currently new networks are developed and relevant existent relationships are carefully maintained and are used to create strategic alliances with multinational firms and international organizations. Furthermore, networks play an important a role in enhancing global brand reputation. Trust and commitment are essential for successfully operating the business in order to assure optimal cooperation and coordination between international business partners. According to the managing director, trust has to be maintained and enhanced for assuring the longevity and success of the relationships. Messier has experienced few cases of conflict with international business partners. However, they were considered to be the exceptions to the rule. Some of the few broken ties were restored over time. Networks are recognized as being key to international opportunity identification, foreign market entry and implementing changes in foreign entry modes.

Case 2 – Omega

The founder of Omega devoted a limited focus to firm growth, yet this depended on the specific firm context, which modified in later as compared to early stages. Initially, most networks instrumental for international activity were derived from export orders from unsolicited enquiries placed on its website. Limited time and resources were devoted to network building for international operations in the early internationalization stages. Some resources were invested in product catalogues and limited participation in domestic trade fairs, resulting, nevertheless, in a few contacts in foreign markets. Consequently, slight network enhancement took place in the later stages of internationalization as a result of a growth in the internal resources of the company and the identification of new high-growth opportunities. The founder of Omega clarifies:

> Our company started with little capital for our sector . . . we first had to invest in purchasing equipment . . . building production capacity and a critical mass . . . we then commissioned a software company to design our website . . . we received a few enquiries from foreign clients . . . that's how we started to sell to some of our European customers. (Founder, Omega)

Omega had a small network size at international start-up, which grew serendipitously yet slowly over time. Direct ties are predominant; nonetheless, a few indirect ties were developed in later internationalization stages, simultaneously with dedicating greater attention to network development. Network content is restricted to basic business- and international-related information and knowledge regarding pricing terms and logistic requirements. Trust is recognized as key for international business relationships, but it appears to be seen as somewhat static, strictly related to each individual transaction. Specifically, the founder of Omega emphasizes the importance of trust regarding respecting delivery times and order specifications. No particular efforts seem to be made to maintain relationships over time other than respecting the specifications of the export–import contract. However, this is not without its exceptions regarding a few relationships with lead customers and foreign distributors. Networks are perceived as playing a part in international opportunity identification and foreign market entry.

Case 3 – Triangulum

The founder of Triangulum has deliberately devoted attention to international expansion based on network development since early internationalization stages. Resources were specifically allocated to attending trade fairs and industry events and visiting foreign markets and business partners. Most networks useful for internationalization are interorganizational ties developed explicitly for this business. Strategically important networks also become interpersonal ties over time:

> Creating a large and reliable international business network has always been one of our top priorities . . . it used to take a lot of effort when we first started networking abroad . . . now we are known in our field . . . we have made a trusted brand name and good reputation for ourselves . . . now foreign business comes on our door step. (Founder, Triangulum)

Network size, limited in early stages, experienced constant growth, presently reaching over 1500 foreign contacts, as explained by the founder. Direct ties were predominant in the early stages; however, indirect ties increased in later stages. Centrality has improved incrementally, although more work needs to be done in this respect, according to the founder of the firm.

Triangulum initially sought interorganizational networks to obtain legitimacy; later on information, knowledge and tangible resources were exchanged, thus increasing the likelihood of identifying foreign market opportunities via its network. The information shared, explicitly in later stages, led to accessing new business partners in new foreign markets and collaboration for joint product customization and development. The knowledge and information flow is fostered by trustworthy relationships, built in time, which frequently results in involvement in high commitment foreign entry modes. In the later stages of internationalization, the founder noticed a snowballing effect in terms of network contact development. Consequently, less effort was required to identify suitable network partners as compared to the early stages of internationalization, given its increase in network centrality. Due to its already established reputation as well as a rather large network of contacts meticulously built since start-up, further network developments seem to take place partially by themselves.

The findings presented above are summarized in Table 8.2.

DISCUSSION AND CONCLUSIONS

The research question addressed by this study was: how does the managerial attitude affect the development of networks for internationalization? In order to answer this question three key dimensions related to network development – content, structure and governance (Hoang and Antoncic, 2003) – have been investigated. The qualitative research method adopted enabled the classification of the investigated SMEs according to two distinct behavioural patterns related to managerial attention to network development. Messier and Triangulum generally adopted a proactive attitude towards network building ever since start-up. Conversely, Omega demonstrated an overall reactive behaviour with little change in the later stages. The aproach followed by Messier and Triangulum for network building is similar to that of 'the strategist entrepreneur' (Freeman and Cavusgil, 2007) who systematically aims to build business networks in key markets and regions for her/his industry with a long-term focus. Omega, on the other hand, resembles 'the respondent entrepreneur' characteristics (ibid.) as this firm is generally content to fulfil unsolicited orders from abroad; yet, due to the lack of clear focus towards international growth combined with resource constraints it generally does not proactively seek to further build international relationships. Taken together, these findings corroborate prior contributions in the SME internationalization literature (Freeman et al., 2006; Sullivan-Mort and Weerawardena, 2006; Freeman and Cavusgil, 2007) in that managerial passion/drive for internationalization is associated with network development. By comparing and contrasting the evidence provided by the three cases investigated, interesting findings were revealed regarding network development (structure, content and governance) for internationalization.

Related to network structure, this research corroborates early findings by Sullivan-Mort and Weerawardena (2006), who found that owner/managers cultivate networking capabilities for fulfiling the strategic vision of reaching global markets. Specifically, this study illustrates that

Table 8.2

	Managerial attitude to network development for international expansion	Network development for international expansion
Messier	*Managerial attitude:* Proactive *Managerial attention:* Medium-high early stages; high later stages *Key staff time and resource allocated for:* Attendance at international trade events, market research visits, initiating contacts with multinational players and international institutions	*Structure:* Limited network size at international start-up; larger network size during later stages; both direct and indirect ties increasingly in later stages *Content:* Initially sought interorganizational networks for obtaining financial resource to rapidly expand internationally and build a global reputation; later on information and knowledge and tangible resources were exchanged with network partners. Networks are currently used to create strategic alliances with multinational firms and international organizations as well as to build a global brand reputation *Governance:* Trust and commitment are essential for assuring an optimal cooperation and coordination between (international) business partners. A good sense of trust should exist from the beginning of the relationship; however trust has to be maintained and enhanced over time. Few cases of conflict or misunderstanding with international business partners were reported
Omega	*Managerial attitude:* Reactive *Managerial attention:* Low early stages; medium-low later stages *Key staff time and resource allocated for:* Limited time and resources available for network building for internationalization; company website development, product catalogues	*Structure:* Small network size at international start-up grew slightly over time. Both direct and a few indirect ties (mainly in later stages), with direct ties being predominant *Content:* Basic business and international-related information and knowledge is exchanged via network ties *Governance:* Trust is recognized as key for international business relationships and efforts are made to respect delivery times and contract specifications to maintain it

Triangulum	*Managerial attitude:* Proactive *Managerial attention:* High early stages; medium-high later stages *Structural distribution on attention:* Attendance at international trade events, market research visits, meeting business partners and enhancing relationships with strategic business partners	*Structure:* Limited network size at international start-up; however, it grew considerably; mainly direct ties were developed in early stages, and both direct and indirect ties in later stages *Content:* Initially sought interorganizational networks to obtain legitimacy; later on information and knowledge and tangible resources were exchanged. The information shared, specifically in later stages led to access new business partners in existent and new foreign markets *Governance:* Trust built over time governs business relationships; the knowledge and information flow is contingent upon a trustworthy relationship and involvement in high commitment foreign entry modes

the firms whose decision-makers explicitly focus attention and dedicate time and resources to network development have experienced an increase in the size of their network (Hoang and Antoncic, 2003; Coviello, 2006). In a similar vein to Agndal et al. (2008) or Kontinen and Ojala (2011) the empirical evidence shows that this is particularly due to the incremental development of indirect ties derived from the direct ties generated in the later internationalization stages.

In terms of network content, information, knowledge and, ocasionally, tangible resources, arise from the exchange flow with network partners (Johanson and Vahlne, 2006, 2009). Nevertheless, similar to Coviello (2006), the empirical evidence for this study reveals that tie content is idiosyncratic to each firm. Managers who do not dedicate special attention to building and maintaining networks may only use their contacts for obtaining basic information for international activity. Little change in network content is experienced over time by these firms. On the contrary, proactive network developers show an increase in the strategic orientation of the information, knowledge and resources that form the network flow. This type of firm would collaborate with its network partners for securing joint large projects on international markets, would discuss its brand strategies, and would innovate within the network. Thus, support is provided to previous findings by Sepulveda and Gabrielsson (2013) in that significant transformations in the exchange flow were observed between early and later internationalization stages, ranging from a basic flow of information to a more strategic content.

The decision-makers in the three investigated firms collectively agreed that trust is the most important mechanism that governs their international business relationships (Hoang and Antoncic, 2003). All three trust elements identified by Mayer et al. (1995), namely 'ability', 'benevolence' and 'integrity', were considered relevant. Interviews reported only sporadic episodes of opportunistic behaviour in international business relationships (Chetty and Agndal, 2007). Particular emphasis was given to 'ability' and 'integrity', and comparably less to 'benevolence'. In accord with Mayer et al. (1995), the 'benevolence' element of trust has to do with a specific attachment of the other party and the intention to do good besides egocentric profit-making. It is then sensible to argue that while in a few close relationships, which may have gained a personal touch over the time, 'benevolence' may be a prominent characteristic that governs the interactions, most of the ties are positioned at the interorganizational level, and so is the corresponding trust (Zaheer et al., 1998). SMEs that purposely dedicated attention to network building also paid attention to maintaining and enhancing trust through constant interaction (Larson, 1992). Therefore, they were able to foster cooperation and coordination and long-term commitment with their business partners (Johanson and Vahlne, 2009; Vahlne and Johanson, 2013). However, in the case of Omega, maintaining trust was only mentioned in relationship to a few critical partners with whom they engaged in longer-term relationship building.

In conclusion, the findings of this study enrich our understanding of the theme analysed and are briefly summarized in what follows. Managerial attitude to network development for international expansion significantly influences network structure, content and governance. Specifically, the empirical evidence shows that devoting attention to network building in a calculative and sustained manner will influence network structure by leading to an increase in interorganizational and indirect ties, and overall network size respectively. A proactive attitude to network development will also lead to an increase in the diversity and strategic orientation of resources shared with other actors. As far as network governance is concerned, emphasis will be placed on trust enhancement with other actors in the network; sustained efforts will be dedicated to fostering cooperation and collaboration with the business partners for internationalization purposes. Thus, this study contributes to the SME internationalization literature by investigating network development in a more comprehensive manner, examining the influence of managerial attitude on three key elements previously highlighted by the mainstream entrepreneurship literature regarding network structure, content and governance (Hoang and Antoncic, 2003).

The empirical findings reveal a few relevant managerial implications. SME decision-makers who seek to expand the firm's operations internationally should pay particular attention to interorganizational network development in a consistent and proactive manner. They should specifically allocate time and financial resources to identifying and attending the most important international industry events in their sector on a regular basis. SME managers ought to be efficient in building and maintaining relationships, considering the time and financial effort required. Moreover, managers may find it useful to prepare and present their new products/services in specific foreign markets of interest to the firm in workshops where potential business partners and/or customers would be invited to join.

As with all research, this study has its limitations. This investigation is based on three study cases in the UK. Hence, the findings should be interpreted with caution when attempting to extend them beyond this specific context. It would be interesting for future research to explore the validity of the findings revealed by this investigation in considerably different contexts in developed and emerging economies. Cross-cultural studies with SMEs from both individualistic and collectivistic cultures as well as immigrant entrepreneurial businesses are also encouraged. This will lead to enhancing present knowledge regarding managerial attitude to network building for SME internationalization by considering the increased diversity, multiculturalism, transnational mobility and linkages of the twenty-first-century entrepreneur. Moreover, the results clearly demonstrate that managerial attitude to network building for international expansion has a positive influence on network development, which in turn may lead to broader internationalization outcomes and a higher degree of international involvement. Further research should examine the association between managerial attitude, network development for international expansion and internationalization, thus simultaneously investigating the causes and consequences of networks in the context of internationalized SMEs. Furthermore, network development and dynamics are dependent upon the characteristics and changes of the environment. Scholars may find it interesting to investigate exogenous factors together with managerial attitude as antecedents of networks beneficial for internationalization.

NOTES

1. In this study, we use the terms founder, owner, entrepreneur, manager when referring to the SME's main decision-maker.
2. An SME is defined by the European Commission as an enterprise that employs fewer than 250 persons, and whose annual turnover does not exceed EUR50 million or whose annual balance-sheet total does not exceed EUR43 million (European Commission, 2003).

REFERENCES

Agndal, H. and S. Chetty (2007), 'The impact of relationships on changes in internationalisation strategies of SMEs', *European Journal of Marketing*, **41**(11/12), 1449–74.

Agndal, H., S. Chetty and H. Wilson (2008), 'Social capital dynamics and foreign market entry', *International Business Review*, **17**(6), 663–75.

Aldrich, H.E. and E. Auster (1986), 'Even dwarfs started small: liabilities of size and age and their strategic implications', in B.M. Staw and L.L. Cummings (eds), *Research in Organizational Behavior* (Vol. 8), Greenwich, CT: JAI Press, pp. 65–98.

Blankenburg-Holm, D., K. Ericksson. and J. Johanson (1996), 'Business networks and cooperation in international business relationships', *Journal of International Business Studies*, **27**(5), 1033–53.

Borgatti, S.P. and P.C. Foster (2003), 'The network paradigm in organizational research: a review and typology', *Journal of Management*, **29**(6), 991–1013.

Borgatti, S.P., C. Jones and M.G. Everett (1998), 'Network measures of social capital', *Connections*, **21**(2), 36–45.

Brass, D.J., J. Galaskiewicz, H.R. Greve and W. Tsai (2004), 'Taking stock of networks and organizations: a multilevel perspective', *Academy of Management Journal*, **47**(6), 795–817.

Burt, R.S. (1992), *Structural Holes*, Cambridge, MA: Harvard University.

Burt, R.S. (2000), 'The network structure of social capital', in R.I. Sutton and B.M. Staw (eds), *Research in Organizational Behaviour* (Vol. 22), Greenwich, CT: JAI Press, pp. 345–423.

Caligiuri, P., M. Lazarova and S. Zehetbauer (2004), 'Top managers' national diversity and boundary spanning', *Journal of Management Development*, **23**(9), 848–59.

Chetty, S. and H. Agndal (2007), 'Social capital and its influence on changes in internationalization mode among small and medium-sized enterprises', *Journal of International Marketing*, **15**(1), 1–29.

Chetty, S. and D. Blankenburg-Holm (2000), 'Internationalisation of small to medium-sized manufacturing firms: a network approach', *International Business Review*, **9**(1), 77–93.

Chetty, S.K. and L.M. Stangl (2010), 'Internationalization and innovation in a network relationship context', *European Journal of Marketing*, **44**(11/12), 1725–43.

Ciravegna, L., L. Lopez and S. Kundu (2014), 'Country of origin and network effects on internationalization: a comparative study of SMEs from an emerging and developed economy', *Journal of Business Research*, **67**(6), 916–23.

Coviello, N.E. (2006), 'The network dynamics of international new ventures', *Journal of International Business Studies*, **37**(5), 713–31.

Coviello, N.E. and H.J. Munro (1995), 'Growing the entrepreneurial firm', *European Journal of Marketing*, **29**(7), 49–61.

Coviello, N.E. and H.J. Munro (1997), 'Network relationships and the internationalisation process of small software firms', *International Business Review*, **6**(4), 361–86.

Dimitratos, P., J. Johnson, J. Slow and S. Young (2003), 'Micromultinationals: new types of firms for the global competitive landscape', *European Management Journal*, **21**(2), 164–74.

Dimitratos, P., S. Lioukas, K.I.N. Ibeh and C. Wheeler (2010), 'Governance mechanisms of small and medium enterprise international partner management', *British Journal of Management*, **21**(3), 754–71.

Eberhard, M. and J. Craig (2013), 'The evolving role of organisational and personal networks in international market venturing', *Journal of World Business*, **48**(3), 385–97.

Eisenhardt, K.M. (1989), 'Building theories from case study research', *The Academy of Management Review*, **14**(4), 532–50.

Eisenhardt, K.M. (1991), 'Better stories and better constructs: the case for rigor and comparative logic', *Academy of Management Review*, **16**(3), 620–27.

Eisenhardt, K.M. and M.E. Graebner (2007), 'Theory building from cases: opportunities and challenges', *The Academy of Management Journal*, **50**(1), 25–32.

European Commission (2003), 'Commission recommendation', *Official Journal of the European Union*, L 124/36.

Fernhaber, S.A. and D. Li (2013), 'International exposure through network relationships: implications for new venture internationalization', *Journal of Business Venturing*, **28**(2), 316–34.

Freeman, S. and S.T. Cavusgil (2007), 'Toward a typology of commitment states among managers of born-global firms: a study of accelerated internationalization', *Journal of International Marketing*, **15**(4), 1–40.

Freeman, S., R. Edwards and B. Schroder (2006), 'How smaller born-global firms use networks and alliances to overcome constraints to rapid internationalization', *Journal of International Marketing*, **14**(3), 33–63.

Ghauri, P.N. (2004), 'Designing and conducting case studies in international business research', in R. Marschan-Piekkari and C. Welch (eds), *Handbook of Qualitative Research Methods for International Business*, Cheltenham, UK and Northampton, MA, USA: Edward Elgar Publishing, pp. 109–24.

Ghauri, P.N. and K. Grønhaug (2010), *Research Methods in Business Studies* (4th edition), London: FT Pearson.

Harris, S. and P.N. Ghauri (2000), 'Strategy formation by business leaders: exploring the influence of national values', *European Journal of Marketing*, **34**(1/2), 126–42.
Harris, S. and C. Wheeler (2005), 'Entrepreneurs' relationships for internationalization: functions, origins and strategies', *International Business Review*, **14**(2), 187–207.
Hilmersson, M. and H. Jansson (2012), 'International network extension processes to institutionally different markets: entry nodes and processes of exporting SMEs', *International Business Review*, **21**(4), 682–93.
Hoang, H. and B. Antoncic (2003), 'Network-based research in entrepreneurship: a critical view', *Journal of Business Venturing*, **18**(2), 165–87.
Hymer, S.H. (1976), *A Study of Direct Foreign Investment*, Cambridge, MA: MIT Press.
Johanson, J. and L.G. Mattsson (1988), 'Internationalization in industrial systems: a network approach', in N. Hood and J.-E. Vahlne (eds), *Strategies in Global Competition*, New York: Croom Helm, pp. 287–314.
Johanson, J. and L.G. Mattsson (1993), 'Internationalization in industrial systems – a network approach, strategies in global competition', in P.J. Buckley and P.N. Ghauri (eds), *The Internationalization of the Firm: A Reader*, London: Academic Press, pp. 303–22.
Johanson, J. and J. Vahlne (2006), 'Commitment and opportunity development in the internationalization process: a note on the Uppsala internationalization process model', *Management International Review*, **46**(2), 165–78.
Johanson, J. and J. Vahlne (2009), 'The Uppsala internationalization process model revisited: from liability of foreignness to liability of outsidership', *Journal of International Business Studies*, **40**(9), 1411–31.
Kontinen, T. and A. Ojala (2011), 'Social capital in relation to the foreign market entry and post-entry operation of family SMEs', *Journal of International Entrepreneurship*, **9**(2), 133–51.
Laanti, R., M. Gabrielsson and P. Gabrielsson (2007), 'The globalization strategies of business-to-business born global firms in the wireless technology industry', *Industrial Marketing Management*, **36**(8), 1104–17.
Larson, A. (1992), 'Network dyads in entrepreneurial settings: a study of the governance of exchange relationships', *Administrative Science Quarterly*, **37**(1), 76–104.
Lindstrand, A., S. Melén and E.R. Nordman (2011), 'Turning social capital into business: a study of the internationalization of biotech SMEs', *International Business Review*, **20**(2), 194–212.
Lloyd-Reason, L. and T. Mughan (2002), 'Strategies for internationalisation within SMEs: the key role of the owner-manager', *Journal of Small Business and Enterprise Development*, **9**(2), 120–29.
Loane, S. and J. Bell (2006), 'Rapid internationalisation among entrepreneurial firms in Australia, Canada, Ireland and New Zealand: an extension to the network approach', *International Marketing Review*, **23**(5), 467–85.
Madhok, A. (2006), 'How much does ownership really matter? Equity and trust relations in joint venture relationships', *Journal of International Business Studies*, **37**(1), 4–11.
Manolova, T.S., I.M. Manev and B.S. Gyoshev (2010), 'In good company: the role of personal and inter-firm networks for new-venture internationalization in a transition economy', *Journal of World Business*, **45**(3), 257–65.
Mayer, R.C., J.H. Davis and F.D. Schoorman (1995), 'An integrative model of organizational trust', *The Academy of Management Review*, **20**(3), 709–34.
Miles, M.B. and A.M. Huberman (1994), *Qualitative Data Analysis*, Thousand Oaks, CA: Sage.
Ojala, A. (2009), 'Internationalization of knowledge-intensive SMEs: the role of network relationships in the entry to a psychically distant market', *International Business Review*, **18**(1), 50–59.
Oviatt, B.M. and P.P. McDougall (1994), 'Toward a theory of international new ventures', *Journal of International Business Studies*, **25**(1), 45–65.
Patton, M.Q. (2002), *Qualitative Research and Evaluation Methods* (3rd edition), Thousand Oaks, CA: Sage.

Piekkari, R., E. Plakoyiannaki and C. Welch (2010), '"Good" case research in industrial marketing: insights from research practice', *Industrial Marketing Management*, **39**(1), 109–17.

Poulis, K., E. Poulis and E. Plakoyiannaki (2013), 'The role of context in case study selection: an international business perspective', *International Business Review*, **22**(1), 304–14.

Provan, K.G., A. Fish and J. Sydow (2007), 'Interorganizational networks at the network level: a review of the empirical literature on whole networks', *Journal of Management*, **33**(3), 479–516.

Sepulveda, F. and M. Gabrielsson (2013), 'Network development and firm growth: a resource-based study of B2B born globals', *Industrial Marketing Management*, **42**(5), 792–804.

Spiggle, S. (1994), 'Analysis and interpretation of qualitative data in consumer research', *Journal of Consumer Research*, **21**(3), 491–503.

Sullivan-Mort, G. and J. Weerawardena (2006), 'Networking capability and international entrepreneurship', *International Marketing Review*, **23**(5), 549–72.

Vahlne, J.E. and J. Johanson (2013), 'The Uppsala model on evolution of the multinational business enterprise – from internalization to coordination of networks', *International Marketing Review*, **30**(3), 189–210.

Yin, R. (2014), *Case Study Research: Design and Methods* (5th edition), London: Sage Publications Inc.

Zaheer, A., R. Gözübüyük and H. Milanov (2010), 'It's the connections: the network perspective in interorganizational research', *Academy of Management Perspectives*, **24**(1), 62–77.

Zaheer, A., B. McEvily and V. Perrone (1998), 'Does trust matter? Exploring the effects of interorganizational and interpersonal trust on performance', *Organization Science*, **9**(2), 141–59.

9. A process view of new ventures' internationalization: exploring the 'black box'

Nuno Fernandes Crespo, Vítor Corado Simões and Margarida Fontes

INTRODUCTION

International entrepreneurship (IE) is a field of research that emerged about 20 years ago, considering Oviatt and McDougall's (1994) article as the starting point (Autio, 2005; Keupp and Gassmann, 2009). The phenomenon of new ventures' (NVs') internationalization since or soon after their foundation was found to be poorly explained by extant international business (IB) theories. Therefore, the IE field originally focused on small and young ventures that launched their internationalization early in their lifecycles (Keupp and Gassmann, 2009). These firms were perceived as outliers of the traditional process theory of internationalization (Johanson and Wiedersheim-Paul, 1975; Johanson and Vahlne, 1977).

Therefore, the definition of international new venture (INV) provided by Oviatt and McDougall (1994) is still dominant in the literature: 'a business organization that, from inception, seeks to derive significant competitive advantage from the use of resources and the sale of outputs to multiple countries' (p. 49). Afterwards, McDougall and Oviatt (2000) extended their 1994 definition, to envisage IE as 'a combination of innovative, proactive and risk-seeking behavior that crosses national borders and is intended to create value in organizations' (p. 903). They included international comparisons of entrepreneurial behaviours within the boundaries of the IE field. More recently, those authors defined it as 'the discovery, enactment, evaluation, and exploitation of opportunities – across national borders – to create future goods and services' (Oviatt and McDougall, 2005a, p. 540; 2005b, p. 7).

Looking at the various streams of IE literature, Jones et al. (2011) clustered the key themes of the IE field into three groups: (1) entrepreneurial internationalization, regarding entrepreneurship activities that go beyond country borders; (2) international comparisons of entrepreneurship, which cover the studies that compare entrepreneurship characteristics and initiatives across borders; and (3) comparative entrepreneurial internationalization, which includes studies that analyse entrepreneurial internationalization from a cross-national perspective.

Although the literature on NV internationalization has boomed (Keupp and Gassmann, 2009; Jones et al., 2011), several voices have questioned its static nature. Several authors have pointed out the need to better understand the dynamic processes leading INVs or born globals (BGs) to evolve over time (Coviello, 2006; Simões et al., 2011). Others have criticized the dominant pattern of cross-sectional approaches focusing on the study of the direct relationships between the antecedents of IE and the outcomes of the internationalization process, without addressing the process as such (Aspelund et al., 2007; Keupp and Gassmann, 2009).

This chapter provides an encompassing perspective of NVs' internationalization process, highlighting the relevance of managerial decisions or actions in the context of such a process. More specifically, it is intended to respond to the pleas for more research about the nature of managerial decision-making and organizational behaviour of early internationalizing firms (Rialp et al., 2005). It also addresses Keupp and Gassmann's (2009) demand for the development of an integrated framework to analyse NVs' internationalization process. Our purpose is to address the organizational processes through which antecedents – such as entrepreneurs' characteristics, environment elements and NVs' characteristics – are related to internationalization and performance outcomes. This is expected to contribute to opening the 'black box' of NVs' internationalization process dominant in the mainstream analysis, focused on the direct cause–effect relationship between antecedents and outcomes.

This chapter is organized into seven sections, including this introduction. The next section synthesizes the traditional view regarding the NVs' internationalization. This is followed by the presentation of the methodology regarding the development of the framework. The fourth section provides the rationale for the inclusion of the three main sets of variables (antecedents, actions and outcomes) as well as the moderating variables. The process-oriented framework is presented next. This is followed by a brief discussion. The last section outlines the main conclusions.

IE AND PERFORMANCE: THE TRADITIONAL VIEW

The dominant approach in IE empirical research so far has focused on the analysis of the direct relationships between the antecedents of IE – concerning the entrepreneur, the firm or the environment – and the outcomes of the internationalization process, without addressing

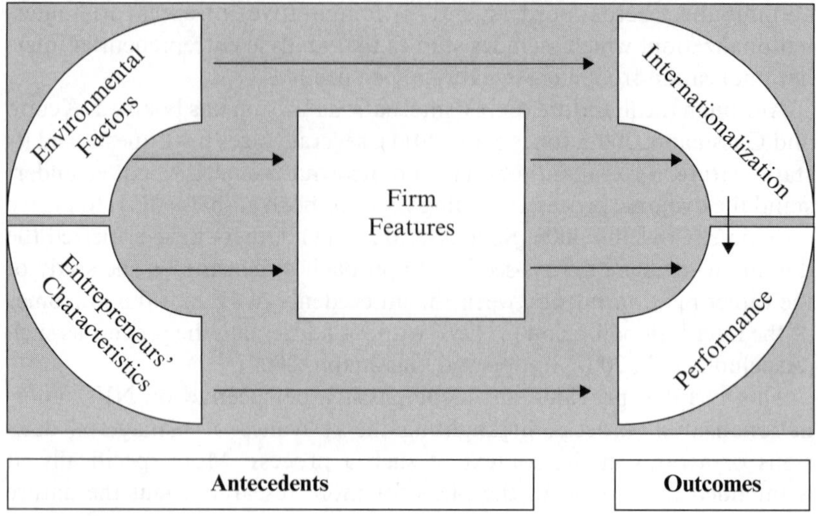

Source: Designed by the authors.

Figure 9.1 A traditional view of new ventures' internationalization

the process inherent to those relationships (e.g., McDougall, 1989; McDougall et al., 2003; De Clercq et al., 2005; Acedo and Florin, 2006; Belso-Martínez, 2006; Mudambi and Zahra, 2007; Zucchella et al., 2007; Jantunen et al., 2008). The bulk of the literature on NVs' internationalization processes addresses the direct and causal relationships between one or several types of antecedents (regarding antecedents related to the entrepreneur, the environment and the firm itself), displayed mainly side by side, and the performance or pattern and degree of internationalization (Figure 9.1). The dependent variables are mainly related to performance (e.g., firm performance, international performance, export performance, or financial measures) and internationalization (degree, pattern, speed and scope of internationalization, export intensity or propensity to internationalize). This research explores the antecedents related particularly to entrepreneurs' characteristics (e.g., McDougall et al., 1994; Acedo and Florin, 2006; Sambasivan et al., 2009) or environmental factors (e.g., Zahra et al., 1997; Andersson, 2004). Other contributions address several types of antecedents, adopting theoretical (e.g., Madsen and Servais, 1997; Andersson and Wictor, 2003; Freeman et al., 2006) and empirical (e.g., McDougall, 1989; McDougall et al., 1994, 2003; Belso-Martínez, 2006; Mudambi and Zahra, 2007; Zucchella et al., 2007) approaches.

Meanwhile, several researchers have called for a process view of NVs' internationalization, espousing a holistic view of the IE process (Jones and Coviello, 2005; Rialp et al., 2005; Aspelund et al., 2007; Jones, 2009; Keupp and Gassmann, 2009). They reject the idea of a linear model merely providing a direct relationship between a set of antecedents and a set of performance outcomes, as indicated in Figure 9.1. According to Keupp and Gassmann (2009, p. 608), 'very little research has so far addressed the why question of IE, that is, the elements . . . which enable entrepreneurial firms to internationalize their business in an entrepreneurial manner over time'.

This opens an interesting opportunity for research. We intend to contribute towards filling the gap by providing a holistic framework in which intermediate factors, namely managerial actions and decisions, are envisaged as intermediate elements that shape the process leading from individual and environmental characteristics to internationalization outcomes. Before presenting the basic tenets of the framework, a brief methodological note will be provided.

METHOD

As pointed out above, our contribution is aimed at developing an integrated framework of NVs' internationalization processes. This section explains the method adopted to carry out this research work. The procedure followed entailed three main steps: (1) establishing a research protocol; (2) conducting the literature review; and (3) designing the process framework. These are briefly described below.

Establishing a Research Protocol

A research protocol was developed to identify the relevant issues regarding NVs' internationalization process, with a view to defining appropriate guidelines for conducting a literature research. Another purpose of the protocol was to enable the replicability of the approach by other researchers. The steps of the protocol are presented in the Appendix to this chapter, and will be briefly described below. The main literature reviews of the IE field have provided the basis for our endeavour. They led to the identification of a large set of research on IE, which were subject to review to capture the key characteristics of the variables considered. Then, a joint analysis was carried out to unveil the main research gaps still existing in the IE literature. The focus has been put on the scarce attention given to company behaviour and decisions; this is, in our opinion, an essential element to developing a more encompassing view of the IE process. The last step corresponds to the design of the framework itself.

Conducting the Literature Review

The starting point was the assessment of the most recent IE literature reviews to identify the blocks of variables relevant to understand NVs' internationalization process. The thorough review of the literature undertaken led to identifying the major types of variables or themes that have been dominant in IE research. This enabled us to assess the density, and the relevance and the shortcomings of extant literature as well as the relationships among the main blocks of variables. It was found that most of the literature has adopted very streamlined approaches, establishing direct relationships between antecedents and outcomes, confirming the findings by Keupp and Gassmann (2009). Therefore we have delved into the identification of relevant firm actions or decisions that are an integral part of the international entrepreneurship process. This led to the identification of a set of variables regarding firms' actions that might contribute to building a more encompassing and realistic view of the IE process.

Designing a Process Framework

The review of the literature along the lines presented above laid the basis to develop a framework intended to provide a holistic understanding of the process of NVs' internationalization. This framework combines multiple levels of analysis (namely the entrepreneur, the firm and the environment) and provides a time-led understanding of how IE processes unfold, including antecedents, actions and outcomes. The design of such a framework will be explained more in detail in the remainder of this chapter.

However, it is important to underline that our intention is not to provide an all-encompassing framework. We just identified what are, from our perspective, the building blocks and aimed at establishing relationships among them. Other frameworks may be designed to highlight issues that have not been detailed enough in our contribution. By the same token, partitions of our framework might be considered to carry out research on more focused issues.

DESIGNING THE FRAMEWORK: A PROCESS VIEW

The framework design includes Jones and Coviello's (2005) key elements of the entrepreneurial internationalization process: the time, the firm, the entrepreneur, the environment, the internationalization behaviour, and performance. It intends, however, to go further insofar as it provides a closer look at specific managerial actions, which Jones and Coviello

(2005) include within the 'internationalization behaviour' category. Our framework is also in line with the suggestions of Aspelund et al. (2007), who called for integrating internal factors (related to the firm and the entrepreneur), external factors (associated to the industry and market) and strategic or organizational factors (here called 'firms' actions').

Antecedents

Entrepreneurs' characteristics

The entrepreneur is the 'match' that fires the entrepreneurial process (Gartner, 1988). Entrepreneurs' characteristics are highlighted as relevant to the founding process of early internationalizing firms (e.g., McDougall et al., 1994; Knight and Cavusgil, 1996; Madsen and Servais, 1997; Andersson and Wictor, 2003; Sharma and Blomstermo, 2003). The entrepreneur, or the entrepreneurial team, may provide the newborn firm with the experience, knowledge and linkages enabling it to succeed in the international arena (McDougall et al., 2003; Simões, 2012).

A positive relationship has been shown between firms' early internationalization and entrepreneurs' characteristics, such as open-minded attitudes, international orientation, global mindset, international experience, networking and risk tolerance (e.g., Madsen and Servais, 1997; Preece et al., 1998; Kuemmerle, 2002). The existence of a relationship between firms' international development and entrepreneurial team members' personal characteristics or life experiences has also been pointed out; these include knowledge of foreign languages, foreign education or work experience abroad, birth in a foreign country and interest in travelling (e.g., McDougall et al., 1994, 2003; Bloodgood et al., 1996; Reuber and Fischer, 1997; Belso-Martínez, 2006; Acedo and Jones, 2007; Zucchella et al., 2007).

Entrepreneurs or management teams' prior international knowledge is especially relevant for NVs, since these organizations, due to their newness, usually lack a knowledge heritage. It may be argued that in the very early years there is some overlap between entrepreneurs' and firms' knowledge (Simões, 2012), especially in 'experiential knowledge', considered by Madsen and Servais (1997) as the most critical type of knowledge for international activities.

The perspective of direct relationships between entrepreneurs' characteristics and the degree or speed of internationalization or performance seems, however, to be excessively coarse, a more fine-grained analysis indicates that such links may be explained through several indirect relationships. There is evidence that the owner/manager profile influences the learning capabilities of the firm, which afterwards impact upon both the design of knowledge-intensive products and marketing capabilities, thereby leading to accelerated internationalization (Weerawardena et al., 2007). Prior knowledge and entrepreneurs' experience bears on how external stimuli are recognized and often lays the basis to figure out new opportunities (Di Gregorio et al., 2008).

Entrepreneurs' characteristics also play a role in shaping strategic decisions (Madsen and Servais, 1997; Reuber and Fischer, 1997; Weerawardena et al., 2007). By the same token, several characteristics of the founders/entrepreneurs (such as previous international experience, international knowledge or social networks) may facilitate the access to specific international partners or networks (McDougall et al., 1994; Reuber and Fischer, 1997). Founders may even activate 'dormant' linkages to push for firms' international expansion (Simões and Câmara, 2006).

The arguments presented above lead to the first proposition:

P1: Regarding the NVs' internationalization process, entrepreneurs' characteristics do influence firms' features.

Environmental antecedents

The external environment corresponds to the 'forces and elements external to the organization's boundaries that affect and are affected by an organization's actions as well as more general economic, socio-cultural, political-legal, and technological forces which provide the broader context for the organization's operations' (Covin and Slevin, 1991, p. 11).

There is a large body of IE research that envisages industry factors as antecedents of IE processes, for instance, distinguishing INVs from domestic ones (McDougall, 1989; McDougall et al., 2003) or explaining superior performance (McDougall et al., 1992; Robinson and McDougall, 1998) and higher survival levels of INVs (Mudambi and Zahra, 2007). Oviatt and McDougall (2005a) suggest that industry competition accelerates the internationalization process. Fernhaber et al. (2007) identified a set of industry structure variables that influence the probability of NVs' internationalization, namely: industry evolution, industry concentration, knowledge intensity of industry, local industry internationalization, global integration of industry, industry venture capital and the appropriability regime.

Research on knowledge-intensive industries (e.g., Preece et al., 1998) and on high-tech businesses implicitly acknowledges the relevance of the industry structure. It is usually considered that these businesses deal more critically with globalization effects (e.g., Fontes and Coombs, 1997; Autio et al., 2000; Zahra et al., 2000; Jones, 2001). Industry's technological turbulence has a positive relationship to firms' performance (Su et al., 2011).

Nevertheless, it has been argued that the body of evidence regarding the impact and the role of industry structure factors on NVs' internationalization process is still modest (Zahra and George, 2002b; Fernhaber et al., 2007).

Markets' (home and foreign) characteristics have also been considered as determinants of both the emergence of INVs. A positive relationship between environmental uncertainty and entrepreneurship was found (Miller, 1983; Balabanis and Katsikea, 2003). Interestingly, there is evidence that entrepreneurial firms operating in uncertain and hostile environments are likely to achieve superior performance (Covin and Slevin, 1989; Covin and Slevin, 1991; Zahra and Covin, 1995). Zahra et al. (1997) found that hostility, dynamism and heterogeneity of firms' domestic competitive environment positively influence export intensity, internationalization scope and international performance. But firms with an entrepreneurial behaviour are better prepared to handle hostile conditions in foreign markets (Hitt et al., 1997). Shrader et al. (2000) also found that several features of the foreign market (degree of market revenue exposure and country risk) as well as the degree of entry mode commitment are negatively related to the number of countries in which a firm operates. These arguments lead to the second proposition:

P2: Regarding the NVs' internationalization process, environmental factors (related to the industry and the home and foreign markets) do influence firms' features.

Firms' features

This set of factors is influenced by entrepreneurs' characteristics and environmental antecedents. They may been envisaged as second-order antecedents. However, we have included them together with the previous items, since they have often been considered as antecedents to IE performance. Jones et al. (2011) point out that several firm-specific factors can be identified as relevant to explain internationalization degree, scope and speed. These factors may be clustered into three groups: general resources, knowledge and firm orientation. A brief presentation follows. To avoid overlaps, the derivation of such factors into research propositions is not developed now, but in the following section, dealing with firms' actions.

According to the resource-based view (RBV), firms with resources (including assets, processes, capabilities, routines and knowledge) that are valuable, rare, non-imitable and non-substitutable have an advantage over their competitors, in both domestic and foreign markets; this leads to improved performance (Wernerfelt, 1984; Barney, 1991). Firms with unique combinations of these resources may also have higher international orientation (Bloodgood et al., 1996), particularly in the case of NVs (McDougall et al., 1994).

There is a wide body of research showing the effect of different types of resources on NVs' internationalization patterns and outcomes. For instance, entrepreneurial orientation was found to be relevant to explain internationalization (Preece et al., 1998; Knight, 2001) and international performance (Knight, 2001; Knight and Cavusgil, 2004). Higher international orientation of NVs is positively related to internationalization performance (Jantunen et al., 2008) and speed (Belso-Martínez, 2006). Knowledge intensity is expected to have a positive effect on both internationalization degree and performance (Autio et al., 2000). Similarly, technological capabilities exhibit a positive relationship to internationalization (Zou et al., 2010).

In spite of the above arguments, it may be argued that the relationships between firms' features and internationalization/performance are mediated by a set of firms' decisions or actions. Such mediation effects are dealt with in the following section.

Firms' Actions

Four main variables regarding decisions or actions are considered to impact upon NVs' internationalization and performance: absorptive capacity, generic competitive strategies, networking decisions and entrepreneurial alertness. The rationale for the selection of these variables is explained below.

Absorptive capacity

The literature on technological development and organizational learning shows that learning has path-dependent, evolutionary features: capabilities developed in the past do shape future learning patterns. Cohen and Levinthal's (1990) concept of absorptive capacity is one of the most classical expressions of this evolutionary thinking. Absorptive capacity was defined as the firm's ability to recognize the value of new information from external sources, and to assimilate and apply it in its operations to commercial ends (Cohen and Levinthal, 1990; Zahra and George, 2002a; Zahra, 2005). Transforming the potential into action, requires action. This is underlined by Autio et al. (2000), who found that firms' success is likely to be strongly influenced by their initial options, focus and effort. Evolutionary processes take time, however, and INVs do not have the time to learn about foreign markets through a long, time-consuming process, as the standard internationalization literature suggests. Learning occurs more rapidly, particularly in the context of aggressive and hyperactive strategies (Chetty and Campbell-Hunt, 2004). Likewise, it may be argued that the ability to learn by actively seeking knowledge about foreign markets, international opportunities, potential customers and operations in foreign markets is inherent to the entrepreneurial nature of INVs (Knight and Cavusgil, 1996; Oviatt and McDougall, 1997, 2005a).

There is evidence supporting a relationship between firms' characteristics and absorptive capacity. The size of accessible resources, the scope of relationships and firms' routines influence firms' behaviours, such as learning or knowledge absorption (Ocasio, 1997). This suggests that absorptive capacity plays a mediating role in NVs' internationalization process. IE research has put emphasis on the role of learning itself (Autio et al., 2000; Zahra et al., 2000) as well as on the relevance of absorptive capacity for learning. Nevertheless, the research on *how* INVs learn (Zahra, 2005) and *how* their absorptive capacity is acquired and nurtured (Zahra and George, 2002a) is still limited.

The literature has pointed out absorptive capacity as an antecedent to internationalization, namely through the increase in foreign market knowledge (Eriksson and Chetty, 2003). Additionally, it was found that absorptive capacity has a moderating effect on the relationship between international venturing and financial performance (Zahra and Hayton, 2008). This leads to the third proposition:

P3: Regarding the NVs' internationalization process, firms' absorptive capacity mediates the relationship between firms' features and their internationalization and performance outcomes.

Generic competitive strategy

Recent literature reviews (Rialp et al., 2005; Keupp and Gassmann, 2009; Rialp-Criado et al., 2010; Jones et al., 2011) converge in showing that competitive strategy is an under-researched topic. There are, however, empirical contributions that provide support to the central role of strategy in INVs, as a mediating factor between antecedents on the one hand, and internationalization and performance outcomes on the other.

Drawing on the resource- and knowledge-based views, it may be argued that firms undertake strategic actions or decisions in line with the resources and knowledge available to them (Cohen and Levinthal, 1990; Wiklund and Shepherd, 2003). International orientation and entrepreneurial orientation were found to be positively related to strategic decision-making, namely to innovativeness and flexibility (Knight, 2000, 2001; Knight and Cavusgil, 2004). International marketing orientation is an antecedent of business strategies to improve performance in international markets (Knight and Cavusgil, 2004).

Freeman and Cavusgil (2007) found that different strategic orientations make a difference in internationalization patterns. Using Porter's (1980) generic strategies, Namiki (1988) suggests that exporting SMEs generally adopt one of four main strategies: marketing differentiation, segmentation differentiation, innovation differentiation and product-oriented service (customer service and high-quality products). Exporting SMEs following the segmentation differentiation and innovation differentiation strategies seem to achieve higher performance (ibid.).

Strategy decisions have a positive and significant influence on SMEs' performance (Bloodgood et al., 1996; Knight, 2000, 2001) as well as on INVs' survival (Mudambi and Zahra, 2007). They may also influence the degree and the speed of internationalization (Bloodgood et al., 1996; McDougall et al., 2003).

Niche strategies were identified as a very relevant factor to explain internationalization speed, since they reduce the risks of competing against global players (e.g., Bloodgood et al., 1996; Madsen and Servais, 1997; Knight and Cavusgil, 2004; Rialp et al., 2005; Zucchella et al., 2007). For our purposes, the key point is to underline the relevance of the strategic posture followed by the NV for its performance and internationalization. Therefore, the fourth proposition is the following:

P4: Regarding the NVs' internationalization process, firms' generic competitive strategy mediates the relationship between firms' features and their internationalization and performance outcomes.

Networking

There is a consensus in INV/BG literature that networks play a key role as facilitators of fast internationalization (Oviatt and McDougall, 1994), by providing access to critical external resources, capabilities, information, knowledge and opportunities (e.g., Oviatt and McDougall, 1994; Madsen and Servais, 1997; Andersson and Wictor, 2003; Sharma and Blomstermo, 2003; Freeman et al., 2006). Therefore, networks may help NVs to overcome the liabilities of newness and smallness and the related resources and knowledge constraints (Freeman et al., 2006; Tang, 2009). Network connections are often used as an explanatory factor of early or accelerated internationalization processes (Belso-Martínez, 2006; Yiu et al., 2007; Zucchella et al., 2007). There is, however, evidence that, at organizational level, the role of networking is *prima facie* envisaged as related to managerial decision-making and to competitive strategy, and not so much as a direct antecedent of the IE process (Freeman et al., 2006; Zhou et al., 2010). Freeman et al. (2006) argue that when NVs face constraints such as lack of knowledge and financial resources, aversion to risk taking and poor access to economies of scale, they develop networking and alliance strategies to enable faster access to international markets.

Network ties may be activated to enable access to resources or knowledge needed for the firm to compete internationally and to enter specific markets (Chetty and Wilson, 2003). Therefore, the network relationship characteristics may influence the degree, scope and speed of internationalization (Belso-Martínez, 2006; Weerawardena et al., 2007; Yiu et al., 2007; Zucchella et al., 2007) as well as the firm's international performance (Mort and Weerawardena, 2006; Zhou et al., 2007). Therefore, the fifth proposition is as follows:

P5: Regarding the NVs' internationalization process, the firm's networking profile mediates the relationship between firm's features and their internationalization and performance outcomes.

Entrepreneurial alertness (EA)

The emergence of new ideas and opportunity identification have been recognized as important issues in both entrepreneurship (Shane and Venkataraman, 2000; Baron, 2006; Short et al., 2010) and IE fields (Mainela et al., 2014). Extant literature points out a host of factors to explain the opportunity recognition or identification process, such as prior knowledge or experience (Venkataraman, 1997), information analysis (Kirzner, 1973), personal awareness, skills and insights (Kirzner, 1999) and EA (Kirzner, 1973; Busenitz, 1996).

The concept of EA was developed by Kirzner (1973, 1979, 1982), being defined as 'the ability to notice without search opportunities that have hitherto been overlooked' (Kirzner, 1979, p. 48). McMullen and Shepherd (2006) go a step further, arguing that entrepreneurship involves action. In their view, EA 'is what happens when the market presents a profitable situation that is successfully exploited by an individual [or company] who "fits" the necessary profile' (McMullen and Shepherd, 2006, p. 144). Therefore, alertness is not entrepreneurial unless it involves both judgement and a drive towards action.

EA may be envisaged as a mediating variable between firms' features and outcomes (internationalization and performance), being therefore influenced by NVs' features, while impacting upon their internationalization and performance. EA may be contingent on firms' resources (Di Gregorio et al., 2008), and also on entrepreneurial orientation or international orientation levels. Firms' knowledge, expertise and experience may act as a trigger for the motivation to search for new opportunities (Cohen and Levinthal, 1990), while the latter may be expected to impact on alertness. Organizations' prior experiential knowledge also influences the internationalization process, through its relationship to search processes or alertness (Eriksson et al., 1997).

There is still a modest stream of research relating this variable to firm performance and internationalization. Sambasivan et al. (2009) concluded that EA mediates the relationship between personal skills and venture performance. Westhead et al. (2005) report that experienced portfolio entrepreneurs, when compared with novice ones, present higher EA, identify a larger number of opportunities, and achieve increased performance than novice entrepreneurs. Based on this rationale, the sixth proposition is the following:

P6: Regarding the NVs' internationalization process, firms' EA mediates the relationship between firms' features and their internationalization and performance outcomes.

Outcomes

In IE research the concept of internationalization of the firm has been given various meanings, thereby leading to different implications (Zahra and George, 2002b). When researchers refer to internationalization as an outcome, they may address the degree or extent, the speed or the scope of internationalization (McDougall, 1989; McDougall et al., 1994; Bloodgood et al., 1996; McDougall and Oviatt, 1996; Fontes and Coombs, 1997; Reuber and Fischer, 1997; Zahra et al., 2000). These internationalization dimensions may be related to firm performance in different ways. However, performance is a construct that is amenable to operationalization in a holistic form, since it may refer to different aspects of firms' organizational efficiency.

Research on NVs' internationalization suggests the existence of a positive link between the level of internationalization and firm performance (e.g., Bloodgood et al., 1996; McDougall and Oviatt, 1996; Zahra et al., 2000; Zahra and Hayton, 2008).

There is a wide array of internationalization and performance measures. Addressing internationalization in general may undermine the comparability and the consistency of the findings. For instance, Lu and Beamish (2001) conclude that internationalization (measured by the level of foreign direct investment [FDI] activity) has a non-linear relationship to SMEs' performance (measured by return on assets), performance decreases for initial FDI activity, while it increases after reaching a higher level of FDI. Bloodgood et al. (1996) also identify a relationship between the level of internationalization and performance, but operationalize it as internationalization extent (percentage of primary activities of the firm that are engaged in foreign markets), while using return on sales (ROS) and earnings before interest and tax (EBIT) as performance measures. Therefore, it is important to clearly identify how internationalization is measured (degree, scope or speed).

Taking into account the latter observation and based on the arguments developed above, a seventh proposition is presented:

P7: Regarding the NVs' internationalization process, firms' performance is influenced by the degree, scope and/or speed of its internationalization.

Environmental Factors as Moderators

To fully understand the IE process, moderating variables should be taken into account. Covin and Slevin (1991) identified a set of moderating factors (classified as environmental, internal and strategic) that may affect the relationship between entrepreneurial characteristics and firm performance. Two moderating factors, related to environmental conditions, were considered. These factors will affect both the relationships between the antecedents and firm actions, and the relationship between these actions and the outcomes of IE process. A brief description of the moderating factors and the rationale for their inclusion is presented below.

Industry structure

Although the industry structure plays a role in shaping initial firms' features, industry variables also moderate several relationships in the IE process. Lumpkin and Dess (2001) found that the stage of industry lifecycle moderates the relationship between proactiveness (one of the dimensions of entrepreneurial orientation) and firm performance. In a meta-analysis on the relationship between entrepreneurial orientation and performance, Rauch et al. (2009) found that industry's technological intensity may play a moderating role between these two variables. Home industry competition was found to moderate the relationship between firm-specific advantages and international venturing (Yiu et al., 2007). Paladino (2008) also concluded that technological turbulence moderates the relationship between the resource and market orientation of firms' organizational learning and firms' performance. Therefore the following propositions are suggested:

P8a: Regarding the NVs' internationalization process, the relationships between firms' characteristics and managerial actions are stronger when competitive intensity and technological turbulence are high than when they are low.

P8b: Regarding the NVs' internationalization process, the influence of firms' managerial actions (specifically absorptive capacity and competitive generic strategies) on internationalization and performance outcomes are stronger when competitive intensity and technological turbulence are high than when they are low.

Market characteristics

Both home and foreign market characteristics were found to moderate the relationship between entry mode selection and entrepreneurial orientation on the one hand, and international performance on the other (Covin and Slevin, 1989; Lumpkin and Dess, 2001; Rasheed, 2005). Lumpkin and Dess (2001) concluded that environmental dynamism moderates the relationship between proactiveness and firm performance, while environmental hostility moderates the relationship between competitive aggressiveness (another entrepreneurial orientation dimension) and firm performance. Zahra and Garvis (2000) found that international environment hostility plays a moderating role on the relationship between international corporate entrepreneurship and international performance. There is also evidence that home market dynamism has a positive influence on the relationship between non-equity entry modes and international performance, while foreign market risk has a negative effect (Rasheed, 2005). Dimitratos et al. (2004) also found that home country environmental uncertainty moderates the relationship between entrepreneurship orientation and international performance. Therefore the following propositions are suggested:

P9a: Regarding the NVs' internationalization process, the relationships between firms' characteristics and managerial actions are stronger when hostility, dynamism and heterogeneity of the markets (domestic and foreign) are high than when they are low.

P9b: Regarding the NVs' internationalization process, the influence of firms' managerial actions (specifically absorptive capacity and competitive generic strategies) on internationalization and performance outcomes are stronger when hostility, dynamism and heterogeneity of the markets (domestic and foreign) are high than when they are low.

A PROCESS-ORIENTED FRAMEWORK

Taking the set of propositions developed above together, a holistic, process perspective of the IE process emerges, as depicted in Figure 9.2.

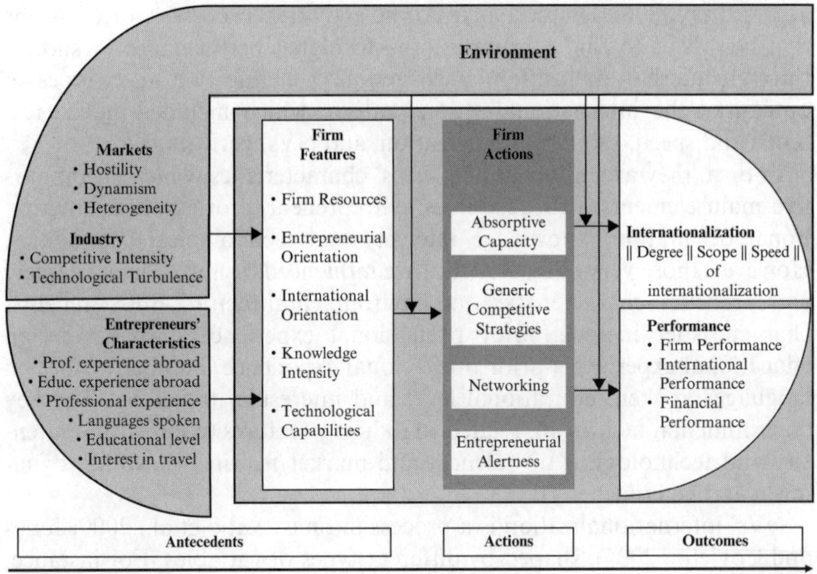

Source: Designed by the authors.

Figure 9.2 A developed framework of new ventures' internationalization

This is in line with the calls by Aspelund et al. (2007), Jones (2009) and Keupp and Gassmann (2009). In particular, it addresses the role of several managerial decisions or actions in the context of the IE process.

Contrary to the Jones and Coviello (2005) model, in which the entrepreneur and the firm were represented side by side, we argue that entrepreneurs' characteristics will influence the NV's features (Simões, 2012). NVs are designed in line with entrepreneurs' knowledge, experience and personality. The way the NV is managed is also influenced by industry (McDougall, 1989; McDougall et al., 2003; Oviatt and McDougall, 2005a) and market characteristics (Miller, 1983); therefore, the environment is another antecedent to firms' features.

At the core of the conceptual framework are firm managerial actions, capabilities or decisions envisaged as key to enable the 'conversion' of firms' features or antecedents into internationalization and performance outcomes. It is further expected that industry structure and market patterns play a role as moderators of some of the relationships hypothesized. Four types of managerial features and actions were identified: absorptive capacity, competitive strategies, EA and networking. These actions may be understood as dynamic activities, processes, or decisions that help NVs to find a route leading to higher performance or success through internationalization. Such actions generate two main types of outcomes: the internationalization pattern, which includes the degree, scope and speed of internationalization, and NVs' performance.

In turn, they are influenced by firms' characteristics, which encompass five main elements: firm resources, entrepreneurial orientation, international orientation, knowledge intensity and technological capabilities. However, those very characteristics are influenced by antecedents, namely entrepreneurs' characteristics and environmental factors. Entrepreneurs' characteristics include: prior professional experience abroad, foreign educational experience, prior professional experience, number of foreign languages spoken, educational level and interest in travelling. The key environmental factors are related to industry features (competition intensity and technological turbulence) and market features (hostility, dynamism and heterogeneity).

NVs' internationalization is a process in time (Autio et al., 2000; Jones and Coviello, 2005), shaped by different types of variables. For instance, when the NV is created, it will be to a large extent influenced by entrepreneurs' characteristics and environmental factors. However, as time goes by, aspects related to firm's resources, capabilities and entrepreneurial orientation will play a stronger role in their managerial and strategic decisions and actions. By the same token, the influence of environmental features will change, becoming a moderating factor in the relationships between firm features, managerial decisions and actions, and performance outcomes.

To sum up, since SME internationalization is a complex process, it is difficult to develop a framework to fully explain it (Jones and Coviello, 2005). However, distinct but inter-related approaches may help to better understand the internationalization process of NVs. The proposed framework is intended to do so, by providing a broad understanding of the complex phenomenon of NVs' internationalization. It highlights seven main issues: (1) how entrepreneur's characteristics contribute to shape firm's features; (2) the role of environmental factors in influencing firms' early features and the effects of managerial factors at later stages of a firm's life; (3) the dynamic process through which firms' features influence their actions or decisions; (4) how firms' actions lead to internationalization and performance outcomes; (5) the fact that internationalization patterns will further impinge upon firms' performance features; (6) the moderating role played throughout the process by environmental factors on the relationships between both firms' characteristics – firms' features and firms' actions – and internationalization pattern/performance; and

(7) the role of time as a relevant variable, since NVs' conditions, capabilities and knowledge change as they take actions and the internationalization process unveils.

DISCUSSION

A host of researchers (Jones and Coviello, 2005; Keupp and Gassmann, 2009; Rialp-Criado et al., 2010; Jones et al., 2011) have demanded an integrated or holistic approach, adopting a process view to explain the level and the speed of internationalization of NVs. This chapter develops a framework that is intended to answer such a demand.

The framework includes four main blocks of variables: antecedents, actions, outcomes and moderators. It is deeply rooted in the IE field, building upon Jones and Coviello's (2005) key constructs: the firm, the entrepreneur, the environment and the performance. Performance indicators are related to both firms' overall performance and internationalization performance. It intends, however, to go further than Jones and Coviello (2005) insofar it provides a closer look into firms' capabilities, strategy and behaviour.

Concerning the blocks of variables, there are a few issues that deserve a brief reference. Several researchers have presented the *entrepreneur* or the *entrepreneurial team* as the key antecedent of INVs (McDougall et al., 1994; Madsen and Servais, 1997). From the company foundation event onwards, there is a new player in the process: *the firm*. It has a specific set of *features* that may drive the internationalization process and, at a later stage, are influenced by it. The framework takes into account the existence of a relationship, especially in the very early years, between the entrepreneurs and the firm itself, as pointed out by Madsen and Servais (1997) and Simões (2012). The *environment* is considered to influence the entrepreneurial internationalization process as an antecedent (near foundation) and as a moderator (later in the NV's life). Therefore, this framework intends to reconcile the approach of Dimitratos et al. (2004) and Yiu et al. (2007) with that of Oviatt and McDougall (2005a), Shrader et al. (2000) and Zahra and Covin (1995), by highlighting reference time as an element that defines environmental characteristics as antecedent or moderator.

The core of the framework is, however, the set of constructs intended to express the managerial 'actions' (including decisions, capabilities, behaviours and strategies) leading to internationalization behaviours. Little research has so far addressed the following question: which organizational 'actions' are central to NVs' internationalization process?

Such 'actions' may be envisaged as dynamic activities, processes or decisions that enable the NV to find a way in the international scene. Taking into account firm youth, such 'actions' are influenced by NVs' characteristics, which have been previously influenced by entrepreneurs' characteristics and environmental factors.

The organizational processes or strategic decisions that are considered in the framework as mediating the relationship between the antecedents and the outcomes of IE included in the framework are the following: absorptive capacity, competitive strategies, EA and networking. All these elements have already been considered in IE research, but, to the best of our knowledge, extant literature has never approached them together as mediating variables in the internationalization process. By highlighting company decision and behaviour elements, we are confident that the framework might contribute to stimulating new empirical research in the field, improving our understanding of how managerial decisions impinge upon internationalization patterns and performance.

With regard to the outcomes, the framework was designed with a logic similar to Oviatt and McDougall's (2005a) model explaining internationalization speed. In fact, besides antecedent variables, mediating variables are also included to explain NVs' internationalization patterns and performance. However, Oviatt and McDougall's model includes entrepreneurial opportunity, technology (called enabling force) and competition (called motivation force) as antecedents. Another difference concerns the fact that these authors considered knowledge (as a process: related to absorption capacity) and network relationships as moderating constructs, whereas these elements are envisaged in our framework as managerial actions that are vital to shaping the internationalization process and to enhancing firms' performance.

The proposed framework has relevant managerial implications. It draws attention to the fact that the outcomes of NVs' internationalization processes are not exclusively dependent on NVs' antecedents. They are also contingent upon the decisions taken by company management during the first years of existence. The framework suggests that both antecedents and 'actions' contribute to shape the NVs' internationalization pattern and performance. Managerial decisions and the development of endogenous firms' capabilities and relationships are essential ingredients of internationalization processes. The dialectics between managerial drive and company capabilities and resources is a central issue in guiding NVs' decision-making processes.

CONCLUSIONS

This chapter was intended to respond to the demands for an integrated analysis of NVs' internationalization processes (Aspelund et al., 2007; Keupp and Gassmann, 2009). The framework proposed herein focuses on the organizational and managerial elements through which the antecedents impact on internationalization outcomes. It provides a foundation for a deeper understanding of NVs' internationalization process by identifying four groups of managerial issues (absorptive capacity, competitive strategy, EA and networking) impinging upon firms' internationalization patterns and performance. It also provides a clear perspective of the path leading from IE antecedents to outcomes, and highlights environmental factors that play an antecedent role in firms' characteristics and a moderating role in the relationships between the various sets of variables.

This work has two main limitations. First, the managerial and organizational actions, which are at the core of the conceptual framework, do not encompass all the possible managerial actions that might be taken. In particular, for the sake of economy, dimensions concerning business models and entry modes were left aside. Second, the framework is very complex, encompassing a large number of constructs. It is recognized that there is scope for additional research to develop less parsimonious models.

In spite of this, we expect that the proposed framework might contribute to stimulating further research to enhance our knowledge about the 'black box' of NVs' internationalization processes. This is a promising and exciting avenue in which progress demands additional work on both the theoretical and the empirical fronts.

REFERENCES

Acedo, F.J. and J. Florin (2006), 'An entrepreneurial cognition perspective on the internationalization of SMEs', *Journal of International Entrepreneurship*, **4**(1), 49–67.

Acedo, F.J. and M.V. Jones (2007), 'Speed of internationalization and entrepreneurial cognition: insights and a comparison between international new ventures, exporters and domestic firms', *Journal of World Business*, **42**(3), 236–52.

Andersson, S. (2004), 'Internationalization in different industrial contexts', *Journal of Business Venturing*, **19**(6), 851–75.

Andersson, S. and I. Wictor (2003), 'Innovative internationalisation in new firms: born globals – the Swedish case', *Journal of International Entrepreneurship*, **1**(3), 249–76.

Aspelund, A., T.K. Madsen and Ø. Moen (2007), 'A review of the foundation, international marketing strategies, and performance of international new ventures', *European Journal of Marketing*, **41**(11/12), 1423–48.

Autio, E., H.J. Sapienza and J.G. Almeida (2000), 'Effects of age at entry, knowledge intensity, and imitability on international growth', *Academy of Management Journal*, **43**(5), 909–24.

Balabanis, G.I. and E.S. Katsikea (2003), 'Being an entrepreneurial exporter: does it pay?', *International Business Review*, **12**(2), 233–52.

Barney, J.B (1991), 'Firm resources and sustained competitive advantage', *Journal of Management*, **17**(1), 99–120.

Baron, R.A. (2006), 'Opportunity recognition as pattern recognition: how entrepreneurs "connect the dots" to identify new business opportunities', *Academy of Management Perspectives*, **20**(1), 104–19.

Belso-Martínez, J.A. (2006), 'Why are some Spanish manufacturing firms internationalizing rapidly? The role of business and institutional international networks', *Entrepreneurship and Regional Development*, **18**(3), 207–26.

Bloodgood, J.M., H.J. Sapienza and J.G. Almeida (1996), 'The internationalization of new high-potential US ventures: antecedents and outcomes', *Entrepreneurship: Theory and Practice*, **20**(4), 61–76.

Busenitz, L.W. (1996), 'Research on entrepreneurial alertness', *Journal of Small Business Management*, **34**(4), 35–44.

Chetty, S. and C. Campbell-Hunt (2004), 'A strategic approach to internationalization: a traditional versus a "born-global" approach', *Journal of International Marketing*, **12**(1), 57–81.

Chetty, S.K. and H.I.M. Wilson (2003), 'Collaborating with competitors to acquire resources', *International Business Review*, **12**(1), 61–81.

Cohen, W.M. and D.A. Levinthal (1990), 'Absorptive capacity: a new perspective on learning and innovation', *Administrative Science Quarterly*, **35**(1), 128–52.

Coviello, N. (2006), 'The network dynamics of international new ventures', *Journal of International Business Studies*, **37**(5), 713–31.

Covin, J.G. and D.P. Slevin (1989), 'Strategic management of small firms in hostile and benign environments', *Strategic Management Journal*, **10**(1), 75–87.

Covin, J.G. and D.P. Slevin (1991), 'A conceptual model of entrepreneurship as firm behavior', *Entrepreneurship Theory and Practice*, **16**(1), 7–25.

De Clercq, D., H. Sapienza and H. Crijns (2005), 'The internationalization of small and medium-sized firms', *Small Business Economics*, **24**(4), 409–19.

Di Gregorio, D., M. Musteen and D.E. Thomas (2008), 'International new ventures: the cross-border nexus of individuals and opportunities', *Journal of World Business*, **43**(2), 186–96.

Dimitratos, P., S. Lioukas and S. Carter (2004), 'The relationship between entrepreneurship and international performance: the importance of domestic environment', *International Business Review*, **13**(1), 19–41.

Eriksson, K. and S. Chetty (2003), 'The effect of experience and absorptive capacity on foreign market knowledge', *International Business Review*, **12**(6), 673–95.

Eriksson, K., J. Johanson, A. Majkgård and D.D. Sharma (1997), 'Experiential knowledge and cost in the internationalization process', *Journal of International Business Studies*, **28**(2), 337–60.

Fernhaber, S.A., P.P. McDougall and B.M. Oviatt (2007), 'Exploring the role of industry structure in new venture internationalization', *Entrepreneurship: Theory and Practice*, **31**(4), 517–42.

Fontes, M. and R. Coombs (1997), 'The coincidence of technology and market objectives in the internationalisation of new technology-based firms', *International Small Business Journal*, **15**(4), 14–35.

Freeman, S. and S.T. Cavusgil (2007), 'Toward a typology of commitment states among managers of born-global firms: a study of accelerated internationalization', *Journal of International Marketing*, **15**(4), 1–40.

Freeman, S., R. Edwards and B. Schroder (2006), 'How smaller born-global firms use networks and alliances to overcome constraints to rapid internationalization', *Journal of International Marketing*, **14**(3), 33–63.

Gartner, W.B. (1988), '"Who is an entrepreneur?" is the wrong question', *American Journal of Small Business*, **12**(4), 11–32.

Hitt, M.A., R.E. Hoskisson and H. Kim (1997), 'International diversification: effects on innovation and firm performance in product-diversified firms', *Academy of Management Journal*, **40**(4), 767–98.

Jantunen, A., N. Nummela, K. Puumalainen and S. Saarenketo (2008), 'Strategic orientations of born globals – do they really matter?', *Journal of World Business*, **43**(2), 158–70.

Johanson, J. and J.-E. Vahlne (1977), 'The internationalization process of the firm – a model of knowledge development and increasing foreign market commitments', *Journal of International Business Studies*, **8**(1), 25–34.

Johanson, J. and F. Wiedersheim-Paul (1975), 'The internationalization of the firm – four Swedish cases', *Journal of Management Studies*, **12**(3), 305–22.

Jones, M.V. (2001), 'First steps in internationalisation: concepts and evidence from a sample of small high-technology firms', *Journal of International Management*, **7**(3), 191–210.

Jones, M.V. (2009), 'Conclusion. SME internationalization: where do we go from here?', in M.V. Jones, P. Dimitratos, M. Fletcher and S. Young (eds), *Internationalization, Entrepreneurship and the Smaller Firm: Evidence from Around the World*, Cheltenham, UK and Northampton, MA, USA: Edward Elgar Publishing.

Jones, M.V. and N.E. Coviello (2005), 'Internationalisation: conceptualising an entrepreneurial process of behaviour in time', *Journal of International Business Studies*, **36**(3), 284–303.

Jones, M.V., N. Coviello and Y.K. Tang (2011), 'International entrepreneurship research (1989–2009): a domain ontology and thematic analysis', *Journal of Business Venturing*, **26**(6), 632–59.

Keupp, M.M. and O. Gassmann (2009), 'The past and the future of international entrepreneurship: a review and suggestions for developing the field', *Journal of Management*, **35**(3), 600–633.

Kirzner, I.M. (1973), *Competition and Entrepreneurship*, Chicago, IL: University of Chicago Press.

Kirzner, I.M. (1979), *Perception, Opportunity, and Profit: Studies in the Theory of Entrepreneurship*, Chicago, IL: University of Chicago Press.

Kirzner, I.M. (1982), *Method, Process, and Austrian Economics*, Lexington, MA: Lexington Books.

Kirzner, I.M. (1999), 'Creativity and/or alertness: a reconsideration of the Schumpeterian entrepreneur', *The Review of Austrian Economics*, **11**(1), 5–17.

Knight, G.A. (2000), 'Entrepreneurship and marketing strategy: the SME under globalization', *Journal of International Marketing*, **8**(2), 12–32.

Knight, G.A. (2001), 'Entrepreneurship and strategy in the international SME', *Journal of International Management*, **7**(3), 155–71.

Knight, G.A. and S.T. Cavusgil (1996), 'The born global firm: a challenge to traditional internationalization theory', in S.T. Cavusgil and T. Madsen (eds), *Advances in International Marketing* (Vol. 8), Greenwich, CT: JAI Press, pp. 11–26.

Knight, G.A. and S.T. Cavusgil (2004), 'Innovation, organizational capabilities, and the born-global firm', *Journal of International Business Studies*, **35**(2), 124–41.

Kuemmerle, W. (2002), 'Home base and knowledge management in international ventures', *Journal of Business Venturing*, **17**(2), 99–122.

Lu, J.W. and P.W. Beamish (2001), 'The internationalization and performance of SMEs', *Strategic Management Journal*, **22**(6/7), 565–86.

Lumpkin, G.T. and G.G. Dess (2001), 'Linking two dimensions of entrepreneurial orientation to firm performance: the moderating role of environment and industry life cycle', *Journal of Business Venturing*, **16**(5), 429–51.

Madsen, T.K. and P. Servais (1997), 'The internationalization of born globals: an evolutionary process?', *International Business Review*, **6**(6), 561–83.

Mainela, T., V. Puhakka and P. Servais (2014), 'The concept or international opportunity in international entrepreneurship: a review and a research agenda', *International Journal of Management Reviews*, **16**(1), 105–29.

McDougall, P.P. (1989), 'International versus domestic entrepreneurship: new venture strategic behavior and industry structure', *Journal of Business Venturing*, **4**(6), 387–400.
McDougall, P.P. and B.M. Oviatt (1996), 'New venture internationalization, strategic change, and performance: a follow-up study', *Journal of Business Venturing*, **11**(1), 23–40.
McDougall, P.P. and B.M. Oviatt (2000), 'International entrepreneurship: the intersection of two research paths', *Academy of Management Journal*, **43**(5), 902–6.
McDougall, P.P., B.M. Oviatt and R.C. Shrader (2003), 'A comparison of international and domestic new ventures', *Journal of International Entrepreneurship*, **1**(1), 59–82.
McDougall, P.P., R.B. Robinson and A.S. DeNisi (1992), 'Modeling new venture performance: an analysis of new venture strategy, industry structure, and venture origin', *Journal of Business Venturing*, **7**(4), 267–89.
McDougall, P.P., S. Shane and B.M. Oviatt (1994), 'Explaining the formation of international new ventures: the limits of theories from international business research', *Journal of Business Venturing*, **9**(6), 469–87.
McMullen, J.S. and D.A. Shepherd (2006), 'Entrepreneurial action and the role of uncertainty in the theory of the entrepreneur', *Academy of Management Review*, **31**(1), 132–52.
Miller, D. (1983), 'The correlates of entrepreneurship in three types of firms', *Management Science*, **29**(7), 770–91.
Mort, G.S. and J. Weerawardena (2006), 'Networking capability and international entrepreneurship', *International Marketing Review*, **23**(5), 549–72.
Mudambi, R. and S.A. Zahra (2007), 'The survival of international new ventures', *Journal of International Business Studies*, **38**(2), 333–52.
Namiki, N. (1988), 'Export strategy for small business', *Journal of Small Business Management*, **26**(2), 32–7.
Ocasio, W. (1997), 'Towards an attention-based view of the firm', *Strategic Management Journal*, **18**(S1), 187–206.
Oviatt, B.M. and P.P. McDougall (1994), 'Toward a theory of international new ventures', *Journal of International Business Studies*, **25**(1), 45–64.
Oviatt, B.M. and P.P. McDougall (1997), 'Challenges for internationalization process theory: the case of international new ventures', *Management International Review*, **37**(2), 85–99.
Oviatt, B.M. and P.P. McDougall (2005a), 'Defining international entrepreneurship and modeling the speed of internationalization', *Entrepreneurship: Theory and Practice*, **29**(5), 537–53.
Oviatt, B.M. and P.P. McDougall (2005b), 'The internationalization of entrepreneurship', *Journal of International Business Studies*, **36**(1), 2–8.
Paladino, A. (2008), 'Analyzing the effects of market and resource orientations on innovative outcomes in times of turbulence', *Journal of Product Innovation Management*, **25**(6), 577–92.
Porter, M.E. (1980), *Competitive Strategy: Techniques for Analyzing Industries and Competitors*, New York: Free Press.
Preece, S.B., G. Miles and M.C. Baetz (1998), 'Explaining the international intensity and global diversity of early-stage technology-based firms', *Journal of Business Venturing*, **14**(3), 259–81.
Rasheed, H.S. (2005), 'Foreign entry mode and performance: the moderating effects of environment', *Journal of Small Business Management*, **43**(1), 41–54.
Rauch, A., J. Wiklund, G.T. Lumpkin and M. Frese (2009), 'Entrepreneurial orientation and business performance: an assessment of past research and suggestions for the future', *Entrepreneurship: Theory and Practice*, **33**(3), 761–87.
Reuber, A.R. and E. Fischer (1997), 'The influence of the management team's international experience on the internationalization behaviors of SMEs', *Journal of International Business Studies*, **28**(4), 807–25.
Rialp-Criado, A., I. Galván-Sánchez and Sonia Suárez-Ortega (2010), 'A configuration-holistic approach to born-global firms' strategy formation process', *European Management Journal*, **28**(2), 108–23.

Rialp, A., J. Rialp and G.A. Knight (2005), 'The phenomenon of early internationalizing firms: what do we know after a decade (1993–2003) of scientific inquiry?', *International Business Review*, **14**(2), 147–66.

Robinson, K.C. and P.P. McDougall (1998), 'The impact of alternative operationalizations of industry structural elements on measures of performance for entrepreneurial manufacturing ventures', *Strategic Management Journal*, **19**(11), 1079–100.

Sambasivan, M., M. Abdul and Y. Yusop (2009), 'Impact of personal qualities and management skills of entrepreneurs on venture performance in Malaysia: opportunity recognition skills as a mediating factor', *Technovation*, **29**(11), 798–805.

Shane, S. and S. Venkataraman (2000), 'The promise of entrepreneurship as a field of research', *Academy of Management Review*, **25**(1), 217–26.

Sharma, D.D. and A. Blomstermo (2003), 'The internationalization process of born globals: a network view', *International Business Review*, **12**(6), 739–53.

Short, J.C., Jr, D.J. Ketchen, C.L. Shook and R.D. Ireland (2010), 'The concept of "opportunity" in entrepreneurship research: past accomplishments and future challenges', *Journal of Management*, **36**(1), 40–65.

Shrader, R.C., B.M. Oviatt and P.P. McDougall (2000), 'How new ventures exploit tradeoffs among international risk factors: lessons for the accelerated internationalization of the 21st century', *Academy of Management Journal*, **43**(6), 1227–47.

Simões, V.C. (2012), 'Portuguese BGs: founder's linkages, company evolution and international geographic patterns', in M. Gabrielsson and V.H.M. Kirpalani (eds), *Handbook of Research on Born Globals*, Cheltenham, UK and Northampton, MA, USA: Edward Elgar Publishing.

Simões, V.C. and F. Câmara (2006), 'Social networks as drivers of internationalization patterns: a case study of fish exports', in *Proceedings of the 32nd EIBA Conference*, Fribourg.

Simões, V.C., J. Antunes and L. Laranjeira (2011), 'Born globals: evolution and revolution as organisations grow', in *Proceedings of the 37th European International Business Academy (EIBA) Conference*, Bucharest.

Su, Z., E. Xie, D. Wang and Y. Li (2011), 'Entrepreneurial strategy making, resources, and firm performance: evidence from China', *Small Business Economics*, **36**(2), 235–47.

Tang, Y.K. (2009), 'Networks and the internationalization of firms: what we believe and what we might have missed', in M.V. Jones, P. Dimitratos, M. Fletcher and S. Young (eds), *Internationalization, Entrepreneurship and the Smaller Firm: Evidence from Around the World*, Cheltenham, UK and Northampton, MA, USA: Edward Elgar Publishing.

Venkataraman, S. (1997), 'The distinctive domain of entrepreneurship research: an editor's perspective', in J.A. Katz and R.H. Brockhaus (eds), *Advances in Entrepreneurship, Firm Emergence, and Growth*, Greenwich, CT: JAI Press.

Weerawardena, J., G.S. Mort, P.W. Liesch and G. Knight (2007), 'Conceptualizing accelerated internationalization in the born global firm: a dynamic capabilities perspective', *Journal of World Business*, **42**(3), 294–306.

Wernerfelt, B. (1984), 'A resource-based view of the firm', *Strategic Management Journal*, **5**(2), 171–80.

Westhead, P., D. Ucbasaran and M. Wright (2005), 'Decisions, actions, and performance: do novice, serial, and portfolio entrepreneurs differ?', *Journal of Small Business Management*, **43**(4), 393–417.

Wiklund, J. and D. Shepherd (2003), 'Knowledge-based resources, entrepreneurial orientation, and the performance of small and medium-sized businesses', *Strategic Management Journal*, **24**(13), 1307–14.

Yiu, D.W., C.M. Lau and G.D. Bruton (2007), 'International venturing by emerging economy firms: the effects of firm capabilities, home country networks, and corporate entrepreneurship', *Journal of International Business Studies*, **38**(4), 519–40.

Zahra, S.A. (2005), 'A theory of international new ventures: a decade of research', *Journal of International Business Studies*, **36**(1), 20–28.

Zahra, S.A. and J.G. Covin (1995), 'Contextual influences on the corporate

entrepreneurship–performance relationship: a longitudinal analysis', *Journal of Business Venturing*, **10**(1), 43–58.
Zahra, S.A. and D.M. Garvis (2000), 'International corporate entrepreneurship and firm performance: the moderating effect of international environmental hostility', *Journal of Business Venturing*, **15**(5–6), 469–92.
Zahra, S.A. and G. George (2002a), 'Absorptive capacity: a review, reconceptualization, and extension', *Academy of Management Review*, **27**(2), 185–203.
Zahra, S.A. and G. George (2002b), 'International entrepreneurship: the current status of the field and future research agenda', in M.A. Hitt, R.D. Ireland, S.M. Camp and D.L. Sexton (eds), *Strategic Entrepreneurship: Creating a New Mindset*, Oxford: Blackwell Publishing.
Zahra, S.A. and J.C. Hayton (2008), 'The effect of international venturing on firm performance: the moderating influence of absorptive capacity', *Journal of Business Venturing*, **23**(2), 195–220.
Zahra, S.A., R.D. Ireland and M.A. Hitt (2000), 'International expansion by new venture firms: international diversity, mode of market entry, technological learning, and performance', *Academy of Management Journal*, **43**(5), 925–50.
Zahra, S.A., D.O. Neubaum and M. Huse (1997), 'The effect of the environment on export performance among telecommunications new ventures', *Entrepreneurship: Theory and Practice*, **22**(1), 25–46.
Zhou, L., B.R. Barnes and L. Yuan (2010), 'Entrepreneurial proclivity, capability upgrading and performance advantage of newness among international new ventures', *Journal of International Business Studies*, **41**(5), 882–905.
Zhou, L., W.-P. Wu and X. Luo (2007), 'Internationalization and the performance of born-global SMEs: the mediating role of social networks', *Journal of International Business Studies*, **38**(4), 673–90.
Zou, H., X. Liu and P. Ghauri (2010), 'Technology capability and the internationalization strategies of new ventures', *Organizations and Markets in Emerging Economies*, **1**(1), 100–119.
Zucchella, A., G. Palamara and S. Denicolai (2007), 'The drivers of the early internationalization of the firm', *Journal of World Business*, **42**(3), 268–80.

APPENDIX

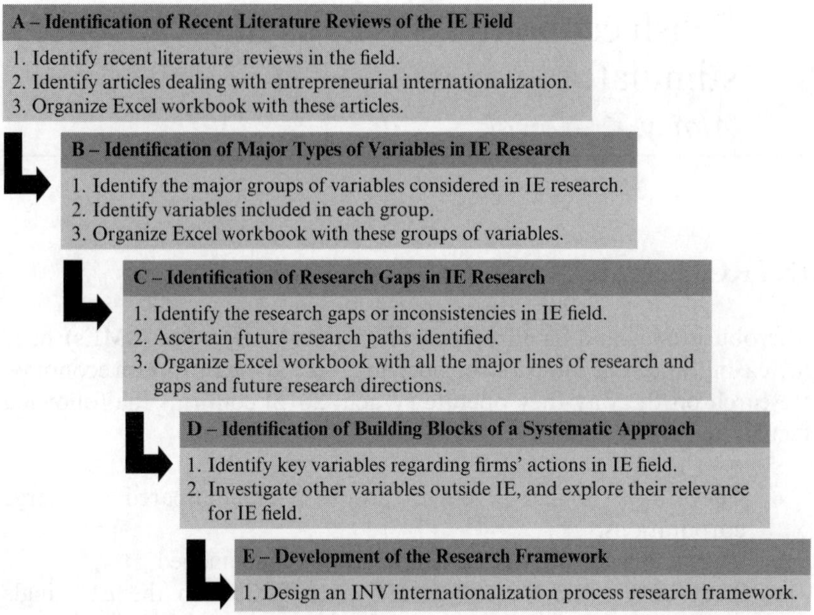

A – Identification of Recent Literature Reviews of the IE Field

1. Identify recent literature reviews in the field.
2. Identify articles dealing with entrepreneurial internationalization.
3. Organize Excel workbook with these articles.

B – Identification of Major Types of Variables in IE Research

1. Identify the major groups of variables considered in IE research.
2. Identify variables included in each group.
3. Organize Excel workbook with these groups of variables.

C – Identification of Research Gaps in IE Research

1. Identify the research gaps or inconsistencies in IE field.
2. Ascertain future research paths identified.
3. Organize Excel workbook with all the major lines of research and gaps and future research directions.

D – Identification of Building Blocks of a Systematic Approach

1. Identify key variables regarding firms' actions in IE field.
2. Investigate other variables outside IE, and explore their relevance for IE field.

E – Development of the Research Framework

1. Design an INV internationalization process research framework.

Figure 9A.1 Methodological procedures

10. How to enhance competitiveness of the Polish economy? SMEs as innovativeness stimulator

Alojzy Z. Nowak

INTRODUCTION

Microbusinesses and small and medium-sized enterprises (SMEs) have increasingly become quite a strong driving force in the European economy. Research on the way they operate (Wach, 2012) confirms the following facts:

- They have higher average productivity compared to large corporations.
- They are usually better and more effectively managed.
- They have a chance to operate more flexibly in the EU single market. The last programme of the European Commission for the Competitiveness of Enterprises and SMEs – COSME – provides key priorities for SMEs, for instance, better access to external sources of financing, loan funds for high-risk investments and long-term investment funds.
- They generate an extra synergy through various forms of cooperation with other businesses, for example, through clustering. For instance, the Polish Aviation Valley cluster located in Southeastern Poland, is known for its aerospace industry. This cluster consortium is cooperating with small innovative firms and local science centres. Polish Aviation Valley is acting within the framework of the Enterprise Europe Network, which is responsible for the aviation industry. Another example is the cluster of innovative manufacturing technologies founded in 2009 in Poland, which provides production services, education, research, development and consultancy. An important task of that cluster is to promote economic development of the region and strengthening the competitiveness of companies in the manufacturing sector. Additionally, the SMEs involved also gain from the experience of operation of such businesses.

SMEs are distinguished in their local environments by:

- being really active in new job creation;
- contributing to development of regions;
- being more resistant to political changes;
- revealing greater social responsibility.

Also, the latter aspect of conducting ethical business has been especially emphasized in the face of the recent financial crisis. There were rules and practices relating to ethical business applied to large companies – those reckoned too big to fail – but cases of those suffering imminent bankruptcy led to governmental intervention. These interventions led to serious charges on the budgets of a number of states. Thus, regular taxpayers ultimately had to pay the cost and public perception of the malpractices of large companies rose significantly.

THE ROLE AND IMPORTANCE OF SMEs IN THE EUROPEAN ECONOMY

SMEs are the leading sector in the European Union's economy. They account for nearly 99 per cent of all business entities in the EU and they employ over 74 million people, generating around 60 per cent of the EU's GDP and providing almost 70 per cent of jobs throughout the EU territory. They are vital source of innovation, true entrepreneurship and economic growth (Buzek, 2011). Dynamic growth of the SME sector in the European Union should be attributed significantly to the adoption of the European Charter for Small Enterprises, approved by the European Union leaders at the Santa Maria da Feira European Council in June 2000. This was a document presenting the key assumptions of policy concerning SMEs, in which emphasis was put upon acknowledging the needs of small businesses in the process of creating the EU legislation. At the same time, as new technologies are developed and IT revolutions proceed, the need emerged for having more precise definitions of both microbusinesses and SMEs. Table 10.1 presents the European Commission's definition of SMEs.

One of the principal objectives for the new definitions was to ensure that measures given in support of businesses were only provided to the types of entities that actually need them. The new definitions included methods of calculation of employment and financial-level thresholds in order to obtain a true picture of an enterprise's economic condition. To this end, the following categories of businesses are introduced: an autonomous, a partnership and a related/linked enterprise. It was specified in detail how to regard particular types of links between SMEs and other businesses or investors while

Table 10.1 Definition of small and medium-sized enterprises by European Commission Regulation 800/2008

Criteria	Microenterprises	Small Enterprises	Medium-sized Enterprises
Maximum employment	9	49	249
Maximum annual turnover	2 million euros	10 million euros	50 million euros
The maximum amount of the annual statement of all assets	2 million euros	10 million euros	43 million euros
Relationships	An autonomous (independent) enterprise Partnership enterprises The related enterprises		

Source: Regulation of the European Commission, No. 800/2008, 6 August 2008.

calculating financial indices and employment levels. The new definitions also clarify the issue of an SME's ability to acquire external financing sources, for example, enterprises linked with other entities where the latter have significant financial resources that may exceed specified limits are denied SME status. The actual purpose of all those measures undertaken in the European Union is to foster the SME's sector competitiveness.

Furthermore, SMEs have particular importance in the European Union's regional policy. Due to their strong ties with the local environment and the influence they have upon it, they came to be perceived as the key link in regional development. Accordingly, promotion of entrepreneurial culture as well as creation and development of innovative, competitive SMEs increasingly become one of the most important domains of public intervention policy in regional local categories.

In the process of SME sector growth, the role played by regional and local-level governments in individual EU member states is diversified but undeniably increasing (Buzek, 2011). Very significant in this respect is a network of Euro Info Centres, which act as local information providers to SMEs. The European Commission, through its policy, supports creation and operation of Euro Info Centres, in particular in such areas as:

- counselling in acquiring financial resources from structural funds, provision of information concerning particular sales markets and combining business partners;
- aid provided to businesses, especially over initial stages of their development;

- creating and active participation in all sorts of seminars and conferences concerning business innovativeness and competitiveness;
- publication of documents and brochures useful for SMEs.

The Lisbon Strategy

A special role in the strategy for modernization and reform of the European economy was attributed by the European Union to the SME sector in the so-called Lisbon Strategy, adopted in 2000. The EU leaders had little doubt that initiatives and actions aiming at the generation of a modern, competitive economy could only be successful when the development of entrepreneurship was real rather than just declared. Indeed, the SME sector has grown to become over time the principal driving force in the growth of innovativeness, growth of employment and social integration in Europe.

Measures undertaken by the European Commission and the EU Council, with 14 years of operation of the Lisbon Strategy taken into account, seem just partial and not entirely satisfying from today's perspective. However, it would be wrong and oversimplified to say no success has been achieved toward strategy implementation by member states with respect to SME-related policy. Actually, progress was largely attained in ten principal directions of planned action, namely the following:

- development of education and training in the field of entrepreneurship;
- development of occupational and sustained education;
- improvement of access to electronic services;
- cheaper and faster process of businesses' registering;
- simplification of legal regulations;
- improvement of conditions for SME sector operation in the EU single market;
- simplification of the tax system and improvement of access to financing sources;
- improvement of access to new technologies;
- promotion of effective cases of application of e-business and advanced companies' support systems;
- better representation of SME sector interests, both in individual member states and at the EU level.

SMEs IN POLISH ECONOMY DEVELOPMENT

As far as problems of SMEs in Poland are concerned, this issue should largely be considered from the point of view of the need for improving the competitiveness of Polish companies on global markets (PARP, 2013). It is beyond argument that decisive progress is needed in the following areas:

- Improvement of the economy competitiveness.
- Sustainable development stimulation of a knowledge-based economy model.
- Introduction of a new system of education based on creativity, creation of new skills and competence, including language and cultural skills, in order to provide a solid foundation for releasing intellectual capital. This has a special relationship with the continuation of the reform of higher education in Poland, which should be more compatible with the needs of an innovative economy.
- Consolidation of fundamentals for a friendly and efficient state with respect to individuals and entities undertaking business activity.
- Equalization of opportunities and social and economic potential all over Poland, in recognition that more sustainable growth, oriented in social needs, also contributes to SME sector development.
- Promotion of attitudes aimed at mutual trust and ability to cooperate rather than confrontation, which is especially important for small and medium-sized enterprises for which reliability, legitimacy and positive image rank among crucial strengths, the ultimate aim being to build clusters.

In the area of practical solutions available to authorities at all levels, in particular to central government, this translates, among other things, into the following necessities:

- To achieve a real breakthrough in levels of R&D activities financing – at present the state only allocates around 0.65 per cent of Poland's GDP to that end. Companies from the SME sector should become crucial beneficiaries of this form of financial support to a much higher extent than it is nowadays.
- Modernization of the system and provisions concerning intellectual property, with the aim of gradual renouncement of the present model of imitation-based development to the benefit of one based on a higher degree of original solutions. The role of SMEs in this context is much underrated (Wilczarski and Zurek, 2008).
- Bringing such changes to regulations, legal regulations included, that promote better linking of EU funds with Poland's development priorities, including those related to specificity of SMEs' nature

Table 10.2 Frequency of use of financing sources

	Regularly %	Sporadically %	Never %
Own equity	73	23	4
Bank loans	13	39	48
Leasing	6	31	63
EU subsidies	2	10	88
Budget subsidies	1	8	91
Factoring	1	1	98
Loans from loan funds		8	92
Guarantees given by guarantee funds		3	97
Issuance of shares or bonds		2	98
Money from venture capital funds		1	99

Source: Wolański (2013b).

and activities. It is also necessary, in this context, to achieve better linking of local governments to the business environment and its more pronounced involvement in creation of new cooperation and legal solutions that can help the formation of clusters.

- Activating the policies of many state institutions, among other things to enable the implementation of the Small Business Act for Europe, adopted by the European Parliament in 2008. Its key elements include ten common guiding principles applicable in the EU member states, such as provision, on a permanent basis, of more business-friendly conditions of active measures to be taken by states to ensure the SME sector better access to financing, both from the EU funds and from member states' resources.

The capital structure of Polish small and medium-sized enterprises is determined by the frequency of use of different financing sources (Table 10.2).

The main source of SME financing is their own equity – almost all SMEs make use of this source. External sources are used much less frequently, and are mostly represented by bank loans followed by leasing. Other external sources are less predominant than these two, and are used on a small scale. In view of the above financing structure, one should determine why SMEs hardly use external sources of financing. The study by Wolański (2013b) indicates that SMEs do not see the need for external financing, as shown in Table 10.3.

It seems that this situation stems from the fact that financial needs in the SME sector are relatively small and can be covered from own equity. Or,

Table 10.3 Percentage of enterprises that do not make use of a given financing source due to the lack of need

Source of Finance	%
Bank loans	67
Leasing	86
EU subsidies	40
Budget subsidies	60
Factoring	85
Loans from loan funds	70
Guarantees given by guarantee funds	73
Issuance of shares or bonds	78
Money from venture capital funds	70

Source: Wolański (2013b).

alternatively or simultaneously, it is due to inhibitions arising from lack of awareness and attitudes emanating from lack of trust of outsiders versus the inability to recognize benefits.

EU FUNDS – OPPORTUNITIES AND THREATS: THE POLISH PERSPECTIVE

European funds have provided a stimulus for companies from the SME sector, in particular for start-ups and young undertakings seeking proper market entry. As a preferential financing source for enterprises, they have contributed to improvement of Polish business competitiveness, including the SME sector. However, according to conclusions from research carried out by the Faculty of Management at the University of Warsaw in cooperation with the Office of the Marshall of Mazowieckie Province, the State School of Higher Professional Education in Płock, and Płock Scientific Society on relevant factors and barriers to business development in Mazovia, institutional, legal and procedural obstacles in Poland are still seriously hampering the process of acquiring aid resources provided by the European Union. In Poland there are almost 150 offices and institutions involved in management of financial resources and in many cases beneficiaries of such funds from the sector of small and medium-sized companies complain about the following:

- basically low quality of service of applicants and beneficiaries, poor customer orientation;

- the bureaucracy of the process of application for subsidies, resulting from excessive complexity and level of detail in competition regulations;
- bureaucratic rigors in offices – lengthy periods for verifying the applications for disbursement;
- poor level of preparation of some public institution personnel to implement the objectives of operational programmes;
- imposing on beneficiaries obligations contradictory to provisions of generally applicable law, for example, vague guidelines concerning expenditure eligibility or financing principles;
- inadequate operation of mechanism of investment project coordination on both local and central levels;
- the lack of consistent information policy covering the entire area of issues regarding the implementation of projects co-financed from European funds.

The above are just some of the barriers most frequently signalled in the research. However, pressure from public opinion has recently led to simplification of procedures for applying for the EU aid funds and shortening of periods until actual payment, Poland has generally experienced no problems with absorption of resources from the EU budget for the years 2007–13. Still, further improvement in the system of the EU funds management is certainly needed. It would also be quite desirable to develop a public ranking of the work quality of managing institutions, including those acting as agencies and involved in the implementation of funds. This ranking could be arranged according to specific criteria, mainly with respect to time limits for activities performed.

SMEs AND INNOVATIVE ECONOMY

As we witness the present efforts aimed at alleviating the consequences of financial crisis or of turbulence occurring in the Eurozone, it becomes clear how individual governments actively undertake a variety of measures to overcome economic stagnation and its negative results, further, to give a fresh impulse for growth in the sphere of real economy (Orłowski et al., 2010). On the one hand, traditional methods, including budgetary and fiscal discipline restriction of public spending and tax increases, and on the other hand, stimulation of economy, fiscal loosening and efforts to increase consumption and reduce unemployment, are becoming more and more popular.

However, what we are witnessing as well is that some governments go further than standard procedures and either raise or resist from restricting public expenditure on the needs of the elderly population in such areas as biomedicine, health care, or social care, because it is in the development of these specialties that they also see potential sources of creation of new, prospective products or innovative technologies. Indeed, it seems that systematic endeavours to stimulate competitiveness and productivity of any given economy is the key to achieving more stable economic growth.

In these conditions, innovations and innovativeness become the following:

- the driving force of contemporary economy;
- an important modernization-fostering factor that improves economic efficiency;
- the foundation for permanent economic growth, the factor promoting economic potential;
- a factor that crucially determines not only the growth of enterprises, but also improves living standards of consumers.

That's why governments, as they opt for this development model, aim for:

- extending the area of knowledge-based economy and services;
- implementation of an educational system in which priority is given to creative attitudes and creation of new competence;
- reforms in academic education in order to link universities to a greater extent with needs and challenges of local and global economy and with provision of stable foundation for releasing intellectual capital;
- support for public education where electronic media, Internet and e-learning are capable of playing a significant role in promotion of innovative attitudes;
- creation of legal and institutional frameworks for efficient state innovation-fostering policies.

In this development model much importance is attributed to the SME sector. This is because these types of businesses fit very well within the above-mentioned governmental priorities. And, furthermore, it is exactly SMEs that most readily and aptly grasp the new twenty-first-century trends in the area of desirable economic policy and development strategy (Bielawska, 2012). The trends are increasingly as follows:

- Giving up the hitherto prevailing model of creation of innovation-fostering policy based on a single company to the benefit of a model relying upon collaboration between many companies, operating in a number of complementary areas of entrepreneurship. It becomes more and more popular to create clusters of new technologies or consortia whose cooperation is not only confined to similar levels of research or technology, but relies on better recognition of the specific nature of a given local market, including its cultural aspect as well.

- It is the region that increasingly becomes a place of interactions necessary for emergence of modernization processes while the characteristics and specific potential of such region makes it easier to reduce the risk inherent in innovation, to absorb various types of knowledge and enables interactive learning and the exchange of experience.
- SMEs increasingly gain a role – not decisive perhaps, but significant nonetheless – in innovation, since their principal driving force is not only the level of spending on research, but also their creativeness and an ability to apply a high degree of development of exact sciences that may be used by individuals or relatively small groups to utilize innovation and innovativeness. Hence it becomes of increasing importance for innovative use in family businesses on the market.
- The increasing complexity as well as costs and risk related with innovation are going to highlight the value of links and ties among entities reaching further than regular market relations – links between businesses and academic establishments, research laboratories, providers of counselling or technological services. Share of SMEs in cooperation with such entities is growing, though not sufficiently (PARP, 2007).
- A concept of demand-based approaches to innovation, oriented at creation of new ideas and solutions, becomes a significant method of implementing innovation. This is based on better reconnaissance into and understanding of demands, both hidden and manifested, of consumers' needs. Its implementation happens through creation of effective mechanisms of acquiring and using of information originating from consumers as well as – quite often – through taking advantage of their ideas or even ready solutions. Flexibility of the SME sector in this respect is more and more appreciated.
- Innovative activities of companies in the twenty-first century are not going to be exclusively oriented to profit maximization. Instead, they will also take into account human needs, variable over time. Small and medium-sized enterprises are best fitted to meet this kind of expectation. Therefore, one should expect a new dynamics in

development of areas in which the following factors will play important roles: green technologies, medical technologies, information technologies, biotechnologies and nanotechnology.

It seems that the awareness of such trends, if still insufficient, becomes more and more universal in Poland. Innovations become a real driving force of contemporary economy; a modernization-fostering factor that can stimulate economic efficiency, consolidates economic potential and through export, lays foundations for sustainable growth.

Considering the issue from the perspective of Polish experience, there is a problem of knowledge transfer from science to economy that warrants closer inquiry. This also includes the elements making up a so-called knowledge triangle (research & technology, education & innovation, links with business, including in the SME sector). There are reasons to argue that as technological progress becomes more and more dynamic, requirements asked of scientific centres concerning forms, types, ways and means of knowledge transfer from the world of science and technology and its implementation to business would increase accordingly. Obviously, it is really since their beginnings, centuries ago, that academic institutions have significantly contributed to economic progress. Today, expectations from them are greater than ever in the past. However, also on the part of those most interested in the transfer, that is, on the part of companies, a genuine demand is needed for innovative solutions – innovativeness and ideas to emerge from research circles. So far, this 'aspiration' of knowledge and new technologies by companies in Poland has been insufficient. On the other hand, it would be oversimplification and a mistake to underrate positive changes taking place in this respect. In many cases such positive changes occur thanks to European Union schemes and programmes promoting innovative projects, also – or perhaps quite largely – to the benefit of the SME sector.

IMPORTANCE OF FINANCIAL AND TAX POLICY TO SMEs

Absorption of funds by the SME sector from EU funds is not without its problems but is still an important factor alleviating another serious economic barrier to that sector operation. Depending on developments of business cycles, a number of sources from which capital is acquired increases or decreases and – from companies' point of view – the role played by less or (desirably!) more stable fiscal policy run by the state institutions becomes more important.

Research by the European Commission and carried out by Gallup among 15 000 small and medium-sized enterprises operating in the European Union territory, indicates that their most serious concerns are related to limited demand, but also with uncertain financial markets conditions, as a result of the global financial crisis (Gallup, 2008). This situation then tends to largely translate into the policies applied by banks, which – facing uncertain prospects and the troubled condition of European economies – restrict access to credit of which businesses are beneficiaries. One of the key barriers hindering the growth of either a small or a growing entrepreneur is the lack of capital for a start-up and then for necessary investments. This phenomenon becomes further aggravated over periods of turbulence in financial markets. We are yet to see whether we will have to deal with this aggravating phenomenon in Poland over the next couple of years. The present economic slowdown makes such a scenario seem quite likely. To acquire capital is probably going to become more difficult and expensive. We also have to reckon with the access to micro-loans, which is becoming more restricted, and is so important to entities from the SMEs sector.

As shown by the outcomes of studies carried out by TNS Pentor, one of the principal research agencies in the Polish market specialized in corporate research, the economic slowdown that affected Poland in the years 2008–09 as an echo of the global financial crisis, had negative impact upon relations between banks and corporate customers, especially SMEs. TNS Pentor (2011, p. 16) argues:

> [B]anks caused a great damage in this respect, by losing – sometimes just overnight – the trust and companies' confidence in being able to regulate their liabilities toward banks . . . In the effect of abrupt depreciation of Polish zloty some banks, especially those with prevailing foreign capital, started verification of credit contracts made, demanding additional collateral from their contractors and in certain cases rendering them immediately due and payable. At the same time, due to the lack of liquidity in the inter-banking market, credit activity all but stagnated. Credit became a good in deficit and companies seeking credit were experiencing tremendous difficulties. Banks' credit committees were extending the procedures, increasing means of security required, raising the prices of credit and so on. Credit availability was abruptly reduced with corresponding increase of a number of businesses refused credit by banks. The breakdown of trust in relations between banks and enterprises was seriously aggravated by the problem of the so-called foreign currencies options, that is, losses suffered by companies on derivatives securing foreign currencies exchange rates-related risk. Two thirds of businesses perceived that the financial crisis deteriorated their access to banking products and services while eight out of ten declared they faced raised prices of banking services and sharpened criteria in applying for credit. According to 60 per cent of entrepreneurs the principal reason behind tightened credit policy toward business circles was in banks' apprehension about solvency of their clients.

While the year 2013 was slightly better for the SMEs sector and the problem of its access to credit was, accordingly, less serious than during the recent slowdown of the years 2008–09, still any further deterioration of business outlooks may change the attitude revealed by banks in this respect. However, according to at least some part of the small business environment, at present banks seem to show some effort to better understand the specificity of SMEs and their needs, and, even more importantly, they also seem to better perceive an increasing potential in that sector than they did until quite recently.

Another aspect, just as important for the SME sector and crucial for some entities in it is that of tax policy. In particular over periods of worse economic conditions (Matejun and Kaczmarek, 2010), when narrowly treated, tax policy is only of a fiscal nature reduced to collection of taxes to maintain the stability of public finance. However, when perceived broadly and in the long run, it may actively support the state social and economic policy and favour the pursuit of its goals. This latter approach is vastly more advantageous to the SME sector. The Polish tax system is perceived by SMEs as complicated, abounding in vague and incomprehensive provisions and rather unstable. Additionally, they are irritated by an excessive number of legal acts applied therein – worse still, such regulations tend to become more and more extensive and, unnecessarily, increasingly detailed. Their ever-present weakness is too many references to other provisions, as is the lack of statutory definitions and the use of terms and notions having unequivocal or inconsistent meaning. Taxes on SMEs in Poland are at the level of the EU average and the OECD – see Figure 10.1; however, it should be noted that labour taxes are the largest part of the structure of the taxation regarding SMEs in Poland. Financial experts also point out that Poland needs the development of e-taxation and greater possibility of electronic contact with the tax office.

CONCLUSIONS

Some problems that make life difficult for the SME sector stem from poor company management. Research so far and a number of analyses indicate that one crucial factor hindering innovativeness and competitiveness of Polish businesses from that sector is their lack of properly skilled and competent staff. The problem is serious, considering how the research, carried out by Polish Agency for Enterprise Development, among others, concludes that in the processes of globalization we are witnessing competent and properly skilful personnel as having the potential of becoming a new and most effective source of competitive advantage. Therefore,

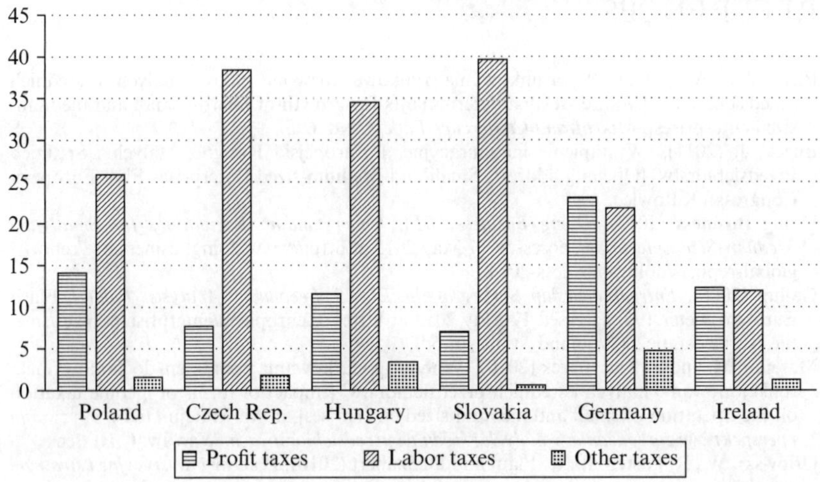

Source: Doing Business (2013).

Figure 10.1 Total tax rate, in %, selected countries

it seems very important and urgent to recognize the actual demand for trained human resources, in particular in sectors featuring the largest potential of innovation and innovativeness. Another development barrier lies in the mixed and rather reserved attitude of small businesses to external sources of finance. However, as underlined in the research conclusions, banks and financial institutions recently seem to better perceive the increasing potential in the SME sector (Wolański, 2013a).

Looking from the SMEs' perspective, this environment tends to emphasize that the process of delivering the Polish economy from the excess of legal regulation and bureaucracy should be accelerated and accompanied by the introduction of simple and transparent principles concerning business activity. From the point of view of the interests of Polish economy it is also necessary to foresee trends that are likely to happen in the global economy and its individual sectors and to develop, on that basis, potential development scenarios with small business adequately taken into account. Despite some weaknesses, the SME sector remains a significant opportunity for the Polish economy to raise its efficiency and to improve its competitiveness in Europe's single market.

REFERENCES

Bielawska, A. (2012), 'Uwarunkowania rynkowe rozwoju mikro, małych i średnich przedsiębiorstw' [Market-related determinants for growth of micro-, small and medium-sized enterprises], *Mikrafirma Conference Papers*, No. 695.

Buzek, J. (2011), 'Wystąpienie inauguracyjne, I Europejski Kongres Małych i Średnich Przedsiębiorstw' [Opening address, Small and Medium-sized Enterprises First European Congress), Katowice.

Doing Business (2013), *Doing Business 2014, Understanding Regulations for Small and Medium-Size Enterprises*, accessed 17 May 2015 at http://www.doingbusiness.org/reports/global-reports/doing-business-2014.

Gallup (2008), *Entrepreneurship Survey of the EU-25, Secondary Analysis: Poland*, Flash Eurobarometer 192, accessed 17 May 2015 at http://ec.europa.eu/enterprise/policies/sme/files/survey/static2008/poland_static_en.pdf.

Matejun, M. and E. Kaczmarek (2010), 'Wpływ opodatkowania podatkiem dochodowym na funkcjonowanie małych i średnich przedsiębiorstw' [Impact of forms of income taxation on the operation of small and medium-sized enterprises], in M. Matejun (ed.), *Wyzwania i perspektywy zarządzania w małych i średnich przedsiębiorstwach*, Warsaw: C.H. Beck.

Orłowski, W., R. Pasternak, K. Flaut and D. Szubert (2010), *Procesy inwestycyjne i strategie przedsiębiorstw w czasach kryzysu* [Investment Processes and Corporate Strategies at the Time of Crisis], Warsaw: PARP (Polish Agency for Enterprise Development).

PARP (Polish Agency for Enterprise Development) (2007), 'Cooperation between scientific entities and the economy', in *Innovative Economy Operational Programme, 2007–2013*, accessed 17 May 2015 at http://www.mg.gov.pl/NR/rdonlyres/88D2599D-B8CE-4279-922D-E906617A20AE/44401/POIG_po_negocjacjach_ENG_28_01_08.pdf.

PARP (Polish Agency for Enterprise Development) (2013), *15 Raport o stanie sektora małych i średnich przedsiębiorstw w Polsce* [15th Report on the Condition of Small and Medium-sized Enterprises Sector in Poland], Warsaw: PARP.

TNS Pentor (2011), *Investment Climate in Poland*, The report of the study by TNS Pentor, Warsaw, Poland: TNS Pentor.

Wach, K. (2012), *Europeizacja Małych I Średnich Przedsęibiorstw* [The Europeanization of Small and Medium-Sized Enterprises], accessed 17 May 2015 at http://www.wach.uek.krakow.pl/images_books/2012_europeizacja_MSP_spis_tresci.pdf.

Wilczarskim, T. and J. Żurek (2008), *Dobre praktyki z zakresu ochrony własności intelektualnej* [Good Practices for the Protection of Intellectual Property], accessed 17 May 2015 at http://www.wktir.pl/owi/dobre_praktyki.pdf.

Wolański, R. (2013a), *Wpływ otoczenia finansowego na konkurencyjność małych i średnich przedsiębiorstw* [The Impact of the Financial Environment on the Competitiveness of Small and Medium-sized Enterprises], Warsaw: Wolters Kluwer.

Wolański, R. (2013b), 'The capital structure of Polish small and medium-sized enterprises and its impact on their competitiveness', University of Warsaw, Faculty of Management Working Paper Series **1**(1), accessed 17 May 2015 at http://www.wz.uw.edu.pl/portaleFiles/5630-Faculty%20of%20M/WP/FMWPS1May2013Wolanski.pdf.

PART II

INTERNATIONALIZATION OF SMEs AND SELECTED STATE SUPPORT

11. Internationalization of European SMEs

Irene Mandl and Funda Celikel Esser

INTRODUCTION

Small and medium-sized enterprises (SMEs), that is, companies with fewer than 250 employees and a turnover of up to EUR50 million or a balance sheet total of up to EUR43 million (European Commission, 2003), are the backbone of the European economy. The more than 20 million SMEs represent more than 99 per cent of businesses, about two-thirds of private sector employment and about half of the total value added created by businesses. Consequently, European SMEs are considered as a key driver for economic growth, innovation and social integration.[1]

Against this considerable importance of SMEs for the European economy and in an economic situation in which the member states of the European Union are seeking recovery from the most severe downturn since World War II, fostering SMEs' growth gains attention on the policy agendas at European and national levels. Internationalization, both within Europe and beyond, is widely recognized as a potential pathway to recovery (European Commission, 2011, 2012) while at the same time there is some evidence that comparatively few SMEs engage in international activities, particularly beyond the EU (Wymenga et al., 2013). In the period 2006–08, about 30 per cent of European SMEs were importers (14 per cent beyond the internal market), 26 per cent exporters (13 per cent beyond the internal market), less than one in ten had technical cooperations or international subcontracting relationships and only 2 per cent have conducted foreign direct investment (FDI) (Figure 11.1; EIM Business and Policy Research, 2010).

In general, internationalization activity increases with company size. While, for example, less than one-quarter of microenterprises (fewer than ten employees and a turnover or a balance sheet total of up to EUR2 million) have been found to be exporters and 2 per cent to have realized investments abroad, the shares are as high as 53 per cent and 16 per cent respectively for medium-sized firms (49–249 employees and a turnover of up to EUR50 million or a balance sheet total of up to EUR43 million). However, there are some country differences. For example, in Slovakia the share of small firms (10–49 employees and a turnover or balance sheet total of up to EUR10 million) among exports is higher than that for

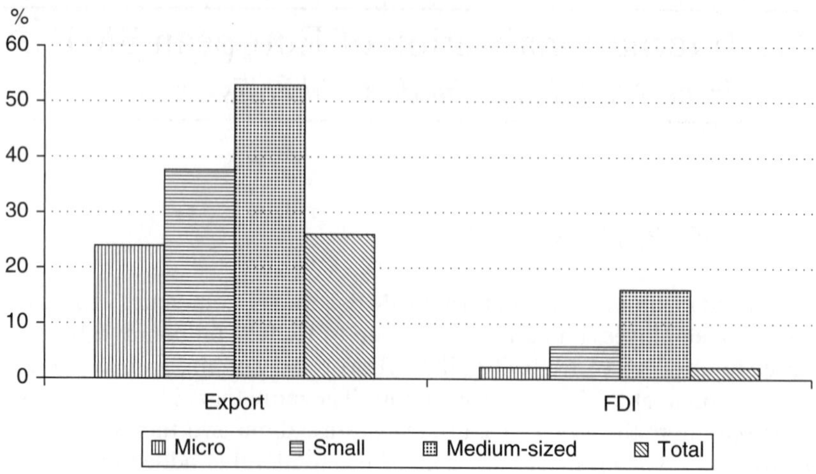

Source: EIM Business and Policy Research (2010).

Figure 11.1 European SMEs with exports and foreign direct investment (both within and beyond Europe), 2006–08, by size

medium-sized companies, and in Austria, Denmark, Finland, France and Romania the share of microenterprises among exports exceeds that for small firms (OECD, 2011).

European SMEs are particularly little engaged in offshoring and delocalization activities. Fragmented national data show that the share of SMEs' offshoring or planning to offshore tasks ranges below 10 per cent.

Nevertheless, an increasing offshoring tendency is observed, not least driven by the need to reduce costs to maintain and increase competitiveness in the aftermath of the global financial and economic crisis (Eurofound, 2013a). Similarly, several European governments are increasingly engaging in supporting SMEs' internationalization, which was also highlighted as one of the priority areas of Europe's Small Business Act (SBA), aiming at improving the business environment for SMEs and the related SME policy. Accordingly, it is worth investigating the main characteristics of the internationalization of European SMEs, including the drivers and barriers for such, the outcomes of SMEs' internationalization and the currently available public support to assist SMEs in their cross-border activities in order to derive some policy pointers for improvement potentials.

BOX 11.1 COST OPTIMIZATION AS DRIVER FOR SMEs' INTERNATIONALIZATION

The Czech textile company H&D a.s. offshored production to China as the increasing labour costs in the Czech Republic made the firm less competitive. Management assumed that the global competition in the industry will further increase due to the establishment of vertical production chains and the weaker negotiation power of SMEs towards suppliers. Hence, internationalization was initiated as a means to optimize costs.

Source: Eurofound's database on restructuring in SMEs case studies: http://www.eurofound.europa.eu/observatories/erm/restructuring-in-smes/hd-czech-republic; accessed 17 May 2015.

CHARACTERISTICS OF INTERNATIONALIZATION ACTIVITIES OF EUROPEAN SMEs

Drivers of SMEs' Internationalization

European SMEs' internationalization activities are strongly driven by the entrepreneur's personality and intrinsic motivation to further develop the business (Eurofound, 2013a). Next to this pull factor, general globalization trends, public policies and the macroeconomic situation and technological progress are relevant push factors. KPMG (2007), for example, found that tax optimization and lower administrative costs abroad are major drivers for internationalization of SMEs (see Box 11.1, for example) and in Estonia it was observed that government policy specifically targeting export-oriented enterprises caused restructuring in many SMEs to benefit from government support (Eurofound, 2013a). Sakai (2002) pinpoints that the increasing level of outsourcing of large multinational companies opens up (international) business opportunities for SMEs as first- and second-tier suppliers while at the same time increasing competition in the domestic market. This, in turn, might trigger outsourcing in SMEs to focus on specific core competencies and become internationally competitive niche players.

Patterns of SMEs' Internationalization

Internationalization modes

Internationalization of European SMEs generally follows a 'waterfall strategy', cascading from one country to the next, starting with geographically and culturally closer markets to more distant ones and from

BOX 11.2 FOREIGN DIRECT INVESTMENT AS SMEs' INTERNATIONALIZATION STRATEGY

The Slovenian medium-sized retail company Blažič acquired its German supplier firm as it was interested in insourcing production. Buying the company that already had the required technology and know-how was considered to be the better alternative to investing in technology development itself.

Source: Eurofound's database on restructuring in SMEs case studies: http://www.eurofound.europa.eu/observatories/erm/restructuring-in-smes/blai-robni-trakovi-slovenia; accessed 17 May 2015.

more advanced to less developed economies (Eurofound, 2013a). EIM Business and Policy Research (2010) finds that for exporting SMEs, other European Union countries are the most important target markets (76 per cent), followed by other European countries (27 per cent), North America (17 per cent), Middle East and North Africa (14 per cent each).

Furthermore, it often takes place in consecutive stages from export to more integrated modes like foreign direct investment (Box 11.2) or joint ventures. Italian and Estonian data, for example, clearly indicate a dominance of SME exports over international outsourcing or the establishment of own commercial or productive units abroad (Corò and Gurisatti, 2011; Ministry of Economic Affairs and Communication, 2011). Nevertheless, across Europe there are numerous examples of SMEs engaging more intensively at international level than 'just exporting'.

The first exports are often rather random and unplanned while internationalization activities going beyond exports tend to be accompanied by market research on the legal framework, demand, competitive situation, availability of raw materials and suppliers and the search for local cooperation partners and expert staff (Eurofound, 2013a). This can be considered as a comparatively advanced managerial behaviour against the finding that SMEs in general tend to be weak in anticipating and planning restructuring, even with regard to events that could be well prepared for in advance (like, for example, business transfers and successions for age reasons) (ibid.). The better preparation of such higher-level internationalization modes can be attributed to the anticipated high costs involved if the move abroad fails (Box 11.3).

Regarding activities that are offshored by European SMEs, no coherent picture can be given. While it is found for the Netherlands, for example, that SMEs offshore product development, Czech, Greek or Italian SMEs rather offshore labour-intensive (manufacturing) activities, and Danish as well as Irish SMEs are observed to particularly source distribution, sales/

BOX 11.3 PREPARATION FOR INTERNATIONALIZATION

In striving to realize his vision to expand to China, the owner of the Danish Sjølund company, which specializes in aluminium and steel section bending and employs about 65 workers (and now 45 in China), established a business plan for internationalization. As a first step, the company hired a Chinese engineer working at that time in Denmark and familiarized him for three months with the company strategies, culture and working procedures at headquarters. In the meantime, the company management visited various potential sites in China and contacted potential customers. After they had found a suitable location and recruited local staff, they sent a Danish blacksmith to China for three months to train the Chinese workforce.

Source: Eurofound's database on restructuring in SMEs case studies: http://www.eurofound.europa.eu/observatories/erm/restructuring-in-smes/sjlund-denmark; accessed 17 May 2015.

marketing and engineering internationally (Karagianni and Labrianidis, 2001; Giusti, 2007; RSM Erasmus University, 2007).

Networks and born globals

Many SMEs engage in networks to share knowledge and resources with partners to overcome their inherent size constraints, and these networks are quite extensive, based on trust, and hence need time to be established (De Magalhaes, 2001; Onkelinx and Sleuwaegen, 2008; Istituto Guglielmo Tagliacarne, 2011; Kontinen, 2011).

Networks seem to be particularly important for SMEs not following the above-described traditional internationalization strategies, but intensively engaging in global markets (that is, also beyond the EU) already briefly after inception, without first developing a stable domestic market. Such 'born global enterprises' constitute about one-fifth of all young enterprises (entrepreneurs trying to start a business or who have done so within the last three-and-a-half years) in Europe, albeit with considerable differences across countries (Eurofound, 2012): while in Romania, Belgium and Denmark born globals represent between 40–50 per cent of young enterprises, the share is as low as 7 per cent in Hungary (Figure 11.2).

Born globals tend to be innovative, and not only with regard to their products/services, but also with regard to their market penetration strategy. While born globals are observed to use any of the stages identified for 'traditional internationalization' (occasional exports; exports via independent representatives; sales subsidiaries; foreign direct investment) they are widely assumed to search for less resource-intensive entry modes (Pock and Hinterhuber, 2011). The reason for this is that they aim at quickly establishing a foothold in multiple international markets while at the same

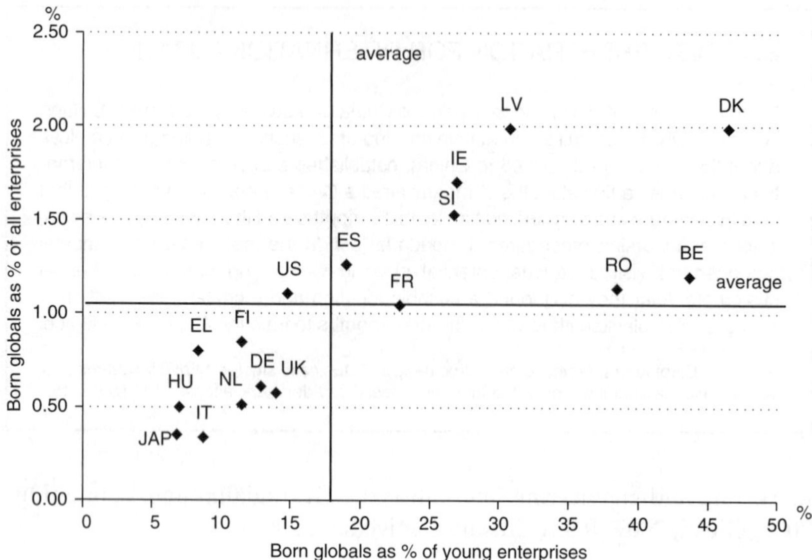

Source: Global Entrepreneurship Monitor, own calculations and presentation.

Figure 11.2 Born globals as share of young and all enterprises, selected EU member states, USA and Japan, 2008

BOX 11.4 COLLABORATION AS ENTRY MODE INTO FOREIGN MARKETS

InterNations GmbH, a German born global, provides a platform for people living and working abroad. Its aim is to facilitate business and leisure networking. Hundreds of 'ambassadors' are active on a voluntary basis in more than 300 cities around the world. They represent the organization and execute marketing activities in their local community, organize events, collect the money raised from these events and liaise with the German headquarters. As of 2014, the network unites about 1 million expats and 'global minds'.

Sources: www.internations.org; Eurofound (2012).

time being characterized by resource constraints due to their small size. Consequently, anecdotal evidence also highlights alternative collaborative governance structures like licensing, franchising or even volunteering as market entry modes (Box 11.4; Leonidou and Samiee, 2012; Söderqvist and Chetty, 2013).

No clear indication can be found regarding the field of activity of born global enterprises. While several publications highlight them as being active in high-technology sectors, others show that born globals can also be found in traditional manufacturing and service sectors (Eurofound, 2012).

EFFECTS OF INTERNATIONALIZATION ACTIVITIES ON EUROPEAN SMEs

Economic Performance

As an introductory note it needs to be mentioned that data showing the performance of international SMEs in Europe are scarce. There is no systematic and regular monitoring tool, so available evidence is based on individual studies. In general, these indicate that European SME exporters have higher levels of productivity and competitiveness than non-exporters (Jakobsen and de Voss, 2003; Burger et al., 2008; Onkelinx and Sleuwaegen, 2008; BIS, 2010; EIM Business and Policy Research, 2010; Istituto Guglielmo Tagliacarne, 2011). Italian data, for example, show that 52 per cent of SMEs that delocalized or increased their foreign activities benefited from an increased turnover, to be attributed to increased demand (66 per cent), improved quality or product range (31 per cent), access to new markets (25 per cent), more competitive prices (20 per cent) and investments (14 per cent) (Istituto Guglielmo Tagliacarne, 2011). In line with this, anecdotal evidence also hints towards internationalization as a sound pathway for some European SMEs to cope with the effects of the global economic and financial crisis, as working abroad could help them lower production costs and attract new/additional customers, and hence retain competitiveness, when confronted with a depressed home market (Box 11.5).

Data for French born globals highlight that these young international businesses on average are more profitable than other young firms and are characterized by better financial sustainability (Eurofound, 2012): some 48 per cent of the French born globals achieve a profit margin of at least 5 per cent, while this amounts to 44 per cent of young enterprises in general. This better performance is attributed to their 'pioneer character' in terms of being superior to competitors with regard to the products and services they offer. The available data also show that about two-thirds of French born globals can be considered to be 'financially healthy' (and consequently financially sustainable), compared to 52 per cent of young enterprises in general. Similarly, the share of 'financially risky' French

BOX 11.5 INTERNATIONALIZATION IMPROVES SMEs' ECONOMIC PERFORMANCE

The Greek small construction company Aktis S.A. decided to set up a joint venture with a Romanian partner during the recession. This resulted in the retention of all jobs in Greece and the creation of ten jobs in Romania in spite of the difficult economic situation. The internationalization improved the firm's financial performance: the company management indicates that about 50 per cent of the turnover during 2011 was produced on the Romanian market and a 30 per cent reduction in total operating costs could be achieved. They are convinced that the company would not have been able to survive in the recession if it had not been for the internationalization of the production process to Romania.

Source: Eurofound's database on restructuring in SMEs case studies: http://www.eurofound.europa.eu/observatories/erm/restructuring-in-smes/aktis-greece; accessed 17 May 2015.

born globals is about 5–6 percentage points lower than for young enterprises in general.

Furthermore, and not least the above-mentioned importance of business networks for born globals' activities; valuable knock-on effects on other businesses are assumed. The global networks are considered to facilitate international and national knowledge transfer and skills development and to contribute to the development of clusters of high value-added activities. Also, the higher level of profitability of born globals results in a higher level of tax revenues. At the same time it needs to be mentioned that little is known about born globals' capacity to survive economic shocks and there are some pointers towards them being hit harder due to their strong dependency on external capital (Eurofound, 2012; Sleuwaegen and Onkelinx, 2014).

Innovation

While some authors advocate the perspective that international companies are per se more innovative than domestically oriented firms as the pure act of going international is an innovation in itself, there is also some data available to show European SMEs' innovation capacity regarding new product, service or process development.

International SMEs in Europe have been found to be more innovative than their domestically oriented counterparts. EIM Business and Policy Research (2010) highlight that almost half of the internationally active SMEs introduced new products or services in the past three years (compared to about one-third of enterprises on average), and about one-third

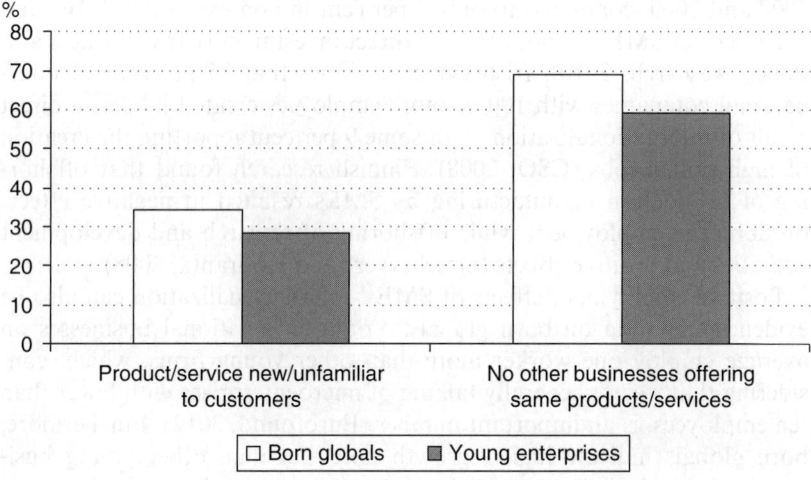

Source: Global Entrepreneurship Monitor, own calculations and presentation.

Figure 11.3 Share of born global and young enterprises indicating innovation, selected EU member states, USA and Japan, 2008

had process innovations (compared to about 22 per cent on average). Similarly, Eurofound (2012) finds that 34 per cent of born globals indicate that all or some of their potential customers consider their products or services as new and unfamiliar (compared to 28 per cent on average) and 69 per cent assume that there are no other businesses offering the same product or service to their potential customers (compared to 59 per cent on average) (Figure 11.3). Nevertheless, it is not known whether the higher innovation level fosters internationalization or vice versa (Lamotte and Colovic, 2013).

Furthermore, born globals are highlighted as providing benchmark orientations and strategies for other firms, including well-established large multinationals (Vapola et al, 2008; Vapola, 2012) that can learn from born globals about new technological and market opportunities, which eventually leads to enhanced innovation performance also in these related firms.

Employment

Regarding employment effects, it was found that on average exporting European SMEs and SMEs with foreign direct investment experienced an employment growth of 7 per cent and 16 per cent, respectively, between

2007 and 2009, compared to only 3 per cent in non-exporting SMEs and 4 per cent in SMEs without foreign direct investment (EIM Business and Policy Research, 2010). Irish evidence shows that 15 per cent of international companies with 100 or more employees created jobs as a direct result of internationalization, with some 9 per cent reporting the creation of high-skilled jobs (CSO, 2008). Finnish research found that offshoring of production manufacturing by SMEs resulted in negative effects on domestic employment while offshoring of research and development activities had positive effects (Deschryvere and Kotiranta, 2008).

Positive employment effects of SMEs' internationalization can also be evidenced by data on born globals. Young international businesses on average employ one worker more than other young firms, which, considering that we are generally talking of microenterprises with fewer than ten employees, is an important number (Eurofound, 2012). Furthermore, born globals indicate higher growth potential than other young businesses when asked about their planned number of employees in the future (Figure 11.4).

Similar to the economic effects, regarding employment effects it is not

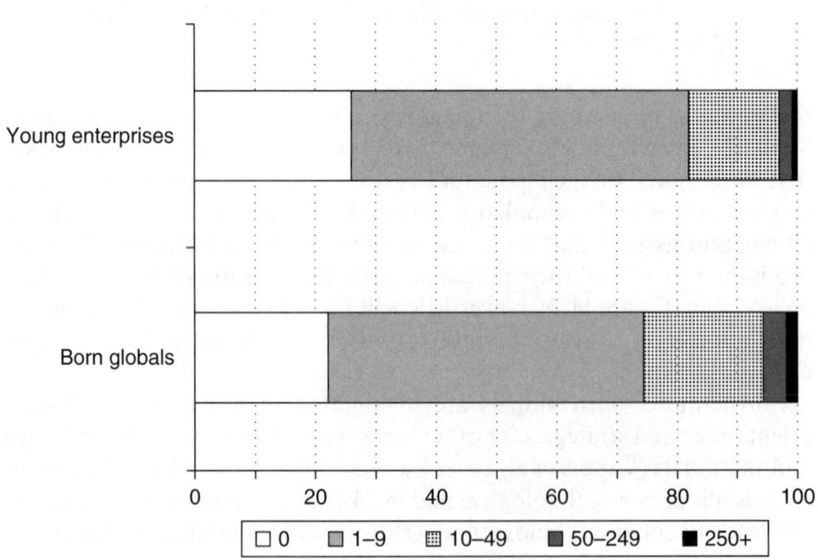

Source: Global Entrepreneurship Monitor, own calculations and presentations.

Figure 11.4 Share of born globals and young enterprises by planned number of employees in five years, selected EU member states, USA and Japan, 2008

only direct outcomes that should be considered. Dynamically growing international SMEs might have important knock-on effects on other businesses, both in their home market and abroad. This is to be attributed to network and supply chain effects, where other firms benefit from the good development of the international SME in terms of receiving outsourced orders, getting access to new markets/clients or being involved in joint distribution activities. Consequently, domestic firms might also create jobs as a result of SMEs' international activities.

PUBLIC SUPPORT FOR INTERNATIONALIZATION OF SMEs

The Need

Supporting SMEs' internationalization is in the public interest as available evidence shows that exporting SMEs show higher turnover and employment growth and are more innovative than domestically oriented businesses (European Commission, 2007; EIM Business and Policy Research, 2010; Wymenga et al., 2013). However, there exists a range of barriers hindering European SMEs in becoming (more) internationally active, which, interestingly, is perceived to be more severe by those SMEs just planning or thinking about going international than by those already active at international level (European Commission, 2007; EIM Business and Policy Research, 2010). Some of these barriers are strongly related to the specific characteristics of SMEs (particularly the limited resources) and the business model or the entrepreneur and staff:

- high costs of internationalization;
- quality and price as well as specifications of the products and services offered;
- lack of qualified personnel and language skills (Box 11.6);
- lack of managerial time to realize the internationalization activities;
- difficulties in identifying foreign business opportunities and/or locating potential target markets;
- difficulties in identifying and approaching foreign customers and business partners.

Next to those internal barriers, European SMEs report encountering challenges related to the business environment, the institutional framework and the 'foreignness' inherent in international activities (Box 11.7):

BOX 11.6 SUPPORT NEEDS IN SMEs' INTERNATIONALIZATION

A medium-sized Dutch manufacturing company selling its products throughout Europe, with the main markets being Spain, Belgium, Germany, France and Austria, highlights that when opening an office abroad, the most important aspect is local knowledge. It was not a big problem when expanding to Belgium because the legislation there was not very dissimilar from the Netherlands, and language was also less of an issue. However, when setting up a small industrial location in Spain, it realized the importance of working with someone knowing about the work mentality in Spain while at the same time involving someone from the home-based core team in the new subsidiary to ensure that the foreign plant follows the strategies and working methods of the headquarters.

Source: Eurofound's database on restructuring in SMEs case studies: http://www.eurofound.europa.eu/observatories/erm/restructuring-in-smes/manufacturing-company-the-netherlands; accessed 17 May 2015.

BOX 11.7 CHALLENGES IN SMEs' INTERNATIONALIZATION

The export manager of the Latvian manufacturing SME PAA Baths pinpoints that for them the most challenging issue about doing business abroad was uncertainty and, as a consequence, highlights the relevance of planning. However, he mentions that internationalization plans might need to be adjusted due to changing market conditions, including changes in supply and demand, price fluctuations, the political situation at home and abroad, inflation and the activities of the government.

Source: Eurofound's database on restructuring in SMEs case studies: http://www.eurofound.europa.eu/observatories/erm/restructuring-in-smes/paa-baths-latvia; accessed 17 May 2015.

- lack of capital;
- lack of adequate public support;
- lack of adequate information;
- costs or bureaucracy related to transport and foreign legislation as well as tariffs;
- cultural differences.

The Supply

Being aware of such barriers, public support of SMEs' internationalization has a longstanding tradition in Europe. The first Internationalization Agency was founded in Finland in 1919 (European Commission, 2007),

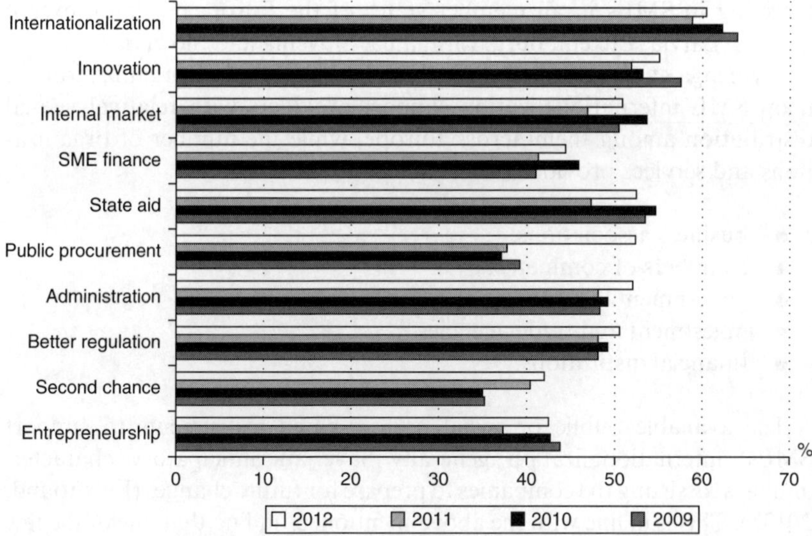

Note: Ideally, all values should reach 100 per cent.

Source: UEAPME (2012).

Figure 11.5 European Small Business Act Scoreboard, 2009–12

and nowadays across Europe there exists a comparatively wide range of public or social partner-based support for internationalization, also explicitly addressing SMEs. At European level, the 'Europe 2020'[2] strategy aiming at achieving smart, sustainable and inclusive growth, explicitly pinpoints internationalization as a priority of the European Commission. In 2008, the Small Business Act (SBA) was approved, aiming at a general improvement of SMEs' business environment through a general commitment to a 'Think Small First' principle in policy-making and ten priority areas for an improved SME policy. One of these areas refers to internationalization. In its SBA Scoreboard, UEAPME (2012) (Figure 11.5) analyses whether national measures have been taken in the areas defined by the SBA and what impact these have had on SMEs. It finds that initiatives related to SME internationalization rank highest among all priority areas, but in 2012 shows the lowest improvement compared to other fields.

In line with the comparatively high level of available SME internationalization support as shown by the SBA Scoreboard, Eurofound (2013b) finds public or social partner-based internationalization support explicitly targeting in SMEs in all member states of the European Union except Cyprus, Latvia, Luxembourg, Lithuania, Slovenia and Slovakia.

Wymenga et al. (2013) identify the following types of organizations as main SME internationalization support providers with relatively equal distribution among them across Europe, while the number of organizations and services provided differs across countries:

- business associations;
- chambers of commerce;
- governmental organizations;
- investment and trade agencies;
- financial institutions.

The available public or social partner-based instruments to support SMEs' internationalization generally have an anticipatory character, aiming at assisting the companies to prepare for future changes (Eurofound, 2013b). This is in line with the above-mentioned finding that one of the few restructuring forms in which SMEs intensively engage in anticipation, preparation and planning is internationalization going beyond exports. In spite of that, about half of the available SME internationalization support instruments in Europe seem to target exporting, followed by technical cooperation and becoming a subcontractor (about one-quarter and one-fifth of the instruments) and setting up a subcontract, FDI and importing (around 15 per cent each) (Wymenga, 2013; note that several instruments targeted various internationalization forms, consequently the sum totals more than 100 per cent). About two-thirds of the analysed instruments are available to all SMEs, without size class differentiation in the offered services. This entails the risk that the programmes do not pay sufficient attention to the specific needs of the smaller enterprises (Wymenga et al., 2013).

Regarding the content of provided support, the types of support instruments explicitly or implicitly targeting SMEs could be identified (Table 11.1).

The necessity of awareness raising and providing SMEs with information not only about the opportunities internationalization offers, but also about the existing public support instruments becomes obvious when looking at the comparatively low shares of international SMEs in Europe. Respective instruments highlight the benefits of internationalization for individual companies and the national/regional economy to attract (more) SMEs to go global and take advantage of the inherent potentials. Such measures do not necessarily target already existing entrepreneurs, but could also focus on students or pupils still in education to trigger an early understanding of cross-border business activities. Some of the available

Table 11.1 Types of public and social partner-based internationalization support for SMEs

Type of Support	Description	Example
Awareness raising	Advocating higher levels of internationalization through highlighting the benefits of internationalization, but also promoting the available support programmes	Internationalisierungs-offensive, AT[a]
Access to finance	Subsidies, loans, guarantees, liaising with potential investors	Business Expansion Grant, IE[b] Confidi, IT[c]
Advice and consultancy	Provision of information on target markets and internationalization strategies, feedback to/evaluation of internationalization plans, coaching/accompanying foreign market entry	BornGlobal, DK[d]
Networking assistance	Support in identifying and approaching potential business partners (incl. suppliers and clients) and investors abroad	Finpro, FI[e]
Qualification	Education and training of management and staff related to internationalization, theoretical and practical familiarization with internationalization	Erasmus for Young Entrepreneurs, EU-wide[f] Go:Global Slovenia, SI[g]
Comprehensive international business incubators	Provision of premises, shared back-office services, education and training opportunities, networking with peers, potential investors, suppliers and clients, information about (financial) support programmes	Go Silicon Valley, AT[h]
One-stop shops for internationalization support	Platforms providing an overview of available support instruments relevant for internationalization	Ventanilla Única Empresarial, ES[i]

Table 11.1 (continued)

Type of Support	Description	Example
Instruments combining several of the above, and also providers from several countries		Econet, AT/CZ/SK[j] 1, 2, 3 GO, BE/DE/FR/LU[k]

Notes:
a. See http://www.bmwfw.gv.at/Aussenwirtschaft/internationalisierungsoffensive/Seiten/default.aspx.
b. See https://www.localenterprise.ie/Discover-Business-Supports/Financial-Supports/Business-Expansion-Grant/.
c. See http://www.confidiprovincelombarde.it.
d. See http://usa.um.dk/en/the-trade-council/the-trade-council-offers1/get-off-to-a-good-start/export-preparation/bornglobal.
e. See http://www.finpro.fi/web/english-pages/export-partner-groups/guide-to-export-partner-groups.
f. See http://www.erasmus-entrepreneurs.eu/.
g. See http://www.goglobal.si/.
h. See http://www.ots.at/presseaussendung/OTS_20131029_OTS0051/go-silicon-valley-201314-last-minute-call.
i. See http://www.ventanillaempresarial.org/.
j. See http://www.econet-platform.at/.
k. See http://www.123go-networking.org/.
All accessed 18 May 2015.

Sources: European Commission, 2007; Eurofound, 2012; Eurofound, 2013b; ERM database on restructuring support instruments: http://www.eurofound.europa.eu/observatories/emcc/erm/support-instruments; accessed 18 May 2015.

awareness-raising instruments also focus on increasing firms' knowledge about the provided internationalization support. This seems to be important, bearing in mind the comparatively wide variety of support and the respective lack of transparency for SMEs: survey findings show that only 15 per cent of microenterprises, 20 per cent of small firms and 27 per cent of medium-sized enterprises know about public support instruments that could be used for internationalization (EIM Business and Policy Research, 2010). In line with this, some European countries have established one-stop shops for internationalization. These platforms offer general theoretic information on internationalization, practical information on target markets as well as an overview of available support instruments. In many cases these platforms are not supposed to provide very detailed and comprehensive information, but rather a first entry point that then refers the interested SME further on to more specific information or experts who could give individualized consultancy.

Access to finance is a general challenge for SMEs and as shown above is also perceived as an important barrier to internationalization. This holds particularly true for born globals who are deemed to have a higher monetary demand (as they are starting up, innovating and internationalizing at the same time), but lower levels of own resources (due to their young age and hence limited opportunities to reinvest already realized profits) and more limited access to external finance (as due to their 'newness' and innovative and dynamic business model they are often perceived as a more risky investment). Financial support for internationalization can take the forms of loans or subsidies as well as export or foreign direct investment guarantees limiting the SMEs' financial risks. Another pathway of support in this context refers to attracting investors or mediating between the SME and potential financial sources (also see networking support below).

Another important internationalization barrier identified above refers to SMEs' lack of information. Consequently, advice and consultancy constitutes an important field of external support. Governmental authorities, chambers of commerce and business organizations as well as specialized internationalization agencies across Europe offer a wide range of general information on internationalization modes and pathways, including recommendations regarding processes and procedures. Furthermore, they provide specific information about individual target markets regarding legal, administrative and institutional frameworks and requirements and economic development and market situations, potential clients, suppliers, business partners and competitors. Furthermore, some instruments follow a very individualistic approach in terms of checking a particular firm's readiness for internationalization, assessing a specific internationalization plan or accompanying the process of going global.

This is often combined with assistance in finding suitable local partners abroad, be it potential investors, clients, suppliers or other types of cooperation partners. As shown above, such international networking is deemed important for SMEs as due to their limited financial and human resources they have more difficulties in establishing international business relationships than larger firms. Particularly, born globals who have been found to strongly rely on international networks in their rapid and intensive internationalization activities could benefit from this form of support.

Several of the identified barriers hindering SMEs' internationalization are related to qualification deficiencies. Management might lack competencies to strategically plan and prepare the internationalization project, and staff might lack skills to implement them. This refers on the one hand to 'hard skills' like management or language competences, and on the other hand to 'soft skills' related to doing business in a multicultural environment. Across Europe, several support instruments can be found supporting SMEs in improving the skills and competences of both management and staff for their internationalization. This ranges from short seminars to long-term courses. Also, and similar to the above-described awareness-raising measures, such initiatives are not exclusively focused on company management and staff, but also schools and universities increasingly offer an international orientation in their curricula. Furthermore, the provision of qualification is not limited to theoretical knowledge. A range of support instruments available across Europe offer practical/operational internationalization qualifications in terms of offering current or future entrepreneurs or management staff the opportunity of gaining hands-on experience in international exchange or internship programmes.

Finally, a rather innovative and recent approach in internationalization support refers to the establishment of international business incubators. In many cases linked to chambers of commerce or business organizations, these not only offer cheap premises and back office services to SMEs (often targeting young enterprises), but several of the above-mentioned other support types. Formal advice and qualification instruments assist the firms in their preparation for internationalization, and the incubator facilitates networking with peers on the premises as well as with business partners and investors abroad. Such an environment also offers the opportunity to test international business ideas and in a few examples they also facilitate access to financial support programmes as having been accepted into such an incubator is considered as a 'quality criterion' by the financial support providers.

The Demand

EIM Business and Policy Research (2010) finds considerable differences regarding SMEs' use of public support in internationalization. While, for example, only 1 per cent of Dutch SMEs avail themselves of financial support, the share is as high as 47 per cent in Austria. In general, however, there is a negative relationship between firm size and use of public internationalization support, and private consultants are much more often approached than public instruments. This might be explained by the following aspects (Eurofound, 2013a):

- Due to their more limited resources and lack of experience, SMEs have difficulties identifying measures suitable for their specific needs among the wide variety of available support instruments.
- Applications are often administratively burdensome, and it might take a long time until operational support is provided. This is often

not feasible for SMEs as they tend to lack resources to bridge the periods until public support becomes operationally available.

- SMEs have doubts about whether the advice would be tailored enough to their needs or whether it could cover more complex and specific issues, as the available support in many cases covers 'SMEs as such' with little consideration of the heterogeneity among the SME population and the resulting individual support needs.

CONCLUSIONS AND POLICY RECOMMENDATIONS

European SMEs are not very active in engaging in internationalization. Bearing in mind that available data pinpoint that international SMEs show a high level of contribution to the economy and the labour market, this can be seen as unused potential that could be better exploited. Public and social partner-based support is needed to enhance and improve SMEs' internationalization activities. That such public investment realizes satisfactory returns on investment is, for example, shown by the finding that government support of SME internationalization produces a high level of additionality; that is, a significant number of SMEs would not have internationalized without public support (European Commission, 2007).

To counteract SMEs' reluctance to go global, several policy recommendations can be derived. First of all, to better promote a global mindset of (future) entrepreneurs and raise awareness about the business and economic potential inherent to internationalization, the internationalization aspect could be given a stronger emphasis in entrepreneurship training, be it at school or university level or in training addressed to practitioners (Mettler and Williams, 2011). This refers to enhancing theoretical knowledge (for example, about internationalization strategies, intercultural management, languages), but probably even more important would be the provision of opportunities to gain first-hand international experiences and build up international networks early on, for example through international internships (Mascherpa, 2012).

Second, due to their more limited resources, SMEs tend to have more difficulties in acquiring the relevant information needed for proper internationalization decisions. Hence, more tailor-made support in terms of offering information about the economic, legal and institutional setting in various target markets (understood as country–client–product combinations) seems to be necessary, as is the opportunity of having the internationalization idea and plan reviewed by experts before investing in the endeavour. Similarly, assistance in identifying and approaching potential business partners (suppliers and clients) and investors abroad is deemed important as SMEs often depend on local partners in their internationalization.

As internationalization should be considered as a process rather than an event, one-off support at the start of international activities might not be sufficient for SMEs. Experts accompanying SMEs' internationalization in the form of continuous monitoring, coaching and the provision of advice when needed could prevent SMEs from making mistakes in the decisive phases of internationalization. Another solution to this challenge could be facilitating SMEs' access to staff availing them of specialist knowledge in the field of internationalization and/or the target market. This could be realized by offering employment incentives for international recruitment. Examples are tax or social security reductions for hiring research and development staff or managers from abroad.

The available research also shows that born globals, that is, enterprises that intensively engage in international business briefly after inception, hardly receive any policy attention across Europe. Bearing in mind that they are not a small phenomenon and show some potential to contribute to job creation and economic recovery, raising awareness of the existence of such businesses, their specific characteristics and support needs seems to be necessary. One particularity of born globals is that they are innovating, starting up and internationalizing more or less at the same time, resulting in a comprehensive challenge. While there is a multitude of start-up, innovation and internationalization support available across Europe, instruments combining these three elements are rare but would be essential for born globals in order to reduce administrative burden and enable them to go global quickly. Such could be realized, for example, through the establishment of comprehensive business incubators, offering born globals not only a 'company hotel', but also educational, networking and financial support.

Finally, it should be pinpointed that more differentiation in SMEs' internationalization support would be recommended. The SME population is very heterogeneous, as are their potential internationalization pathways. This results in a variety of support needs that should be more specifically addressed rather than offering 'one size fits all' solutions. For such, also more information about the characteristics of international SMEs, their internationalization strategies and modes and the challenges they encounter when doing business globally would be required as a basis for sound policy-making.

NOTES

1. See http://ec.europa.eu/enterprise/policies/sme/index_en.htm and http://ec.europa.eu/enterprise/policies/sme/facts-figures-analysis/index_en.htm; accessed 18 May 2015.
2. See http://ec.europa.eu/europe2020/index_en.htm; accessed 18 May 2015.

REFERENCES

BIS (2010), 'Internationalisation of innovative and high growth SMEs', *BIS Economics Paper No. 5*, London: Department for Business, Innovation and Skills.

Burger, A., A. Jaklič and M. Rojec (2008), 'Exporting and company performance in Slovenia: self selection and/or learning by exporting?', *Ekonomicky časopis*, **56**(2), 131–53.

Corò, G. and P. Gurisatti (2011), 'Piccolo è ancora bello? Il ritratto die PMI in Confindustria' [Small is beautiful? A portrait of SMEs in the General Confederation of Italian Industry], *Costruire il Futuro PMI Protagoniste: Sfide e Strategie*, Rome: Confindustria Piccola Industria, Servizio Italiano Pubbblicazioni Internazionali.

CSO (Central Statistics Office) (2008), 'International sourcing: moving Irish business activity abroad', press release, Dublin: CSO.

De Magalhaes, C.S. (2001), 'International property consultants and the transformation of local markets', *Journal of Property Research*, **18**(2), 99–121 [online], accessed 17 May 2015 at http://www.tandfonline.com/doi/abs/10.1080/09599910110014156.

Deschryvere, M. and A. Kotiranta (2008), 'Domestic employment effects of offshoring: empirical evidence from Finland', *Discussion Papers No. 1166*, Helsinki: Elinkeinoelaman tutkimuslaitos.

EIM Business and Policy Research (2010), *Internationalisation of European SMEs*, Zoetermeer/Brussels: European Commission, Directorate-General for Enterprise and Industry.

Eurofound (2012), *Born Global: The Potential of Job Creation in New International Businesses*, Luxembourg: Publications Office of the European Union, accessed 17 May 2015 at http://eurofound.europa.eu/sites/default/files/ef_publication/field_ef_document/ef1265en.pdf.

Eurofound (2013a), *Restructuring in SMEs in Europe*, Luxembourg: Publications Office of the European Union, accessed 17 May 2015 at http://www.eurofound.europa.eu/sites/default/files/ef_publication/field_ef_document/ef1247en.pdf.

Eurofound (2013b), *Public Policy and Support for Restructuring in SMEs*, Dublin: Eurofound, accessed 18 May 2015 at https://eurofound.europa.eu/sites/default/files/ef_files/docs/erm/tn1208013s/tn1208013s.pdf.

European Commission (2003), *Commission Recommendation of 6 May 2003 Concerning the Definition of Micro, Small and Medium-sized Enterprises*, 2003/361/EC, Brussels: European Commission.

European Commission (2007), *Supporting the Internationalisation of SMEs. Good Practice Selection*, Luxembourg: Publications Office of the European Union.

European Commission (2011), *European Economic Forecast – Autumn 2011, European Economy 6/2011*, Brussels: European Commission.

European Commission (2012), *Communication from the Commission: Towards a Job-rich Recovery*, COM(2012) 173 final, Brussels: European Commission.

Giusti, M. (2007), 'L'esperienza italiana di delocalizzazione produttiva all'estero tra incentivi e dissuasioni' [The Italian experience of relocation of production abroad: incentives and disincentives], Pisa: Department of Public Law, University of Pisa.

Istituto Guglielmo Tagliacarne (2011), *Le Relazioni Internazionali della Piccola e Media Imprenditoria Italiana* [International Relations of Italian Small and Medium Entrepreneurship], Rome: Istituto Guglielmo Tagliacarne.

Jakobsen, L. and V. de Voss (2003), *Internationalisation of SMEs, Observatory of European SMEs 2003, No. 4*, Brussels: European Commission.

Karagianni, S. and L. Labrianidis (2001), 'The pros and cons of SMEs going international', *Eastern European Economics*, **39**(2), 5–28, Armonk, NY; M.E. Sharpe.

Kontinen, T. (2011), 'Internationalization pathways of family SMEs', *Jyväskylä Studies in Business and Economics*, Vol. 100, Jyväskylä: University of Jyväskylä.

KPMG (2007), 'Thinking big!, SME Action Day', Brussels: BusinessEurope/KPMG.

Lamotte, O. and A. Colovic (2013), 'Innovation and internationalization of young entrepreneurial firms', *Management International*, **18**(1), 87–103.

Leonidou, A.C. and S. Samiee (2012), 'Born global or simply rapidly internationalising? Review, critique, and future prospects', in M. Gabrielsson and V.H.M. Kirpalani (eds), *Handbook of Research on Born Globals*, Cheltenham, UK and Northampton, MA, USA: Edward Elgar Publishing.

Mascherpa, S. (2012), 'Born global companies as market driven organisations: an empirical analysis', PhD thesis, Milan: Università degli Studi di Milano-Bicocca.

Mettler, A. and A.D. Williams (2011), 'The rise of the micro-multinational: how freelancers and technology-savvy start-ups are driving growth, jobs and innovation', *Lisbon Council Policy Brief*, **5**(3), Brussels: Lisbon Council.

Ministry of Economic Affairs and Communication (2011), *Estonian Enterprise Policy 2007–2013*.

OECD (2011), *Entrepreneurship at a Glance 2011*, Paris: OECD.

Onkelinx, J. and L. Sleuwaegen (2008), *Internationalization of SMEs*, Flanders: Flanders District of Creativity and Vlerick Leuven Gent Management School.

Pock, M. and H. Hinterhuber (2011), 'Born globals – Wie aus Start-ups internationale Unternehmen werden' [Born globals – how start-ups become international companies], *Zeitschrift für KMU und Entrepreneurship*, **59**(2), 141–7.

RSM Erasmus University (2007), 'Erasmus entrepreneurship outlook 2007: Dutch SMBs turn "en masse" to offshoring but business intelligent in lacking', press release, 27 September, accessed 17 May 2015 at http://www.rsm.nl/about-rsm/news/detail/2020-erasmus-entrepreneurship-outlook-2007-dutch-smbs-turn-en-masse-to-offshoring-but-bus/.

Sakai, K. (2002), 'Global industrial restructuring: implications for small firms', *OECD Science, Technology and Industry Working Papers, 2002–2004*, Paris: OECD.

Sleuwaegen, L. and J. Onkelinx (2014), 'International commitment, post-entry growth and survival of international new ventures', *Journal of Business Venturing*, **29**(1), 106–20.

Söderqvist, A. and S. Chetty (2013), 'Strength of ties involved in international new ventures', *European Business Review*, **25**(6), 536–52.

UEAPME (European Association of Craft, Small and Medium-sized Enterprises) (2012), *UEAPME Think Small Test and Small Business Act Implementation Scoreboard*, Brussels: UEAPME Study Unit, accessed 18 May 2015 at http://www.ueapme.com/IMG/pdf/Scoreboard_2012_final.pdf.

Vapola, T.J. (2012), 'Battleship strategy for managing MNC-born global innovation networks', in M. Gabrielsson and V.H.M. Kirpalani (eds), *Handbook of Research on Born Globals*, Cheltenham, UK and Northampton, MA, USA: Edward Elgar Publishing, pp. 161–84.

Vapola, T.J., P. Tossavainen and M. Gabrielsson (2008), 'The battleship strategy: the complementing role of born globals in MNCs' new opportunity creation', *Journal of International Entrepreneurship*, **6**(1), 1–20.

Wymenga, P., N. Plaisier and J. Vermeulen (2013), *Study on Support Services for SMEs in International Business*, Rotterdam: ECSIP Consortium/DG Enterprise and Industry.

12. Using national export promotion programs to assist smaller firms' international entrepreneurial initiatives

Leonidas C. Leonidou, Saeed Samiee and Valeska V. Geldres

INTRODUCTION

Encouraging firms to engage in exporting is an ongoing thrust by governments around the world. An important governmental policy tool for motivating firms to consider exporting is export promotion programs (EPPs). These initiatives are aimed at motivating firms, especially smaller ones that tend to be internationally inactive, to begin exporting. The process of internationalization generally begins with exporting and involves entry into a foreign market outside normal operational scope of the firm. Like other new business initiatives, the first international market entry involves both innovation and risk (Samiee et al., 1993). As innovation and risk-taking are intertwined with entrepreneurship, new internationalization initiatives, especially by first-time exporters, are entrepreneurial (Ibeh and Young, 2001; Lu and Beamish, 2001; Chandra et al., 2009). In fact, EPPs are intended to induce international entrepreneurial aspirations in smaller non-exporting firms, while encouraging current exporters to penetrate deeper into existing markets and target new export markets (cf. Shamsuddoha et al., 2009b). Thus, whether aimed at initiating exporting for the first time or expanding international business activities among current exporters, EPPs must contain important entrepreneurial content to be effective.

Although the process of internationalization may begin with any market entry mode, exporting is the first step in the firm's foreign market venture. Indeed, it remains the most frequently used vehicle for smaller firms to enter foreign markets because as compared to other entry mode options: (1) exporting places little or no pressure on the firm to change its organizational structure (e.g., adding a new department) and (2) it is both less risky and only minimally resource dependent (Leonidou and Katsikeas, 1996).[1] Exporting also offers significant benefits for both the national economy (e.g., increasing employment, earning foreign currency to finance imports, creating backward and forward linkages) and the individual firm (e.g., developing new technologies, facilitating organizational growth, enhancing financial position) (Leonidou et al., 2007). These positive 'side benefits' of exporting offer additional incentives for firms to pursue new customers in markets abroad, while country-level benefits arising from increased levels of exporting justify governmental efforts to promote export-related entrepreneurship via EPPs.

However, involving small firms in exporting activities is not an easy task. Smaller firms are hindered by numerous internal obstacles (e.g., insufficient financial resources) and external challenges (e.g., intense foreign market competition), as well as domestic hurdles (e.g., inadequate infrastructural facilities) and barriers abroad (e.g., imposition of tariff/non-tariff barriers) (Leonidou, 2004). These obstacles can seriously inhibit firms at any stage of the export development process and seriously harm their performance. Non-exporters may lose interest and never begin or become skeptical or reluctant to engage in exporting altogether, neophyte exporters may interrupt or withdraw completely from foreign activities and experienced exporters may delay or even hold back future export expansion plans (Leonidou and Katsikeas, 1996).

In light of the above, governments frequently offer assistance to firms in the private sector (especially smaller ones) in an attempt to overcome these hurdles, as well as encourage firms to develop initiatives to better exploit export market opportunities (Lages and Montgomery, 2005). Such assistance usually takes the form of export promotion programs, which may range from loan guarantees and tax benefits to provision of foreign country data and trade mission sponsorship (Jaramillo, 1992; Cavusgil and Yeoh, 1994). However, to be successful, national government export assistance should be properly targeted at and clearly understood by current and would-be exporters (Seringhaus and Rosson, 1990). Although these programs may differ according to the idiosyncratic economic, political-legal and cultural environments prevailing in each country, their correct use can enhance the firm's entrepreneurial attributes, which can subsequently contribute to heightened export performance (Leonidou et al., 2011).

This chapter aims to shed light on the instrumental role of national EPPs in helping smaller firms to enhance their international entrepreneurial initiatives and expand into exporting in a successful way. In doing so, we first explain the nature of entrepreneurship and its link with exporting and export performance. We then provide an overview of extant empirical research on national EPPs. In the next section, we analyze various types of EPPs and explain how these can strengthen the entrepreneurial abilities of small firms. Finally, we derive some conclusions, as well as implications for business managers and public policy-makers.

THE NATURE OF ENTREPRENEURSHIP AND EXPORTING

There is no common definition for entrepreneurship, which involves *a process leading to change* and is frequently associated with new ventures, including export market entry and new product development (Rundh, 2011). Generically, entrepreneurship is a value creation process within an organization that aims to assemble a unique set of resources to exploit business opportunities (Caruana et al., 1998; Rundh, 2011). As such, it involves a number of stages, ranging from the identification of opportunities and development of new business concepts, to the deployment of the necessary resources (and capabilities) to implement the concept and the exploitation of the resultant business venture (Morris et al., 1993; Caruana et al., 1998). By default, the entrepreneurship process is applicable to any type of organization, irrespective of industry, size or legal status (Covin and Slevin, 1991). Although scholars in the field have operationalized entrepreneurship in multiple ways, the convergence of their views leads to three major dimensions, namely, risk-taking, innovativeness and proactiveness, which are important in developing export activities (Covin and Slevin, 1989; Miles and Arnold, 1991; Zahra and Garvis, 2000).

With regard to *risk-taking*, the undertaking of any new business venture involves certain risk elements (e.g., personal, social, psychological and financial) that need to be systematically managed or mitigated in order to yield successful results (Caruana et al., 1998). Thus, risk-seeking behavior facilitates the exploitation of business opportunities, even though there is a strong possibility of it resulting in seriously expensive failure (Knight, 2000). In a similar vein, the firm's propensity to export has been associated with managers who have high levels of risk tolerance, as opposed to managers of non-exporting firms who are mainly risk averse (Simmonds and Smith, 1968; McConnell, 1979; Dichtl et al., 1990). Since a large number of studies (e.g., Simpson and Kujawa, 1974; Wiedersheim-Paul et al., 1978; Cavusgil and Naor, 1987) reveal that there is a tendency by firms to perceive greater risks when selling to foreign markets because of the high volatility and complexity of the international business environment, managers' perception of risk is particularly critical in exporting.

Despite the broad agreement regarding the close relationship between entrepreneurship and innovativeness (see, for example, Ayranci and Çolakoglu, 2013), *innovativeness* lacks a unique definition. It is generally agreed, however, that innovativeness refers to a conscious and deliberate effort to make economic, social or other changes within an organization, such as the development of new products/services, unique technologies and novel processes (Dibrell et al., 2011). To achieve this, it is important for individuals to develop high levels of intuition, creativity, independence, autonomy and open-mindedness (Caruana et al., 1998). Innovativeness is also central to the firm's export behavior, in the sense that export initiation is regarded by some scholars as an innovation, as in the case of adopting new production processes or introducing new products (Simmonds and Smith, 1968). In fact, many studies (e.g., Dichtl et al., 1990; Holzmüller and Kasper, 1990) showed that, as opposed to non-exporters, exporting firms have managers who are more innovative and ready to break away from existing norms and behavioral patterns.

Proactiveness is the extent to which people and organizations take pre-emptive actions to influence their environment beneficially, usually expressed in terms of constantly taking initiatives, aggressively seeking new opportunities and experimenting with potential responses to environmental changes (Venkatraman, 1989; Bateman and Crant, 1993). As such, it involves elements of adaptability to changing conditions, considerable persistence and pushing to get things done and willingness to bear the costs of a failure (Caruana et al., 1998). Proactiveness has also been an issue of concern in exporting, especially within the sphere of export stimuli, with proactive stimulation denoting export involvement characterized by an interest in exploring unique internal competences (e.g., possession of a financial competitive advantage) and/or foreign market opportunities (e.g., exclusive information about a specific foreign market) (Leonidou, 1995). As opposed to reactive export stimulation, proactively stimulated firms were found to exhibit a more aggressive, positive and long-term approach to exporting (Czinkota and Johnston, 1983).

The aforementioned entrepreneurial dimensions are essential, not only in facilitating the firm's export behavior, but also in enhancing its performance in foreign markets (McDougall and Oviatt, 2000; Dimitratos and Plakoyiannaki, 2003). Limited empirical evidence on the subject reveals that: (1) the firm's entrepreneurial activity in export operations has an instrumental effect on export performance (both financial and non-financial); (2) certain organizational factors (e.g., size, age and structure) moderate the firm's ability to adopt an entrepreneurial posture in approaching export markets; and (3) contextual factors, such as the degree of complexity of the foreign market, may moderate the effect of entrepreneurship on export performance (e.g., Zahra et al., 1997; Caruana et al., 1998; Jones and Coviello, 2005).

METHODOLOGY

Our goal in this chapter is to review and synthesize scholarly knowledge as articulated in the export promotion program literature. To accomplish this objective, we examined published scholarly works on national export promotion programs as means of inciting entrepreneurial export activity in smaller firms. The crucial role of these programs has given rise to a large number of studies since its debut in the early 1960s. In reviewing EPPs, we paid close attention to published empirical research. Overall, these studies address 54 types of export promotion vehicles in use. For the purposes of this chapter, we have classified these EPP types into seven groups. These include programs related to export financing, information, education and training, legal issues, market selection, marketing strategy and miscellaneous. In the paragraphs that follow, we closely examine these categories. Key empirical articles used in this study are shown in the Appendix at the end of the chapter.

NATIONAL EXPORT PROMOTION PROGRAMS

Entrepreneurial processes share many similarities with the firm's export development process, in the sense that both deal with the identification/exploitation of opportunities, the deployment of appropriate resources (and capabilities) and the creation of value to the firm, through the adoption of risk-taking, innovative and proactive behavior (McDougall and Oviatt, 2000; Dimitratos and Plakoyiannaki, 2003). National export promotion programs can facilitate the firm's entrepreneurial initiatives in exporting, by providing 'external resources' (and capabilities) that are essential to overcoming the various obstacles found at different stages of the export development process (Seringhaus, 1986; Seringhaus and Rosson, 1990).

One set of studies dealt with the awareness, usage and usefulness of EPPs by non-exporters (Kumcu et al., 1995), exporters (Kedia and Chhokar, 1986), or both (Albaum, 1983). The literature has particularly centered on: (1) the use and effectiveness of specific EPPs, such as participation in trade missions (Seringhaus, 1987); (2) the areas of government export assistance (e.g., marketing, finance, information) specifically required by firms (Czinkota and Ricks, 1981); and (3) adjustments to EPPs needed to suit the characteristics of individual firms (e.g., firm size) (Moini, 1998) or their management (e.g., previous experience) (Gray, 1997).

Another group of studies focused on segmenting firms receiving export assistance programs according to the stage they had reached along the internationalization path (Crick and Czinkota, 1995; Ahmed et al., 2002). In particular, these studies perceive firms as being at different stages of export development (i.e., non-exporters, sporadic exporters, regular exporters and advanced exporters), with each stage requiring a different type of government assistance (Czinkota and Johnston, 1981; Naidu and Rao, 1993). For example, in the early export stages, firms have a greater need for export training services, guidance in handling documentation and information on obtaining foreign sales leads. However, as they evolve to more advanced stages, the emphasis is on services pertaining to communications, logistics and sales support (Francis and Collins-Dodd, 2004).

Some studies also emphasized the link between EPPs and factors that stimulate (e.g., possession of unique products) or obstruct (e.g., inadequate overseas representation) the firm's efforts to initiate and develop export operations (Albaum, 1983; Vanderleest, 1996). Here, national export promotion assistance helps increase or complement management knowledge and experience (Singer and Czinkota, 1994). In many exporting studies (e.g., Rabino, 1980; Koh, 1989), government export assistance is also regarded as a stimulus per se, driving firms to initiate or expand export operations, although, compared with other export stimuli, its impact is relatively low. Various other studies have also identified the specific obstacles firms encounter in overseas markets and measured the degree to which EPPs can alleviate them (Kotabe and Czinkota, 1992).

Another group of studies viewed national EPPs as instrumental in enhancing organizational (e.g., technical skills, foreign market knowledge, overseas business contacts) and/or managerial (e.g., export commitment, international orientation, expertise in export activities) competence (Seringhaus and Rosson, 1990). Thus, the government is a 'change agent', whose assistance facilitates the adoption of a more proactive, systematic and planned approach to exporting by private sector firms (Seringhaus, 1986). Though not clearly stated, studies falling under this group implicitly consider EPPs a helpful external hand extended to the firm to enhance its resources and capabilities.

A final (and more recent) group of studies explores the effect of EPPs on the firm's export performance, either directly (Wilkinson and Brouthers, 2000; Gillespie and Riddle, 2004; Lages and Montgomery, 2005) or through the intervening effect of other factors (Shamsuddoha and Ali, 2006; Shamsuddoha et al., 2009a). In the former case, organizational (e.g., company size) and managerial (e.g., international outlook) factors are crucial to becoming aware of and using EPPs. In the latter case, these programs enhance managerial perceptions, knowledge and commitment, which in turn help to effectively design an export marketing strategy and/or improve the firm's competitive advantage in international markets. Regardless of how EPP use interacts with the individual firm and its management, the outcome is the achievement of superior export performance.

NATIONAL EXPORT PROMOTION PROGRAMS AND ENTREPRENEURIAL ACTIVITY

Various national export promotion programs reported in empirical studies on the subject are summarized in Figure 12.1. These programs

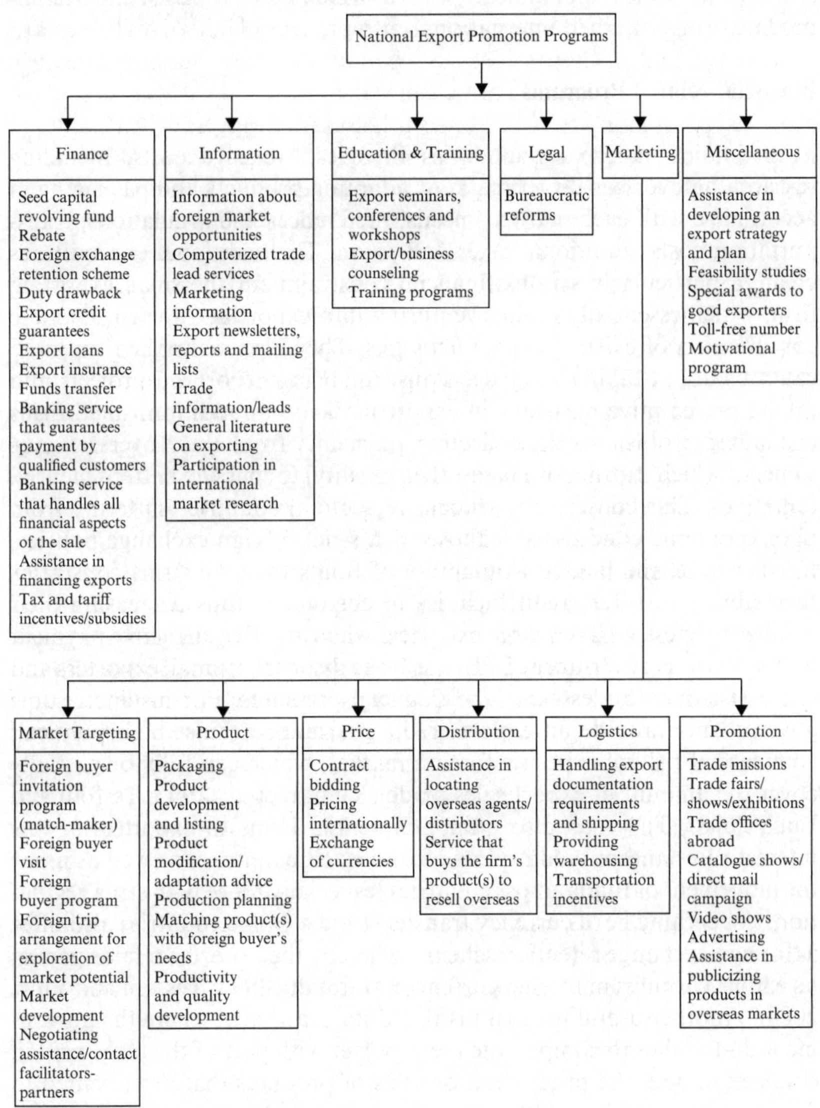

Figure 12.1 Classification of export promotion programs

are universally aimed at motivating firms, especially non-exporters, to become entrepreneurial with respect to exporting.[2] Altogether, seven major categories of government export assistance programs are identified, including financial, informational, educational, legal, targeting, marketing and miscellaneous issues. We discuss and analyze these programs in the sections that follow and indicate ways in which they can assist and accommodate firms with their international entrepreneurial initiatives to export.[3]

Financial-related Programs

Transcending national boundaries involves excessive costs, including researching overseas target markets, adapting products and packaging in accordance with each market's needs, preferences and regulations, transportation costs, additional taxes and so on. The additional expenditures create a particularly serious financial constraint for the small exporting firm, which essentially inhibit venturing into exporting or even the mere continuation of existing export activities. They also make the firm more cautious about taking risky decisions, financing export-led projects and taking pre-emptive measures in export markets. In addition, small firms encounter problems with collecting payments from their overseas customers, which further weakens their ability to pursue entrepreneurial initiatives. This concern is particularly acute in countries suffering from poor economic conditions or those with strict foreign exchange policies. Furthermore, the limited availability of funds to small firms constrains their ability to offer credit facilities to customers, thus decreasing their competitiveness vis-à-vis large exporters who can offer attractive payment terms. Various government EPPs are at the disposal of small exporters and can assist them by lessening the financial pressures. For instance, some governments provide an export credit guarantee against high political/commercial risk in a specific foreign market, which can fully or partially cover the amount of export sales made (Kumku et al., 1995; Tesfom and Lutz, 2008). They can also offer preferential loans to exporters at low interest rates and/or credit quotas for selected countries, as well as assist the movement of funds across countries (especially those with strict regulations concerning hard currency transfer) (ibid.). Some countries also offer a 'foreign exchange retention scheme' whereby the exporter retains part of its export earnings in foreign currency (Marandu, 1995; Tesfom and Lutz, 2008). Another useful program is the 'duty drawback' where the government undertakes to compensate the exporter with part of the taxes paid in connection with the production or sales of products that are oriented to foreign markets (ibid.). Although recently banned by international organizations (such as the World Trade Organization), the governments of some countries still provide export subsidies in certain sectors of the economy (i.e., offering money to reduce export prices) in order to increase the competitiveness of their exporters in international markets (Marandu, 1995).

Information-related Programs

Many firms admit that one of the strongest motives encouraging them to embark on export activities is the existence of attractive business opportunities abroad, which can yield profitable sales and sustainable growth (Kaynak and Kothari, 1984; Barker and Kaynak, 1992; Trimeche, 2002). However, identifying, selecting and exploiting these opportunities is not an easy task, mainly because of information deficiencies confronted by many exporters, especially those of smaller size that have limited financial resources. For example, small firms tend to have: (1) limited familiarity with and knowledge of the available sources of information (either domestically or abroad) about foreign markets; (2) an unclear picture about the nature and importance of information necessary to successfully carry out their export operations; (3) insufficient financial means to acquire information, especially that of a primary nature because it is more expensive to collect; and (4) less competence at easily retrieving, analyzing and interpreting export-related information (Samiee and Walters, 1991b; Katsikeas and Morgan, 1994; Morgan and Katsikeas, 1997). This situation is becoming even more acute due to source (e.g., manipulative data collection), quality (e.g., inaccurate/incomplete data) and comparability (e.g., different classification and measurement systems) problems associated with international business research (Leonidou and Theodosiou, 2004). Despite these difficulties, possessing adequate, relevant and accurate information is of paramount importance for the exporting firm, due to the high uncertainty, heterogeneity and volatility characterizing the international business environment (Welch and Wiedersheim-Paul, 1980). Such information would help to enhance the firm's proactiveness and innovativeness in approaching export markets, as well as make its progression along the internationalization path less risky and more committed (Johanson and Vahlne, 1977). Government assistance can prove useful in this respect through the provision of certain programs, such as manuals explaining export mechanics, special country profile reports and 'how to do business' manuals. Computerized trade lead services, coupled with mailing lists of foreign distributors/dealers, provide additional supportive information about establishing a presence abroad. In addition, the sophisticated and idiosyncratic handling of marketing activities in international markets has been responsible for some governments offering specialized marketing information, such as that focusing on market size and growth, key competitor profiles and consumer characteristics. Some countries also subsidize the execution of primary marketing research and/or feasibility studies in foreign countries.

Education and Training-related Programs

Exporting involves unique rules and regulations, specific shipping arrangements and cumbersome bureaucratic procedures that usually discourage small firms from engagement and/or expansion into international business activities. Many small exporters are also unfamiliar with the business practices prevailing in different countries, such as time, space and formality perceptions, the role of interpersonal relations and the way interfirm negotiations are conducted. Moreover, the personnel of these companies usually face problems with speaking foreign languages, understanding the nuances of foreign cultures and having limited international exposure. Furthermore, some firms have little knowledge of export-related procedures, marketing tools and analytical methods. All the above points to the need for educating potential and current exporters to gain these skills, knowledge and experience, which are essential to successfully conducting their international business dealings. To this end, government export assistance can be useful by offering: (1) *specialized seminars*, *conferences* and *workshops*, aiming to help firms to better understand export mechanics, handle export documentation and develop export marketing plans; (2) *business counseling*, aiming to provide advice on specific aspects of exporting, such as selecting and targeting foreign markets, approaching foreign customers and adjusting the elements of the export marketing mix; and (3) *training schemes*, aiming to improve exporters in certain critical areas, such as learning foreign languages, managing time effectively and developing negotiating skills.

Legal-related Programs

Many firms engaged in export operations face numerous rules and regulations, in both home and host markets. Domestically, the government may impose restrictions on exporting to specific overseas markets, as well as on certain goods that are critical for the country's national security and/or foreign policy. Host country restrictions may take several forms: (1) *entry restrictions*, which delay or restrict the flow of the product in the market; (2) *price controls*, which limit the firm's profitability, particularly when operating in inflationary economies; (3) *special tax rates*, which increase the export price of the product in the foreign country; and (4) *exchange controls*, which create difficulties in repatriating the firm's profits. To help exporters accommodate these restrictions, many governments have proceeded with internal bureaucratic reforms, such as consolidating various scattered export-related formalities under the umbrella of a single government agency (Kumku et al., 1995). In addition, special export assistance programs offer legal advice on various issues, such as how to handle disputes associated with foreign distributor agreement, tax authorities and repatriation of funds.

Market Selection-related Programs

A serious obstacle faced by export entrepreneurs in entering new markets relates to the difficulties in identifying and/or contacting appropriate foreign customers (Samiee and Walters, 1991b). In fact, this problem is perceived as by far the most pressing issue by entrepreneurial exporters (Samiee et al., 1993). A number of factors contribute to this, such as: (1) the large geographic distance separating exporters from their customers, which makes the interaction process between the two parties difficult; (2) the limited availability of information sources offering lists of buyers with an interest in purchasing goods from abroad; (3) the lack of systematic efforts made by many exporters to visit and research foreign markets; and (4) the lack of available time and money to make personal visits abroad for the purpose of finding buyers. In fact, plenty of empirical evidence (e.g., Samiee et al., 1993) in the pertinent literature indicates that many firms initiate exports as a response to unsolicited orders from foreign customers, rather than as a result of their own systematic efforts to explore foreign markets. However, such a reactive engagement in export operations usually creates problems (e.g., failure to adapt the marketing mix) associated with an indifferent, half-hearted and short-term approach to the foreign market. To alleviate these problems, a number of government assistance programs can be found, which can take two major forms: (1) *outgoing*, whereby a trip is organized for the exporter (or would-be exporter) in order to explore the foreign market and identify promising customers; and (2) *incoming*, whereby targeted foreign buyers are invited to visit the exporter (or would-be exporter) in order to explore the possibility of initiating business together. The ultimate purpose of these programs is to provide a sound 'matchmaking' service between the exporter and potential import buyers that will guarantee a prosperous, long-term working relationship. Other programs focus on market development, whereby guidelines are offered on how to obtain a foothold in the foreign market and the necessary steps that need to be taken to expand the exporter's presence there.

Marketing Strategy-related Programs

A major source of problems encountered by small firms in export markets relates to the marketing mix, namely the product, price, distribution, logistics and promotion. In the sections that follow, we detail various marketing considerations and export promotional tools made available to international entrepreneurial firms.

Product emphasis

Differences in economic systems, sociocultural contexts, demographic structures, climatic conditions and technical standards are some of the many reasons for the variations in customer preferences across countries (Theodosiou and Leonidou, 2003). All these necessitate product adjustments in the design, construction and functioning of the product, or even the development of entirely new products to cater for the specific needs of buyers in foreign markets. The unique conditions characterizing transportation, storage and handling of goods abroad are also responsible for packaging adjustments, while the use of different languages across countries requires changes on labeling and usage instructions. However, small firms face difficulties in making product changes because of limitations in both resources (e.g., working capital, technical knowledge, production equipment) and capabilities (e.g., new product development, market sensing, cost control) (McConnell, 1979). To overcome these problems, some governments offer a range of specialized EPPs, such as a service to match the company's products with foreign buyers' needs, assistance in developing new products for specific overseas markets, advice on product modification requirements, provision of information on packaging configuration across countries and guidance in properly planning production activity and improving product quality for export purposes.

Price emphasis

As opposed to a firm's home market, selling to international markets usually involves higher prices, mainly because of additional costs associated with product/package alterations, excess transportation/shipping costs, extra marketing costs and tariffs, taxes and other fees charged by foreign authorities. These costs, coupled with the existence of other internal (e.g., lack of economies of scale) and external (e.g., host government actions to subsidize local firms) factors, are responsible for hampering the international price competitiveness of small firms. The fact that international business transactions are conducted in different currencies can further lessen the firm's competitiveness because of difficulties in dealing with unstable foreign exchange rates, foreign exchange restrictions and unconvertible hard currencies. Furthermore, smaller firms tend to avoid marginal pricing in export markets, on the basis of their implied sense that importing customers should fully pay their share of the firm's fixed costs. Larger firms with more exporting experience, on the other hand, understand that they only need to recoup their overheads once; that is, when the domestic market is fully covering fixed costs, it offers the firm substantial flexibility to be price competitive in exporting (Samiee and Walters, 1990). Government assistance to exporters can take the form of providing guidance in: (1) setting the firm's prices in different countries, taking into consideration their idiosyncrasies in terms of cost structures, buyer disposable incomes and competitors' prices; (2) finding the right currency to be used in transactions with foreign buyers, as well as in accommodating foreign exchange risks; and (3) determining the right prices to increase the chances of successful contract bidding.

Distribution emphasis
Obtaining reliable representation in a foreign market is one of the major challenges facing small exporters, mainly because of their limited availability (since most of them are already appointed or controlled by competitors), the tendency to carry multiple (and sometimes competing) products and brands and difficulties in finding the right structural, operational and behavioral characteristics to match the firm's requirements. Difficulties also exist when a small firm has to design its own distribution system in a foreign market, usually caused by variations across countries in terms of: (1) distribution structures and types of intermediaries; (2) range and level of quality of the services offered by intermediaries; (3) behavioral dynamics (e.g., control) among distribution channel members; and (4) degree of penetration of the Internet and other direct methods in the country's distribution system. When small firms operate in foreign markets, other serious problems may arise, such as maintaining control over the foreign intermediaries, providing the right incentives to attract attention to the company's products and establishing proper procedures to enhance communication. Many governments offer assistance to exporters in locating distributors/agents in foreign markets and provide highlights as to their economic (e.g., financial) and non-economic (e.g., reliability) position (Wilkinson and Brouthers, 2000). In some countries, a special government service undertakes to sell the firm's products in foreign markets.

Logistics emphasis
One of the most frequently cited obstacles confronted by small firms in international markets relates to the difficulties in preparing the necessary documentation when fulfilling orders from foreign customers.

To overcome this problem, some governments provide assistance in completing the necessary export documentation, while others offer more simplified documentation and shipping requirements. The long geographic distances between home and host countries (coupled with the poor economic infrastructure and limited transportation options in most less developed countries) are also responsible for excessive transportation costs, which are particularly critical in impeding the international business competitiveness of small firms. Some governments have introduced a special scheme involving a network of local shipping companies, whereby exporters can get lower transportation fees (Kumku et al., 1995; Tesfom and Lutz, 2008). Another serious logistics problem encountered by small firms relates to difficulties in finding adequate warehousing facilities in foreign markets, as well as the high warehousing fees charged in certain countries. The role of government agencies here is to assist local exporters to identify proper warehouses in international markets and secure low warehousing fees.

Promotion emphasis

Although many small firms are reluctant to engage in promotional activities in foreign markets due to financial constraints, others face difficulties associated with legal restrictions in advertising messages and media, clearly defined target audiences and unavailable promotional tools. Certain EPPs deal with this issue, such as providing guidance in: (1) designing advertising campaigns for specific foreign markets; (2) preparing product catalogues targeting international customers; and (3) launching direct mail and/or electronic marketing campaigns. The organization of trade missions is also another useful export promotion tool that helps to establish business contacts and enhance communication with foreign customers. This can take two forms: *inward*, where exporters are given money and other facilities to invite business people, government officials, journalists and other influential people from abroad to visit their home country and *outward*, where exporters receive financial assistance to personally visit foreign markets, in order to explore business opportunities, identify prospective buyers and obtain good representation (Jaramillo, 1992). Another type of governmental assistance to exporters is given through the sponsoring of participation in foreign trade fairs (usually taking the form of covering rental and/or decoration expenses of a space in the exhibition to display the firm's products), where the firm exchanges information with potential customers and gathers market intelligence (Wilkinson and Brouthers, 2006).

Miscellaneous Programs

A series of other government programs aims to encourage exports by small firms and have mainly a motivational or facilitating nature. A very common program is the National Export Award Scheme, which is offered to firms that have excelled in their export activities within a specific time period (Marandu, 1995). This public recognition offered by the government and/or other professional associations to successful exporters provides incentives not only for them, but also for other exporters to enhance their own operations (Kumku et al., 1995). The establishment by the government of trade offices abroad is another useful export promotion tool, since they are vital in helping to establish business contacts, collect foreign market information and provide country insights to current and potential exporters (Wilkinson and Brouthers, 2000; Tesfom and Lutz, 2008). Many governments also supply a toll-free number and/or electronic service (usually located within the Ministry of Commerce and Industry) to give export-related assistance to firms interested in entering foreign markets.

CONCLUSIONS

This chapter has amply demonstrated the critical role of national export promotion programs in assisting smaller-sized firms to boost entrepreneurial activity in international markets. This supports the notion that government assistance can act as an 'external resource' (and capability) for the internationalization of small exporters (Seringhaus, 1986; Seringhaus and Rosson, 1990). Such assistance, if properly used, helps firms to overcome financial, informational, marketing and other hurdles that hinder their export development, while strengthening organizational processes, like market-sensing, organizational learning and product development, which are vital in the successful implementation of export operations. Export promotion assistance is particularly crucial nowadays due to the intense competition, high volatility and great complexity that characterizes today's international marketplace. However, the relative absence of an international mindset in smaller firms somehow inhibits awareness and usage of EPPs, which subsequently hampers the adoption of international entrepreneurial activities.

The appropriate use of national export promotion programs can help strengthen each of the components comprising export entrepreneurship, namely risk tolerance, innovativeness and proactiveness and induce firms to enter international markets via exporting. At the very least, creating awareness of these programs, particularly among smaller firms, should be given high priority. Beyond that, programs can do much to ignite exporting entrepreneurship in firms. First, they can help increase the *risk tolerance* of small firms in foreign markets, especially through the adoption of programs pertaining to information, education and training and legal issues. This is critical in light of the high financial, political, social and other risks incurred when the firm transcends its national boundaries to serve unknown foreign markets, which are sometimes perceived by small business managers as being too restrictive and/or prohibitive to do business with. Thus, even though there is a strong possibility of costly failure when undertaking such high risks, the knowledge, skills and other tools gained from government export assistance can improve the exporting firm's ability to successfully exploit opportunities and properly handle the threats deriving from an international business environment.

Second, by its very nature, export market entry is characterized by many new things, such as new markets and unfamiliar buyer behavior, new tasks and macroenvironments and new marketing approaches and methods. Thus, *innovativeness* is critical both for initial market entry, as well as for achieving success in international markets. National EPPs can act as a facilitator to instill and promote this important characteristic, especially by the provision of rigorous education and training, financial support and assistance for each of the elements of the marketing mix. Government agencies can act as 'change agents' in the export organization, because their assistance programs can provide many new insights, ideas and tools to provoke new thinking within the small firm. An important prerequisite for this, however, is to begin with the right leadership and managerial mindset. In other words, managers who are internationally oriented, determined and receptive to new ideas, are more willing to explore new opportunities and proceed with the necessary export-led adjustments in their organizations.

Third, national EPPs (e.g., information-related, education and training, target marketing) are vital to energize the firm's *proactiveness* in export markets. Such programs help small firms identify and exploit promising foreign market opportunities, design and implement appropriate plans and strategies and adapt promptly to changes in the micro and macro environment abroad. To reap the benefits accrued from government export assistance, however, it is essential to recruit managers characterized by long-term orientation, an aggressive spirit and persistence in their actions. No less important is the firm's continued commitment to and support of exporting, as with any entrepreneurial activity, pay-offs will not be quick. It is also necessary to cultivate a climate in the export organization that is geared toward 'thinking outside the box', promotes free communication across organizational levels, coordinates effectively in key functional areas and seeks and receives constant feedback from markets abroad.

IMPLICATIONS

Our coverage of EPPs as an entrepreneurial activity has several implications for small business managers. Since national EPPs can be instrumental in reigniting and energizing entrepreneurial initiatives in markets abroad, they should first explore the full range of programs offered by other governments, evaluate their content, select those that are more suitable for overcoming specific export barriers and make recommendations to government authorities for new programs currently not available. Given that knowledge regarding these programs is generally limited or lacking among firms that need it the most, initiatives to raise awareness should be a first step. Furthermore, research has demonstrated that the type of assistance that firms need during various stages of export development changes and EPPs can complement (but not fully replace) the critical resources (and capabilities) necessary for successfully operating in foreign markets. In this context, it is essential for business managers to develop a clear checklist of their specific needs to plan and implement their exporting initiatives and to identify gaps that government assistance should fill.

On the other hand, government agencies should provide assistance to small firms to carry out their export operations in a more effective and efficient way. However, in light of the growing diversity, complexity and volatility of the international business environment, government export assistance needs to be both attractive and flexible in enhancing the entrepreneurial abilities of small firms in international markets. In doing so, it is crucial to restructure certain already provided EPPs, introduce innovative new programs and eliminate others that have been ineffective or are outdated. Drawing comparisons between the country's current export promotion programs and those offered by other foreign governments would also help to identify new types of programs that have proved successful elsewhere. Most importantly, it is critical to increase awareness and appreciation of these programs among small business firms through appropriate methods that target these firms, including articles in trade journals and newspapers, organization of open seminars, workshops and conferences and the provision of a hotline service with easy access to government export specialists.

NOTES

1. Growing globalization trends, the reduction in or removal of trade and investment barriers and intensified competition and saturation within traditional home markets provide additional motivation for smaller enterprises to seek business opportunities in markets abroad (Knight, 2000; Pope, 2002). Although small firms may not immediately embrace exporting opportunities, knowledge of environmental change around them is unavoidable, which, in turn, may make exporting a more viable option.
2. Paradoxically, firms needing to use such programs are the most ill-equipped to benefit from them. It is thus not surprising that some entrepreneurial firms that engage in exporting remain sporadic exporters (cf. Samiee and Walters, 1991a, 2002), whereas the ultimate goal of national export promotion programs is to elevate firms to become regular exporters with increasing commitment to exploiting markets abroad. Nevertheless, EPPs are critical in reinforcing an exporting drive. As the world has commercially converged and firms are increasingly internationalizing and globalizing, greater reliance on exporting is the norm. As such, national export promotion initiatives provide useful vehicles for encouraging firms to become more internationally entrepreneurial.
3. All third party involvement in export promotion, especially by governmental bodies and institutions, is subject to regulations that dampen the types and magnitude of export assistance tools. For example, all international trade among the 159 members of the World Trade Organization (WTO) is regulated. Various forms of assistance sponsored by governments to promote exports are viewed as export subsidy and are therefore restricted by WTO. The position held by WTO is that export promotion and, in general, foreign trade promotion to support the competitiveness of companies and countries should be generic and for the benefit of free trade everywhere (Casanueva, 2008). The WTO has taken a much closer look at export promotion activities, identified trade-distorting practices and devised rules that permit countervailing practices (by importing nations) of restricted or prohibited EPPs.

REFERENCES

Ahmed, Z.U., O. Mohamed, J.P. Johnson and L.Y. Meng (2002), 'Export promotion programs of Malaysian firms: an international marketing perspective', *Journal of Business Research*, **55**(10), 831–43.

Albaum, G. (1983), 'Effectiveness of government export assistance for US smaller-sized manufacturers: some further evidence', *International Marketing Review*, **1**(1), 68–75.

Alvarez, R. (2004), 'Sources of export success in small- and medium-sized enterprises: the impact of public programs', *International Business Review*, **13**(3), 383–400.

Ayranci, E. and N. Çolakoglu (2013), 'The linkage between Turkish managers' leadership orientations and their innovativeness feature: an empirical study', *International Business Research*, **6**(8), 26–37.

Barker, A.T. and E. Kaynak (1992), 'An empirical investigation of the differences between initiating and continuing exporters', *European Journal of Marketing*, **26**(3), 27–36.

Bateman, T.S and J.M. Crant (1993), 'The proactive component of organizational behavior', *Journal of Organizational Behavior*, **14**(2), 103–18.

Caruana, A., M. Morris and A. Vella (1998), 'The effect of centralization and formalization on entrepreneurship in export firms', *Journal of Small Business Management*, **36**(1), 16–29.

Casanueva, H. (2008), 'The challenges facing trade promotion in today's world', *Intracen.org*, accessed 18 May 2015 at www.intracen.org/WorkArea/DownloadAsset.aspx?id=58822#sthash.Fb8sD6Bt.dpuf.

Cavusgil, S.T. (1983), 'Public policy implications of research on the export behavior of firms', *Akron Business and Economic Review*, **14**(2), 16–22.

Cavusgil, S.T. and J. Naor (1987), 'Firm and management characteristics as discriminators of export marketing activity', *Journal of Business Research*, **15**(3), 221–35.

Cavusgil, S.T. and P.-L. Yeoh (1994), 'Public sector promotion of US export activity: a review and directions for the future', *Journal of Public Policy and Marketing*, **13**(1), 76–84.

Chandra, Y., C. Styles and I. Wilkinson (2009), 'The recognition of first time international entrepreneurial opportunities: evidence from firms in knowledge-based industries', *International Marketing Review*, **26**(1), 30–61.

Covin, J.G. and D.P. Slevin (1989), 'Strategic management of small firms in hostile and benign environments', *Strategic Management Journal*, **10**(1), 75–87.

Covin, J.G. and D.P. Slevin (1991), 'A conceptual model of entrepreneurship as firm behavior', *Entrepreneurship Theory and Practice*, **16**(1), 7–25.

Crick, D. (1992), 'U.K. export assistance: are we supporting the best programs?', *Journal of Marketing Management*, **8**(1), 81–92.

Crick, D. and S. Chaudhry (2000), 'UK SMEs' awareness, use and perceptions of selected government export assistance – an investigation into the effect of ethnicity', *International Journal of Entrepreneurial Behavior and Research*, **6**(2), 72–89.

Crick, D. and M.R. Czinkota (1995), 'Export assistance: another look at whether we are supporting the best programs', *International Marketing Review*, **12**(3), 61–72.

Czinkota, M.R. and W.J. Johnston (1981), 'Segmenting US firms for export development', *Journal of Business Research*, **9**(4), 353–65.

Czinkota, M.R. and W.J. Johnston (1983), 'Exporting: does sales volume make a difference?', *Journal of International Business Studies*, **14**(1), 147–53.

Czinkota, M.R. and D.A. Ricks (1981), 'Export assistance: are we supporting the best programs', *Columbia Journal of World Business*, **16**(2) 73–8.

Dibrell, C., J. Craig and E. Hansen (2011), 'Natural environment, market orientation and firm innovativeness: an organizational life cycle perspective', *Journal of Small Business Management*, **49**(3), 467–89.

Dichtl, E., H.G. Koeglmayr and S. Mueller (1990), 'International orientation as a precondition for export success', *Journal of International Business Studies*, **21**(1), 23–40.

Dimitratos, P. and E. Plakoyiannaki (2003), 'Theoretical foundations of an international entrepreneurial culture', *Journal of International Entrepreneurship*, **1**(2), 187–215.

Durmuşoğlu, S.S., G. Apfelthaler, D.Z. Nayir, R. Alvarez and T. Mughan (2012), 'The effect of government-designed export promotion service use on small and medium-sized enterprise goal achievement: a multidimensional view of export performance', *Industrial Marketing Management*, **41**(4), 680–91.

Fischer, E. and A.R. Reuber (2003), 'Targeting export support to SMEs: owners' international experience as a segmentation basis', *Small Business Economics*, **20**(1), 69–82.

Francis, J. and C. Collins-Dodd (2004), 'Impact of export promotion schemes on firm competencies, strategies and performance: the case of Canadian high-technology SMEs', *International Marketing Review*, **21**(4/5), 474–95.

Freixanet, J. (2012), 'Export promotion programs: their impact on companies' internationalization performance and competitiveness', *International Business Review*, **21**(6), 1065–86.

Geldres, V.V., M.S. Etchebarne and L.H. Medina (2011), 'Promoción de Exportaciones en el Ambito Público: Su impacto en el Desempeño Exportador a Nivel de la Firma' [Export promotion in the public sector: impact on export performance at the firm level], *Academia Revista Latinoamericana de Administración*, **47**, 1–17.

Gençtürk, E. and M. Kotabe (2001), 'The effect of export assistance program usage on export performance: a contingency explanation', *Journal of International Marketing*, **9**(2), 51–72.

Gillespie, K. and L. Riddle (2004), 'Export promotion organisation emergence and development', *International Marketing Review*, **21**(4/5), 462–73.

Gray, B.J. (1997), 'Profiling managers to improve promotion targeting', *Journal of International Business Studies*, **28**(2), 387–421.

Holzmüller, H.H. and H. Kasper (1990), 'The decision-maker and export activity: a cross-national comparison of the foreign orientation of Austrian managers', *Management International Review*, **30**(3), 217–30.

Ibeh, K. and S. Young (2001), 'Exporting as an entrepreneurial act: an empirical study of Nigerian firms', *European Journal of Marketing*, **35**(5/6), 566–86.

Jaramillo, C. (1987), 'Preparing national export promotion programs', *International Trade Forum*, **23**(3), 24–30.

Jaramillo, C. (1992), 'The basic function of national trade promotion organizations', *International Trade Forum*, No. 3.

Johanson, J. and J.-E. Vahlne (1977), 'The internationalization process of the firm: a model of knowledge development and increasing foreign commitments', *Journal of International Business Studies*, **8**(1), 23–32.

Jones, M.V. and N.E. Coviello (2005), 'Internationalisation: conceptualising an entrepreneurial process of behaviour in time', *Journal of International Business Studies*, **36**(3), 284–303.

Katsikeas, C.S. and R.E. Morgan (1994), 'Differences in perceptions of exporting problems based upon firm's size and export experience', *European Journal of Marketing*, **28**(5), 17–35.

Kaynak, E. and V. Kothari (1984), 'Export behavior of small and medium-sized manufacturers: some policy guidelines for international marketers', *Management International Review*, **24**(2), 61–9.

Kedia, B.L. and J.S. Chhokar (1986), 'An empirical investigation of export promotion programs', *Columbia Journal of World Business*, **21**(4), 13–20.

Knight, G. (2000), 'Entrepreneurship and marketing strategy: the SME under globalization', *Journal of International Marketing*, **8**(2), 12–32.

Koh, A.C. (1989), 'An evaluation of the current export marketing practices of United States firms', in J. Hawes (ed.), *Developments in Marketing Science* (Vol. XII), pp. 198–202.

Kotabe, M. and M.R. Czinkota (1992), 'State government promotion of manufacturing exports: a gap analysis', *Journal of International Business Studies*, **23**(4), 637–58.

Kumku, H.T., T. Harcar and M.E. Kumcu (1995), 'Managerial perceptions of the adequacy of export incentive programs: implications for export-led economic development policy', *Journal of Business Research*, **32**(2), 163–74.

Lages, F.L. and B.D. Montgomery (2005), 'The relationship between export assistance and performance improvement in Portuguese export ventures: an empirical test of the mediating role of pricing strategy adaptation', *European Journal of Marketing*, **39**(7/8), 755–84.

Leonidou, L.C. (1995), 'Empirical research on export barriers: review, assessment and synthesis', *Journal of International Marketing*, **3**(1), 29–43.

Leonidou, L.C. (2004), 'An analysis of the barriers hindering small business export development', *Journal of Small Business Management*, **42**(3), 279–302.

Leonidou, L.C. and C.S. Katsikeas (1996), 'The export development process: an integrative review of empirical models', *Journal of International Business Studies*, **27**(3), 517–51.

Leonidou, L.C. and M. Theodosiou (2004), 'The export marketing information system: an integration of the extant knowledge', *Journal of World Business*, **39**(1), 12–36.

Leonidou, L.C., D. Palihawadana and M. Theodosiou (2011), 'National export-promotion programs as drivers of organizational resources and capabilities: effects on strategy, competitive advantage and performance', *Journal of International Marketing*, **19**(2), 1–29.

Leonidou, L.C., C.S. Katsikeas, D. Palihawadana and S. Spyropoulou (2007), 'An analytical review of the factors stimulating smaller firms to export: implications for policy-makers', *International Marketing Review*, **24**(6), 735–70.

Lim, J.-S., T.W. Sharkey and K.I. Kim (1996), 'Competitive environmental scanning and export involvement: an initial inquiry', *International Marketing Review*, **13**(1), 65–80.

Lu, J.W. and P.W. Beamish (2001), 'The internationalization and performance of SMEs', *Strategic Management Journal*, **22**(6/7), 565–86.

Marandu, E.E. (1995), 'Impact of export promotion on export performance: a Tanzanian study', *Journal of Global Marketing*, **9**(1/2), 9–39.

McConnell, J.E. (1979), 'The export decision: an empirical study of firm behavior', *Economic Geography*, **55**(3), 171–83.

McDougall, P.P. and B.M. Oviatt (2000), 'International entrepreneurship: the intersection of two research paths', *Academy of Management Journal*, **43**(5), 902–6.

Miles, M.P. and D.R. Arnold (1991), 'The relationship between marketing orientation and entrepreneurial orientation', *Entrepreneurship Theory and Practice*, **15**(4), 49–65.

Moini, A.H. (1998), 'Small firms and exporting: how effective are government export assistance programs?', *Journal of Small Business Management*, **36**(1), 1–15.

Morgan, R.E. and C.S. Katsikeas (1997), 'Obstacles to export initiation and expansion', *Omega*, **25**(6), 677–90.

Morris, M.H., R.A. Avila and J. Allen (1993), 'Individualism and the modern corporation: implications for innovation and entrepreneurship', *Journal of Management*, **19**(3), 595–612.

Naidu, G.M. and T.R. Rao (1993), 'Public sector promotion of exports: a needs-based approach', *Journal of Business Research*, **27**(1), 85–101.

Naidu, G.M., S.T. Cavusgil, B.K. Murthy and M. Sarkar (1997), 'An export promotion model for India: implications for public policy', *International Business Review*, **6**(2), 113–25.

Pope, R.A. (2002), 'Why small firms export: another look', *Journal of Small Business Management*, **40**(1), 17–26.

Rabino, S. (1980), 'An aptitude evaluation of an export incentive program: the case of DISC', *Columbia Journal of World Business*, **15**, 61–5.

Rundh, B. (2011), 'Linking flexibility and entrepreneurship to the performances of SMEs in export markets', *Journal of Manufacturing Technology Management*, **22**(3), 330–47.

Samiee, S. and P.G.P. Walters (1990), 'Influence of firm size on export planning and performance', *Journal of Business Research*, **20**(3), 235–48.

Samiee, S. and P.G.P. Walters (1991a), 'Segmenting corporate exporting activities: sporadic versus regular exporters', *Journal of the Academy of Marketing Science*, **19**(2), 93–104.

Samiee, S. and P.G.P. Walters (1991b), 'Rectifying strategic gaps in export management', *Journal of Global Marketing*, **4**(1), 7–37.

Samiee, S. and P.G.P. Walters (2002), 'Export education: perceptions of sporadic and regular exporting firms', *International Marketing Review*, **19**(1), 80–97.

Samiee, S., P.G.P. Walters and F.L. DuBois (1993), 'Exporting as an innovative behavior: an empirical investigation', *International Marketing Review*, **10**(3), 5–25.

Seringhaus, F.H.R. (1986), 'The impact of government export marketing assistance', *International Marketing Review*, **3**(2), 55–66.

Seringhaus, F.H.R. (1987), 'The use of trade missions in foreign market entry', *Industrial Marketing and Purchasing*, **2**(1), 43–60.

Seringhaus, F.H.R. (1993), 'Export promotion in developing countries: status and prospects', *Journal of Global Marketing*, **6**(4), 7–28.

Seringhaus, F.H.R. and G. Botschen (1991), 'Cross-national comparison of export promotion services: the views of Canadian and Austrian companies', *Journal of International Business Studies*, **22**(1), 115–33.

Seringhaus, F.H.R. and P.J. Rosson (1990), *Government Export Promotion: A Global Perspective*, London: Routledge, p. 238.

Shamsuddoha, A.K. and M.Y. Ali (2006), 'Mediated effects of export promotion programs on firm export performance', *Asia Pacific Journal of Marketing*, **18**(2), 93–116.

Shamsuddoha, A.K., M.Y. Ali and N.O. Ndubisi (2009a), 'Impact of government export assistance on internationalization of SMEs from developing nations', *Journal of Enterprise Information Management*, **22**(4), 408–22.

Shamsuddoha, A.K., M.Y. Ali and N.O. Ndubisi (2009b), 'A conceptualisation of direct and indirect impact of export promotion programs on export performance of SMEs and entrepreneurial ventures', *International Journal of Entrepreneurship*, **13**(Supplement), 87–106.

Shipley, D., C. Egan and K.S. Wong (1993), 'Dimensions of trade shows exhibiting management', *Journal of Marketing Management*, **9**(1), 55–63.

Simmonds, K. and H. Smith (1968), 'The first export order: a marketing innovation', *European Journal of Marketing*, **2**(2), 93–100.

Simpson, C.L. and D. Kujawa (1974), 'The export decision process: an empirical enquiry', *Journal of International Business Studies*, **5**(1), 107–17.

Singer, T.O. and M.R. Czinkota (1994), 'Factors associated with effective use of export assistance', *Journal of International Marketing*, **2**(1), 53–71.

Spence, M.M. (2003), 'Evaluating export promotion programs: U.K. overseas trade missions and export performance', *Small Business Economics*, **20**(1), 83–103.

Spence, M.M. and D. Crick (2001), 'An investigation into UK firms' use of trade missions', *Marketing Intelligence and Planning*, **19**(7), 464–74.

Tesfom, G. and C. Lutz (2008), 'Evaluating the effectiveness of export support services in developing countries. A customer (user) perspective', *International Journal of Emerging Markets*, **3**(4), 364–77.

Theodosiou, M. and L.C. Leonidou (2003), 'Standardization versus adaptation of international marketing strategy: an integrative assessment of the empirical research', *International Business Review*, **12**(2), 141–71.

Trimeche, M. (2002), 'Towards an actualization of the factors determining the firm's export expansion: insights from the literature', Working Paper, Kyoto: Kyoto University, pp. 1–21.

Vanderleest, H.W. (1996), 'What new exporters think about US government sponsored export promotion services and publications', *Multinational Business Review*, **4**(2), 21–9.

Venkatraman, N. (1989), 'Strategic orientation of business enterprises: the construct, dimensionality and measurement', *Management Science*, **35**(8), 942–62.

Weaver, K.M., D. Berkowitz and L. Davies (1998), 'Increasing the efficiency of national export promotion programs: the case of Norwegian exporters', *Journal of Small Business Management*, **36**(4), 1–11.

Welch, L.S. and F. Wiedersheim-Paul (1980), 'Initial exports – a marketing failure?', *Journal of Management Studies*, **17**(3), 333–44.

Wiedersheim-Paul, F., H.C. Olson and L.S. Welch (1978), 'Pre-export activity: the first step in internationalization', *Journal of International Business Studies*, **9**(1), 47–58.

Wilkinson, T.J. and L.E. Brouthers (2000), 'An evaluation of state sponsored promotion programs', *Journal of Business Research*, **47**(3), 229–36.

Wilkinson, T. and L.E. Brouthers (2006), 'Trade promotion and SME export performance', *International Business Review*, **15**(3), 233–52.

Zahra, S.A. and D.M. Garvis (2000), 'International corporate entrepreneurship and firm performance: the moderating effect of international environmental hostility', *Journal of Business Venturing*, **15**(5), 469–92.

Zahra, S.A., D.O. Neubaum and M. Huse (1997), 'The effect of the environment on export performance among telecommunications new ventures', *Entrepreneurship Theory and Practice*, **22**(1), 25–46.

APPENDIX: EMPIRICAL STUDIES FOCUSING ON EXPORT PROMOTION PROGRAMS

(https://www.e-elgar.com/edward-elgar-handbook-of-research-on-international-entrepreneurship-strategy-companion-site)

	Empirical studies											
Export promotion programs	Cavusgil (1983) USA	Seringhaus (1986) Canada	Kedia & Chhokar (1986) USA	Seringhaus & Botschen (1991) Austria and Canada	Crick (1992) UK	Samiee et al. (1993) USA	Seringhaus (1993) LDCs	Naidu & Rao (1993) USA	Shipley et al. (1993) UK	Singer & Czinkota (1994) USA	Kumcu et al. (1995) Turkey
Financially related											
Seed capital revolving fund											●
Rebate											●
Foreign exchange retention scheme											
Duty drawback											
Export credit guarantees against political/commercial risk			●								
Export loans				●							●
Export insurance				●	●						●
Funds transfer											
Banking service that guarantees payment by qualified customer											
Banking service that handles all financial aspects of the sale			●								
Assistance in financing exports				●						●	
Tax & tariffs incentives/subsidies											●

Export promotion programs	Empirical studies										
	Cavusgil (1983) USA	Seringhaus (1986) Canada	Kedia & Chhokar (1986) USA	Seringhaus & Botschen (1991) Austria and Canada	Crick (1992) UK	Samiee et al. (1993) USA	Seringhaus (1993) LDCs	Naidu & Rao (1993) USA	Shipley et al. (1993) UK	Singer & Czinkota (1994) USA	Kumcu et al. (1995) Turkey
Information related											
Information about foreign market opportunities											
Information on particular foreign firms or countries			●			●					
Computerized trade lead services								●			
Marketing information							●				
Export newsletters, reports mailing lists and other publications			●	●		●					
Trade information/leads	●		●			●	●				
Participation in international market research	●			●			●			●	
Feasibility studies			●				●				
Education & training											
Export seminars, conferences and workshops			●					●		●	
Export/business counseling	●	●	●	●			●	●		●	
Training programs				●							

Legal aspects							
Bureaucracy reforms							●
Market targeting							
Foreign buyer invitation program (match-maker)							
Foreign buyer visit	●						
Foreign buyer program							
Completely arrange foreign trips for exploiting market potential	●	●	●				
Market development							
Negotiating assistance/contact facilitators-partners							
Product							
Packaging				●	●		
Product development and listing							
Product modification/adaptation advice					●		
Production planning							
Matching your product(s) with foreign buyers needs				●	●		
Productivity and quality development							
Pricing							
Contract bidding	●						
Pricing internationally				●	●		
Distribution							
Assistance in locating overseas agents/ distributors	●		●	●		●	
Service that buys the firm's product(s) to resell overseas							

Export promotion programs	Cavusgil (1983) USA	Seringhaus (1986) Canada	Kedia & Chhokar (1986) USA	Seringhaus & Botschen (1991) Austria and Canada	Crick (1992) UK	Samiee et al. (1993) USA	Seringhaus (1993) LDCs	Naidu & Rao (1993) USA	Shipley et al. (1993) UK	Singer & Czinkota (1994) USA	Kumcu et al. (1995) Turkey
	Empirical studies										
Logistics											
Handling export documentation requirements and shipping			●		●		●				
Providing warehousing					●						
Transportation incentives				●			●				●
Promotion											
Trade missions		●								●	
Trade fairs/shows/exhibitions	●	●		●				●	●	●	●
Trade offices abroad											
Catalog show/direct mail campaign										●	
Advertising	●			●	●						
Assistance in publicizing products in overseas market			●				●				
Miscellaneous											
Assistance in developing an export strategy and plan											
Feasibility studies											
Special awards to good exporters											●
Toll-free number			●								
Motivational program											

Export promotion programs	Empirical studies											
	Crick & Czinkota (1995) USA & UK	Marandu (1995) Tanzania	Vanderleest (1996) USA	Lim et al. (1996) USA	Naidu et al. (1997) India	Moini (1998) USA	Weaver et al. (1998) Norway	Wilkinson & Brouthers (2000) USA	Crick & Chaudhry (2000) UK	Gençtürk & Kotabe (2001) USA	Spence & Crick (2001) UK	Ahmed et al. (2002) Malaysia
Financially related												
Seed capital revolving fund		●										
Rebate		●										
Foreign exchange retention scheme		●			●							
Duty drawback		●										
Export credit guarantees against political/commercial risk					●							
Export loans												
Export insurance					●					●		
Funds transfer		●										
Banking service that guarantees payment by qualified customer						●						
Banking service that handles all financial aspects of the sale						●						
Assistance in financing exports	●				●		●		●			●
Tax & tariffs incentives/subsidies					●							●

Export promotion programs	Empirical studies											
	Crick & Czinkota (1995) USA & UK	Marandu (1995) Tanzania	Vanderleest (1996) USA	Lim et al. (1996) USA	Naidu et al. (1997) India	Moini (1998) USA	Weaver et al. (1998) Norway	Wilkinson & Brouthers (2000) USA	Crick & Chaudhry (2000) UK	Gençtürk & Kotabe (2001) USA	Spence & Crick (2001) UK	Ahmed et al. (2002) Malaysia
Information related												
Information about foreign market opportunities			●	●				●	●			
Information on particular foreign firms or countries				●		●						
Computerized trade lead services								●				
Marketing information												
Export newsletters, reports mailing lists and other publications			●		●	●						
Trade information/leads				●				●		●		
General literature on exporting	●					●				●		●
Participation in international market research	●	●	●		●	●		●	●	●		
Education & training												
Export seminars, conferences and workshops	●		●	●	●	●			●	●		
Export/business counseling	●		●		●	●				●		
Training programs		●										●

Legal aspects									
Bureaucracy reforms									
Market targeting									
Foreign buyer invitation program (match-maker)	●					●	●		
Foreign buyer visit									
Foreign buyer program						●		●	
Completely arrange foreign trips for exploiting market potential					●				
Market development									●
Negotiating assistance/contact facilitators-partners			●	●					
Product									
Packaging									
Product development and listing		●		●			●		●
Product modification/adaptation advice			●	●					
Production planning				●					
Matching your product(s) with foreign buyers needs					●				
Productivity and quality development									●
Pricing									
Contract bidding									
Pricing internationally									
Distribution									
Assistance in locating overseas agents/distributors				●	●	●			
Service that buys the firm's product(s) to resell overseas					●				

Export promotion programs	Empirical studies											
	Crick & Czinkota (1995) USA & UK	Marandu (1995) Tanzania	Vanderleest (1996) USA	Lim et al. (1996) USA	Naidu et al. (1997) India	Moini (1998) USA	Weaver et al. (1998) Norway	Wilkinson & Brouthers (2000) USA	Crick & Chaudhry (2000) UK	Gençtürk & Kotabe (2001) USA	Spence & Crick (2001) UK	Ahmed et al. (2002) Malaysia
Logistics												
Handling export documentation requirements and shipping			●			●						
Providing warehousing												
Transport incentives												
Promotion												
Trade missions			●					●	●	●	●	●
Trade fairs/shows/exhibitions	●	●			●			●	●	●		●
Trade offices abroad								●		●		
Catalog show/direct mail campaign												
Advertising												
Assistance in publicizing products in overseas market								●		●		
Miscellaneous												
Assistance in developing an export strategy and plan												
Feasibility studies					●							●
Special awards to good exporters												
Toll-free number						●						
Motivational program												

Promotion programs	Fischer & Reuber (2003) Canada	Spence (2003) UK	Alvarez (2004) Chile	Francis & Collins Dodd (2004) Canada	Lages & Montgomery (2005) Portugal	Wilkinson & Brouthers (2006) USA	Tesfom & Lutz (2008) Eritrea (Africa)	Freixanet (2012) Spain	Geldres et al. (2011) Chile	Leonidou et al. (2011) UK	Durmuşoğlu et al. (2012) Turkey
	Empirical studies										
Financially related											
Seed capital revolving fund											
Rebate											
Foreign exchange retention scheme											
Duty drawback											
Export credit guarantees against political/commercial risk											
Export loans											●
Export insurance							●				●
Funds transfer											
Banking service that guarantees payment by qualified customer											
Banking service that handles all financial aspects of the sale											
Assistance in financing exports							●	●			
Tax & tariffs incentives/subsidies							●				

Promotion programs	Empirical studies										
	Fischer & Reuber (2003) Canada	Spence (2003) UK	Alvarez (2004) Chile	Francis & Collins Dodd (2004) Canada	Lages & Montgomery (2005) Portugal	Wilkinson & Brouthers (2006) USA	Tesfom & Lutz (2008) Eritrea (Africa)	Freixanet (2012) Spain	Geldres et al. (2011) Chile	Leonidou et al. (2011) UK	Durmuşoğlu et al. (2012) Turkey
Information related											
Information about foreign market opportunities							●	●		●	
Information on particular foreign firms or countries				●						●	
Computerized trade lead services				●							
Marketing information			●							●	
Export newsletters, reports mailing lists and other publications				●				●		●	
Trade information/leads				●							●
General literature on exporting										●	●
Participation in international market research			●								●
Education & training											
Export seminars, conferences and workshops				●				●		●	●

Export/business counseling								●		●	●
Training programs	●			●				●		●	
Legal Aspects											
Bureaucracy reforms											
Market targeting											
Foreign buyer invitation program (match-maker)			●								
Foreign buyer visit											
Foreign buyer program											●
Completely arrange foreign trips for exploiting market potential											
Market development	●										
Negotiating assistance/contact facilitators-partners											
Product											
Packaging											
Product development and listing											
Product modification/adaptation advice											
Production planning											
Matching your product(s) with foreign buyers needs											
Productivity and quality development											

Promotion programs	Empirical studies										
	Fischer & Reuber (2003) Canada	Spence (2003) UK	Alvarez (2004) Chile	Francis & Collins Dodd (2004) Canada	Lages & Montgomery (2005) Portugal	Wilkinson & Brouthers (2006) USA	Tesfom & Lutz (2008) Eritrea (Africa)	Freixanet (2012) Spain	Geldres et al. (2011) Chile	Leonidou et al. (2011) UK	Durmuşoğlu et al. (2012) Turkey
Pricing											
Contract bidding											
Pricing internationally											
Distribution											
Assistance in locating overseas agents/distributors						•					
Service that buys the firm's product(s) to resell overseas											
Logistics											
Handling export documentation requirements and shipping											
Providing warehousing											
Transport incentives							•				

Promotion											
Trade missions	●	●	●	●		●		●	●	●	●
Trade fairs/shows/exhibitions			●	●		●	●	●	●	●	●
Trade offices abroad				●				●	●	●	●
Catalog show/direct mail campaign											
Advertising								●			
Assistance in publicizing products in overseas market											
Miscellaneous											
Assistance in developing an export strategy and plan					●						●
Feasibility studies											
Special awards to good exporters											
Toll-free number									●		
Motivational program											

13. The role of government in encouraging entrepreneurship in emerging economies: the case of Korean ventures

Seung Hoon Jang, Jung Seek Kim and Jonathan Ohn

INTRODUCTION

Recently, entrepreneurship has been considered as an increasingly significant topic in the study of management (Bygrave and Hofer, 1991; Busenitz et al., 2003). It is expected that entrepreneurs and their business activities will boost the economy and employment availability. A newly formed venture with innovative technology will hire employees and nurture professionals, while increasing tax revenue of local and central governments. In addition, several firms seek fundamental innovations that may dominate future society and its markets, while others pursue by-products of such an evolution. Entrepreneurial activities occupy a crucial portion of business activities today. The discussions on this research topic are centered on how individual entrepreneurs recognize and thus, are able to exploit business opportunities through new ventures (Gartner, 1985).

Scholars like Fayolle (2007) have focused on the role of entrepreneurship in explaining new value creation. Particularly, new high-tech ventures have been considered as major ways in which entrepreneurs challenge traditional technology and achieve financial gains (Zahra and Bogner, 2000). In the early twenty-first century, firms, such as Amazon, experimented with a new business model based on IT technology. The sales volume of USD74 452 million in 2013[1] exhibits that Amazon successfully utilized the Internet, establishing precedence and leading the new market. This case exemplifies the potential of entrepreneurial mindsets discovering a new industry to achieve competitive advantage and thereby attain business success. It is imperative to recognize how entrepreneurs can generate value by taking advantage of new technologies.

In order to be fully acknowledged and recognized for its significance, the field of entrepreneurship requires further discussion among scholars to establish validity. Despite the vital role that entrepreneurs have in the economy, the definitions of entrepreneurship are varied (Bygrave and

Hofer, 1991). Schumpeter (1934), one of the initiators of this field, focused on the innovativeness of entrepreneurs and entrepreneurial activities. New entrepreneurial leaders are expected to develop innovative technologies, products or processes such as those that have led to the initiation of the Walkman, Prius and iPhone. Several other researchers like Gartner (1985) and Fauchart and Gruber (2011) have argued that the creation of a new firm is the core of entrepreneurship. Newly formed ventures are able to better capitalize on future or existing business opportunities through their products or services (Choi and Shepherd, 2004). Pharmaceutical giants often merge smaller businesses in order to better utilize newly developed products or technologies. In doing so, they can acquire the new technology, while simultaneously avoiding the risk of investing additional time and effort. Given the effects of new and innovation-centered firms, scholars need to further examine the nature of entrepreneurship to deepen the understanding within the context of the new market and economy.

The importance of global evaluations when considering business implications becomes increasingly relevant as economies around the world continually set new standards through the growth that is evident in many developing countries. Bruton et al. (2008) focus on entrepreneurial activities of emerging economies. The rapid growth in such economies indicates the need for scholars to examine the role of entrepreneurial activities on not only the domestic front, but also on a global scale. The use of new technologies has transformed local and traditional markets by enabling local ventures to introduce and promote their products and services to the global consumers with minimal effort and costs involved. Businesses can now reach and market to consumers everywhere. Smartphone users can now easily access and download Polaris Office, a mobile office application developed by InfraWare – a Korean start-up – regardless of their remote locations. Given the transformative effects of local start-up businesses and their prevalent role in the new global market the conditions that act to encourage new ventures in emerging economies should be closely evaluated to continuously stimulate the development of new ventures and innovation, which is essentially to promote entrepreneurship.

The goal of this study is to examine and identify the factors that encourage the formation of Korean start-up ventures. The prevalence of Korean firms in many key industries reflects the success of Korean entrepreneurs having initiated innovation through their products, services and technologies. Korea has become one of the major economies of the world (Gupta et al., 2012); and although the Korean economy has long been characterized by its '*chaebol*' or conglomerate-driven economy (Kim et al., 2004), Korean start-up ventures play an increasingly significant role in explaining the innovative results of various high-tech industries (Lee, 2000). The country's entrepreneurial business leaders are able to thrive within the culture that the Korean economy fosters, contributing to its success (Kim et al., 2004). In order to dissect and fully comprehend the influences that enable the success of Korean ventures, the literature of entrepreneurship and related topics of the theoretical background of entrepreneurship are reviewed. The study continues on to examine the motivators and supporting mechanisms that nurture the formation and success of Korean ventures, based on the literature review, then finally, conclusions can be made from the implications and limitations of the research. The success that has led Korea to become one of the locomotives of the global economy is explained by exploring the sources that culminate in the development of innovation by Korean firms, providing insight into understanding the global business practices of today.

THEORETICAL BASIS OF ENTREPRENEURSHIP

Researchers like Begley and Boyd (1987) and Marco and Kritikos (2012) have focused on personal characteristics of entrepreneurs as major factors explaining entrepreneurial activities. In other words, people with specific personal characteristics are expected to be successful entrepreneurs. Certain types of traits have been expected to explain how and why several individuals initiate new ventures while others do not. For instance, people who are favorable to new ideas are thought to be more likely to pioneer new business opportunities. According to this perspective, efforts in understanding entrepreneurship should be focused on studying individuals with specific characteristics that may predetermine the individuals to become entrepreneurs. However, Gartner (1985) recognized that differences in characteristics among entrepreneurs can exceed the heterogeneity between entrepreneurs and non-entrepreneurs, which implies that we need to examine distinctive factors of successful entrepreneurs and new ventures rather than limit our studies to a few personal characteristics.

Since Gartner (1985) focused on the interrelationships among individual, environment, process and organization in the processes of new venture creation, the literature of entrepreneurship has examined various factors in explaining how and why several entrepreneurs successfully exploit new business opportunities despite various limitations. For instance, most newly formed firms are required to overcome their relative weaknesses, including weak brand image or low credit, as Aldrich and Auster (1986) and Fackler et al. (2013) showed in their study of the 'liability of smallness'. Since many entrepreneurial opportunities have not existed before, entrepreneurs need to implement a business model without knowing the role models or even the probability of success. Potential job applicants may not be attracted to such businesses because of their uncertain future.

Information asymmetry across different people has been considered as another major stimulant of entrepreneurial opportunities (Shane, 2000; Dimov, 2011). Since some business leaders recognize business opportunities before others would, they are more likely to benefit from the opportunities. Steve Jobs, the entrepreneur in the IT era, understood the potential of personal computers, graphic user interface (GUI) and touchscreen-based smartphones and initiated the markets and value creation in the industry. Morita Akio, the founder of SONY, also saw the opportunities in hand-held music devices, which resulted in gigantic financial profits and a dominant brand image. Although these products or services have been considered as essential commodities of modern living, people may not recognize such needs prior to the commercial launching of the products and services. These cases exhibit that several individuals have the potential to collect better information or predict future consumer needs before others do, which lead to successful entrepreneurial activities.

The study on entrepreneurship has focused on the formation of firms by corporations as well as individuals. Zahra (1995) examined how existing firms create new businesses and reported that new start-ups from established businesses are shown to affect the financial performance of parent organizations. This type of business is expected to have advantages from better financial and managerial resources from the support of its larger corporation. The existing credits and business practices enable newly formed businesses to utilize abundant capital at its disposal. New ventures supported by GE are more likely to retain better tangible and intangible assets. In comparison to the conventional ventures initiated by individual entrepreneurs, these types of firms can more easily achieve competitive advantage due to the availability of their superior resources, as Barney (1991) suggested. In addition to financial capital or experienced talent, these firms can refer to previous business experiences or know-how of the original firm easily. Furthermore, they can recognize and exploit business opportunities ahead of others by utilizing their networks with original firms. A new start-up based on the capital and human resources of Apple can access the business projects of Apple Corporation from the official or unofficial relationships, resulting in better chances of successful business performance.

Additionally, the role of government and other institutional support can increase business conditions that encourage entrepreneurial activities, as Lerner (2002) suggested. Government in these days initiates various forms of mechanisms that support entrepreneurs and new ventures. A form of such supporting mechanisms is the public fund that encourages new venture creation, as seen in the example of the Russian Venture Company (Todosiichuk, 2011). Russian government provided approximately 28 billion rubles to support new future business leaders to establish their own business entities. The National Fund for Entrepreneurship and Development (ETEAN) was established to encourage entrepreneurship in Europe (Balomenou and Maliari, 2013).

Government–industry–academia collaboration is another form of practice that supports entrepreneurship. While large, established firms may initiate drastic, breakthrough innovation projects, smaller start-ups may not be able to afford such ambitious endeavors, as described in the 'liability of smallness' by Aldrich and Auster (1986). Smaller firms are more likely to address issues that include how to accumulate sufficient capital or how to retain human resources. Ordinary ventures initiated by individual entrepreneurs are less likely to retain their own capital or credits required to attract other funds in order to accomplish successful innovative results. In addition, such firms must operate strategically to overcome the lack of experience and know-how that comes with their newness. Even if they are able to borrow funds to overcome such issues, they should take more risks financially and credit-wise. If the government promotes the collaborative and cooperative relationships among these new ventures, large firms, universities and public supporting mechanisms these entrepreneurs can overcome the 'liability of smallness' with minimal risk because they can utilize their tangible or intangible assets for entrepreneurial activities from other collaborators.

Universities have been considered as a major supporter of entrepreneurial activities (Menzies, 2000). Three major areas of entrepreneurial centers include education, the support of entrepreneurs and the scholarship of entrepreneurship (Kurato, 2005). In Canada, university entrepreneurship centers encourage students to start their own businesses. Finkle et al. (2006) mentioned that universities can utilize their entrepreneurship centers as new sources of growth based on their by-products like patents. Alumni entrepreneurs provide universities with the fame of being associated with a technological innovator as well as monetary contribution through donations. Students may choose universities with better funding, extensive alumni networking and innovation projects for their future. Therefore, it is advantageous for universities to consider entrepreneurial activities to continue to survive, grow and prosper.

In addition, various civil organizations provide funding that aims to create new ventures. Since these organizations reflect the intentions of donors that are interested in entrepreneurship, they can accomplish their mission in contributing to the formation of new businesses. The mission of the Kauffman Foundation,[2] a major private fund in this field, lies in helping individual entrepreneurs that seek financial stability through entrepreneurial activities. For this purpose, the institution invested more than USD44 million in 2013 and has managed several entrepreneurial institutions. Kauffman Founders School, Kauffman FastTrac, 1 Million Cups and the Ice House Entrepreneurship program all aim to enhance the capabilities of individual entrepreneurs. Kauffman FastTrac has educated more than 300000 participants. In 2012, the Kauffman Foundation in collaboration with the Lorain County Community College, also initiated the Innovation Fund America to encourage community colleges to support high-tech ventures. This case exhibits the role of private entrepreneurial funds in explaining the prosperity of entrepreneurial firms these days.

In explaining the support for entrepreneurship in developing economies, the role of government is shown to be quite significant. Anglo-American governments as well as those of non-Western countries have played important roles in managing business activities when they drastically develop their economies (Wade, 1990). For instance, East Asian countries, including Korea, have continued government-driven economic development for decades and in a number of most Eastern European countries the governmental role has been quite significant especially in the process of privatization. It implies that scholars and practitioners need to examine the role of the governments in nurturing ventures and entrepreneurs to further understand entrepreneurial activities and vitality in these countries. Considering the significant governmental support in creating entrepreneurial businesses and large business conglomerates in Korea, which then has led to dramatic economic development for decades, this study will focus more on the role of government in encouraging new venture creation in Korea.

CONTRIBUTION OF ENTREPRENEURSHIP TO ECONOMIC DEVELOPMENT IN KOREA

In the mid-1950s, following the Korean War, South Korea was one of the poorest countries in the world with a per capita income of only USD64, earnings lower than those of most Latin American and some Sub-Saharan countries (List-Jensen, 2008). However, Korea has shown spectacular economic growth since then. It now belongs to the Organisation for Economic Co-operation and Development (OECD), the group of the world's wealthiest nations, and is also a member of Group 20 (G-20), consisting of the 20 major economies in the world. In 2009, Korea officially became the first major recipient of official development assistance (ODA) from the OECD to have ascended to the status of being a major donor of ODA. In 2012,

Korea was landmarked to become the seventh member, followed by Japan, the United States, France, Italy, Germany and the UK, of the 20-50 Club, which includes countries with the population over 50 million and maintaining a per capita income of USD20000 (*Yonap*, 2012).

Having almost no natural resources and a tiny domestic market in the small territory of the country, Korea adapted an export-oriented development strategy to fuel its economy. In 2012, Korea was the sixth largest exporter and seventh largest importer in the world. Much of Korea's economic success is credited to entrepreneurs. Many early entrepreneurs in different fields during the 1960s and 1970s have become world-class large conglomerates such as Samsung, Hyundai and LG, which account for more than 30 percent of the nation's GDP. The new generation has made great strides towards becoming forerunners in the global market for emerging businesses.

In spite of the outstanding early successes in entrepreneurship and venture companies, there remain some barriers to entrepreneurship in Korea. For example, there are high set-up costs and administration fees. The prevailing attitude towards venture firms and entrepreneurship has not been all positive. The cultural attitude towards risk and failure is that risk is avoided, stability is revered and failure is unacceptable. Moreover, governmental bureaucracy and inefficiency in coordinating and implementing policies have been criticized often, as well as discontinuity in governmental policies across successive administrations. However, considerable efforts are being made to reduce or remove these barriers to promote the entrepreneurial spirit, which will be discussed later. The organizations in Korea work hard to streamline inter-office communication and collaboration (Beach and Hanks, 2010). The continuing efforts in Korea for deregulation, local autonomy and entrepreneurial activities will produce a more transparent, competitive and user-friendly business environment, thereby contributing to a more robust growth in start-up and high-tech venture companies in the fastest-growing business sectors. These significant efforts in both the government and private sectors will be fully discussed later.

Government's Active Role in Boosting Large Conglomerates, or *Chaebols*

The Korean economy was predominantly agricultural until the mid-1960s. General Park Chung-hee, who became the third president by military coup in 1961, implemented economic development plans to achieve industrialization in South Korea. President Park utilized his military leadership to lead the government to achieve and sustain the rapid economic growth. One of the notable outcomes under his administration was the creation of *chaebols*. A *chaebol* can be referred to as a highly diversified Korean business group under a charismatic chairman (Jung, 2004). The authoritarian government under Park's leadership forced major firms in the early 1960s to invest in export-oriented and capital-intensive manufacturing sectors and created and nurtured *chaebols* by channeling resources into them. Specifically, Park's regime designated 'strategic sectors' (steel, petrochemical, heavy and export-driven industries) on which his administration concentrated scarce resources; companies in such sectors that followed governmental initiatives were offered negotiated access to foreign technologies, subsidies and low-interest loans (mostly backed by repayment guaranteed by the government) (Kim et al., 2004). The supremacy of the state over *chaebols* prevailed until the mid-1980s; since then, however, the state dominancy was gradually undermined and *chaebols* had become more powerful and less dependent on direct or conspicuous assistance from the state (Lee et al., 2000). Although there have been continual criticisms of *chaebols*, it is commonly understood that the *chaebols* have been particularly effective in generating economic development in the form of a non-Western model of state-driven economic growth (Murillo and Sung, 2013).

GOVERNMENT'S ACTIVE ROLE IN BOOSTING THE VENTURE SECTOR

From the 1980s to the mid-1990s

Over the past few decades, the Korean government has implemented policies that promote high-tech venture firms. The definition of Korean small and medium-sized enterprises (SMEs) varies across its industries as described in the Table 13.1. In the manufacturing industry, firms can be considered SMEs when they retain fewer than 300 employees and capital worth USD8 million or less. Technologies accumulated during the 1970s and 1980s were being transferred from big enterprises to these SMEs and many small enterprises began to develop their own technologies. As a result, few successful technology-based SMEs emerged in the 1980s (Chung, 2007). Qnix, established in 1981, was the first Korean high-tech venture; Mirae Corporation, established in 1983, produced semiconductor equipment; Medison, established in 1985, manufactured ultrasonic devices and medical equipment; and Humax I, established in 1986, marketed digital set-top boxes. There were a handful of very successful entrepreneurs during the 1980s and early 1990s, but the term 'venture' remained strange and unfamiliar to the general public. It was considered out of the

Table 13.1 Definition of Korean SMEs

	SMES	
	No. of employees	Capital & sales
Wholesale and product intermediation, machinery equipment rent for industrial use, R&D for natural science, public performance, news provision, botanical gardens, zoos and natural parks, wastewater treatment, waste disposal and cleaning-related services	100 or less	Sales worth USD10 million or less
Seed and seedling production, fishing, electrical, gas and waterworks, medical and orthopedic products, wholesales, fuel and related products, mail order sales, door-to-door sales, tour agencies, warehouses and transportation-related services, professional, science and technology services, business support services, movie, amusement and theme park operation	200 or less	Sales worth USD20 million or less
Large general retail stores, hotels, recreational condominium operation, communications, information processing and other computer-related industries, engineering services, hospitals and broadcasting	300 or less	Sales worth USD30 million or less
Manufacturing	300 or less	Capital worth USD8 million or less
Mining, construction and transportation	300 or less	Capital worth USD3 million or less
Other sectors	50 or less	Sales worth USD5 million or less

Source: Based on: 'Criteria of Korean SMSs' table, Small and Medium Business Administration website: http://www.smba.go.kr/eng/smes/scope.do?mc = usr0001146; accessed 22 May 2015.

norm to start one's own company upon graduating college. Additionally, a large number of small and mid-sized manufacturing and technology businesses were dependent on the resources of *chaebols*, as they acted as subcontractors and suppliers. Governmental support, in the forms of tax credits, grants and special loans, were made available to assist SMEs, but policies aimed to explicitly promote venture firms in the technology sectors from 1980 to 1995 were limited (Bae and Cha, 2008). For instance, an SME that recorded profits the first time in its tax return could receive corporate income tax credit of as much as 50 percent for the tax year and two subsequent years. Qualified property, plant and equipment were subject to tax credits of as much as 50 percent. Dividends income received from qualified SMEs were taxed at a lower rate than those from bigger companies. Also, gain on the sale of stocks for qualified SMEs was tax exempt. In addition, the government provided credit guarantees to SMEs through government-funded agencies.

From the Mid-1990s to 2000: KOSDAQ

Start-ups and high-tech ventures in Korea have boomed since the mid-1990s. Korean Securities Dealers Automated Quotations (KOSDAQ) has played a significant role in enabling the 'venture boom'. Korea Financial Investment Association (KOFIA) established an over-the-counter (OTC) market in 1986 after the government announced its 'Plan to Organize a Market that Facilitates Stock Trading for Small and Medium-Sized Enterprises'. The plan addressed the financial difficulties of raising capital by giving SMEs the opportunity to be listed on the Korea Stock Exchange (KSE), the security exchange index of Korea. On 15 April 1987, KOFIA opened the OTC market and the first three firms, Aero Systems, Beom-Yang Keon-Young and Hankuk Mul-San, were registered. However, the OTC market was criticized for being an inefficient attempt to provide equity financing to SMEs. To revitalize SMEs and computerize trading, KOFIA established the KOSDAQ Securities Exchange, benchmarked from NASDAQ, on 1 July 1996. Since its inception, KOSDAQ has been providing a way for SMEs to raise long-term capital, especially to fuel high-tech ventures. For a company's stock to be listed and traded on KOSDAQ, the company should have at least three years of business operation and equity of KRW0.5 billion (approximately USD0.6 million) (with other conditions being met). The requirements are considerably less stringent than those imposed on firms to be listed on the KSE, which require five years of operation and equity of at least KRW3 billion (approximately USD2.8 million). Government policies continued to complement KOSDAQ. In 1995, the government relaxed registration requirements for KOSDAQ and even large corporations began to capitalize on the market. The government also began to offer tax benefits for companies whose shares were listed in KOSDAQ to further attract promising SMEs and high-tech venture companies. KOSDAQ helped diversify and balance the Korean economy.

Asian Financial Crisis and Venture Boom

When the 1997 Asian financial crisis devastated the Korean economy, much of the criticism centered on *chaebols* and their malfunctioning business practices. Such practices included a lack of transparency and accountability on the management's part, mutual payment guarantees, high debt–equity ratio and unfair trading practices with subcontractors, most of them being SMEs. A number of *chaebols* went bankrupt, disproving long-held beliefs that corporations can be 'too big to fail' and that *chaebols* could never collapse. Koreans began to realize the *chaebols*' detrimental influence on the national economy and how dependent the nation had become on them. The new administration of 1998 made efforts to resuscitate the economy through massive restructuring of the economic system that so heavily depended on *chaebols*, also investigating new stimulants to trigger economic growth.

New government policies ensued to provide a more efficient and effective market environment for start-up businesses and ventures. Substantial benefits were offered in the forms of direct and indirect subsidies, exemptions, tax credits and relaxation of regulations. For instance, in 1999, the government's direct loan to start-ups and SMEs amounted to KRW750 billion (approximately USD659) (Chung, 2007). The rapid advancement of the Internet and information technology (IT) of the late 1990s fostered the idea of creating high-risk, high-return ventures in the IT industry, primarily appealing to young entrepreneurs and college students. Additionally, employment prospects of large corporations were reduced as they had become extremely cautious in hiring new employees and had broken the implicit pledge for lifetime employment since the financial crisis and the IMF bailout. Key policy-makers of the administration and most Korean business leaders envisioned that venture companies would not only increase employment, but also convert the economy into one that is knowledge and IT based.

Burst of Venture Boom or Bubble in 2000

The government assumed the role of 'initiator' of the venture system in the late 1990s, as it employed most of its available resources directly towards venture firms. Its aim was to support the 'full cycle' of new venture creation and development (Bae et al., 2007; Bae and Cha, 2008). However, its direct market intervention has been criticized for having the possibility of distorting economic incentives. Though well-intentioned in supporting entrepreneurs through preferential measures, the benefits of entering high-tech sectors can attract companies lacking a competitive edge just to qualify to receive governmental subsidies. Such propping up of incompetent ventures may well entail increases in screening and monitoring costs to investors and the administration (Lee, 2013). Unfortunately, the venture craze produced a large number of start-ups that did indeed attempt to capitalize on business opportunities in IT, but did not have clear core competencies. As expected, many of those venture firms created in the late 1990s, especially dot.com companies, foundered and dissolved quickly, giving rise to the so-called burst of the venture bubble in 2000. The KOSDAQ Index hit a record high of 2843 on 10 March 2000, but plummeted to approximately 530 in a matter of only nine months (Keum, 2000); as of 9 June 2014 it is approximately 524. Private investment by venture capital companies hit a record high of KRW2.075 trillion (approximately USD1.6 billion) in 2000 and sharply decreased in 2001–02 to 0.889 and 0.617 trillions (approximately USD0.6 billon and 0.5 billion respectively) (KOTRA, 2004).

Similar to large conglomerates in the late 1990s, after the bubble burst in 2000, the venture sector faced a mandate for structural reform. Venture companies sought to enhance profitability by downsizing, outsourcing and focusing on core business domains. Strategic alliances and M&A became more commonplace as a means of creating synergy, acquiring new technology and diversifying into new areas. Start-ups and incumbent ventures focused more on the development of superior technologies. Venture companies strived to succeed on the global front, rather than settling for the smaller domestic market (Chung, 2007). Consequently, an increasing number of venture companies grew their businesses, making for notable success stories.

Government Policies in the 2000s

As the Korean economy continued on its progression towards stabilization and growth, government policies adjusted to support market mechanisms with the utmost concern for how to help high-tech SMEs enhance their competitiveness. Traditional measures, such as tax incentives for venture capital companies and angel investors and direct loans to start-ups, continued to be available. But policy-makers sought ways to further bolster the venture sector. The number of business incubation centers had grown from 30 in 1998 to 361 in July 2003; the government had spent approximately KRW360 billion (approximately USD347.8 million) to support those incubation centers from 1998 to 2003 (KOTRA, 2004). More importantly, the government promoted the clustering of venture companies in certain regions, creating Venture Company Promotion Districts and Venture Company Clustering Facilities: the former nests colleges and research institutes where venture companies tend to aggregate while the latter provides tax and other incentives for buildings with a certain number of venture companies as tenants (KOTRA, 2004). Bae et al. (2007) point out that such habitats include (1) physical infrastructure (convention centers, incubators, office buildings, lodging, etc.); (2) financial infrastructure (venture capital firms, banks, angel investors); (3) special services (accounting and law firms); (4) consulting services; (5) education and training sectors; and (6) research sectors (universities, corporate R&D laboratories and government-supported research institutes). In addition, it loosened regulations to facilitate M&As between ventures and large established companies. While the number of venture capital firms had decreased from 147 since 2000, the central and local governments remained the main financial contributor. Out of KRW455 billion (approximately USD381.5 million) that was raised for the start-up investment funds in 2003, the governments accounted for 30 percent, start-up investment firms 15.6 percent, pension funds 30 percent and individual and institutional investors 23.5 percent. The enhancement of the infrastructure and ecosystem for ventures has been the major concern of policies coming into the new millennium. In the 2000s, successful venture companies in Korea became more diverse, innovative, customer-driven, marketing savvy and globalized, covering diverse business sectors with high growth potentials, including IT, biotechnology, online games and entertainment.

'Creative Economy'

The tradition of providing strong governmental support continues into the current regime, which began in February 2013, when President Park Geun-hye took office. Park proposed to initiate 'Creative Economy' as one of the new national economic agendas meant to overcome the sluggish growth and troublesome unemployment of the past years. The theme underlying Creative Economy, according to the Ministry of Science, ICT and Future Planning (MSIP), is that creativity is the asset in deriving the new growth engine for the Korean economy by combining creative ideas, imagination and information/communication technologies. Park and her administration propose that smaller, innovative firms with creative ideas and technologies will create more jobs and boost exports, thus stimulating growth in the long run (Park, 2013b). Some key aspects of the Creative Economy proposal include (1) creating an ecosystem that facilitates start-ups by breaking down obstacles that inhibit them and to help entrepreneurs revive their businesses after failures; (2) supporting and cultivating ventures and SMEs by providing financial support to help them evolve into globalized companies, ensuring large companies and SMEs to share the benefits of economic prosperity; and (3) expanding information/communication and science/technology sectors to a level unmatched by the rest of the world. The major difference from the previous administration's economic policy for start-up is that the Park government is trying to encourage the private sector to lead efforts to create venture firms and expand their lifecycle (Park, 2013a). In July 2013, the government set up the third stock market, Korea New Exchange (KONEX), a specialized bourse for start-up and young venture firms. KONEX specifically caters to young companies that do not meet the IPO requirements (e.g., sales and paid-in capital) of the tech-savvy KOSDAQ. KONEX-listed companies can also be transferred to KOSDAQ, dependent on their performance.

THE STATUS OF THE VENTURE SECTOR

In order to be eligible to receive the perks provided by the government, a firm must be in accordance with the legal definition of being classified as a venture company. Under the Special Law to Promote Venture Companies, venture companies are defined as SMEs (1) in which venture capital investment firms have at least a 10 percent equity stake, (2) that are certified by the Korea Technology Finance Corporation or Small and Medium Business Corporation, or (3) that have high R&D expenses in comparison to revenues (5–10 percent). Other conditions should be met in addition to the above. Once issued, a certification will be valid for two years without renewal. At the year end of 2013, 29 135 SMEs were certified as venture companies, with about 72 percent classified as manufacturing and 16 percent as IT/software companies, respectively. See Table 13.2 for more details on other types of companies and changes in the numbers from the years 2000 to 2013. Table 13.3 provides trading information on KOSDAQ from December 2013: 998 firms were listed on KOSDAQ; 284 of them, about 28 percent, were listed under venture segment. The venture companies accounted for approximately 19 percent and 30 percent of total market capitalization and daily volume, respectively, of KOSDAQ.

Table 13.2 Venture companies by industry sectors

Sector/Year	2000	2005	2010	2011	2012	2013
Manufacturing	5363	6754	18485	19400	20581	20892
IT/Software	2925	2054	3293	3632	4271	4664
R&D/Service	213	410	281	287	299	332
Construction/Logistics	144	194	410	405	396	414
Wholesaling/Retailing	74	184	396	393	347	354
Other	79	136	1780	2031	2299	2479
Total	8798	9732	24645	26148	28193	29135

Source: Based on Small and Medium Business Administration (SMBA) website data: http://www.smba.go.kr/eng/index.do; accessed 23 May 2015.

Table 13.3 Venture companies listed on KOSDAQ

	Total	Venture
Number of listed companies	998	284
Market capitalization (in billion KRW)	119 292 (approximately USD113 billion)	22 233 (approximately USD21 billion)
Volume (in billion KRW)	992 (approximately USD939.9 million)	299 (approximately USD283.3 million)

Source: Based on the Korea Venture Business Association (KOVA) website data: http://www.venture.or.kr/kova/index.jsp; accessed 23 May 2015.

DISCUSSION AND CONCLUSIONS

Exploring entrepreneurial activities is essential in seeking to explain the momentum of the Korean economy of the present day. Korean business leaders, government and other stakeholders have dedicated efforts to foster an economic culture that not only supports, but also sustains individual entrepreneurs and new ventures to fuel the economic mechanism that is entrepreneurship. Led by self-seeking interests, entrepreneurs are encouraged to pursue business agendas that simultaneously act to bolster the development of the national economy. Newly created value that derives from innovative products or services encourages business activities in the economy, resulting in increase in tax revenue. However, there remain issues that require further examination among future scholars and practitioners in order to maintain the initiation of entrepreneurial activities. Since appropriate utilization of new market opportunities for innovation is crucial for Korea and its businesses to retain competitive advantage, it is crucial to recognize areas where business activities can be more effective and efficient.

In efforts to give rise to entrepreneurship, public opinion within the Korean cultural context should also be considered. A priority in nurturing entrepreneurship is the encouragement of job applicants to work for new ventures or create their own. As large business groups have traditionally dominated the Korean economy, many deem careers with large organizations as stable, guaranteed and socially honorable. The 'liability of newness' (Freeman et al., 1983) can discourage new or small ventures from attracting and retaining talent necessary for success. The prestige that is associated with established organizations drives the majority of job applicants to abide by the social pressures from family, teachers and other sources of influences. Based on this perspective, more efforts need to be made to establish a positive impression of entrepreneurs and their businesses to gain the favor of public opinion, made possible through improved education and instruction on the matter. Education on entrepreneurship provided by private and administrative entities is essential to accomplishing this purpose. In addition to being accustomed to the traditional career path within large organizations, students should also be provided with understanding of their own capabilities in creating their own businesses to make them more inclined to favor new ventures. Civil funds and public budgets can be utilized to support various seminars or lectures that delve into what entrepreneurship is and how one goes about starting such ventures.

The coordination of various new venture funds across regional provinces is another issue in considering the long-term success of new ventures. Various local governments have implemented their own venture parks or similar supportive institutions, which can result in the inefficiency of investment when lacking proper management. Such venture projects have a high possibility of overlapping with other similar projects. If several new firms that market similar items are created in a short amount of time, they will be forced to compete fiercely with each other in still-developing areas. Many firms will hardly be able to survive and overcome the over-competitive business environment. Therefore, central government must act to monitor entrepreneurship projects that are initiated by local administration. Given the fact that most Korean regional governments have been dependent on the budgeting of central government, the authority and accountability of the central government come into question in coordinating the procedures and outcomes of such projects.

Clarification on the standards of how to measure the successes of entrepreneurial funds or projects is also required. The priorities of entrepreneurial efforts lie in creating new ventures that can outlast at least three years or until the time of attaining the complete return of investment. While the economic return on investment from such projects is important, not all outcomes and situations can be measured quantitatively. Without the fulfillment of specific criteria, both public and private entities that encourage entrepreneurship may fail to sustain their business activities. When questioning the legitimacy of measuring change within the field of entrepreneurship, surveys can be conducted to receive feedback from the community. However, even if the survey can be used to examine this opinionated trend to some degree, the actual sphere of influences of people over those who do consider undertaking new ventures can hardly be quantified. Therefore, both practitioners and scholars in the field of entrepreneurship need to examine how to evaluate the economic conditions and outcomes that act as supporting activities, as well as the government and social factors that influence the direction of entrepreneurship as a field.

NOTES

1. Source: www.hoovers.com.
2. See www.kauffman.org.

REFERENCES

Aldrich, H. and E.R. Auster (1986), 'Even dwarfs started small: liabilities of age and size and their strategic implications', in B. Staw and L. Cummings (eds), *Research in Organizational Behavior* (Vol. 8), pp. 165–86.

Bae, Z. and M. Cha (2008), 'Promoting "Venture 2.0" firms in Korea: a comparison of the venture habitat of two decades', paper at the International Council for Small Business World Conference, accessed 22 May 2015 at http://sbaer.uca.edu/research/sbi/2008/chald22f.html.

Bae, Z., J. Bae, J. Kim, K.B. Lee, S. Suh and S.O. Par (2007), 'The tale of two valleys: Daeduk and Teheran', in H.S. Rowen, M.G. Hancock and W.F. Miller (eds), *Making IT: The Rise of Asia in High-Tech*, Stanford, CA: Stanford University Press, pp. 175–94.

Balomenou, C. and M. Maliari (2013), 'Support of local entrepreneurship: an empirical investigation for Serres-Greece', *Spatium*, **29**, 16–21.

Barney, J. (1991), 'Firm resources and sustained competitive advantage', *Journal of Management*, **17**(1), 99–120.

Beach, J. and C. Hanks (2010), 'Entrepreneurship in South Korea', *International Entrepreneurship.com*, accessed 22 May 2015 at http://www.internationalentrepreneurship.com/asia/south-korea.

Begley, T.M. and D.P. Boyd (1987), 'Psychological characteristics associated with performance in entrepreneurial firms and smaller businesses', *Journal of Business Venturing*, **2**(1), 79–83.

Bruton, G.D., D. Ahlstrom and K. Obloj (2008), 'Entrepreneurship in emerging economies:

where are we today and where should the research go in the future', *Entrepreneurship Theory and Practice*, **32**(1), 1–14.

Busenitz, L.W., G.P. West III., D. Shepherd, T. Nelson, G. Chandler and A. Zacharakis (2003), 'Entrepreneurship research in emergence: past trends and future directions', *Journal of Management*, **29**(3), 285–308.

Bygrave, W. and C. Hofer (1991), 'Theorizing about entrepreneurship', *Entrepreneurship Theory and Practice*, **16**(2), 13–33.

Choi, Y.R. and D.A. Shepherd (2004), 'Entrepreneurs' decisions to exploit opportunities', *Journal of Management*, **30**(3), 377–95.

Chung, H.H. (2007), 'Lessons from the Korean venture industry development', *World Bank Working Paper No. 39379*, Washington, DC: World Bank, accessed 22 May 2015 at http://documents.worldbank.org/curated/en/2007/01/7527396/lessons-korean-venture-industry-development.

Dimov, D. (2011), 'Grappling with the unbearable elusiveness of entrepreneurial opportunities', *Entrepreneurship Theory and Practice*, **35**(1), 57–81.

Fackler, D., C. Schnabel and J. Wagner (2013), 'Establishment exits in Germany: the role of size and age', *Small Business Economics*, **41**(3), 683–700.

Fauchart, E. and M. Gruber (2011), 'Darwinians, communitarians and missionaries: the role of founder identity in entrepreneurship', *Academy of Management Journal*, **54**(5), 935–57.

Fayolle, A. (2007), *Entrepreneurship and New Value Creation: The Dynamic of the Entrepreneurial Process*, New York: Cambridge University Press.

Finkle, T.A., D.F. Kurato and M.G. Goldsby (2006), 'An examination of entrepreneurship centers in the United States: a national survey', *Journal of Small Business Management*, **44**(2), 184–206.

Freeman, J., G.R. Carroll and M.T. Hannan (1983), 'The liability of newness: age dependence in organizational death rates', *American Sociological Review*, **48**(5), 692–710.

Gartner, W. (1985), 'A conceptual framework for describing the phenomenon of new venture creation', *Academy of Management Review*, **10**(4), 696–706.

Gupta, V.K., C. Guo, M. Canever, H.R. Yim, G.K. Sraw and M. Liu (2012), 'Institutional environment for entrepreneurship in rapidly emerging major economies: the case of Brazil, China, India and Korea', *International Entrepreneurship and Management Journal*, **10**(2), 1–18.

Jung, D. (2004), 'Korean *chaebol* in transition', *China Report*, **40**(3), 299–303.

Kurato, D.F. (2005), 'The emergence of entrepreneurship education: development, trends, and challenges', *Entrepreneurship Theory and Practice*, **29**(5), 577–97.

Keum, D.-K. (2000), 'The stock market in 2000: the collapse of KOSDAQ', *Dong-A Ilbo*, 27 December, accessed 22 May 2015 at http://news.naver.com/main/read.nhn?mode=LSDand mid=secandsid1=101andoid=020andaid=0000041021.

Kim, H., R.E. Hoskisson, L. Tihanyi and J. Hong (2004), 'The evolution and restructuring of diversified business groups in emerging markets: the lessons from *chaebols* in Korea', *Asia Pacific Journal of Management*, **21**(1–2), 25–48.

KOTRA (2004), *Venture Companies in KOREA*, accessed 23 May 2015 at http://news.naver.com/main/read.nhn?mode=LSD&mid=sec&sid1=101&oid=020&aid=0.

Lee, C.H., K. Lee and K. Lee (2000), '*Chaebol*, financial liberalization and economic crisis: transformation of quasi-internal organization in Korea', Working Paper, Honolulu: Department of Economics, University of Hawaii at Manoa.

Lee, J. (2000), 'Challenges of Korean technology-based ventures and governmental policies in the emergent-technology sector', *Technovation*, **20**(9), 489–95.

Lee, J. (2013), 'The South Korean government and venture capital: the costs of planned growth', *Michigan Journal of Private Equity and Venture Capital Law* [blog], accessed 23 May 2015 at http://mjpvl.org/the-south-korean-government-and-venture-capital-the-costs-of-planned-growth/.

Lerner, J. (2002), 'When bureaucrats meet entrepreneurs: the design of effective "public venture capital" programs', *Economic Journal*, **112**(477), F73–F84.

List-Jensen, A.S. (2008), 'Economic development and authoritarianism – a case study on

the Korean developmental state', *Diiper Research Series Working Paper No. 5*, Aalborg: Aalborg University.
Marco, C. and A. Kritikos (2012), 'Searching for the entrepreneurial personality: new evidence and avenues for further research', *Journal of Economic Psychology*, **33**(2), 319–24.
Menzies, T.V. (2000), 'An exploratory study of university entrepreneurship centers in Canada: a first step in model buildings', *Journal of Small Business and Entrepreneurship*, **15**(3), 15–38.
Murillo, D. and Y.-D. Sung (2013), 'Understanding Korean capitalism: *chaebols* and their corporate governance', *ESADEgeo Position Paper No. 33*, accessed 22 May 2015 at http://www.esadegeo.com/position-papers.
Park, H. (2013a), 'Park's creative economy vision takes shape', *Korea Herald*, 5 May, accessed 23 May 2015 at http://www.koreaherald.com/view.php?ud=20130505000291.
Park, H. (2013b), 'Korea's creative economy aims at venture ecosystem', *Korea Herald*, 14 August, accessed 23 May 2015 at http://www.koreaherald.com/view.php?ud=20130814000546.
Schumpeter, J. (1934), *The Theory of Economic Development: An Inquiry into Profits, Capital, Credit, Interest and the Business Cycle* (Vol. 55), New Brunswick, NJ: Transaction Publishers.
Shane, S. (2000), 'Prior knowledge and the discovery of entrepreneurial opportunities', *Organization Science*, **11**(4), 448–69.
Todosiichuk, A. (2011), 'Conditions for transition to an innovation economy', *Problems of Economic Transition*, **53**(10), 3–25.
Wade, R. (1990), *Governing the Market: Economic Theory and the Role of Government in East Asian Industrialization*, Princeton, NJ: Princeton University Press.
Yonhap (2012), 'S. Korea joining "20-50 Club" marks new chapter in development history', *YonHap News*, 23 June, accessed 22 May 2015 at http://english.yonhapnews.co.kr/national/2012/06/23/56/0302000000AEN20120623001200320F.HTML.
Zahra, S.A. (1995), 'Contextual influences on the corporate entrepreneurship–performance relationship: a longitudinal analysis', *Journal of Business Venturing*, **10**(1), 43–58.
Zahra, S.A. and W.C. Bogner (2000), 'Technology strategy and software new ventures' performance: exploring the moderating effect of the competitive environment', *Journal of Business Venturing*, **15**(2), 135–73.

14. International entrepreneurship among Finnish SMEs

Olli Kuivalainen, Sami Saarenketo, Lasse Torkkeli and Kaisu Puumalainen

INTRODUCTION

Small and medium-sized enterprises (SMEs) play an important part in the Finnish economy as they do in many other economies. More than 99 per cent of Finnish firms are SMEs and they provide most new jobs (Lindholm et al., 2013; SVT, 2014). When compared to the situation in the early 1990s, only SMEs have increased their workforce whereas larger companies or microenterprises now have fewer employees (SVT, 2014).

It is evident that the global recession of 2008 and the challenging business environment have affected the behaviour of Finnish SMEs. Many of them feel that they need to develop to be able to stay competitive in the future. This development is often related to growth aspirations; approximately every tenth Finnish SME is looking for rapid growth whereas more than one-third are aiming for moderate growth (Lindholm et al., 2013). However, most of the Finnish early-stage entrepreneurs (55 per cent) have no international orientation and among the innovation-driven economies Finnish early-stage entrepreneurs have a rather mediocre international orientation level (Stenholm et al., 2012). This means that a lot more could be done to increase the number of international success stories from Finland. This leads to questions such as how Finnish SMEs have eventually internationalized, how they should internationalize and what factors lead to international growth and entrepreneurial-oriented behaviour.

In this chapter we provide an overview of the internationalizing Finnish SMEs, their strategies, resources, product offerings and international growth orientation. For this we use both primary and secondary data. On the basis of primary data collected from the Finnish SMEs in five industries (N = 298 of which 110 had international experience) we are able to describe and profile their internationalization strategies. We especially highlight the firms that can be seen as successful international entrepreneurial SMEs, that is, which have internationalized early and which have been able to sell their products in a number of countries. We also look at existing support organizations in Finland. Finally, we give recommendations for both managers and public policy providers on how to improve SMEs' international performance in the future.

FINNISH SMEs AS INTERNATIONALIZERS

The major strengths that give Finnish SMEs that are starting to internationalize advantages over others include high educational level (see e.g., Dutta and Bilbao-Osorio, 2012) and readiness to use English as a company language. Finnish SMEs tend to possess expertise and superiority in technology and engineering, with flat and flexible organizational culture that enables fast decision-making. This also means that internationalization is seen as a natural way to grow among growth-oriented companies (see e.g., Ruokonen et al., 2008; Ruokonen and Saarenketo, 2009), and there are recent success stories in new emerging industries, for example, mobile gaming and cleantech. We have talked with a number of Finnish start-ups that have started to operate in English even before any foreigners are recruited, which is clearly a strength among these firms.

Simultaneously, there are some disadvantages that internationalizing Finnish SMEs face. These include limited resources and revenues from the small domestic market and scarce financing opportunities – common limitations in SMEs from small open economies (see Bell, 1995; Madsen and Servais, 1997; Loane and Bell, 2006). Domestic SMEs also tend to lack marketing skills and are faced with a Finnish business culture that does not provide the best background for international marketers (quiet and modest style of communication, for example). The development of the Finnish economy in general, or the lack of or just recently implemented 'one-stop shop' support for rapid internationalizers (cf. e.g., Kuivalainen et al., 2008) may pose an additional threat to SMEs seeking foreign market expansion. Moreover, there has been no recent large diaspora of workers in the society, a development that would result in limited expatriate networks in international markets, and the threat posed by small investments from the domestic venture capital (VC) market. For example, the median venture capital investment in Finland for high-tech firms was EUR400000 in 2013 and most of the funding came from international investors (see International VC Zone Report, 2014). Finland as a country also tends to suffer globally from a vague country image and its remote geographic location, which with the addition of generally high salary levels in a number of support/'lower-level' jobs tend to hinder possibilities to recruit new personnel. Finnish firms seem to assess logistics in Finland as competitive, with one problematic issue being the timeliness of deliveries in international trade (Arvis et al., 2012).

However, Finland has regularly been ranked among the world's top performers in numerous studies and indexes such as the WEF (World Economic Forum) *Global Competitiveness Report (2012–2013)* and the Organisation for Economic Co-operation and Development (OECD) *Science, Technology and Industry Scoreboard (2013)*. Therefore, to a certain extent Finnish SMEs may overcome these weaknesses by exploiting to their advantage the internationalization support that is widely available. There are also additional related opportunities, such as a strong national innovation system, one of the world's most innovation-friendly business environments, sophisticated technological infrastructure (see e.g., Dutta and Bilbao-Osorio, 2012) and a society that is among the least corrupt in the world.

INTERNATIONALIZATION OF FINNISH SMEs: ENTREPRENEURIAL CULTURE AND GROWTH

Statistics Finland (SVT, 2014) reports that there are 322 184 enterprises in the country, out of which 99.8 per cent are SMEs employing up to 250 workers. In 2012 Finnish SMEs' turnover was approximately 53 per cent of the turnover of all Finnish enterprises, which reflects around 40 per cent of the country's total GDP (Suomen Yrittäjät, 2013). However, these SMEs account for only 28 per cent of Finnish exports and consequently international trade from Finland is concentrated in certain large firms and industries (Confederation of Finnish Industries, 2014). Most Finnish exports are within the domains of metal, machine and transport equipment industry products, chemical industry products and the forest industry (Tulli, 2014). The share of the electric and electronic industry products has gone down recently, which seems to relate to the demise of the Nokia cluster. This can be seen to make Finland vulnerable to changes in global demand, especially when the country is one of the so-called small open economies. Thus, strategies to support SMEs' internationalization are required (cf. e.g., Luostarinen and Gabrielsson, 2006 for small, open economies – SMOPECs).

However, there are some encouraging signs – it can be seen that Finland is moving towards a more entrepreneurial society. After the downfall of Nokia many university graduates are choosing start-up jobs over corporate careers. Global Entrepreneurship Monitor (GEM) concludes that Finland is a relatively business-friendly, innovation-driven economy where entrepreneurship acts as an essential part of the engine advancing economic performance in the country (Stenholm et al., 2012).

Finland currently holds the number 3 position in the World Economic Forum's Global Competitiveness Index, and number 11 in the World Bank's Ease of Doing Business Index. These are regularly used to compare economies and show that Finland offers a fairly decent environment for starting and expanding a business. However, the GEM results also indicate that among the innovation-driven economies Finnish early-stage entrepreneurs have only mediocre international orientation. Autio (2009) notes that Finland lags significantly behind most of its European and all of its Scandinavian peers in prevalence of high-growth entrepreneurial activity. Furthermore, that this weak performance in high-growth entrepreneurship goes together with the country being a world leader in per capita investment in R&D is a paradox (ibid.). It seems that Finnish government policies are supportive of entrepreneurship in general but the fundamental challenge is to gear the system more towards supporting rapid growth and internationalization of new ventures. This is significant as the economy is highly dependent on internationalization and exports.

Finland needs to become more supportive of growth firms and international entrepreneurship. One reason behind the Finnish paradox (ibid.) mentioned earlier is the lack of international orientation and growth orientation (Nummela et al., 2005; Stenholm et al., 2012) among Finnish SMEs. Thus, in order to advance the entrepreneurial ecosystem and to direct the scarce resources available, it is crucial to identify and support the firms aspiring to grow their businesses internationally.

INTERNATIONALIZATION STRATEGIES OF SMEs: INTERNATIONALIZATION PATHS

Before knowing how to support the firms we need to understand how these firms actually grow and internationalize, the latter being one possible method to grow. Internationalization of SMEs has been recognized to occur through various patterns. Jones and Coviello (2005, p. 292) suggest that 'internationalization may be captured as patterns of behaviour, formed by an accumulation of evidence manifest as events at specific reference points in time'. There is now a rather extensive amount of literature studying the internationalization of SMEs. Most SMEs internationalize after a rather long period of operation in a domestic market, and make their first international entry into nearby markets. This type of internationalization trajectory or path is often called the 'traditional internationalization model' and it is explained by the internationalization process models of which the so-called

Uppsala model is probably the most well known (cf. e.g., Johanson and Wiedersheim-Paul, 1975; Johanson and Vahlne, 1977, 1990, 2003, 2009). The Uppsala model and the network approach (Johanson and Mattsson, 1988) have recognized a gradual process of increasing commitment to foreign markets, conceptualizing the internationalization phenomenon as a step-by-step, gradually intensifying learning process through business network relationships. This view implies that the accumulation of foreign market knowledge necessary to enter those markets will take time. Thus, traditional internationalizing SMEs will not engage in internationalization directly from their foundation and when they do start their internationalization process, will tend to take a risk-averse approach and enter only a few of their geographically and culturally closest markets first.

In contrast to this, rapidly internationalizing SMEs have been defined through several conceptualizations. First, 'born globals' (BGs: Rennie, 1993; Madsen and Servais, 1997; Knight and Cavusgil, 2004) are SMEs that tend to internationalize rapidly and intensely directly from their foundation, a result of them often facing insufficient domestic markets due to either their geographic location, their niche orientation or the general industry dynamics they are surrounded by. While Gabrielsson et al. (2008) note that BGs have been defined in several ways, those definitions in general have in common the notion that BGs are firms that start internationalizing within three years of their foundation, and in doing so enter several foreign markets in quick succession. BGs in general tend to be characterized by differing decision-making logic (Nummela et al., 2014b), and by the high importance of managerial capabilities as a means of preventing failure (Nummela et al., 2014a).

Another, separate trajectory can be found in so-called 'born international firms' (BIs, e.g., Kandasaami, 1998; Kundu and Katz, 2003), which internationalize soon after the foundation of the firm but to a limited extent in relation to the market diversification of the firm. Hence these are companies that have started to internationalize rapidly but do not have business in a variety of foreign markets. Contextually, the cut-off country criterion has, for example, been defined as 'five or less countries' for a firm to qualify as a BI in the earlier research (e.g., Kandasaami, 1998; see also Kuivalainen et al., 2012).

Finally, a 'born-again global' (BAG) is accordingly a company that waits longer before starting to internationalize, but once it does make the decision to do so, enters various foreign markets in quick succession (Bell et al., 2001, 2003). BAGs are 'late internationalizers', but after their initial internationalization resemble BGs (Bell et al., 2003; Kuivalainen et al., 2012). Both firms should, by definition, operate in a large number of foreign markets and gain a significant share of their turnover from international operations.

The existing literature has often studied the motives or factors that lead SMEs to follow a different type of internationalization path (cf. e.g., the review by Jones et al., 2011). In the case of BGs, the goals or mindset, such as international growth orientation (IGO) (Nummela et al., 2005) and international experience, unique resources/capabilities (Knight and Cavusgil, 2004), and networking (Torkkeli et al., 2012), have been found to explain the development. In the case of the BAGs there is often a 'critical incident' such as a new product or change in the management that has triggered the internationalization (Bell et al., 2001). In the next section we study the differences between Finnish SMEs that have followed different paths in their internationalization.

CONCEPTUAL FRAMEWORK

Based on our assessment of the extant context and theory of SME internationalization, a conceptual framework is presented in Figure 14.1. In particular, we examine the impact of international growth orientation (as a managerial mindset; see Nummela et al., 2005) and the type of the growth orientation of the company (Autio et al., 2000) on the internationalization trajectories of SMEs. Our proposition is that they both would affect the type of trajectory that the companies tend to follow.

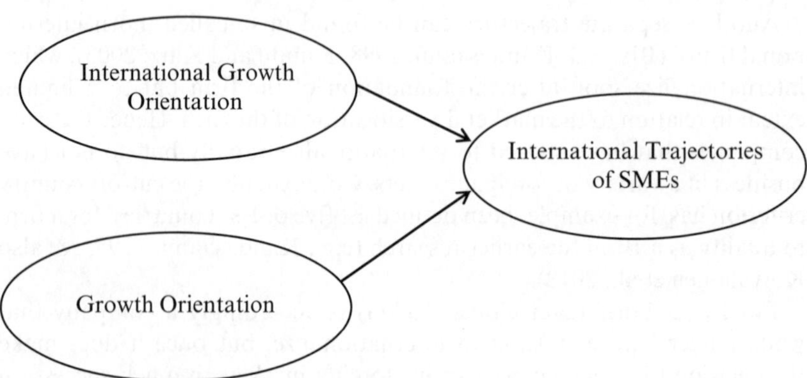

Figure 14.1 Conceptual framework

METHOD AND DATA COLLECTION

We highlight the differences and similarities between the internationalization strategies of Finnish SMEs by examining the underlying differences in their internationalization paths in terms of their target markets and entry modes, the composition of their turnover and budget investments, the extent of their partnership networks, as well as the extent of their international operations and the level of growth-oriented managerial mindset. In doing so, we employ a cross-sectional survey sample of SMEs. The data were collected during the first half of 2008, and consisted of Finnish SMEs outside of microenterprises (i.e., those employing less than ten people). The initial sample was drawn from the Amadeus database and consists of five industry sectors (metal, food, furniture and software industries, and knowledge-intensive business services). By including firms from both more traditional manufacturing fields as well as those from the more knowledge- and service-intensive high-technology fields, we aimed to gain a sample that would include born globals, born again globals, born internationals and traditional internationalizers, that is, a wide variety of companies that could be expected to follow a variety of internationalizing patterns.

The randomly selected firms (N = 1147) were contacted by a group of researchers from the Lappeenranta University of Technology starting first by phone in February 2008. Consequently, an e-mail including a link to the survey was sent to those managers who indicated their agreement to participate in the study. The survey was presented online in the Webropol system and included an additional section for the internationally operating respondents, one that further inquired upon the scale, scope and timing of their foreign expansion. Finally, e-mails were sent to non-respondents one month after the first contact to remind them of the survey, and these were later supplemented with a second reminder e-mail two weeks later to those that still had not given their response. Most of the individual respondents (final N = 298, 26 per cent response rate; 110 of the respondent firms had international experience) identified themselves as managing directors (191) or owners (59), with 40 selecting the option 'other key person' in the survey. We conducted ANOVA (analysis of variance) tests to ensure that the type of respondent did not significantly affect the validity of the responses.

SCALE MEASURES

The survey included items inquiring about the timing of both firm foundation and first foreign market entry, making it possible to differentiate between rapid and correspondingly slower internationalizing firms. In addition, the respondents were asked the extent of foreign operations in which their firm was involved, including the number of countries in which they had operations. This made it possible for us to differentiate between the four types (born global, born international, born again global and slower traditional) internationalizing firms. In addition, we included domestic companies in the sample for our analysis. Accordingly, in line with Kuivalainen et al. (2012), we defined the following four types of paths or patterns among internationalizing SMEs as follows:

1. Born global pattern: started international operations within three years of firm foundation and operate in five or more countries in addition to their originating one (Finland).
2. 'Sporadic' born international pattern: started international operations within three years of firm foundation but operate in less than five countries in addition to their country of origin.
3. Born again global pattern: started international operations later than three years after firm foundation but operate in five or more countries in addition to their country of origin.
4. Traditional pattern: started international operations later than three years after firm foundation and operate in less than five countries in addition to their country of origin.

We examined the relationship between the four internationalization paths with the managerial mindset conducive to international entrepreneurship strategies through contrasting the four types of paths to the levels of growth orientation prevalent in the firm. While growth orientation can be seen as a crucial precedent for international growth in general (Yli-Renko et al., 2002), international entrepreneurship and SME internationalization may require specifically *international* growth orientation (IGO) (Nummela et al., 2005). As IGO may have an effect on both the internationalization paths of SMEs and on their geographical diversification (Tuppura et al., 2008), IGO remains a central concept potentially distinguishing between different paths of internationalization among SMEs. Consequently, we applied Nummela et al.'s (2005) IGO measure, resulting in a four-item scale explaining 85.6 per cent of the total variation within a single factor, with a Cronbach's alpha value of 0.94. The items were as follows:

- Internationalization is the only way to achieve our growth objectives.
- It is important for our company to internationalize rapidly.

- We will have to internationalize in order to succeed in the future.
- The growth we are aiming at can be achieved mainly through internationalization.

We consequently assessed the overall strategies in terms of their perceived importance to the firms, by adapting the Autio et al.'s scale (2000) (the study denotes the scale 'growth orientation'). Correspondingly, our survey included seven-point Likert scale items inquiring about the following possible growth orientation options:

- importance of maximizing profitability;
- importance of maximizing sales growth;
- importance of maximizing technical superiority;
- importance of maximizing value of the firm for eventual acquisition;
- importance of maximizing stability and longevity of the firm.

We calculated the performance of SMEs in foreign markets through a measure of their degree of internationalization (DOI). While there is no accepted single de facto scale for measuring DOI (Susman, 2007, p. 281), Sullivan (1994) has suggested applying multifaceted measures. Thus, we calculated a composite measure for DOI, by standardizing the variables of scale (share of turnover the firm derived from foreign markets) and scope (the number of countries in which the firm has operations), dimensions of international expansion, and combining them to comprise our DOI measure. The higher the value of the composite measure the more international the firm.

Additionally, we inquired about different types of partnerships in which the firms were involved (large foreign multinationals and other types of firms), overall turnover and how it comprised sales of products versus sales of services (by percentage of total turnover), investments the companies made in marketing and R&D activities (by percentages of total turnover), and both first foreign market entry mode and the current primary market. The descriptors of these measures are shown in Table 14.1.

RESULTS

In order to shed light on the differing internationalization paths of the SMEs, we first examined the means of the central explanatory variables between the groups, calculated the corresponding Spearman's correlation values, and conducted one-way ANOVA tests in order to examine the differences in IGO of the SMEs. The results overall, illustrated in Table 14.1,

Table 14.1 Descriptives between the different internationalization paths

	1 Born Globals (BG) (N = 27)			2 Born Internationals (BI) (N = 18)			3 Born Again Globals (BAG) (N = 18)			4 Traditionally Internationalizing (TI) (N = 34)			5 Domestic (DF) (N = 179)		
	Mean	SD	Correlation	Mean	SD	Correlation	Mean	SD	Correlation	Mean	SD	Correlation	Mean	SD	Correlation
Firm age	19.33	11.46	–0.26***	19.72	14.72	–0.21**	47.56	32.69	0.34***	29.12	19.28	0.16	26.79	21.08	0.00
Number of employees	55.35	80.46	–0.16	77.28	111.91	0.16	66.28	52.36	0.20**	58.59	100.32	–0.12	27.59	35.59	–0.30***
Partnerships with large foreign multinational enterprises (LFMNEs)	6.70	8.01	0.27**	10.08	16.88	0.18	9.87	25.16	0.05	1.13	1.48	–0.47***	1.43	1.94	–0.31***
Partnerships with non-LFMNEs	115.57	225.11	0.15	52.07	77.08	–0.05	79.47	126.08	0.13	37.44	93.23	–0.23**	55.20	216.10	–0.22***
Overall turnover	6.98	10.08	–0.11	19.08	39.20	0.21**	10.35	10.09	0.10	6.81	8.53	–0.18*	3.43	5.87	–0.42**
Turnover (%) from sales of products	81.31	30.32	0.16	72.39	31.63	–0.07	72.75	39.45	0.08	67.55	39.76	–0.05	52.99	42.74	–0.13**
Turnover (%) from sales of services	18.69	30.32	–0.24**	29.24	31.82	0.05	31.53	42.08	–0.09	40.38	41.43	0.16	49.85	43.09	0.12*

Investment (%) to marketing activities	6.71	6.01	0.10	10.25	14.73	0.16	7.91	7.48	0.07	4.25	4.37	–0.27**	6.25	12.52	–0.14**
Investment (%) to R&D activities	11.10	16.78	0.10	9.75	12.60	0.06	10.07	11.01	0.13	6.59	9.18	–0.16	6.60	9.91	–0.16**
Degree of internationalization	1.09	1.84	0.45**	–0.97	0.78	–0.24**	1.14	2.10	0.28**	–0.97	0.94	–0.54***	–	–	–
International growth orientation	6.88	2.27	0.14 (5)	7.31	2.10	0.19** (4, 5)	7.06	1.73	0.11 (5)	5.40	2.16	–0.34*** (2, 5)	3.30	2.14	–0.56*** (1, 2, 3, 4)

Note: Numbers in brackets show with which type of patterns the value is significantly different from (BG = 1, BI = 2, BAG = 3, TI = 4, DF = 5); ***$p < 0.01$, **$p < 0.05$, *$p < 0.10$.

point toward several outcomes. First, born globals tended to have more large foreign multinational enterprises (LFMNEs) as partners compared to the traditional internationalizers and the domestic SMEs. BIs and BAGs also had, on average, a relatively large number of LFMNEs as partners, although there were no significant correlations found. Similarly, the more traditional internationalizing firms, as well as the domestic ones, had relatively fewer partners in general. In terms of the overall turnover of the firm, no strong tendencies in paths were evident in relation to whether the firms were more product or service oriented. This may also have been due to the fact that some of the service-oriented firms were notably domestically oriented by nature; the respondents from knowledge-intensive business services in particular consisted mostly of small accounting firms, for which rapid internationalization tends not to be a necessity.

Notably, BGs and BAGs had achieved more expansive internationalization compared to BIs and TIs (traditionally internationalizing firms), as BAGs had the highest average DOI value (1.14), and there existed a positive correlation of 0.28 ($p < 0.05$). The second highest DOI had been achieved on average by BGs (1.09), and higher levels of DOI correlated positively (0.45, $p < 0.05$) with the dichotomous BG variable. Correspondingly, the BIs (−0.97) and TIs (−0.97) were lagging behind with their foreign market expansion when the DOI was measured with our composite variable taking both the scale and scope of internationalization into consideration.

Second, as seen in Table 14.1, IGO was more prevalent with the managers from rapid internationalizers (BGs, BIs and BAGs). We further conducted ANOVA tests between the groups in relation to their IGO, in order to shed further light on how significant these differences were. A prerequisite of the ANOVA test is for the dependent variable to be normally distributed and that its variances between the different classes (in this case, the five classes consisting of the four internationalization paths and the group of domestic SMEs) to be equal. In order to establish that these prerequisites were met we conducted Levene's test for IGO. The result (0.86, $p > 0.05$) indicated sufficient prerequisites for conducting the actual ANOVA test. The test proved significant ($F = 38.02$, $df = 271$, $p < 0.01$) and we found some significant differences in IGO between the different types of firms. The rapid internationalizers (BGs, BIs, BAGs) differed greatly from the domestic SMEs, by virtue of possessing significantly higher levels of IGO. Second, IGO in BIs also differed significantly from that in the traditionally internationalizing SMEs group, again by being remarkably higher. And third, no significant differences between the rapidly internationalizing groups were found in relation to their IGO levels.

Next, we examined the firm groups in relation to their first foreign market entries in terms of their selected countries and entry modes. These are illustrated in Table 14.2 and indicate relatively conservative strategies in firms when they were selecting their first foreign markets. In particular, geographically close markets were preferred, with Sweden and Russia being the most popular choices for first foreign markets in all cases. However, it has to be noted that Russia especially has been seen as a big opportunity for Finnish firms, as since the collapse of the Soviet Union it has been a market in transition with lots of potential in many sectors, and with high perceived value for Finnish goods, for example, in groceries. The first entry modes the firms had employed when entering those markets were most often based on their own or project exporting. Export activities through retailers or distributors were overwhelmingly the next most often used entry modes. As seen in Table 14.2, their present primary operation modes had largely remained similar. This is not surprising as most of the SMEs tend to use exporting as an operation mode (cf. e.g., Dalli, 1994; Brouthers and Nakos, 2004).

Finally, we examined the differences in strategic focus (i.e., growth orientation, as per Autio et al., 2000), through the differences in means and correlations between the different SME types. As seen in Table 14.3, no statistically significant difference between groups was found in relation to emphasis on profit or sales growth maximization. Sales and profits are important for all SMEs. However, the more traditional companies (i.e., the domestic firms and the traditionally internationalizing firms) did not place as much emphasis on achieving technical superiority in comparison to the more rapidly internationalizing firms, in particular BGs. Similarly, BGs placed correspondingly higher emphasis on value maximization for potential acquisition of the company, and conversely were not as concerned with maximizing the stability and longevity of the firm. In contrast, managers of BAGs valued the stability and longevity facets particularly highly, mirroring perhaps their mindset in also delaying their internationalization decisions beyond the first few years. This type of behaviour can be seen as comparatively higher tendency for risk averseness.

As the international and domestic SMEs differed in their level of international growth orientation, we consider it essential to consider how this type of managerial mindset can be developed not only on the organizational, but also on the societal level. A major area of support in the Finnish context comes via expert assistance provided by governmental organizations and the national policy outlined to be encouraging international expansion of SMEs.

Table 14.2 The most common target countries and entry modes among the SMEs

	Born Globals			Born Internationals		
	1st	2nd	3rd	1st	2nd	3rd
First foreign country (n. of cases)	Sweden (7)	Germany; Norway (3)		Sweden (6)	Russia/ Soviet Union (4)	UK (2)
First mode of entry (n. of cases)	Own export/ project export (12)	Export through retailer/ distributor (8)	Licensing or other contractual cooperation (2)	Own export/ project export (8)	Export through retailer/ distributor (4)	Licensing or other contractual cooperation (3)
Current mode of operation (n. of cases)	Own export/ project export (13)	Export through retailer/ distributor (7)	Own sales/ marketing unit in target country (3)	Export through retailer/distributor; acquisition/imports from foreign countries; own export/project export (2)		

POLICIES SUPPORTING INTERNATIONALIZING SMEs IN FINLAND

As in other countries both the Finnish national government, regional administrations and various trade associations have created and are currently developing many types of services that aim to provide support for firms that are looking for growth and have begun or plan to begin to operate in international markets. Many of these new services are targeted at SMEs. The expected benefits include, for example, economic development of the home country of the assisted firms, higher employment rate and improved foreign trade positions (Morgan and Katsikeas, 1997; McNaughton and Bell, 2001). The typical support services focus on broad areas of (1) motivational (e.g., 'how to create the right mindset for internationalization'), (2) informational (e.g., 'how to find information regarding chosen potential target markets') and (3) operational (e.g., 'how to find customers or distributors from the market') needs of firms (Cavusgil, 1984; Seringhaus, 1987; Diamantopoulos et al., 1993).

Born Again Globals			Traditionally Internationalizing		
1st	2nd	3rd	1st	2nd	3rd
Sweden (5)	Russia/Soviet Union; UK (3)		Russia/ Soviet Union (12)	Sweden (10)	Japan; Norway; USA (2)
Own export/ project export (11)	Export through retailer/ distributor (4)		Own export/ project export (13)	Export through retailer/ distributor (12)	Acquisition/ imports from foreign countries (3)
Export through retailer/ distributor (7)	Own export/ project export (6)	Own sales/ marketing unit in target country; acquisition/ imports from foreign countries; licensing or other contractual cooperation (1)	Own export/ project export (9)	Export through retailer/ distributor (5)	Acquisition/ imports from foreign countries (4)

Finland has a long history in internationalization support services as the first trade promotion service was established there in 1919 (European Commission, 2008). All types of internationalization support/export assistance are provided by a large number of providers such as Tekes (the Finnish Funding Agency for Innovation) and Finpro (the national trade, internationalization and investment development organization in Finland) as well as by smaller operators. Several implemented support activities, such as 'export partnerships' in which a number of SMEs cooperate in a market entry with a joint project manager recruited by Finpro, can be seen as best practices (ibid.).

The suitability and impact of domestic support organizations in the case of early and rapidly internationalizing firms have been questioned in the past, however. For example, Kuivalainen et al. (2008) studied 25 Finnish software firms that had international growth aspirations or were already in the latter phases of their internationalization. Most of the respondents did not consider support services important in the latter stages of international growth at all and there was clear evidence that national support organizations are often considered being capable of assisting the rapidly growing firms only in the early stages of internationalization if at all. This

Table 14.3 Descriptives of strategic imperatives (type of growth orientation) for different types of SMEs

	Importance of maximizing profitability			Importance of maximizing sales growth			Importance of maximizing technical superiority			Importance of maximizing value of the firm for eventual acquisition			Importance of maximizing stability and longevity of the firm		
	Mean	Std. Dev.	Corr.	Mean	Std. Dev.	Corr.	Mean	Std. Dev.	Corr.	Mean	Std. Dev.	Corr.	Mean	Std. Dev.	Corr.
Domestic	6.34	0.91	–0.04	5.33	1.27	–0.04	4.16	1.53	–0.24***	4.15	1.68	0.07	6.30	0.90	–0.00
Born global	6.52	0.75	0.04	5.44	0.93	–0.03	5.33	1.00	0.22**	4.56	1.63	0.26***	6.11	0.75	–0.22**
Born international	6.11	1.28	0.11	5.72	1.13	0.12	5.39	0.98	0.16	3.89	1.71	0.00	6.11	1.41	–0.00
Born again global	6.59	0.71	0.07	5.47	0.87	–0.03	5.12	1.17	0.07	3.18	1.59	–0.16	6.82	0.53	0.30***
Traditional	6.42	0.83	–0.04	5.27	1.26	–0.08	4.27	1.55	–0.30***	3.39	1.80	–0.15	6.42	0.61	0.03
Total	6.37	0.89		5.38	1.21		4.43	1.53		4.03	1.71		6.30	0.91	

Note: ***$p < 0.01$, **$p < 0.05$.

may partially still be the case. Although there are numerous activities/services to support the creation of new innovative firms there are still only a few initiatives intended to push innovative firms to grow, the Tekes YIC Programme (Funding for Young and Innovative Companies) and the Vigo Programme of the Ministry of Employment and Economy being some of the existing exceptions to the rule.

The Tekes YIC Programme was established in 2008 to accelerate the growth and internationalization of the most promising innovative new firms in Finland. The aim was to develop the businesses exhibiting good potential for rapid organizational growth in international markets in a hands-on fashion (Tekes, 2013). The Vigo Programme (Vigo, 2013), on the other hand, was launched in 2009 by the decision of the Ministry of Employment and Economy to facilitate the creation of new business accelerators that raise and invest their own funds (and that of other private sector operators) to take equity stakes in the most promising new ventures. By building an effective network of business accelerators, the Vigo Programme aims to boost the provision of 'smart' and 'hands-on' funding for the most potential high-growth ventures in Finland, and bring together instruments that push high potential ventures to proactively and aggressively seek growth. Furthermore, many universities and business schools have taken the initiative in either general entrepreneurship training or even international entrepreneurship. An example of the former could include the 'Entrepreneurship – An Interesting Opportunity?' programme, which was run in Turku among bioscience students, and which has been reported, for example, in Heinonen et al. (2007) whereas the latter includes the International Entrepreneurship Challenge programme run by Lappeenranta University of Technology (2012). In this programme graduate business students work with real-life start-ups and develop international business strategies for these firms.

Consequently, it can be concluded that both the entrepreneurial culture in Finland and related support infrastructure for international entrepreneurship are progressing in a better direction. The policy interventions such as the mentioned initiatives by Tekes and the Ministry of Employment and Economy promote high-growth international entrepreneurship in Finland, and are supposed to enhance the quality of entrepreneurship in the country in the future. However, due to their newness and ongoing nature, the effectiveness of some of the services is yet to be evaluated.

CONCLUSIONS, RECOMMENDATIONS FOR SMEs AND FUTURE PROSPECTS

Our results highlight that IGO and growth orientation do have an effect on internationalization of Finnish SMEs. There are also different types of international entrepreneurship strategies among Finnish SMEs. Our sample consisted of 298 Finnish SMEs, with 179 firms operating domestically and 97 internationally; the latter we were able to divide into the four specific outward internationalization paths on the basis of their timing, market scope and extent/scale of internationalization. The four types of firms (i.e., BGs, BAGs, BIs or TIs) stem from the earlier literature studied. When comparing our results with other studies on SMEs and their internationalization there are several similarities. For example, TIs form the biggest group of firms and most often the firms first enter the nearby markets, which are, in this case, Sweden and Russia. There are many BGs as well, which is often seen in the studies focusing on SMOPECs, and they have many partnerships that help them to operate in global markets. It is evident that many Finnish BGs are operating in the high-tech sector (cf. e.g., Kuivalainen et al., 2012) and utilizing the Finnish education system and innovation culture as a backbone for their internationalization. Our results show that their average R&D spending is higher than that of TIs and domestically operating firms and that these firms emphasize their technological superiority. This is not surprising as high technology has been a focal industry in many international new venture (INV)/BG studies in the past and the need to internationalize early and rapidly stems often from the technological and first-mover advantage (see e.g., the review of Jones et al., 2011 for the high number of high-tech-based studies within the field). It is also clear that rapidly internationalizing firms are much more product-based than the firms that internationalize in a slow incremental manner or stay in domestic markets only. Regarding international growth orientation the results are not surprising either as those SMEs that have either internationalized early or rapidly possess a higher IGO than TIs or domestically operating firms. The difference between BGs and BAGs regarding the 'importance of maximizing stability and longevity of the firm' type of growth orientation is, however, very interesting. This result shows that many BGs are actually growing and internationalizing the firm with the aim of selling the firm in mind. This is in contrast with BAGs, which, after rapid internationalization are actually keen on long-term development of the firm (which is seen from the negative correlation in Table 14.3). BAG firms in the sample are old but it may even be the case that the 'critical incident' that has made them internationalize rapidly after many years is a defensive strategy to safeguard the sustainability of the firm. This difference in the mindset of the entrepreneurs and managers between BGs and BAGs is something that early research on BAGs (e.g., Bell et al., 2001, 2003) has not covered explicitly. Internationalizing firms should, however, take long-term objectives into consideration when building their internationalization strategy and presence.

From the public policy perspective, it is not always an objective to support firms to a certain level when they would be sold to a foreign company and cease their existence as an independent firm. This is something that has happened to many Finnish born global firms, however, as the owners have considered globalization a bridge too far. A small home market may not provide a resource base that is big enough to conquer the US market, for example, and this has been cited as a main reason to sell a mid-sized successful firm to the US competitor in our research interviews. Hence, for the public policy-makers the visualization of the possible outcomes of the firm is of importance. When providing assistance it would also be in their interest to discuss the long-term objectives of the firms carefully and try to tailor the support in the direction of initial public offering, for example. Here the problems related to small domestic VC funding remain in Finland. This is an area that can be hopefully changed in the future when current successful entrepreneurs, such as the founders of Finnish software firms like Supercell and Blancco (who have recently sold their shares or part of their shares to foreign firms), will be investing more in the new Finnish start-ups that are internationally growth oriented and the owners/managers of which are willing to become international entrepreneurs.

The expertise of former Nokia employees who are keen and willing to use their global business experience to develop Finnish SMEs is also another possible resource that may foster Finnish international entrepreneurship. Nokia has, for example, established a 'Bridge' programme in which it supports entrepreneurs who are former employees of Nokia. In this programme 400 start-ups were founded in 2011–13; 40 per cent of these firms are operating in the ICT domain and 18 per cent of all these firms have a licensing agreement with Nokia or have been able to start a business with the idea they already had when working for Nokia (Kiuru et al., 2013). All in all, the recent interest in start-ups and entrepreneurship among Finnish students, for example, is encouraging and with its education and innovation system it is possible that there will be more Finnish international entrepreneurs than in the past although the challenges of making businesses global success stories remain.

REFERENCES

Arvis, J.-F., M.-A. Mustra, L. Ojala, B. Shepherd and D. Saslavsky (2012), *Connecting to Compete 2012, Trade Logistics in the Global Economy, The Logistics Performance Index and its Indicators*, Washington, DC: World Bank.

Autio, E. (2009), 'The Finnish paradox: the curious absence of high-growth entrepreneurship in Finland', *Discussion Papers No. 1197*, Helsinki: Etla.

Autio, E., H.J. Sapienza and J.G. Almeida (2000), 'Effects of age at entry, knowledge intensity, and imitability on international growth', *Academy of Management Journal*, **43**(5), 909–24.

Bell, J. (1995), 'The internationalization of small computer software firms: a further challenge to "stage" theories', *European Journal of Marketing*, **29**(8), 60–75.

Bell, J., R. McNaughton and S. Young (2001), '"Born-again global" firms: an extension to the "born global" phenomenon', *Journal of International Management*, **7**(3), 173–89.

Bell, J., R. McNaughton, S. Young and D. Crick (2003), 'Towards an integrative model of small firm internationalisation', *Journal of International Entrepreneurship*, **1**(4), 339–62.

Brouthers, K.D. and G. Nakos (2004), 'SME entry mode choice and performance: a transaction cost perspective', *Entrepreneurship Theory and Practice*, **28**(3), 229–47.

Cavusgil, S.T. (1984), 'Differences among exporting firms based on their degree of internationalization', *Journal of Business Research*, **12**(2), 195–208.

Confederation of Finnish Industries (EK) (2014), 'Yrittäjyys talouden moottorina' [Entrepreneurship economic engine], accessed 14 May 2014 at http://ek.fi/mita-teemme/yrittajyys/.

Dalli, D. (1994), 'The exporting process: the evolution of small and medium-sized firms towards internationalization', in S. Zou (ed.), *Advances in International Marketing* (Vol. 6), Greenwich, CT: JAI Press, pp. 107–15.

Diamantopoulos, A., B.B. Schlegelmilch and K.Y. Tse (1993), 'Understanding the role of export marketing assistance: empirical evidence and research needs', *European Journal of Marketing*, **27**(4), 5–18.

Dutta, S. and B. Bilbao-Osorio (eds) (2012), *The Global Information Technology Report 2012 – Living in a Hyperconnected World*, Geneva: World Economic Forum.

European Commission (2008), *Supporting the Internationalisation of SMEs – Good Practice Selection*, Luxembourg: Office for Official Publications of the European Communities.

Gabrielsson, M., V.H.M. Kirpalani, P. Dimitratos, C.A. Solberg and A. Zucchella (2008), 'Born globals: propositions to help advance the theory', *International Business Review*, **17**(4), 385–401.

Heinonen, J., S.-A. Poikkijoki and I. Vento-Vierikko (2007), 'Entrepreneurship for bioscience researchers – a case study of an entrepreneurship programme', *Industry and Higher Education*, **21**(1), 21–30.

International VC Zone Report (2014), *Summary of Finnish Hi-tech Capital Raising Activity in 2013*, accessed 23 May 2015 at http://www.vczone.fi/wp-content/uploads/2014/01/FINNISH-HI_FY2013_final.pdf.

Johanson, J. and L.-G. Mattsson (1988), 'Internationalisation in industrial systems – a network approach', in N. Hood and J.-E. Vahlne (eds), *Strategies in Global Competition*, New York: Croom Helm, pp. 214–87.

Johanson, J. and J.-E. Vahlne (1977), 'The internationalization process of the firm: a model of knowledge development and increasing foreign market commitments', *Journal of International Business Studies*, **8**(1), 23–32.

Johanson, J. and J.-E. Vahlne (1990), 'The mechanism of internationalisation', *International Marketing Review*, **7**(4), 11–24.

Johanson, J. and J.-E. Vahlne (2003), 'Business relationship learning and commitment in the internationalization process', *Journal of International Entrepreneurship*, **1**(1), 83–101.

Johanson, J. and J.-E. Vahlne (2009), 'The Uppsala internationalization process model revisited: from liability of foreignness to liability of outsidership', *Journal of International Business Studies*, **40**(3), 1411–31.

Johanson, J. and F. Wiedersheim-Paul (1975), 'The internationalization of the firm: four Swedish cases', *Journal of Management Studies*, **12**(3), 305–23.

Jones, M.V. and N.E. Coviello (2005), 'Internationalisation: conceptualising an entrepreneurial process of behaviour in time', *Journal of International Business Studies*, **36**(3), 284–303.

Jones, M., N. Coviello and Y. Tang (2011), 'International entrepreneurship research (1989–2009): a domain ontology and thematic analysis', *Journal of Business Venturing*, **26**(6), 632–59.

Kandasaami, S. (1998), *Internationalisation of Small- and Medium-sized Born-global Firms: a Conceptual Model*, Crawley, WA: Graduate School of Management, University of Western Australia.

Kiuru, P., J. Handelberg and H. Rannikko (2013), 'Bridge it up – työntekijöille tarjottujen start-up -palveluiden vaikuttavuus – Case Nokian Bridge-ohjelma' [Bridge it up – the impact of start-up services offered for employees – the case of Nokia's Bridge Programme], accessed 15 May 2014 at http://pienyrityskeskus.aalto.fi/fi/current/news/2013-10-17/.

Knight, G.A. and S.T. Cavusgil (2004), 'Innovation, organizational capabilities, and the born-global firm', *Journal of International Business Studies*, **35**(2), 124–41.

Kuivalainen, O., S. Saarenketo and K. Puumalainen (2012), 'Start-up patterns of internationalization: a framework and its application in the context of knowledge-intensive SMEs', *European Management Journal*, **30**(4), 372–85.

Kuivalainen, O., J. Lindqvist, M. Ruokonen and S. Saarenketo (2008), 'Use and impact of internationalization support services – the case of Finnish software SMEs', in *Proceedings of the 3rd European Conference on Management of Technology and Innovation*, 17–19 September, Nice–Sophia Antipolis.

Kundu, S.K. and J.A. Katz (2003), 'Born-international SMEs: BI-level impacts of resources and intentions', *Small Business Economics*, **20**(1), 25–47.

Lappeenranta University of Technology (2012), 'International Entrepreneurship Challenge', accessed 14 May 2014 at http://www.lut.fi/web/en/international-entrepreneurship-challenge.

Lindholm, T., P. Malinen and E. Lemmelä (2013), *Pk-yritysbarometri – kevät 2013* [SME-Barometer – spring 2013], Vaasa: Suomen Yrittäjät Ry.

Loane, S. and J. Bell (2006), 'Rapid internationalisation among entrepreneurial firms in Australia, Canada, Ireland and New Zealand: an extension to the network approach', *International Marketing Review*, **23**(5), 467–85.

Luostarinen, R. and M. Gabrielsson (2006), 'Globalization and marketing strategies of born globals in SMOPECs', *Thunderbird International Business Review*, **48**(6), 773–801.

Madsen, T.K. and P. Servais (1997), 'The internationalization of born globals: an evolutionary process?', *International Business Review*, **6**(6), 561–83.

McNaughton, R.B. and J. Bell (2001), 'Competing from the periphery: export development through hard business network programmes', *Irish Marketing Review*, **14**(1), 43–54.

Morgan, R. and C. Katsikeas (1997), 'Obstacles to export initiation and expansion', *OMEGA: The International Journal of Management Science*, **25**(6), 677–90.

Nummela, N., K. Puumalainen and S. Saarenketo (2005), 'International growth orientation of knowledge-intensive SMEs', *Journal of International Entrepreneurship*, **3**(1), 5–18.

Nummela, N., S. Saarenketo and S. Loane (2014a), 'The dynamics of failure in international new ventures: a case study of Finnish and Irish software companies', *International Small Business Journal* [online], accessed 22 May 2015 at http://isb.sagepub.com/content/early/2014/07/10/0266242614539363.abstract.

Nummela, N., S. Saarenketo, P. Jokela and S. Loane (2014b), 'Strategic decision-making of a born global: a comparative study from three small open economies', *Management International Review*, **54**(4), 527–50.

OECD (2013), *OECD Science, Technology and Industry Scoreboard*, accessed 13 May 2014 at http://www.keepeek.com/Digital-Asset-Management/oecd/science-and-technology/oecd-science-technology-and-industry-scoreboard-2013_sti_scoreboard-2013-en#page1.

Rennie, M.W. (1993), 'Born global', *McKinsey Quarterly*, No. 4, 45–52.

Ruokonen, M. and S. Saarenketo (2009), 'The strategic orientations of rapidly internationalizing software companies', *European Business Review*, **21**(1), 17–41.

Ruokonen, M., N. Nummela, K. Puumalainen and S. Saarenketo (2008), 'Market orientation and internationalisation in small software firms', *European Journal of Marketing*, **42**(11/12), 1294–315.

Seringhaus, F.H.R. (1987), 'Export promotion: the role and impact of government services', *International Marketing Review*, **3**(2), 106–16.

Stenholm, P., A. Kovalainen, J. Heinonen and T. Pukkinen (2012), *Global Entrepreneurship Monitor – Finnish 2012 Report*, Turku: Turku School of Economics, University of Turku.

Sullivan, D. (1994), 'Measuring the degree of internationalization of a firm', *Journal of International Business Studies*, **25**(1), 325–42.

Suomen virallinen tilasto (SVT) (2014), 'Yritysrekisterin vuositilasto 2012' [Business Register annual statistics 2012], accessed 7 February 2014 at http://www.stat.fi/til/syr/2012/syr_2012_2013-11-28_tie_001_fi.html.

SuomenYrittäjät (Federation of Finnish Entreprises) (2013), 'Yrittäjyys suomessa' [Entrepreneurship in Finland], accessed 6 February 2014 at http://www.yrittajat.fi/fi-FI/suomenyrittajat/yrittajyyssuomessa.

Susman, G.I. (2007), *Small and Medium-Sized Enterprises and the Global Economy*, Cheltenham, UK and Northampton, MA, USA: Edward Elgar Publishing.

Tekes (2013), 'Rahoitus nuorille innovatiivisille yrityksille' [Funding for young innovative enterprises], accessed 22 May 2015 at http://www.tekes.fi/rahoitus/rahoitusta-yritysten-kehitysprojekteihin/rahoitus-nuorille-innovatiivisille-yrityksille/.

Torkkeli L., K. Puumalainen, S. Saarenketo and O. Kuivalainen (2012), 'The effect of network competence and environmental hostility on the internationalization of SMEs', *Journal of International Entrepreneurship*, **10**(1), 25–49.

Tulli (2014), 'Foreign trade 2013 – Finnish trade in figures', accessed 14 May 2014 at http://www.tulli.fi.

Tuppura, A., S. Saarenketo, K. Puumalainen, A. Jantunen and K. Kyläheiko (2008), 'Linking knowledge, entry timing and internationalization strategy', *International Business Review*, **17**(4), 473–87.

Vigo (2013), Vigo website, accessed 13 May 2014 at http://www.VIGO.fi/etusivu.

World Economic Forum (2013), *The Global Competitiveness Report 2012–2013*, accessed 13 May 2014 at http://www3.weforum.org/docs/WEF_GlobalCompetitivenessReport_2012-13.pdf.

Yli-Renko, H., E. Autio and V. Tontti (2002), 'Social capital, knowledge, and the international growth of technology-based new firms', *International Business Review*, **11**(3), 279–304.

15. The internationalization of SMEs in Italy

Antonella Zucchella and Birgit Hagen

INTRODUCTION

In Italy, the small firm and its internationalization endeavours have always been a central theme in internationalization (export performance) research and of huge importance to practitioners and policy-makers alike. A rich body of literature is available but most of the knowledge has been produced in Italian and has thus remained so far confined to Italy. This body of literature covers multiple aspects of SME internationalization with a particular focus on traditional SMEs, their opportunities and challenges, their distinctive characteristics and their cluster affiliation. However, more recently different research streams also include innovation in foreign growth patterns and new typologies of international SMEs.

In order to account for these contributions and highlight the new research avenues, in the years 2007–09 the Italian Academy of Management (AIDEA) initiated a working group on internationalization. These efforts were presented and discussed at a conference held in 2009 at Pavia University and summarized in a reader on the internationalization of Italian firms (Pepe and Zucchella, 2009).

This contribution is based on a review of the extant literature and on statistical reports, and aims to cluster the different topics, findings and perspectives into key relevant research areas. The latter are defined according to the need of assembling and systematically grouping research and statistical sources with the purpose of elaborating research propositions. At the same time these propositions target some research gaps and controversial issues in the literature and some relevant issues for the practice of management and for policy-makers.

In reviewing the literature, we primarily build on the knowledge produced by the Italian working group and by two literature reviews on Italian firms' internationalization (Genco, 2001; Matarazzo and Rescinti, 2010). We account for the most recent statistical data and link the international contributions on SMEs' internationalization to the knowledge produced by the Italian research community.

The streams identified follow – at least in part – the discussion of the international research community, that is, the emergence of new typologies of international firms, the importance of the internationalization–performance relationship and the process aspects of internationalization. In addition to this, the reviewed contributions reflect Italian specificities and distinctive firm characteristics as related to internationalization. For instance, the discussion about merits and limits of the small size is prominent, as the Italian SME landscape is strongly skewed towards micro- and small dimensions, and about the local environment, for example, districts and the effect of location on international growth. Finally, the institutional environment is a topic of great interest especially in these latest years of recession.

THE INSTITUTIONAL ENVIRONMENT

A basic assumption of much internationalization research has been that firms are embedded in country-specific institutional environments that guide firms' strategic actions and influence their overall competitiveness. Not surprisingly, and especially in the last years of recession, the structure of Italian SMEs and the institutional environment has been a topic of lively discussion and effort in research and policy-making.

In describing the Italian institutional environment we follow the call for the study of domain-specific institutional environments (Kostova, 1999; Busenitz et al., 2000; Descotes et al., 2011) and give account of regulatory, cognitive and normative data and studies related to internationalization.

In general, macroeconomic data and international comparisons portray an Italian SME sector that suffers from structural (mainly size) problems and a non-favourable institutional environment. According to the *Doing Business* report (World Bank-IFC, 2013) on the ease of doing business, Italy ranks 73rd among 185 countries surveyed, well behind other European countries. The ease of doing business is an indicator of a business-friendly environment in terms of efficient regulatory processes and strong legal institutions that protect property and investor rights. Also, the country's overall performance on the Small Business Act (SBA) grid[1] (European Commission, 2013) continues to be below EU average. The cost of starting a new business, for example, is six times the average EU cost and also the cost to close a business is extremely high as compared to an EU benchmark (22 per cent to 10 per cent in the EU). Related to this is the below-average support for a 'second chance'.

In Italy, access to finance has been historically difficult and in general is described as one of the most problematic areas for Italian SMEs. Italian SMEs suffer from a chronic and structurally difficult access to finance well below the EU average, with signs of increasing deterioration (European Commission, 2013; Wehringer, 2014) during the last years of recession.

Also a recent ISTAT (National Bureau of Statistics) survey (2013a) emphasizes access to finance as the most important obstacle to SME growth in general and innovation and internationalization endeavours in particular. The survey, in line with SBA analysis (European Commission, 2013), reports access to finance (40 per cent), level of demand (37 per cent), bureaucracy (35 per cent) and the sociocultural context (23 per cent) as the main obstacles to internationalization.

In terms of internationalization, the available SBA indicators do not capture any significant progress. 'SMEs importing from outside the EU', 'SMEs exporting outside the EU', 'cost required to import/export', 'time required to import/export' all are substantially below EU average. Across the ten dimensions measured in the SBA frame, Italy has made progress on 'entrepreneurship' and the two core indicators in this area – the entrepreneurship rate and the rate of opportunity entrepreneurship – remain close to the EU average.

Global Entrepreneurship Monitor (GEM) data[2] (Muffatto et al., 2012) are partially supportive of the SBA entrepreneurship analysis. Experts agree in their comments with the overall unfavourable context for entrepreneurial activity as described in the SBA analysis, but GEM findings on entrepreneurial attitude, intent and activity are in contrast. Its core indicator 'total early stage entrepreneurial activity' (TEA) ranks Italy second last in the group of the innovation-driven economies. GEM also underlines the low level of opportunity perception, which is around a third of the Northern European countries, and an extremely high fear of failure that positions Italy second behind Greece. A longitudinal analysis shows that TEA has been consistently low in recent years and in particular after 2007. It reached its all time low in 2010 but now shows first signs of recovery of early stage activity. In 2012, early stage activity was mainly found in services to consumers and services to firms (around 60 per cent) and in the manufacturing sector (25 per cent).

The complex relationship between SMEs and their institutional environment needs to be better understood. Smaller firms perceive institutions as hostile to business and they perceive a generalized institutional void. This constraining environment (Secchi, 1985) can be viewed as opposed to an enabling one, which is described crucial especially for small and resource-constrained firms (Volpe and Carballo, 2010). The institutional void has been partially filled by the extraordinary growth from the 1960s to the 1990s of industrial districts and local clusters. The agglomeration of SMEs in the same location – all belonging to the same industry and/or to the same supply chain – permitted the sharing of local knowledge about foreign markets and supported the development of local institutions like export consortia, and dedicated events to promotion and business development like trade fairs (Zucchella et al., 2010). On the public institutions side, regional governments have played an increasing role in export promotion. The latter phenomenon might, however, have determined an increasing gap between the already internationally oriented regions (Northern Italy) and the less dynamic and more internally focused southern regions. For example the Northern Italian region of Lombardy, where most export activity is concentrated, is the one that experienced both traditional and innovative services and incentives to export promotion, like temporary export management schemes and vouchers for internationalization services. Maddaloni (2009) reports that the use and dissemination of export-related information between institutions and exporting SMEs remains limited, although generally appreciated.

Caffarelli and Veronesi (2013) present a recent review of the status of the Italian institutional environment as related to internationalization. The authors conclude that notwithstanding normative efforts and considerable investment dedicated to export promotion over the last years the impact has been limited due to difficulties of coordination and unclear responsibilities of the actors involved.

The data and studies reported above give proof of a weak domain-specific institutional profile. This holds for the regulatory dimension, that is, laws, regulations and governmental policies that support international SMEs and facilitate or hamper their efforts to acquire resources useful to going abroad. Efforts at the national and regional level to sustain internationalization exist (Maddaloni, 2009) but fall short in effective application and use (Caffarelli and Veronesi, 2013). The companies' skills and knowledge related to selling abroad, that is, the cognitive dimension of the institutional frame, do not seem to become 'common knowledge' among businesses, apart from the case of industrial districts, and many firms have difficulties in understanding the basic steps required to begin exporting (Maddaloni, 2009; Zucchella et al., 2010).

Finally, as regards the normative dimension of the institutional frame, that is, whether international firms and their managers are considered exemplars, and how strong is the belief that going international is good, we do not have any hard data at hand. However, being researchers in the field, we are attentive observers of the numerous 'best exporter', 'exporter excellence' awards. Also, the media are full of stories of success and interviews with international and successful firms and entrepreneurs.

We use Busenitz et al. (2010) data to conclude our section on the institutional environment. The authors compare the institutional profiles of the USA, Sweden, Germany, Spain and Italy in a domain that is closely related to internationalization: entrepreneurship. Italy ranks lowest on the cognitive dimension (that is, how to deal with risk, how to manage risk, how to find markets for products), second lowest on the regulatory dimension (that is, laws that support new ventures) yet scores second highest on the normative dimension (that is, innovative and creative thinking is considered a road to success). Their study confirms the macro-data and academic research we have presented and complements it from the entrepreneur's perspective: Italian international SMEs have to overcome more hurdles than their counterparts abroad.

The above review about the institutional frame in which international SMEs are embedded, contains some contrasting views with the mainstream international literature, which is mostly focused on the enabling environment perspective, and provides suggestions for more research on the role of a hostile environment in not only constraining but also in driving foreign expansion. This leads us to our first proposition:

P1: An environment perceived as hostile by smaller firms represents at the same time a constraint to their international growth, for the lack of appropriate institutions, but can also support early and fast internationalization, as escape strategy from a poor domestic operating context for business.

SME CHARACTERISTICS AND TYPES

SME internationalization is a combination of various elements – external and internal to the firm. In this section we aim to describe firm internal characteristics and the bridges between the firm's internal and external environments.

The Role of Firm Size

Many studies – Italian and international – have dealt with the *role of firm size* in internationalization (e.g., Bonaccorsi, 1992; Bugamelli et al., 2001; Ferragina and Quintieri, 2001). SMEs account for 99.9 per cent of enterprises in Italy and for 80 per cent of the industrial and service labour force – figures that position Italy well above the European average. Furthermore, the sector is highly skewed towards a small-scale structure: the share of microenterprises[3] is much higher than the EU average, while the percentage of small and especially medium-sized firms is below average (Eurostat, 2012). In this general frame, international SMEs represent about one-third of small firms and 50 per cent of medium-sized firms. Overall, the average export intensity in 2012 is 31 per cent as compared to 29.4 per cent in 2010 (ISTAT, 2013a). The slight increase is the first sign of recovery during years of heavy recession, which have hit SMEs all over Europe.

The high-performing firms are located mainly in Northern Italy, where about 40 per cent of the population reside: they contribute more than 60 per cent to the overall added value of the Italian economy as compared to 20.7 per cent in Central Italy (19 per cent of population) and 18 per cent (34 per cent of the population) in Southern Italy (European Commission, 2013; ISTAT, 2013a).

Empirical results regarding firm size and international performance remain mixed although much evidence points to the fact that firm size is not significantly related to export performance (Bonaccorsi, 1992; Grandinetti, 1992; for a more detailed discussion please see the section below on 'The internationalization–performance relationship').

For a long time, Italian authors have devoted attention to the general universe of SMEs, treating them as a relatively uniform world. More recently, they are increasingly focusing on the two extremes of this universe: microenterprises on one side and medium-sized on the other.

Medium-sized firms are rated as the best performers internationally (Mediobanca-Unioncamere, 2008; Varaldo et al., 2009; Mariotti and Mutinelli, 2009) with the strongest orientation to operate abroad (Mariotti and Mutinelli, 2008a). These medium-sized firms are frequently leaders in global niches, with a unique portfolio of knowledge and technologies and they are independent of cluster affiliation (Mariotti and Mutinelli, 2008a). Mariotti and Mutinelli (2009) describe them as a new alternative model to district-embedded firms on one side and to the large multinationals on the other. These firms are triggering a new cycle of Italian internationalization and show the typical traits of micro-multinationals (Varaldo et al., 2009).

On the other hand, microenterprises (below ten employees) show understandably a lower international commitment. However, there are international firms also in this segment and their characteristics have been highlighted in recent research by Zucchella and Brugnoli (2014). Only 7 per cent of these firms are engaged in selling abroad and in a number of cases their export activity is marginal and/or occasional. However, some others show high export intensity ratios. The latter are usually fast-growing firms, which will soon move towards a larger scale. The authors conclude their research underlining the huge potential of foreign growth of microenterprises, especially if adequately supported.

What Triggers International Competitiveness of Italian SMEs?

Innovation

It is important to note that international firms – independently of their size – outperform domestic players in all *innovation*-related efforts: international micro- and small firms, for example, introduce new products/services significantly more frequently than do their counterparts (48 or 45 per cent as compared with the average of 41 per cent). They are also able to translate innovation efforts into market success: two-thirds of the smallest and small international firms enter new segments and largely outperform their domestic peers, whose share is around 18 per cent and 38 per cent respectively (ISTAT, 2013b).

SBA indicators are in line with Italian reports: Italian SMEs score well on some of the core indicators such as SMEs introducing product or process innovation, introducing marketing or organizational innovation, and also innovating in-house is above EU average (European Commission, 2013). European Firms in a Global Economy (EFIGE) data (Altomonte et al., 2012) rank Italy above or in line with the seven-country[4] average on 'process innovator', 'market innovator' and 'product innovator' while 'organizational innovator' is slightly below the benchmark.[5] According to the European Commission (2013), however, this general innovation orientation does not seem to fully turn into market value, as SBA scores on 'collaborating with others', 'entry in other markets' and 'sales of new to market and new to firm innovation' remain below average (ibid.). The effect of innovation on the internationalization patterns of firms has been confirmed in recent EFIGE survey data from seven EU member states. Accordingly, and regardless of the country, the share of enterprises that carried out product or process innovation is much higher in the case of international firms (Berthou and Hugot, 2012). Likewise, firms with a high engagement in foreign activities, exhibit better economic and innovative performances. Firms with the highest international involvement, that is, firms with manufacturing activities abroad, are characterized by both higher productivity and higher R&D efforts and innovative performances (Castellani and Zanfei, 2007).

Similar to international literature, the interrelation between internationalization and innovation is also an emerging topic in Italian literature. Traditionally, these two routes to growth have been studied separately and only recently innovation and internationalization are increasingly seen as being strongly interrelated (e.g., Sterlacchini, 1999; Basile et al., 2003; Castellani and Zanfei, 2007; Pla-Barber and Alegre, 2007; Kafouros et al., 2008; Pittiglio et al., 2009; Cassiman and Golovko, 2011; Denicolai et al., 2014; Hagen et al., 2014). This involves that innovation is not necessarily a trigger to international growth, but can also be a consequence of international expansion. A recent study on traditional industries (textile and apparel) reveals that small firms in these sectors also rely on innovation, and notably on design innovation, to compete globally (Zucchella and Siano, 2014).

Networks

Networks in general and strategic partnerships in particular have been described as being a way to overcome resource constraints associated with SMEs and the liability of foreignness (e.g., Gulati et al., 2000; Gabrielsson and Kirpalani, 2004; Coviello, 2006; Gabrielsson et al., 2008).

Statistical data (ISTAT, 2013b) confirm the importance of *networking and cooperation* to Italian SMEs: about 60 per cent of Italian SMEs indicate at least one stable relationship with other organizations. In general, non-contractual forms of collaborations prevail (60 per cent). Here, the overarching objective is the reduction of production costs (60 per cent). Relationships that involve formal contracts instead are established to realize product/process innovation (28 per cent), access to knowledge and technologies (23 per cent) or access to new markets (32 per cent). Flexibility of production and internationalization are mentioned less frequently (8 per cent).

Again, the larger the firm, the more intensive is collaboration and networking and the more formalized is collaboration and cooperation. With increasing size also emerges the increasing importance of relationships that involve investments in knowledge, productive/organizational flexibility and the capacity to redesign the value chain.

Firms that are more active and dynamic in developing collaborations are also pursuing more dynamic and complex strategies: on average, they have twice as many products and services on offer and they approach new markets more frequently than their less active counterparts (27 per cent vs 13 per cent). The positive effect of collaborations also holds with respect to product and process innovation. Microfirms in particular seem to take advantage from partnering with others. While 40 per cent of the connected firms declare they have realized innovations this share diminishes to 23 per cent in their non-connected counterparts. Consistently with literature (Gulati, 1998) small firms overcome size-related disadvantages through networking and collaboration. Most importantly, collaborating firms declare they are more competitive internationally, which is a consistent finding across all categories of firm size – from 20 per cent of microfirms to more than 30 per cent in the case of larger firms – and industry sectors.

Location in clusters and districts

Similar to capturing positive effects through collaboration and networking is embeddedness in a cluster. Studies on *industrial districts* are prominent in Italian literature (e.g., Coro and Grandinetti, 1999; Mariotti and Mutinelli, 2003, 2004b; Rabellotti et al., 2003; Chiarvesio et al., 2006; Mariotti et al., 2006; Musso, 2006; Rullani, 2006; Solinas, 2006; Belussi and Sedita, 2008). SME organization in districts has been a strategy to fill institutional voids and a typical Italian model of SME internationalization but, together with traditional sector specialization and small scale, has also been identified as a major structural weakness in Italian industrial systems (Rabellotti et al., 2003; Mariotti and Mutinelli, 2004, 2008a).

The most recent report by Intesa-San Paolo (2013) highlights that cluster firms are performing better than non-cluster-based firms both in terms of growth of sales (5.8 per cent vs 4.3 per cent) and in terms of international presence (51 per cent vs 45 per cent). Innovation (as expressed in patents and registration of international trademarks) is more frequent (45 vs 32 per 100 firms and 39 vs 20 per 100 firms respectively). Cluster firms also seem to be a step ahead with regard to strategic positioning. Here a recent analysis (ibid.) reveals a shift from a predominant production orientation towards internationalization, innovation, quality, ecology-sustainability, design, brand and distribution.

With globalization, the cluster has to address the danger of the supply/value chain division: subcontracting SMEs are in difficulties because of the ongoing and increasing delocalization of production in cheap-labour countries (Signorini, 2006; Majocchi and Presutti, 2009; Intesa-SanPaolo, 2013). Successful counteraction here comprises innovation, quality and flexibility (which translates into 'time to market'), which compensate for the minor cost of delocalized production to cheap-labour countries, favour long-term relationships and are less subject to price threats (Rabellotti et al., 2003; Varaldo, 2006; Belussi et al., 2010). Belussi and Sedita (2008) report an interesting case of 'inverse delocalization' to counteract the phenomenon with employing immigrant employees from cheap-labour countries.

A second challenge is the ongoing separation between high and low performers in the clusters. In the past, performance was essentially homogeneous due to access to common resources, the possibility to imitate leading competitors through a complex and a delicate balance between competition and cooperation. Winners are mainly larger district firms and they now need to take on the role of the leader, leveraging their capabilities in R&D, in branding and in distribution. Cluster actors here need to address the challenge of developing social capital within the cluster. The social capital of clusters as of today is a heritage from the past but, as the analysis above shows, it needs to be developed and combined with the international growth of cluster leaders and international firms that are located in international markets. Global value chains have their roots 'at home', so that cluster firms are linked to and leveraged by multinational leaders Italian and foreign (Chiarvesio, 2005; Mariotti et al., 2006). In the light of the above we put forward Proposition 2:

P2: The international growth of Italian SMEs has leveraged partially on factors that are similar to other firms and partially on distinctive factors of the Italian socioeconomic scenery, like the embeddedness in industrial districts. The recent evolution of districts suggests that this unique bundle of internationalization drivers is changing: will it converge towards a European model or stay predominantly unique, though with evolving traits?

THE TYPOLOGIES OF INTERNATIONAL SMEs

The universe of SMEs is not homogeneous. We mentioned already the relevance of dividing SMEs into subcategories according to their size. We also discussed some works that specifically describe the internationalization of two extreme groups, the micro- and the medium firms. The latter seems to represent the emerging backbone of Italian internationalization and to converge towards to the micro-multinational model. The former show some cases of fast and high international growth, together with a number of occasional and marginal exporters and a predominant share of 'potential' exporters. It is also worth trying to outline groups of firms according to their internationalization pattern and their strategic orientation.

An analysis of most recent data (2010–12) of international Italian firms shows a nuanced picture (ISTAT, 2013a). The 45000 enterprises included in the sample exported in 2012 products and services of about EUR260 billion and realized about 11 per cent growth as compared with 2010. The overall growth, however, is the result of two opposed performances: on the upside, growth comes from the performance of the 'winners', about 36 per cent of the firms, which grow through global expansion (that is, on European and at least five non-European markets). These highly competitive firms are juxtaposed to 16 per cent of 'losers' that lost presence in both European and non-European markets.

The winners in the international arena are characterized by strategic responses in terms of quality improvements, product diversification and increased technology content, and active partnering, and they tried to maintain price levels while the losers are described as being less strategic, less active and more defensive. This divide between 'winners' and 'losers' in the international arena merits a more nuanced reflection. We approach this reflection by looking at different profiles or types of Italian entrepreneurial firms.

De Girolamo and Piscitello (2010) report first results of a project on competencies, that is, marketing competencies (segmentation, adaptation/standardization, competitor/customer knowledge etc.), organizational competencies (coordination, ICT etc.), and supply chain management competencies (development of partnerships, locally and globally, sharing of best practices etc.) in 53 small multinational organizations with subsidiaries abroad. According to their level and type of competencies four groups of firms are defined: those that exhibit superior values on all competence bundles; those that consistently display inferior levels; and intermediate positions of firms with one/two above average scores. Not surprisingly, firms with above average on all competencies outgrow their counterparts at the international level; likewise, firms with below-average competencies underperform. The authors note an interesting detail: at intermediate levels, the development of marketing and supply chain management competencies seems to be independent from the development of organizational competencies, while the development of organizational competence instead is only possible when marketing and supply chain competence is available.

Esposito (2003) presents a descriptive analysis of the characteristics of three groups of internationalizers, that is, potential, expanding and established internationalizers (3000 SMEs in total). He compares the firms along demographic, performance and strategic (quality, positioning, innovation) variables. Established and expanding internationals essentially share high-end marketing positioning supported by high quality and product innovation, high growth potential, and much attention to human resources.

Still in an Italian context, Hagen et al. (2012) uncover different strategic types of international SMEs. Through cluster analysis, the authors identify four strategic types of firms, namely an entrepreneurial/growth-oriented group of firms; a customer-oriented group; a product/inward-oriented cluster; and a further group of firms that lacks strategic orientation.

The customer-oriented group fosters customer satisfaction and knowledge and offers products and services that address the needs of a global niche. The entrepreneurial/growth-oriented group puts emphasis on product and service innovation and on all growth-related company objectives. Both the customer-oriented and the entrepreneurial/growth-oriented type of businesses score high on management competencies and characteristics being indicative of a high degree of 'international orientation'. An international background, a global mindset as well as motivation and commitment to go international here are of major influence. The product/inward-oriented type concentrates attention towards core manufacturing competence and quality and essentially ignores customers and communication instruments. The last cluster describes a group of enterprises that lack a consistent strategic profile. Logistic regression shows that the four types are related to differentiated international performance.

The growing body of international entrepreneurship inspired some Italian authors to try to identify the existence of born global (BG) firms in Italy and to understand their traits in comparison to traditional exporters. The study by Zanni and Zucchella (2009) compares born globals and traditional internationalizers (144 international SMEs).

The entrepreneurs' education and experience, the positioning in a niche, the presence of interfirm or social networks and their location in clusters discriminate born global firms from traditional internationalizers. The first two characteristics confirm transversal, cross-country drivers of the born global phenomenon (e.g., Madsen and Servais, 1997; Reuber and Fischer, 1997; Rialp et al., 2005; Freeman et al., 2006, 2010 for networks) whereas the last element constitutes a distinct Italian born global characteristic. Moreover, Italian born globals are frequent in mature industries and not necessarily in high-tech ones.

Mascherpa (2011) studies the impact of international entrepreneurial orientation, international market knowledge, marketing capability and networking capability on the status of being a born global, that is, an early and fast internationalizer. She finds that a global mindset and networking capability are discriminating characteristics, in line with extant literature (e.g., Rennie, 1993; Knight and Cavusgil, 1996; Mort and Weerawardena, 2006).

When summarizing the findings reported above, it is clear that the 'average' international firm does not exist. The major part of the explanation regarding internationalization and international performance lies in firm competencies and entrepreneurial activity such as innovation, networking and the design and executing of the (complex) international strategy itself: it is the right combination of firm characteristics and strategy that account for international performance. Policy-makers would be well advised to take this increasing firm heterogeneity into account. However, as Hagen et al. (2010, 2012) underline, the differentiated strategic orientations of international SMEs still remain a poorly understood issue, which requires further investigation. Hence we state in Proposition 3:

P3: The realm of international SMEs is made of heterogeneous typologies of firms. This variety can be reduced through to the identification of strategic groups of international SMEs, according to the purposes of the analysis.

THE INTERNATIONALIZATION PROCESS AND ITS DIMENSIONS

Almost 80 per cent of Italian enterprises are active only in the domestic market. Out of these, one-fifth expand from local/regional to act nationally. According to Welch and Wiedersheim-Paul (1980), who stress the importance of 'domestic internationalizers', these domestically expanding firms might become successful international firms. Their hypothesis is that as the firm moves into more distant regions, it is moving into less familiar territory – that is, more 'foreign' markets. Communication, for example, is more difficult and costly than for the local region. But, as these barriers are overcome, the relative 'foreignness' of distant markets is reduced. Also, the firm is likely to develop skills in marketing a product at a distance that will also necessarily extend its communication network. Ultimately, through the extended network, decision-makers will be exposed to more attention-evoking factors, which are the triggers for exporting. Firms demonstrating active 'pre-export behaviour' on domestic markets will have less difficulty in starting extra-regional expansion and becoming exporters and they will be in a better position to fulfil demands once they have entered foreign markets (ibid.).

These considerations can apply very well to Italian small firms: the domestic-oriented SMEs have to operate in a relatively large and diversified market space, with very relevant regional differentials, involving both geographic and cultural distance. The domestic expansion might thus support and prepare the international growth.

With regard to the scope of international activity, recent data from ISTAT (2013a) report that medium and large firms conquer global markets more frequently, while the smaller firms expand mainly within the European market but they have lost presence in emerging markets.

According to the report, the smaller scale also affects entry mode decisions. The prevailing entry mode to foreign markets is represented by export, while joint ventures and FDI play a less relevant role. The microfirms tend to rely on indirect export modes, delegating the foreign sales process to distributors and trading companies. On the other hand, in the last decade, medium-sized firms have experienced and driven a process of multinationalization, by establishing foreign subsidiaries in a number of countries, including distant emerging economies (Mariotti and Mutinelli, 2008b, 2009).

A subanalysis of the ISTAT competitiveness report (2013a) studies the change in entry modes and market scope as a (re)action to the crisis in a sample of about 5000 international SMEs (active SMEs in 2010–12). Around 12 per cent of the sample chose less complex internationalization modes and foreign markets while about 18 per cent of the firms widened their country portfolio and moved into more complex entry modes. Again, the group of firms that intensified international presence and especially the category of 'global' firms are shown to be associated with increased added value and job creation. Firms that decrease their international presence instead lose in terms of added value and number of employees. The study shows that with increasing 'globalness' and thus with increasing market complexity the firms realize gains in productivity, value added and growth. This finding is generally confirmed in literature, which highlights increasing presence in emerging countries/distant regions and the close association between market reach and international growth (Cerrato and Depperu, 2010; D'Angelo et al., 2013; Hagen and Zucchella, 2014).

In addition to the geographic scope, the *complexity of internationalization modes* is an important trigger for international competitiveness and is associated with superior performance. According to Altomonte et al. (2012) multiple mode firms, particularly the triple mode firms[6] are significantly more likely to introduce product innovations, and possess more sophisticated human capital. Still, in Italy 'simpler' forms of internationalization prevail, that is, only export or export–import modes (ISTAT, 2013a). The period between 2007 and 2010 has not shown much advancement towards more complex modes.

Recent CIS data (ISTAT, 2013b) on FDI and contractual production confirm these findings. Just a handful of SMEs indicate FDI (0.3 per cent) and contractual agreements are also rare (2 per cent). Furthermore, FDI and contractual forms seem to be alternatives more than complementary, as very few firms indicate both options. Non-equity and other flexible modes of entry, which involve minor risk and minor cost, are more common in Italy.

While much international and Italian work reports exporting to be the predominant and persistent SME internationalization mode (Depperu, 1993; Zucchella and Maccarini, 1999) there is also evidence of a more dynamic stance. In support of the CIS analysis that reported moves to more complex modes and markets, Iacobucci and Spigarelli (2007), for instance, note that Italian medium firms typically show remarkable ability to penetrate international markets through 'light' modes of entry, that is, export, but they also find an increase in the level of internationalization (both export and direct investments). In the five-year period (2001–05) dynamism, however, is to be observed mainly in terms of internationalization modes, as most foreign direct investments continue to go to countries within the EU. This reported evidence speaks to the traditional internationalization approach (Johanson and Vahlne, 1977) where firms proceed incrementally regarding both entry mode and market choice and move from the least risky and closest options to more demanding and risky entry mode and market choices.

Especially in the context of SMEs, the stage theory has been challenged and complemented by studies on international new ventures or born global firms. Mascherpa (2011) seeks to understand the differences between traditional Italian internationalizers and born global firms and their internationalization patterns in a sample of 214 SMEs. Her study examines not only the foreign sales intensity, market scope, entry mode choice, but also speed of internationalization.

Born global firms are essentially different from other international SMEs in terms of the time taken to start international activity and the speed at which internationalization develops. The average time to the first foreign market of the enterprises included in Mascherpa's (2011) sample is nine years. On average, the export intensity is around 50 per cent, a ratio that is reported also by Cerrato and Depperu (2010) and that underlines the importance of internationalization to the overall company performance.

In line with ISTAT (2013a) data and earlier studies (e.g., Iacobucci and Spigarelli, 2007; Cerrato and Depperu, 2010), in Mascherpa's study the geographical scope is mainly confined to the EU. About 70 per cent of the companies indicate the first three foreign markets within the single market. The same holds when asked to define the three most important export markets, where the EU remains the most significant area for export activity. However, around one-third of the firms describe Asia, the USA or Australia as their most important markets.

Mascherpa (2011) divided her sample into two different subgroups on the basis of the two dimensions of time, that is, precocity and speed and export intensity, two commonly used criteria to discriminate traditional internationalizers and born global firms (109 born globals and 105 traditional exporters). With respect to the first foreign entries clear differences between the subgroups emerge: BGs enter more frequently geographically and psychically distant markets (such as the USA and Japan, Asia) and only these companies ranked Australia first. Their broader approach to market selection is also reflected in the portfolio they consider their most important markets: while Europe is for both groups the major trading area, BGs are successfully pursuing international activities also beyond EU borders. Again, these findings support ISTAT (2013a) data with regard to the superior performance achieved through 'globalness' mentioned above.

The picture offered by literature and statistical sources about the process aspects of internationalization of Italian SMEs is rather varied and confirms the heterogeneity hypotheses raised in the previous section. In addition to this, it also highlights that some traits of the foreign growth process of Italian firms are persistent over time, and not evolving, as a process perspective tends to suggest. In particular, we find both firms that experience dynamism in their process of internationalization, especially in terms of entry modes, and firms that remain stable exporters over long periods of time. The latter condition is not necessarily the result of a poor international growth strategy, but may be consistent with the best possible exploitation of home-based advantages, like, for example, production in clusters where the needed resources and competencies are available. This is the case for many businesses that benefit from a 'made in' effect, from luxury goods, to designer furniture, food and wine. They can be viewed as location-bound productive systems, which leverage on both firm- and local system-specific drivers to export in global markets. Proposition 4 is therefore as follows:

P4: The international process of Italian SMEs is reflected by different models. In a number of cases we observe a gradual Uppsala-like process, which starts from the domestic expansion, with increasing scope and mode commitment. In other cases, we observe a born global–like foreign growth. Contrary to the mainstream literature, a large number of SMEs are stable exporters over time. Explanations for this peculiar trait are not only found in resources constraints, but also in a global competitive strategy of leveraging on home location–bound advantages.

THE INTERNATIONALIZATION–PERFORMANCE RELATIONSHIP

The relationship between internationalization and performance is one of the major topics in international business literature. However, different studies show contrasting results. Some authors find a positive relationship (Delios and Beamish, 1999), other authors find a negative one (Geringer et al., 2000), or a U-shaped one (Lu and Beamish, 2004), or, again, an inverted-U relationship (Geringer et al., 1989; Hitt et al., 1997). In some works no relationship is found between the two variables (Morck and Yeung, 1991). One of the reasons for these scattered results depends on the operationalization of the variables. Internationalization can be approached in different ways (export, foreign sales, foreign production) and the same holds for the construct of financial performance.

Few studies devote attention to the specificities of small firms in explaining the relationship between profitability and internationalization. SMEs cannot be considered smaller clones of larger enterprises; their strategic management and their internationalization policies differ substantially from those of the big firms (Dana et al., 1999; Wyer and Smallbone, 1999; Zucchella and Maccarini, 1999).

From the point of view of internationalization, SMEs have traditionally been characterized by a predominant exporting approach (Bilkey, 1978) and this is even truer for Italian firms. However, starting from the 1980s, medium-sized firms have demonstrated a growing commitment to FDI and to forming international alliances, thus generating small multinationals (or micro-, or again pocket multinationals, e.g., Mariotti and Mutinelli, 2009; Varaldo et al., 2009).

As mentioned in a previous section the world of Italian international SMEs is highly differentiated and hosts different species, but the prevailing model is still represented by small exporters. The latter tend to persist in this approach to foreign markets over long periods of time and constitute the archetypal category of smaller internationalizers in Italy.

There are a few works regarding the relationship between internationalization and financial performance in Italian SMEs. Majocchi and Zucchella (2003) found no relationship, confirming that this issue is still very open, but also suggesting that the reality of smaller firms needs to be understood using different lenses.

A related open issue is the relationship between size and international performance, mostly measured by foreign sales intensity ratios. According to a number of authors, small firms have more constraints on their international growth, because of the paucity of their financial and managerial resources. As a consequence, their international performance is supposed to be lower than in larger firms. Other studies have demonstrated that firm size and export intensity – as measured by the ratio of exports to sales – are not correlated (Bonaccorsi, 1992; Moen, 1999; Zucchella, 2001). This means that SMEs are not necessarily prevented from being strong exporters. In other words, each country may host both medium-sized firms mainly focused on the domestic market and small and microenterprises with very high export levels. What makes the latter internationally effective is a niche strategy that compensates for small size and resource constraints (Knight and Cavusgil, 1996). The Italian literature has devoted special attention to this issue in the last decades, though these studies have mostly been discussed in the domestic academic community. Zucchella and Maccarini (1999) analysed 40 case studies of SMEs with good international performances and found that the best international performers were pursuing a niche strategy. Zucchella et al. (2007) found that early international growth was also related to the adoption of a niche strategy and Hagen et al. (2012) confirmed recently that a niche strategy is at the heart of successful born global firms. The contribution of the Italian researchers received a recent endorsement in the article by Hennart (2014), who explicitly states that born global firms are 'accidental internationalists', because they are forced to internationalize early and quickly by their global niche positioning. The research by Mascherpa (2011) confirms higher international performance ratios for born global firms and their positioning in market niches.

The analysis in the fourth section above on the differentiated typologies of international SMEs in Italy highlights further relationships with export performance. The work on international SMEs (Hagen et al., 2012) highlights differentiated strategic orientations and relates the four strategic clusters discovered to different international performances. The best performers in foreign markets belong to the entrepreneurial/growth-oriented cluster and to the customer-oriented/niche-oriented group of firms. In the light of the above, Proposition 5 states:

P5: The relationship between financial performance and internationalization in Italian international SMEs is not univocal. The same holds for the relationship between size and international performance. These unclear/nuanced relationships are influenced by the relative importance of smaller firms targeting global customers/global market niches. These firms are pushed into foreign expansion by the natural scope of their business, and domestic expansion does not represent a viable option.

CONCLUSIONS

Italian SMEs show commonalities and specific traits in an international comparison, with reference to their structural characteristics, their orientation to foreign growth, the process of internationalization and their international performance.

This contribution builds on a comparative review of literature and statistical sources, with the aim of confronting both conceptual and empirical findings from different research streams about the issue of SMEs' internationalization. This effort is driven by the intention to highlight the contribution of Italian studies on the subject, which have long remained at least partially unknown abroad. In addition to this, comparing Italian with international research permits us to identify some common trends but also some relevant differences in the internationalization of smaller firms, as we mentioned above. Building on this comparison, we develop some research propositions that target research gaps and controversial issues and may support a further development of international business and international entrepreneurship studies. In addition to this, the propositions contain relevant issues for policy-making and for small firms managers and entrepreneurs, because they address differentiated strategic orientations towards foreign market opportunities, alternative growth paths and their effectiveness in terms of performance.

NOTES

1. Small Business Act for Europe (SBA) is the EU's flagship policy initiative to support small and medium-sized enterprises, comprising a set of policy measures organized around ten principles ranging from 'entrepreneurship' and 'responsive administration' to 'internationalization'.
2. Realized with a representative sample of at least 200 adults (18–64 years) and a panel of 36 experts.
3. Microenterprises are firms with less than ten employees.
4. Countries included in EFIGE: France, Germany, Austria, Hungary, Italy, Spain and the UK.
5. These facts seem to be in conflict with data that report Italian innovation indicators such as R&D expenditure (e.g., EU-27: 2 per cent vs IT: 1.26 per cent R&D expenditure as percentage of GDP) and patenting (EU-27: 108.6; IT 73.3 patent applications × million inhabitants) below EU average (Eurostat, 2013); it has to be noted that these proxies underestimate innovation in the Italian context of industrial specialization (traditional industries – made in Italy) where R&D and patenting is less formalized and used; furthermore, most innovation studies (e.g., the CIS) do not include firms with <10 employees and thus do not account for the Italian SME structure.
6. Combinations across the range of imports, exports, foreign direct investment and international outsourcing.

REFERENCES

Altomonte, C., T. Aquilante and G.I.P. Ottaviano (2012), *The Trigger of Competitiveness – The EFIGE Cross Country Report*, Brussels: Bruegel Blueprint Series.

Basile, R., A. Giunta and J.B. Nugent (2003), 'Foreign expansion by Italian manufacturing firms in the nineties: an ordered probit analysis', *Review of Industrial Organization*, **23**(1), 1–24.

Belussi, F. and S.R. Sedita (2008), 'L'evoluzione del modello distrettuale: la "delocalizzazione inversa" e il caso del distretto della concia di Arzignano' [The evolution of the district model: 'reverse outsourcing' and the case of the tanning district of Arzignano], *Economia e Politica Industriale*, **2**, 51–72.

Belussi, F., A. Samarra and S.R. Sedita (2010), 'Learning at the boundaries in an "open regional innovation system": a focus on firms' innovation strategies in the Emilia Romagna life science industry', *Research Policy*, **39**(6), 710–21.

Berthou, A. and J. Hugot (2012), *How Does Innovation Affect the Internationalization Pattern of Firms? EFIGE Country Report for France*, Brussels: Bruegel.

Bilkey, W. (1978), 'An attempted integration of the literature on the export behavior of firms', *Journal of International Business Studies*, **9**(1), 33–46.

Bonaccorsi, A. (1992), 'On the relationship between firm size and export intensity', *Journal of International Business Studies*, **23**(4), 605–35.

Bugamelli, M., P. Cipollone and L. Infante (2001), 'L'internazionalizzazione delle imprese italiane negli anni 90' [The internationalization of Italian companies in the 90s], in B. Quintieri (ed.), *Le imprese esportatrici italiane: caratteristiche, performance e internazionalizzazione*, Bologna: II Mulino.

Busenitz, L.W., C. Gomez and J.W. Spencer (2000), 'Country institutional profiles:

unlocking entrepreneurial phenomena', *The Academy of Management Journal*, **43**(5), 994–1003.
Caffarelli, F. and G. Veronesi (2013), 'Il sistema paese a support dell'internazionalizzazione' [The country's system to support internationalization], *Questioni di Economia e Finanza, Occasional Paper No. 196*, Rome: Banca d'Italia.
Cassiman, B. and E. Golovko (2011), 'Innovation and internationalization through exports', *Journal of International Business Studies*, **42**(1), 56–75.
Castellani, D. and A. Zanfei (2007), 'Internationalisation, innovation and productivity: how do firms differ in Italy?', *The World Economy*, **30**(1), 156–76.
Cerrato, D. and D. Depperu (2010), 'Internazionalizzazione e competitività delle imprese produttrici di machine utensili: alcune evidenze empiriche' [Internationalization and competitiveness of manufacturers of machine tools: some empirical evidence], *Rivista Piccola Impresa/Small Business*, **3**, 11–37.
Chiarvesio, M. (2005), 'Internazionalizzazione, innovazione e performance delle PMI dei distretti industriali' [Internationalization, innovation and performance of SMEs in industrial districts], *Argomenti*, **15**, 24–61.
Chiarvesio, M., E. Di Maria and S. Micelli (2006), 'Strategia e modelli di internazionalizzazione delle imprese distrettuali italiane' [Strategy and models of internationalization of Italian district industries], *Economia e Politica Industriale*, **3**, 99–126.
Coro, G. and R. Grandinetti (1999), 'Strategie di delocalizzazione e processi evolutivi nei distretti industriali italiani' [Outsourcing strategies and evolutionary processes in Italian industrial districts], *L'industria*, **20**(4), 897–924.
Coviello, N. (2006), 'The network dynamics of international new ventures', *Journal of International Business Studies*, **37**(5), 713–31.
Dana, L.P., H. Etemad and R.W. Wright (1999), 'The impact of globalization on SMEs', *Global Focus*, **11**(4), 93–105.
D'Angelo, A., A. Majocchi, A. Zucchella and T. Buck (2013), 'Geographical pathways for SME internationalization: insights from an Italian sample', *International Marketing Review*, **30**(2), 80–105.
De Girolamo, F. and L. Piscitello (2010), 'Il success internazionale delle PMI italiane: quali competenze distinctive?' [The international success of Italian SMEs: what distinctive skills?], *Economia e Politica Industriale*, **37**(3), 189–200.
Delios, A. and P.W. Beamish (1999), 'Geographic scope, product diversification and the corporate performance of Japanese firms', *Strategic Management Journal*, **20**(8), 711–27.
Denicolai, S., A. Zucchella and R. Strange (2014), 'Knowledge assets and firm international performance', *International Business Review*, **23**(1), 55–62.
Depperu, D. (1993), *L'internazionalizzazione delle piccole e medie imprese* [The Internationalization of SMEs], Milan: Egea.
Descotes, R.M., B. Walliser, H. Holzmueller and X. Guo (2011), 'Capturing institutional home country conditions for exporting SMEs', *Journal of Business Research*, **64**(12), 1303–10.
Esposito, G.F. (2003), 'Segmentazione delle imprese esportatrici e ruolo delle competenze d'impresa nei processi di apertura sui mercati esteri: capitale umano e capacità di connessione' [Segmentation of exporting firms and the role of business skills in the process of opening foreign markets: human resources and capabilities connection], in G.F. Esposito (ed.), *La globalizzazione dei piccoli. Fattori di competizione e promozione dell'internazionalizzazione per le PMI*, Milan: Franco Angeli, pp. 63–90.
European Commission–DG Enterprise and Industry (2013), *2013 SBA Fact Sheet Italy*, accessed 5 February 2014 at http://ec.europa.eu/enterprise/policies/sme/facts-figures-analysis/performance-review/files/countries-sheets/2013/italy_en.pdf.
Eurostat (2012), *Europe in Figures – Eurostat Yearbook 2012 – Industry, Trade and Services*, accessed 3 June 2014 at http://epp.eurostat.ec.europa.eu/portal/page/portal/product_details/publication?p_product_code=CH_07_2012.
Eurostat (2013), *Key Figures on Europe, 2013 Digest of the Online Eurostat Yearbook*, Luxembourg; Publications Office of the European Union.

Ferragina, A.M. and B. Quintieri (2000), 'Caratteristiche delle imprese esportatrici italiane. Un'analisi su dati Mediocredito e Federmeccanica' [Characteristics of Italian exporters. An analysis of data from Mediocredito and Federmeccanica], *Quaderni di Ricerca*, No. 4, Rome: ICE.

Freeman, S., R. Edwards and B. Schroder (2006), 'How smaller born-global firms use networks and alliances to overcome constraints to rapid internationalization', *Journal of International Marketing*, **14**(3), 33–63.

Freeman, S., K. Hutchings, M. Lazarisa and S. Zyngier (2010), 'A model of rapid knowledge development: the smaller born-global firm', *International Business Review*, **19**(1), 70–84.

Gabrielsson, M. and V.H.M. Kirpalani (2004), 'Born globals: how to reach new business space rapidly', *International Business Review*, **13**(5), 555–71.

Gabrielsson, M., V.H.M. Kirpalani, P. Dimitratos, C. Solberg and A. Zucchella (2008), 'Born globals: propositions to help advance the theory', *International Business Review*, **17**(4), 385–401.

Genco, P. (2001), 'Lo stato della ricerca sull'internazionalizzazione delle PMI' [The state of research on the internationalization of SMEs], *Quaderno di Ricerca*, No. 13, 115–19.

Geringer, J.M., P.W. Beamish and R.C. DaCosta (1989), 'Diversification strategy and internationalization: implications for MNC performance', *Strategic Management Journal*, **10**(2), 109–19.

Geringer, J.M., S. Tallman and D.M. Olsen (2000), 'Product and geographic diversification among Japanese multinational firms', *Strategic Management Journal*, **21**(1), 51–80.

Grandinetti, R. (1992), 'Apprendimento ed evoluzione nei percorsi di internazionalizzazione delle piccole e medie imprese' [Learning and development paths of internationalization of small and medium-sized enterprises], *Piccola Impresa*, **5**(1), 79–122.

Gulati, R. (1998), 'Alliances and networks', *Strategic Management Journal*, **19**(4), 293–317.

Gulati, R., N. Nohria and A. Zaheer (2000), 'Strategic networks', *Strategic Management Journal*, **21**(3), 203–15.

Hagen, B. and A. Zucchella (2014), 'Born global or born to run? The long-term growth of born global firms', *Management International Review*, **54**(4), 497–525.

Hagen, B., S. Denicolai and A. Zucchella (2014), 'International entrepreneurship at the crossroads between innovation and internationalization', *Journal of International Entrepreneurship*, **12**(2), 111–14.

Hagen, B., J. Larimo and A. Zucchella (2010), 'Strategy in internationally oriented SMEs', *Economia Aziendale Online*, **1**(4), 345–57.

Hagen, B., A. Zucchella, P. Cerchiello and N. De Giovanni (2012), 'International strategy and performance – clustering strategic types of SMEs', *International Business Review*, **21**(3), 369–82.

Hennart, J.F. (2014), 'The accidental internationalists: a theory of born globals', *Entrepreneurship Theory and Practice*, **38**(1), 117–35.

Hitt, M.A., R.E. Hoskisson and H. Kim (1997), 'International diversification: effects on innovation and firm performance in product diversified firms', *Academy of Management Journal*, **40**(4), 767–98.

Iacobucci, D. and F. Spigarelli (2007), 'I processi di internazionalizzazione delle medie imprese italiane' [The processes of internationalization of Italian SMEs], *L'industria*, **4**, 625–52.

Intesa-SanPaolo (2012), *Economia e finanza dei distretti industriali, rapporto annuale – n. 5* [Economic and Financial Affairs of the Industrial Districts, Annual Report No. 5], Rome: Servizio Studi e Ricerche.

ISTAT (2013a), *Rapporto sulla competitività dei settori produttivi – internazionalizzazione delle imprese e performance* [Report on the Competitiveness of the Productive Sectors – Business Internationalization and Performance], Rome: Istituto nazionale di statistica.

ISTAT (2013 b), *9° Censimento dell'industria e dei servizi e Censimento delle istituzioni non profit*: *Primi risultati* [9th Census of Industry and Services and Non-profit Institutions: First Results], Rome: Centro di stampa dell'Istat.

Johanson, J. and J.-E. Vahlne (1977), 'The internationalization process of the firm: a model of knowledge development and increasing foreign market commitments', *Journal of International Business Studies*, **8**(1), 23–32.

Kafouros, M.I., P.J. Buckley, J.A. Sharp and C. Wang (2008), 'The role of internationalization in explaining innovation performance', *Technovation*, **28**(1–2), 63–74.

Knight, G. and S.T. Cavusgil (1996), 'The born global firm: a challenge to traditional internationalisation theory', in S.T. Cavusgil and T. Madsen (eds), *Advances in International Marketing* (8th edition), Greenwich, CT: JAI Press, pp. 11–26.

Kostova, T. (1999), 'Transnational transfer of strategic organizational practices: a contextual perspective', *Academy of Management Review*, **24**(2), 308–24.

Lu, J. and W.P. Beamish (2004), 'International diversification and firm performance: the s-curve hypothesis', *The Academy of Management Journal*, **47**(4), 598–609.

Maddaloni, D. (2009), 'Processi di internazionalizzazione delle imprese italiane e incentivazione statale: evidenze empiriche' [The internationalization of Italian firms and state incentive: empirical evidence], in C. Pepe and A. Zucchella (eds), *L'internazionalizzazione delle imprese italiane*, Bologna: Il Mulino, pp. 315–37.

Madsen, T. and P. Servais (1997), 'The internationalization of born globals: an evolutionary process?', *International Business Review*, **6**(6), 561–83.

Majocchi, A. and M. Presutti (2009), 'Industrial clusters, entrepreneurial culture and the social environment: the effects on FDI distribution', *International Business Review*, **18**(1), 76–88.

Majocchi, A. and A. Zucchella (2003), 'Internationalization and performance', *International Small Business Journal*, **21**(3), 249–68.

Mariotti, S. and M. Mutinelli (2003), 'L'internazionalizzazione passiva dei distretti italiani' [The passive internationalization of Italian districts], *Economia e Politica Industriale*, **119**, 139–54.

Mariotti, S. and M. Mutinelli (2004), 'L'internazionalizzazione attiva dei distretti italiani' [The active internationalization of Italian districts], *Economia e Politica Industriale*, **123**, 153–62.

Mariotti, S. and M. Mutinelli (2008a), 'Nuove tendenze nell'internazionalizzazione delle imprese italiane' [New trends in the internationalization of Italian companies], *Economia e Politica Industriale*, **1**, 127–44.

Mariotti, S. and M. Mutinelli (2008b), 'Le multinazionali dei paesi emergenti in Italia' [Multinationals from emerging countries in Italy], *Economia e Politica Industriale*, **3**, 181–7.

Mariotti, S. and M. Mutinelli (2009), 'L'evoluzione delle imprese multinazionali italiane e il ruolo del quarto capitalismo' [The evolution of Italian multinationals and the role of the fourth capitalism], *Economia e Politica Industriale*, **1**, 123–34.

Mariotti, S., M. Mutinelli and L. Piscitello (2006), 'Eterogeneita e internazionalizzazione produttiva dei distretti industriali italiani' [Heterogeneity and productive internationalization of Italian industrial districts], *L'industria*, **27**(1), 173–201.

Matarazzo, M. and R. Riscinti (2010), 'Studies on firms' internationalisation in Italian journals: themes, trends and future directions', *Economia e Politica Industriale*, **37**(4), 69–109.

Mascherpa, S. (2011), 'Born global companies as market-driven organizations – an empirical analysis', unpublished doctoral dissertation, Milan: Bicocca University.

Mediobanca-Unioncamere (2008), *Indagine sulle medie imprese industriali italiane* [Survey on Medium Sized Italian Industries], Milan: Ufficio studi Mediobanca-Centro studi Unioncamere.

Moen, Ø. (1999), 'The relationship between firm, size, competitive advantages and export performance revisited', *International Small Business Journal*, **18**(1), 53–72.

Morck, R. and B. Yeung (1991), 'Why investors value multinationality', *The Journal of Business*, **64**(2), 165–87.

Mort, G. and J. Weerawardena (2006), 'Networking capability and international entrepreneurship: how networks function in Australian born global firms', *International Marketing Review*, **23**(5), 549–72.

Muffato, M., P. Giacon and S.S. Saadat (2012), *Global Entrepreneurship Monitor Italia 2012*, Padova: GEM – Università degli studi di Padova.

Musso, F. (2006), 'Strategie di internazionalizzazione fra economie distrettuali e filiere estese' [Internationalization strategies of district economies and extended supply chains], *Sinergie*, **24**(69), 61–85.

Pepe, C. and A. Zucchella (2009), *L'internazionalizzazione delle imprese italiane* [The Internationalization of Italian Firms], Bologna: Il Mulino.

Pittiglio, R., E. Sica and S. Villa (2009), 'Innovation and internationalization: the case of Italy', *Journal of Technology Transfer*, **34**(6), 588–602.

Pla-Barber, J. and J. Alegre (2007), 'Analysing the link between export intensity, innovation and firm size in a science-based industry', *International Business Review*, **16**(3), 275–93.

Rabellotti, R., A. Carabelli and G. Hirsch (2003), 'Italian industrial districts on the move: where are they going?', *European Planning Studies*, 17(1), 19–41.

Rennie, M. (1993), 'Global competitiveness: born global', *The McKinsey Quarterly*, No. 4, 45–52.

Reuber, A. and E. Fischer (1997), 'The influence of the management team's international experience on the internationalization behaviors of SMEs', *Journal of International Business Studies*, **28**(4), 807–25.

Rialp, A., J. Rialp and G. Knight (2005), 'The phenomenon of early internationalizing firms: what do we know after a decade (1993–2003) of scientific inquiry?', *International Business Review*, **14**(2), 147–66.

Rullani, E. (2006), 'L'internazionalizzazione invisibile. La nuova geografia dei distretti e delle filiere produttive' [The invisible internationalization. The new geography of districts and production chains], *Sinergie*, **24**(69), 3–32.

Secchi, C. (1985), 'La regolamentazione del commercio estero italiano e il protezionismo "per conto terzi"' [The regulation of the Italian foreign trade and protectionism 'for third parties'], in S. Cassese and E. Gerelli (eds), *Deregulation: la deregolamentazione amministrativa e legislativa*, Milan: Franco Angeli, pp. 73–92.

Signorini, F. (2006), 'Il modello distrettuale nel contest dei problem dell'economia italiana: sfide competitive e issues di politica economica' [The district model in the context of the problem of the Italian economy: competitive challenges and economic policy issues], in B. Quintieri (ed.), *I distretti industriali dal locale al globale, osservatoria nazionale per l'internazionalizzazione e gli scambi*, Soveria Mannelli: Rubbettino Editore, pp. 19–57.

Solinas, G. (2006), 'Integrazione dei mercati e aggiustamento nei distretti industriali' [Market integration and adjustment in industrial districts], *Sinergie*, **24**(69), 87–114.

Sterlacchini, A. (1999), 'Do innovative activities matter to small firms in non-R&D intensive industries? An application to export performance', *Research Policy*, **28**(8), 819–32.

Varaldo, R. (2006), 'll distretto industriale oltre la fabbrica: come rispondere alla sfida della globalizzazione' [The industrial district over the factory: how to respond to the challenge of globalization], in B. Quintieri (ed.), *I distretti industriali dal locale al globale, osservatoria nazionale per l'internazionalizzazione e gli scambi*, Soveria Mannelli: Rubbettino Editore, pp. 115–41.

Varaldo, R., D. Dalli, R. Resciniti and A. Tunisini (2009), *Un tesoro emergente. Le medie imprese italiane dell'era globale* [An Emerging Treasure: The Medium-sized Enterprise of the Global Era], Milan: Franco Angeli Edizioni.

Volpe, M.C. and J. Carballo (2010), 'Beyond the average effects: the distributional impacts of export promotion programs in developing countries', *Journal of Development Economics*, **92**(2), 201–14.

Wehringer, G. (2014), 'SMEs and the credit crunch: current financing difficulties, policy measures and a review of literature', *OECD Journal: Financial Market Trends*, **2013**(2), 1–34.

Welch, L. and F. Wiedersheim-Paul (1980), 'Initial exports – a marketing failure?', *The Journal of Management Studies*, **17**(3), 333–44.

World Bank-IFC (2013), *Doing Business 2013, Smarter Regulations for Small and Medium Size Enterprises*, Washington, DC: World Bank.

Wyer, P. and D. Smallbone (1999), 'Export activity in SMEs: a framework for strategic analysis', *Journal of the Academy of Business Administration*, **4**(2), 9–24.

Zanni, L. and A. Zucchella (2009), 'I nuovi imprenditori internazionali italiani. I casi delle imprese nate globali e dell'imprenditoria etnica nei distretti industriali' [The new international Italian entrepreneurs. The cases of born globals and ethnic entrepreneurship in the industrial districts], in C. Pepe and A. Zucchella (eds), *L'internazionalizzazione delle imprese italiane. Competitività e attrattività del Made in Italy*, Bologna: Il Mulino, pp. 175–208.

Zucchella, A. (2001), 'The internationalization of SMEs: alternative hypotheses and empirical survey', in J.H. Taggart, M. Berry and M. McDermott (eds), *Multinationals in a New Era*, Basingstoke, UK: Palgrave.

Zucchella, A. and A. Brugnoli (2014), Micro-imprese, imprese artigiane e mercati esteri [Microenterprises, small business and foreign markets], *Quaderni di ricerca sull'artigianato*, No. 1, 3–20.

Zucchella, A. and M. Maccarini (1999), *I nuovi percorsi di internazionalizzazione* [New Paths of Internationalization], Milan: Giuffrè.

Zucchella, A. and A. Siano (2014), 'Internationalization and innovation as resources for SME growth in foreign markets', *International Studies of Management and Organization*, **44**(1), 21–41.

Zucchella, A., A. Brugnoli and A. Dal Bianco (2010), 'Barriers to the internationalization of SMEs – an analysis from the perspective of support service providers', in P. Dimitratos and M. Jones (eds), *Resources Efficiency and Globalization*, New York: McGraw Hill, pp. 310–26.

Zucchella, A., G. Palamara and S. Denicolai (2007), 'The drivers of early internationalization of the firm', *Journal of World Business*, **42**(3), 268–80.

16. Internationalization of SMEs in Scotland

Nicolas Li and Marian V. Jones

> We need to create an entrepreneurial environment in Scotland that is world class, join the dots up, build on synergies and kick down the barriers and silence the naysayers.
>
> (Sir Tom Hunter, 2014, p. 3)

INTRODUCTION

Scotland is a constituent part of the United Kingdom (UK), along with England, Wales and Northern Ireland. It has 8.4 per cent of the UK population, 32 per cent of the land mass and generates 9.1 per cent (£53 billion) of UK tax revenues (Scottish Government, 2014a). The Scottish Parliament was reinstated following the Scotland Act of 1998 and Scots were then empowered with self-governance in domestic affairs such as economic development.

However, the information is sparse on how competitive Scottish small and medium-sized enterprises (SMEs) are as they stand alone. Yet they are not few – as at March 2013, there were 340 840 SMEs operating in Scotland, which accounted for 99.3 per cent of all private sector enterprises in Scotland (Scottish Government, 2014b). With the curtain drawn on the Scotland's independence referendum in September 2014, as it has decided to stay in the Union, it is timely to consider the role of SME internationalization, and speculate on how it might enhance Scotland's efforts to become a prominent entrepreneurial nation in the world economy.

In this chapter, we aim to provide an account of SME internationalization in the Scottish context. The discussion leads to the answer of an important question: are Scottish SMEs internationally active; if so, are they competitive enough? We begin with a brief introduction on the exporting situation in Scotland, its competitors, the entrepreneurial culture of Scottish firms, and government support. We also introduce the ACE model as a template for interventional support of SME internationalization. Next, we discuss key reports and scholarly articles on SME internationalization in the Scottish context. Finally, we conclude with recommendations for improving SME performance globally and future prospects for SMEs.

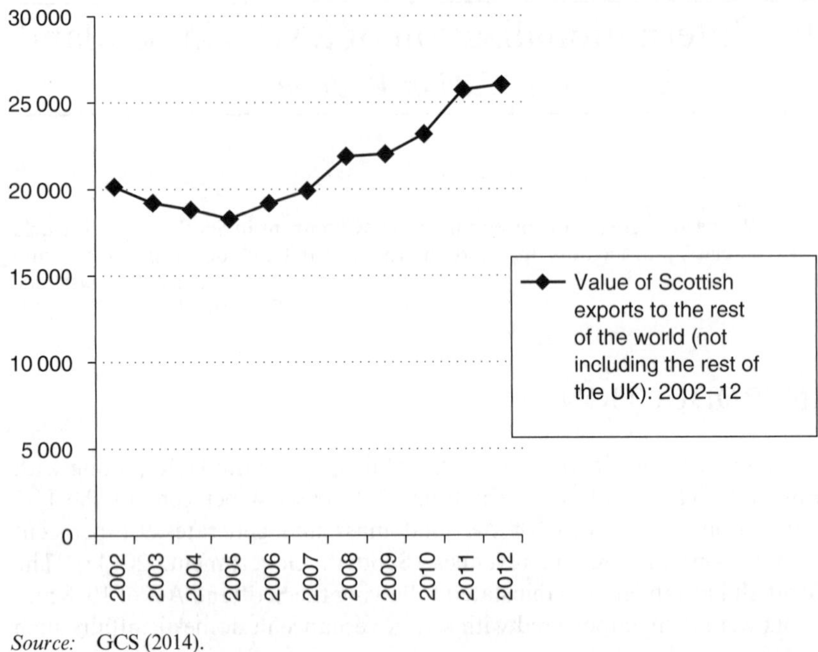

Source: GCS (2014).

Figure 16.1 Value of Scottish exports to the rest of the world (not including the rest of the UK): 2002–12

SME INTERNATIONALIZATION IN SCOTLAND

Exporting in Scotland

Scotland is an innovation-driven economy (Levie, 2014) with a population of 5.3 million (Scottish Government, 2014b), producing world-class products and services that are competitive in global markets. As Figure 16.1 indicates, the total value of Scottish exports has increased each year since 2006 when Scottish exports were valued at £18.8 billion. The value of Scottish exports to the rest of the world between 2006 and 2012 has increased by 38.4 per cent (an average of 5.6 per cent per year). According to the Global Connection Survey (GCS, 2014), an annual survey collecting information on exports and international connections of companies in Scotland, the total value of international exports from Scotland in 2012 (excluding oil and gas) is estimated at £26 billion, of which £15.4 billion was from the manufacturing sector and £8.7 billion from the services sector. This represents an increase of 5.9 per cent on the previous year when Scottish exports were valued at £24.6 billion.

In addition, the top five exporting industries in 2011 were food and beverages (£4.7 billion); manufacture of refined petroleum and chemical products (£4.1 billion); legal, accountancy, management, architecture, engineering, technical testing and analysis activities (£1.7 billion); wholesale retail trade, repair of motor vehicles & motorcycles (£1.7 billion); and financial and insurance activities (£1.4 billion). Furthermore, the top five export destinations in 2012 were the USA (£3.6 billion), Netherlands (£2.7 billion), France (£2.2 billion), Germany (£1.5 billion) and Norway (£0.9 billion). Classified by the destination region, the top five are the EU (£11.7 billion), North America (£3.9 billion), Asia (£2.7 billion), the rest of Europe (£2.5 billion) and Middle East (£1.2 billion). With respect to the rest of the UK, the total value of exports from Scotland in 2012 (excluding oil and gas) is estimated at £47.6 billion, of which £25.3 billion was from the services sector and £12.7 billion from the manufacturing sector (GCS, 2013). On the other hand, Scotland imported £49 billion worth of goods and services from the rest of the UK in 2011 (Scottish Government, 2012).

Competitors

Given the similar size of economy and geographical proximity, Scotland is often compared with Northern Ireland and the Republic of Ireland. In Dimitratos et al.'s (2013) report, for example, SMEs assisted by their respective development agencies (Scottish Enterprise, Invest Northern Ireland and Enterprise Ireland) were surveyed about their innovation-related activities, and about their attitude towards business improvement methods and government support schemes. Their results indicate that SMEs in the three regions have homogeneous attitudes towards those investigated issues.

Comparing Scotland with the rest of the UK, on average, the proportions of Scotland's exporting SMEs are slightly below that of the UK as a whole. Aproximately 43 per cent of SMEs in Scotland export – well below that of the London region but above that of Wales. SMEs are viewed as engines of their regional economies bringing in overseas income into the national and local economies (Blackburn and Wainwright, 2010). Notably, Scotland has become the leader in the life science industry with a 47 per cent increase in the number of firms between 2007 and 2011, but surprisingly medical technology and diagnostics company numbers are falling across the rest of the UK (Mobius, 2012). In contrast, Scotland's proportion of high-tech firms in its business base is the second lowest amongst UK regions, partially accounting for the fact that Scotland performs less well in terms of high-growth firms (Mason and Brown, 2012).

Last, Scotland is a preferred inward foreign direct investment location for non-European MNCs (Dimitratos et al., 2009b). In 2013, Scotland attracted 82 global foreign direct investment (FDI) projects – an increase of 8 per cent on the previous year's figure and only six short of the record number of 88 recorded in 1997 (Ernst & Young, 2014). In addition, the Glasgow 2014 Commonwealth Games and Ryder Cup, both taking place in 2014, are anticipated to enhance Scotland's international profile and boost trade and investment. However, due to the continued enlargement of the European Union (EU), Scotland faces a risk of peripheralization as the EU border moves eastwards. The recent expansion of the EU (Croatia in 2013, Romania and Bulgaria in 2007) offers multinationals cost-effective alternatives to Scotland. The competitive challenge from an expanding EU should be addressed at both institutional and policy levels.

Government Policies and Support

The current government target, as first launched in the Scottish International Trade and Investment Strategy in 2011, is to increase the value of exports by 50 per cent by 2017 (SDI, 2012). The government agencies driving measures to achieve that target are Scottish Enterprise servicing the 'lowland' regions and Highlands and Islands Enterprise operating in Northwestern Scotland.

The international arm is Scottish Development International (SDI), which is a joint venture between the Scottish government, Scottish Enterprise and Highlands and Islands Enterprise. SDI is tasked to stimulate more businesses to internationalize, and ensure they have the knowledge, skills and capability to do so successfully. SDI's effort is needed in two distinct areas (Scottish Enterprise, 2014): (1) deepening the international base: to encourage existing exporters to do more; (2) broadening the base: to encourage more Scottish firms to develop international aspirations, and develop the capacity to trade in international markets. To enable a firm to enter a new market or develop new business relations in key markets, SDI currently operates 29 overseas offices. This is particularly useful in helping Scottish SMEs overcome knowledge deficit and shortcomings in their networking capacity. Crucially, SDI works closely with UK Trade and Investment, and this is important in countries where SDI does not have direct presence.

Amongst programmes that underpin SME internationalization, the Smart Exporter Programme (SEP) has been pivotal in encouraging more Scottish SMEs to begin exporting. Launched in 2010 and funded by

Scottish Enterprise and the European Social Fund, the SEP is an umbrella arrangement of support measures designed to address the market failure of asymmetric information and to help Scottish firms develop skills and capacities required to internationalize successfully.

Entrepreneurial Culture

The entrepreneurial culture in a country is long associated with national and regional economic success (Baumol, 1968; Beugelsdijk, 2007). A society characterized by an entrepreneurial culture is likely to lead to higher levels of entrepreneurship (Beugelsdijk, 2007), subsequently triggering a process of economic dynamism, resulting in economic growth (Carree and Thurik, 2003).

As an innovation-driven economy like Scotland (Levie, 2014), the entrepreneurial culture underpins the nature of internationalization and enables some SMEs to internationalize early, rapidly, and involve themselves in complex entry modes over and beyond exporting. Thus internationalization can be described as entrepreneurial and stimulated not only by the need to diffuse innovations from its research base, but also in the innovative and proactive ways in which some firms engage in international business. Research on the Scottish SME sector, or focused on internationalization more widely but conducted within Scotland, draws attention to the need for early and rapid international market entry, especially in high-technology sectors, and the capability to do so (Bell, 1995; Jones, 1999, 2001; Harris and Li, 2009). Particularly important in enabling SMEs to engage in internationally competitive markets is the appropriate knowledge (Fletcher, 2007; Casulli, 2011; Fletcher and Harris, 2012), the ability to learn vicariously from partners (Fletcher and Harris, 2012), and through reasoned application of experiential knowledge (Jones and Casulli, 2014). In Scotland and elsewhere it is found that most firms that demonstrate rapid commencement of internationalization tend to be, but are not exclusively from high-technology sectors. Equally important for the economy are different venture types from start-up ventures following different internationalization trajectories, to micro-multinationals (Dimitratos et al., 2003) and multinational enterprises (Young et al., 1988), and significant contributions to empirical and theoretical understanding of internationalization has emerged from Scottish universities, often from international teams of researchers.

Scotland is geographically small and benefits from close proximity between SMEs, its higher education establishments and enterprise agencies, and shared dialogue through research projects, secondments and scholarships. The shared understanding of entrepreneurship and

<table>
<tr><td rowspan="7">Inspiration: changing the competitive culture
Marketing Focus</td><td colspan="2">Ambition & Awareness
A</td><td colspan="2">Capability & Capacity
C</td><td colspan="3">Expansion & Extension
E</td></tr>
<tr><td>No Awareness
1</td><td>Some Awareness
2</td><td>Aware & Taking Actions
3</td><td>First Export
4</td><td>Deep 1st Market
5</td><td>Extra Markets
6</td><td>More Complex Forms
7</td></tr>
<tr><td colspan="7">Access to SE/HIE support: e.g., R&D funding, leadership training, investor readiness, e-business, European funding
Access to SE/HIE innovation support</td></tr>
<tr><td colspan="5">First international sale support – Smart Exporter/Scot Exporter</td><td colspan="2"></td></tr>
<tr><td></td><td colspan="4">2nd & 3rd sale support – Export Explorer (?)</td><td colspan="2"></td></tr>
<tr><td colspan="2">Partnership referrals/joint delivery of events (e.g. BG, LAs, Professional Advisors)</td><td></td><td colspan="2">Account Managed Companies Export Support SDI/SD/HIE</td><td colspan="2">Deeper International activity (e.g., JV) SDI/SE/HIE</td></tr>
</table>

Broader ⟷ **Deeper**

Note: BG: born global; HIE: Highlands and Islands Enterprise; JV: joint venture; LA: local authority; SDI: Scottish Development International; SE: Scottish Enterprise.

Source: Slow (2014).

Figure 16.2 The ACE model of Scottish SME internationalization

innovation as processes commensurate with and driving internationalization is reflected in Slow's (2014) ACE model, Figure 16.2, which outlines the exporting behaviour of Scottish SMEs elicited through shared dialogue on internationalization theory and industry practice, between Scottish Enterprise and researchers in higher education. The ACE model is a guide for policy mechanisms to encourage firms to commence exporting and support them through the process of internationalization.

The ACE model is a reflection of the key elements that are important at the pre-export stage of a business and post-first export: Ambition & Awareness, Capacity & Capability and Expansion & Extension, henceforth ACE. The first two are pre-export, the last post-export, although it is essential to note that as a company extends its exporting activity and considers other 'deeper' forms of internationalization (like joint ventures or direct investment overseas) it will need to reconsider the A and C sections again, just in a potentially different way. This model reflects the dynamic internationalization patterns of international new venture (INV) theories (e.g., Oviatt and McDougall, 1994) in that it does not assume a gradual, step-staged approach through indirect exporting to more complex modes. Rather, the assumption is that firms need to have requisite knowledge and capabilities to enable them to make their first international market entry, and the knowledge and capability to support further development whether it involves moving from irregular to regular exports, or a change in operational activity to complex international business arrangements such as joint production ventures. It therefore reflects Vohora et al. (2004) in that firms need to reach a level of capability and readiness to enable them to progress to the next phase of growth. Emphasis in the model is on starting and developing international business activity rather than the particular form it takes, with a focus on exporting as a useful generic form of activity. Essentially, ACE is a capability and competence model rather than a stage model of export development:

1. *Ambition & Awareness (A).* At its most simple this stage is when a pre-exporting business first recognizes that it may have the ability to engage in international business and assess what opportunities are available to enable it to start. At this point in the process, it is not inevitable that the firm will become an exporter, but in developing the ambition companies are opening their perspectives to explore possibilities and are implicitly willing to put the resources into taking it further – this is the ambition stage; it is characterized by motivation, awareness and opportunity.

   Once the firm makes the decision to begin internationalization, exploration includes which products/services, which markets, what mode and so on. Developing an awareness of resource and capability needs and evaluating this against the current position of the company is a crucial step in the process of translating desire into action, qualifying the opportunity and assessing the availability of suitable markets. The outcome of this stage is often a 'go/no-go' decision, albeit one that may be repeated often once a company has made the step of considering exporting as a valid route for its growth.
2. *Capacity & Capability (C).* The Capacity & Capability (C) stage of the model determines in more detail whether the company has the ability to meet overseas demand, and how it will organize itself to best exploit its potential. There is no strict ordering of these elements due to their inter-relatedness and essentially joint development. A company will assess whether it currently has the ability to pursue export opportunities and, assuming a proactive approach to the internationalization process, what it needs to do in order to sustain this position. At any one time a business may have either capacity or capability or both to pursue the opportunities open to it or it may have gaps; and by undertaking a 'long, hard look' it will be able to assess whether it can 'go now' or what needs to be done in order to 'go'.

Once the company has decided to 'go', it will enter the market through its desired route – direct sales, agent, distributor – and seek the first sale. It is important to note here that, for example, firms that have specialized products and services, design or technological capabilities even at this early stage may engage in more complex business arrangements with overseas partners. Moreover, at the 'C' stage a company may also discover that it needs more information before engaging in international business activity; in this case it may revert to the 'A' stage to fill that gap. These points reinforce the idea that the process is iterative, non-linear and that there is no set time period for a company to go through each stage. It can thus be argued that firms that under-resource the 'C' stage are more likely to be 'yo-yo' exporters, and firms that move from A to E without adequately building capabilities and competencies, may fail to sustain their international growth.

3. *Expansion & Extension (E)*. This part of the model is signalled when a firm seeks to extend or deepen its involvement in international business. This might involve extending already successful exporting activity to new export markets (as indicated in traditional theory, e.g., Johanson and Vahlne, 1977), deepening its penetration in its first market, or extending different aspects of its value chain across several countries, through potentially new and innovative forms of business activity (Oviatt and McDougall, 1994; Jones, 1999).

   At this stage and at 'every decision point' within it, the model suggests that a firm will re-work its 'A' and 'C' decisions. However, these will become increasingly intrinsic as the business builds more experience. It is also at this stage that significant productivity enhancement can be seen both through 'learning by exporting' (Harris and Li, 2009; Fletcher and Harris, 2012) and growth in decision-making efficiency (Jones and Casulli, 2014), as found from survey and longitudinal research in the Scottish context.

In summary, the ACE model is an important guiding frame used by SDI, Scottish Enterprise and Highlands and Islands Enterprise for the delivery of support to internationalizing businesses. For companies, completely new to exporting, initiatives like Smart Exporter focus on building the 'A' and 'C' stages with the aim to increase the number of firms involved in exporting, and to enhance their chances of sustained international growth. For account-managed businesses and companies already involved in exporting the focus is more towards competences relevant to the 'E' stage. For A and C interventions, the policy imperative is to 'broaden' the export base, for E it is to 'deepen' the increase international to total sales ratio of firms as they continue to internationalize.

SME INTERNATIONALIZATION AND EXAMPLES OF SCOTTISH OR SCOTTISH-FOCUSED STUDIES

SME Internationalization

Internationalization may be understood as a firm's profit-seeking activities across national borders. From a network perspective, Welch and Luostarinen (1988, p. 36) consider internationalization to be 'the process of increasing involvement in international operations'. This definition implies that internationalization is a linear sequential process of 'increasing' involvement. Similarly, Calof and Beamish (1995, p. 116) define internationalization as 'the process of adapting firms' operations (strategy, structure, resources, etc.) to international environments'.

SME activities abroad embrace several strategic approaches to internationalization, namely international market presence, speed of internationalization and mode of entry (Jones and Coviello, 2005). A central topic in international business research is the choice of foreign countries or regions that form a firm's geographic target market (Papadopoulos and Denis, 1988; O'Farrell et al., 1998). Country choice is a critical step in firms' internationalization (He and Wei, 2013), especially because international markets may provide higher degrees of heterogeneity than the domestic market (Kim, 2013), and therefore more challenge. Countries differ from each other in terms of sociopolitical and cultural aspects (Brouthers et al., 2008), technology and organization (Kogut, 1991), patterns of demand (Fabrizio and Thomas, 2012) and systems of innovation (Nelson and Nelson, 2002). Paradoxically therefore, the heterogeneity across countries creates and encourages unique entrepreneurial opportunities (Kim, 2013).

The internationalization process may be understood as a series of market entry events at disparate points of time (Jones, 1999; Jones and Coviello, 2005) that do not necessarily follow a linear or predetermined pattern. From a management perspective, the speed at which to develop internationally is a key aspect of a firm's international strategy (Chetty et al., 2014). Time of entry is particularly relevant for SMEs since they have limited resources and must utilize them efficiently (Morgan-Thomas and Jones, 2009). Early studies found the internationalization path to be a gradual, staged, patterned and largely export-oriented process (Bilkey and Tesar, 1977). Some recent studies find that while some firms are motivated to take a gradual, staged and export-oriented approach, others undertake a rapid internationalization path utilizing various modes of market entry such as joint ventures, subsidiaries and so on, in addition to the more common export-oriented approach (Oviatt and McDougall, 1994; Bell et al., 2004).

Modes of entry include a range of possibilities from low-commitment exporting, through intermediate collaborative entry modes such as licensing and non-equity alliances, to high-commitment foreign direct investment (FDI) via equity joint ventures or wholly owned subsidiaries (Brouthers et al., 2008). Much research has focused on the entrepreneurial processes of internationalization start-up in new or small ventures, or on large multinational enterprises. Research by scholars in Scotland has drawn attention to a group of firms that are of significant importance to the economy, but fall between those camps and are thus neglected. These firms, now known as micro-multinational enterprises (mMNEs) are internationalizing SMEs that adopt higher-commitment entry modes beyond exporting (Dimitratos et al., 2003, 2014; Prashantham, 2011). Higher-commitment modes include cooperative alliances, joint ventures and wholly owned subsidiaries. These modes are typical in mMNEs, but in comparison to MNEs they may not always own foreign assets. For instance, they may use non-equity alliances through which they control important foreign assets rather than own them outright. Examining organizational attributes using a Chilean sample, Dimitratos et al. (2014) argue that the risk-related element of entrepreneurial orientation (EO) and networking with domestic and international partners increases the likelihood that the firm will go beyond exporting and become an mMNE. It thus seems valuable to dig deeper into what distinguishes mMNEs from those exporters.

Scottish Context

In academic research, Scotland seems to be an appropriate representative of the UK. Many studies have adopted a subsample of Scottish SMEs to represent their UK-context internationalization research (e.g., Hamill and Gregory, 1997; Johnson, 2004; Bell et al., 2001, 2004). However, Scotland is also an ethically and regionally distinct nation that needs to be considered separately (Findlay et al., 2009), especially as the Scottish government has autonomy to deploy business assistance policy. Although Scottish SME internationalization is known to be advantaged by the nation's technological innovation environment and entrepreneurship (Danson et al., 2008), a quick review of the literature reveals that there is a rather small and fragmented body of literature with an explicit focus on the Scottish context.

It should be noted that we did not conduct a comprehensive or systematic review. Rather we were looking for studies that made obvious and explicit reference to the Scottish context. Our quick review for literature explicitly mentioning a (partial) sample of Scottish firms began with a Boolean keyword search for published journal articles ranked by relevance in the ISI Web of Science (WOS) database for the period 1977–2013 (inclusive). The year 1977 was picked as the starting point for the seminal work of Johanson and Vahlne (1977). In particular, we used the terms 'SME', 'small firm', 'internationalization', 'international business', 'Scotland' and 'Scottish'. In addition, the research domain was limited to 'social sciences', the research area to 'business economics' in English language only. We then conducted a supplementary check on Google Scholar for journals not indexed by WOS (e.g., *Journal of International Entrepreneurship*) as well as relevant book chapters. We did not include review papers, media reports and official publications were excluded from the search.

The results are presented in Table 16.1, listed by the alphabetical order of the first author's surname. Our search, which includes 20 studies, confirms Scottish-context research has received relatively less scholarly attention than some of other countries such as Finland, the USA and China, which is not surprising given that to date, Scotland does not have status as an independent country. Few internationalization studies clearly identify an inclusion of Scottish firms in their sampling, even though it is the case (e.g., Jones, 1999, 2001). More often Scotland is implicitly treated as a region within the UK and sharing the same institutional environment. Strikingly, no papers on Scottish SMEs have been published in top-tier journals, such as *Academy of Management Journal*, *Organization Science*, *Journal of International Business Studies*, and so on. However, a few studies on MNEs and their subsidiaries in Scotland emerged during the search (e.g., Young et al., 1988; Dimitratos et al., 2009b). Therefore, there is a gap to be addressed in Scotland-based research.

In conclusion, there is a need for empirical research focusing explicitly on the Scottish context or comparing Scotland with the rest of the UK or other countries. It is also necessary to make datasets of Scottish firms openly available for further research, like the dataset collected on Scotland separately by the Global Entrepreneurship Monitor (Levie, 2014). Government statistics, if made available would provide a valuable resource to researchers interested in extending our knowledge and understanding of the relationship between internationalization and social as well as economic problems in the Scottish economy. For instance, Spain provides detailed and extensive panel data on SME internationalization from which Casillas et al. (2012) proposed and tested the relationship between static patterns and the dynamic configurations of a firm's export behaviour, thus enhancing knowledge on the competitiveness of Spain's SMEs, and providing policy-relevant recommendations.

Table 16.1 Journal articles and book chapters on SME internationalization containing a sample of Scottish firms

No	Study	Keywords	Journal/ Book Chapter	Methodology	Sample
1	Bell et al. (2003)	Integrative model; small firm internationalization	*J Int Ent*	Case studies	An undisclosed number of SE-assisted SMEs along with those from England, N. Ireland, Australia and New Zealand – 50 firms in total
2	Bell et al. (2004)	Internationalization; knowledge-intensive SMEs	*Int Small Bus J*	Case studies	30 UK SMEs from three regions, including Scotland
3	Casulli (2009)	Opportunity creation; SME internationalization	Book chapter	International opportunity creation	Semi-structured interviews with nine internationalizing Scottish SMEs
4	Danson et al. (2008)	SME internationalization; policy effectiveness	Book chapter	Interviews	12 local enterprises that provide services to SMEs wishing to internationalize
5	Diamantopoulos and Inglis (1988)	Differences between high and low involvement exporters	*Int Mar Rev*	Correlation analysis	48 food and beverage exporters
6	Dimitratos et al. (2009a)	Core rigidities; mMNEs	Book chapter	Case study	Case study analysis of 15 Scottish firms
7	Fillis and Wagner (2005)	Competencies; e-business; entrepreneurship; marketing	*Int Small Bus J*	Interviews	21 Scottish small firms conducting e-business
8	Fletcher and Harris (2012)	International knowledge	*Int Bus Rev*	Case study	15 SE-assisted firms
9	Fletcher and Prashantham (2011)	International entrepreneurship; knowledge assimilation; learning	*J Small Bus & Ent Dev*	Longitudinal case study	SE-assisted firms
10	Fletcher et al. (2013)	Knowledge management; market entry;	*J Int Mar*	Case studies	10 internationalizing SMEs

Table 16.1 (continued)

No	Study	Keywords	Journal/ Book Chapter	Methodology	Sample
		interorganizational strategy			
11	Hamill and Gregory (1997)	Internet usage and export involvement	*J Mar Man*	Quantitative	103 SMEs
12	Harris and Li (2009)	Exporting	*Oxford Econ Papers*	Quantitative	An undisclosed number of Scottish SMEs
13	Harris and Wheeler (2005)	Relationships; internationalization	*Int Bus Rev*	Case studies	Owners of profitable young international businesses in central Scotland
14	Ibeh et al. (2004)	mMNE; international entrepreneurship	*J Int Ent*	Descriptive	204 Scottish mMNEs
15	Johnsen and Johnsen (1999)	Network	*Int J Ent B&R*	Case studies	10 smaller knitwear companies
16	Johnson (2004)	Early internationalization; international start-ups; high technology	*J Int Ent*	Case studies	12 semi-structured interviews, 6 with SE-assisted firms
17	Keogh et al. (1998)	Innovation strategy; technology-based firms	*Int Small Bus J*	Case studies	Oil and gas industry based in Aberdeen
18	Mason and Brown (2013)	Regional development; policy	*Small Bus Econ*	Case studies	5 high-growth firms in Scotland
19	McAuley (1999)	Entrepreneurship	*J Int Mar*	Qualitative	15 micro-entrepreneurial arts/craft firms
20	McAuley and Fillis (2005)	Entrepreneurialism; globalization; craft production	*J Small Bus & Ent Dev*	Mixed	Public and private payers in the craft sector
21	Prashantham and McNaughton (2006)	Multinational subsidiary; social capital; public policy; internationalization	*Int Bus Rev*	Single case study	Scottish technology and collaboration initiative

CONCLUSIONS

Recommendations for Improving SME Performance Globally

International business offers fruitful opportunities, but simultaneously presents challenges to Scotland's businesses. On the edge of Europe, Scotland must continue to compete on the basis of knowledge, skills and ingenuity (Dimitratos et al., 2009b). Knowledge management, internationalization and innovation are often regarded as three disconnected activities in the firm that need to be examined as interdependent processes at macro- and micro-levels in the economy, and as interconnected theories and disciplines in education and research (Jones and Coviello, 2005; Jones, 2013). However, the intrafirm consolidation of these activities may result in superior performance internationally. Given that high-tech and knowledge-intensive industries are evidenced to provide the strongest impulse to economic recovery – they are more productive, less energy intensive and more innovative (European Commission, 2013) – Scotland should be devoted to developing its high-tech businesses.

Whatever the results of the referendum, Scotland will continue to encourage and support the internationalization of its SMEs through its development and enterprise agencies. This will require continued policy support measures but also action from the higher and further education sectors to align entrepreneurship, innovation and internationalization in the curriculum, as well as languages and ICT capability. Scottish SMEs along with many others in the EU may struggle to access and participate in global supply chains, therefore SME upgrading in manufacturing and service capabilities is important (ibid.).

Scottish SMEs may consider the growth potential and abundant opportunities from emerging markets, given that the current export volume to Asian and Latin America is relatively low. Of course, the Scottish government has recognized the opportunity (SDI, 2012). For example, it targets doubling the number of Scottish companies (based on 2010 levels) supported to access Chinese markets by 2017 (Scottish Government, 2012).

Future Prospects for Scottish SMEs

Exporting and deeper forms of internationalization among SMEs are fundamental for small nation economies such as Scotland. For Scottish-based researchers, perhaps the Scottish context provides a rich opportunity to extend empirical knowledge and theory as Scotland emerges as an innovative, entrepreneurial and globally oriented nation, whether or not it does so as part of or independently of the UK. Given the strong technological and innovative nature of the Scottish economy, Scotland may constitute a foundation for a new way of understanding of the significance and outcome of SME internationalization to country-level competitiveness.

REFERENCES

Baumol, W. (1968), 'Entrepreneurship in economic theory', *American Economic Review*, **58**(2), 64–71.

Bell, J. (1995), 'The internationalization of small computer software firms: a further challenge to "stage" theories', *European Journal of Marketing*, **29**(8), 60–75.

Bell, J., D. Crick and S. Young (2004), 'Small firm internationalization and business strategy: an exploratory study of "knowledge-intensive" and "traditional" manufacturing firms in the UK', *International Small Business Journal*, **22**(1), 23–56.

Bell, J., R. McNaughton and S. Young (2001), '"Born-again global" firms: an extension to the "born global" phenomenon', *Journal of International Management*, **7**(3), 173–89.

Bell, J., R. McNaughton, S. Young and D. Crick (2003), 'Towards an integrative model of small firm internationalization', *Journal of International Entrepreneurship*, **1**(4), 339–62.

Beugelsdijk, S. (2007), 'Entrepreneurial culture, regional innovativeness and economic growth', *Journal of Evolutionary Economics*, **17**(2), 187–210.

Bilkey, W.J. and G. Tesar (1977), 'The export behaviour of smaller-sized Wisconsin manufacturing firms', *Journal of International Business Studies*, **8**(1), 93–8.

Blackburn, R. and T. Wainwright (2010), 'The eXport factor: British SMEs' approach to doing business overseas', monograph, London: Barclays.

Brouthers, K.D., L.E. Brouthers and S. Werner (2008), 'Real options, international entry mode choice and performance', *Journal of Management Studies*, **45**(5), 936–60.

Calof, J.C. and P. Beamish (1995), 'Adapting to foreign markets: explaining internationalization', *International Business Review*, **4**(2), 115–31.

Carree, M. and R. Thurik (2003), 'The impact of entrepreneurship on economic growth', in Z. Acs and D. Audretsch (eds), *Handbook of Entrepreneurship Research*, Boston, MA: Kluwer, pp. 437–71.

Casillas, J.C., A.M. Moreno and F.J. Acedo (2012), 'Path dependence view of export behaviour: a relationship between static patterns and dynamic configurations', *International Business Review*, **21**(3), 465–79.

Casulli, L. (2009), 'Exploring opportunity creation in internationalizing SMEs: evidence from Scottish firms', in M.V. Jones, P. Dimitratos, M. Fletcher and S. Young (eds), *Internationalization, Entrepreneurship and the Smaller Firm: Evidence from around the World*, Cheltenham, UK and Northampton, MA, USA: Edward Elgar Publishing, pp. 20–36.

Casulli, L. (2011), 'Making internationalization decisions: how heuristics and biases affect the reasoning processes of leaders of small and medium-sized firms', PhD thesis, Glasgow: University of Glasgow.

Chetty, S., M. Johanson and O.M. Martín (2014), 'Speed of internationalization: conceptualisation, measurement and validation', *Journal of World Business*, **49**(4), 633–50.

Danson, M., E.M. Helinska-Hughes, M.D. Hughes and G. Whittam (2008), 'Supporting SMEs in Scotland: strategies for internationalizing', in L.-P. Dana, I.M. Welpe, M. Han and V. Ratten (eds), *Handbook of Research on European Business and Entrepreneurship*, Cheltenham, UK and Northampton, MA, USA: Edward Elgar Publishing, pp. 700–717.

Diamantopoulos, A. and K. Inglis (1988), 'Identifying differences between high- and low-involvement exporters', *International Marketing Review*, **5**(2), 52–60.

Dimitratos, P., J. Finch and N. Li (2013), *The Innovation for Competitive Enterprise Benchmark Survey: Briefing Report II*, research report commissioned by the European Union's the Special EU Programmes Body, Glasgow: University of Glasgow.

Dimitratos, P., J.E. Amorós, M.S. Etchebarne and C. Felzenstein (2014), 'Micro-multinational or not? International entrepreneurship, networking and learning effects', *Journal of Business Research*, **67**(5), 908–15.

Dimitratos, P., J.E. Johnson, K.I.N. Ibeh and J. Slow (2009a), 'Core rigidities of micromultinationals: the Scottish experience', in M.V. Jones, P. Dimitratos, M. Fletcher and S. Young (eds), *Internationalization, Entrepreneurship and the Smaller Firm: Evidence from Around the World*, Cheltenham, UK and Northampton, MA, USA: Edward Elgar Publishing, pp. 139–49.

Dimitratos, P., J. Johnson, J. Slow and S. Young (2003), 'Micromultinationals: new types of firms for the global competitive landscape', *European Management Journal*, **21**(2), 164–74.

Dimitratos, P., I. Liouka, D. Ross and S. Young (2009b), 'The multinational enterprise and subsidiary evolution: Scotland since 1945', *Business History*, **51**(3), 401–25.

Ernst & Young (2014), *EY 2014 Scotland Attractiveness Survey*, accessed 16 June 2014 at http://www.ey.com/Publication/vwLUAssets/EY_UK-Attractiveness-Survey-2014-Scotland-web/$FILE/1485655_Scotland_Attractiveness_Survey_2014_FINAL.pdf.

European Commission (2013), *EU Industrial Structure Report 2013*, accessed 13 July 2014 at http://ec.europa.eu/enterprise/policies/industrial-competitiveness/competitiveness-analysis/eu-industrial-structure/files/report_euis_2013_final.pdf.

Fabrizio, K.R. and L.G. Thomas (2012), 'The impact of local demand on innovation in a global industry', *Strategic Management Journal*, **33**(1), 42–64.

Fillis, I. and B. Wagner (2005), 'E-business development an exploratory investigation of the small firm', *International Small Business Journal*, **23**(6), 604–34.

Findlay, A., C. Mason, D. Houston, D. McCollum and R. Harrison (2009), 'Escalators, elevators and travelators: the occupational mobility of migrants to South-East England', *Journal of Ethnic and Migration Studies*, **35**(6), 861–79.

Fletcher, M. (2007), 'Internationalising small and medium sized enterprises (SMEs): a learning approach', PhD thesis, Glasgow: University of Glasgow.

Fletcher, M. and S. Harris (2012), 'Knowledge acquisition for the internationalization of the smaller firm: content and sources', *International Business Review*, **21**(4), 631–47.

Fletcher, M. and S. Prashantham (2011), 'Knowledge assimilation processes of rapidly internationalising firms: longitudinal case studies of Scottish SMEs', *Journal of Small Business and Enterprise Development*, **18**(3), 475–501.

Fletcher, M., S. Harris and R.G. Richey Jr. (2013), 'Internationalization knowledge: what, why, where, and when?', *Journal of International Marketing*, **21**(3), 47–71.

Global Connection Survey (GCS) (2014), 'Scotland's Global Connections Survey 2012: estimating exports from Scotland', *Statistical Bulletin*, 29 January, accessed 10 May 2014 at http://www.scotland.gov.uk/Resource/0044/00442854.pdf.

Hamill, J. and K. Gregory (1997), 'Internet marketing in the internationalization of UK SMEs', *Journal of Marketing Management*, **13**(1–3), 9–28.

Harris, R. and Q.C. Li (2009), 'Exporting, R&D, and absorptive capacity in UK establishments', *Oxford Economic Papers*, **61**(1), 74–103.

Harris, S. and C. Wheeler (2005), 'Entrepreneurs' relationships for internationalization: functions, origins and strategies', *International Business Review*, **14**(2), 187–207.

He, X. and Y. Wei (2013), 'Export market location decision and performance: the role of external networks and absorptive capacity', *International Marketing Review*, **30**(6), 559–90.

Hunter, T. (2014), 'Foreword', in J. Levie (2014), *Global Entrepreneurship Monitor: Scotland 2013, GEM Report*, Glasgow: University of Strathclyde.

Ibeh, K., J.E. Johnson, P. Dimitratos and J. Slow (2004), 'Micromultinationals: some preliminary evidence on an emergent "star" of the international entrepreneurship field', *Journal of International Entrepreneurship*, **2**(4), 289–303.

Johanson, J. and J.-E. Vahlne (1977), 'The internationalization process of the firm – a model of knowledge development and increasing foreign market commitments', *Journal of International Business Studies*, **8**(1), 23–32.

Johnsen, R.E. and T.E. Johnsen (1999), 'International market development through networks: the case of the Ayrshire knitwear sector', *International Journal of Entrepreneurial Behavior & Research*, **5**(6), 297–312.

Johnson, J. (2004), 'Factors influencing the early internationalization of high technology start-ups: US and UK evidence', *Journal of International Entrepreneurship*, **2**(1–2), 139–54.

Jones, M.V. (1999), 'The internationalisation of small UK high technology firms', *Journal of International Marketing*, **70**(4), 63–85.

Jones, M.V. (2001), 'First steps in internationalisation: concepts and evidence from a sample of small high-technology firms', *Journal of International Management*, **7**(3), 191–110.

Jones, M.V. (2013), 'Growth at the centre of the confluence', *Making It Magazine*, 14 December, accessed 26 May 2015 at http://www.makingitmagazine.net/?p=7836.

Jones, M.V. and L. Casulli (2014), 'International entrepreneurship: exploring the logic and utility of individual experience through comparative reasoning approaches', *Entrepreneurship Theory and Practice*, **38**(1), 45–69.

Jones, M.V. and N.E. Coviello (2005), 'Internationalization: conceptualising an entrepreneurial process of behaviour in time', *Journal of International Business Studies*, **36**(3), 284–303.

Keogh, W., S.L. Jack, D.J. Bower and E. Crabtree (1998), 'Small, technology-based firms in the UK oil and gas industry: innovation and internationalization strategies', *International Small Business Journal*, **17**(1), 57–72.

Kim, M. (2013), 'Many roads lead to Rome: implications of geographic scope as a source of isolating mechanisms', *Journal of International Business Studies*, **44**(9), 898–921.

Kogut, B. (1991), 'Country capabilities and the permeability of borders', *Strategic Management Journal*, **12**(1), 33–47.

Levie, J. (2014), *Global Entrepreneurship Monitor: Scotland 2013, GEM Report*, Glasgow: University of Strathclyde.

Mason, C. and R. Brown (2012), *Technology-based Firms in Scotland*, accessed 26 May 2015 at http://www.scottish-enterprise.com/~/media/SE/Resources/Documents/STUV/Technology-Based-Firms-in-Scotland.pdf.

Mason, C. and R. Brown (2013), 'Creating good public policy to support high growth firms', *Small Business Economics*, **40**(2), 211–25.

McAuley, A. (1999), 'Entrepreneurial instant exporters in the Scottish arts and crafts sector', *Journal of International Marketing*, **7**(4), 67–82.

McAuley, A. and I. Fillis (2005), 'The Orkney based craft entrepreneur: remote yet global?', *Journal of Small Business and Enterprise Development*, **12**(4), 498–509.

Mobius (2012), *UK Life Science Start-up Report*, accessed 14 June 2014 at http://mobiuslifesciences.com/file_download/8.

Morgan-Thomas, A. and M.V. Jones (2009), 'Post-entry internationalization dynamics: differences between SMEs in the development speed of their international sales', *International Small Business Journal*, **27**(1), 71–97.

Nelson, R.R. and K. Nelson (2002), 'Technology, institutions, and innovation systems', *Research Policy*, **31**(2), 265–72.

O'Farrell, P.N., P.A. Wood and J. Zheng (1998), 'Regional influences on foreign market development by business service companies: elements of a strategic context explanation', *Regional Studies*, **32**(1), 31–48.

Oviatt, B.M. and P.P. McDougall (1994), 'Toward a theory of international new ventures', *Journal of International Business Studies*, **25**(1), 45–64.

Papadopoulos, N. and J.E. Denis (1988), 'Inventory taxonomy and assessment of methods for international market selection', *International Marketing Review*, **5**(3), 47–60.

Prashantham, S. (2011), 'Social capital and Indian micromultinationals', *British Journal of Management*, **22**(1), 4–20.

Prashantham, S. and R.B. McNaughton (2006), 'Facilitation of links between multinational subsidiaries and SMEs: the Scottish Technology and Collaboration (STAC) initiative', *International Business Review*, **15**(5), 447–62.

Scottish Development International (SDI) (2012), *Scotland's International Trade and Investment Strategy 2011–2015*, accessed 20 June 2014 at http://www.sdi.co.uk/~/media/

SDI/Files/documents/international-trade/Scotlands%20International%20Trade%20and%20Investment%20Strategy.pdf.

Scottish Enterprise (2014), *Scottish Enterprise Business Plan 2014–2017*, accessed 11 June 2014 at http://www.scottish-enterprise.com/~/media/SE/Resources/Documents/ABC/Business-plan-2014.pdf.

Scottish Government (2012), *Working with China: A Five Year Strategy for Engagement between Scotland and the People's Republic of China*, accessed 20 June 2014 at www.scotland.gov.uk/Resource/0040/00409256.pdf.

Scottish Government (2014a), *Government Expenditure & Revenue Scotland 2012–13*, accessed 15 June 2014 at http://www.scotland.gov.uk/Publications/2014/03/7888/0.

Scottish Government (2014b), 'Latest economy statistics publications', accessed 14 June 2014 at http://www.scotland.gov.uk/Topics/Statistics/Browse/Economy/Q/pno/1.

Slow, J. (2014), 'The ACE model: a staged development model for the internationalization of SMEs', mimeograph, Glasgow: Scottish Enterprise.

Vohora, A., M. Wright and A. Lockett (2004), 'Critical junctures in the development of university high-tech spinout companies', *Research Policy*, **33**(1), 147–75.

Welch, L.S. and R. Luostarinen (1988), 'Internationalization – evolution of a concept', *Journal of General Management*, **14**(2), 34–55.

Young, S., N. Hood and S. Dunlop (1988), 'Global strategies, MNE subsidiary roles and economic impact in Scotland', *Regional Studies*, **22**(6), 487–97.

17. Improving SME performance globally: the Hungarian case

István Molnár and Pál Belyó

INTRODUCTION

SMEs are an important component of economic growth and social welfare and an infinite source of innovation; an important aspect of the spirit of time and space/location. Over the past few decades, Hungarian individual entrepreneurs, small and medium-sized enterprises (SMEs) went through a transformation, which is unique in the Central and Eastern European economies. Within the past century, four major political and economic transitions have occurred – the first two after World War I and II respectively, the third after 1989, following the collapse of the Soviet Union, and the fourth is happening now. During the period between 1920 and 2014 a gradual transformation towards strengthening market economy and within it SMEs occurred, which included denial and elimination, acceptance and legitimization, followed by tolerance and institutional (e.g., governmental and EU) support. In this chapter, the authors apply a historical, economic and political approach by investigating the effect of the business environment on the SMEs and try to determine those policy and regulatory environment elements that enable sustainable SME growth in Hungary. Based on these experiences, policy measures are selected to further improve SME performance.

The case of Hungarian SMEs is a good example for illustrating that in the global economy the use of information technology (IT) should not only be restricted to conducting business (e.g., e-commerce), but also to collect data, analyse market information and generate timely, accurate knowledge for decision-makers. The focus here is rather on the global and macro-view of SMEs, the overall information system and on its efficient use and management. Instead of applying the traditional approach of focusing on SMEs and their strategies, the authors focus on the SME environment and the national or international political and economic system that enable and support SMEs in a global competition. With increased speed of globalization, there is a need to move towards a more complex view of observations that best fits the level of processes and fits the most appropriate (global, regional or national) level of policy intervention into these processes. The authors also think that introducing a historical and macroeconomic view in the analysis of the SMEs is indispensable. It provides solid foundation for policy analysis, comparative studies and helps to create efficient strategies for SME development. It is also helpful to put technology and related developments (e.g., the use of Internet, 'democratization' of establishing businesses, role of 'born global') into a proper perspective.

First, a comprehensive picture is provided about the path that led to the current position of the Hungarian SMEs. By filling the gap of longitudinal research analysis, authors emphasize that without understanding the global, regional and local social, economic and political environment of the SMEs, no comprehensive and objective assessment, consequently, no efficient policy-making and regulation is possible. The authors experienced serious difficulties in introducing longitudinal analysis; data sources, especially those applicable for long-term data analysis are usually missing or incompatible.

Second, for the post-recession period of 2008–13 authors deliver an in depth cross-sectional analysis of the Hungarian SMEs from a regional (EU) and global perspective. The special multilevel regulatory structure and the related information processing will play a significant role in this discussion. The authors argue that any subject – including the SMEs – should be discussed in response to the economic and political debate unfolding across Europe about the future of the EU and more generally, of Europe. This section of the chapter also provides some remarks on the applied methodology and techniques, clarifying under which inherent boundaries are our conclusions valid.

Finally, the generally applicable, effective macroeconomic strategies boosting global performance of SMEs are discussed. Authors argue that without harmonization of national, regional and global regulations, the SMEs cannot develop efficient strategies and improve global performance.

HUNGARIAN SMEs FROM A HISTORICAL PERSPECTIVE

The post-World War II economic and political history of SMEs can be divided into different periods; the periods we perceive reflect the attitude changes of the political and economic environment:[1]

- period 1: establishing the socialist economy (1945–81);
- period 2: co-existence and nursing the market economy (1982–88);
- period 3: free market economy (1989–), with phases:

– phase 1: broadening and stabilizing market economy (1989–2003);
– phase 2: EU membership and integration (2004–08);
– phase 3: economic crisis and recovery (2009–).

Antecedents

The economy prior to World War II[2] was agriculture and small-scale manufacturing oriented, without any significant natural resources. The country had been traditionally relying on foreign trade with negative balance, exporting agricultural goods and textile products, importing raw materials and industrial products. The politically and economically turbulent 1920s and 1930s did not provide an accommodating atmosphere for establishing a solid foundation for a modern free market economy and entrepreneurial culture.

Period 1: Establishing the Socialist Economy (1945–81)

After 1945, and especially after 1948, the socialist government started to nationalize the industry and introduced an agricultural collectivization programme. As a result, most economic activities were conducted by state-owned industrial and services sector firms or in agricultural cooperatives and state farms. The post-World War II economy of the 1950s and 1960s was entirely determined by the 'Cold War' and a forced industrialization aiming to create a self-sufficient, state-controlled economy. The production plans and the resources assigned were given to the state firms and a hierarchical bureaucratic apparatus exercised central control. Prices and the allocation of financial resources (including investments) were also centralized, while the independence of the firms was strictly limited (see Berend, 1999, p. 153; 2006, p. 133).

Starting from 1968, after about 15 years of reform discussions, self-sufficiency was replaced by the New Economic Mechanism (NEM), which reopened the country to foreign trade (also to Western countries)[3] and introduced limited market mechanisms. The reform freed the state-owned firms from strict bureaucratic control and increased their autonomy. Moreover, the NEM allowed the operation of a number of SMEs, mainly in the services sector, generating herewith social changes and opportunity to re-establish an entrepreneurial culture. Nevertheless, the NEM was not only a reform, 'a great experiment, unique in history' (see Kornai, 1980, p. 148),[4] but brought tangible results: production has been growing at an annual rate of about 5 per cent, 'full employment' along with significant productivity increase and real wage growth were achieved and the quality and quantity of consumer supply improved.

At the end of the 1970s, however, it became obvious that 'Some of the original reform ideas have been carried through only partially: forward leaps and retreats alternate' (ibid.). Due to subsidized consumer products, unprofitable state firms, the fiscal deficit along with net foreign debt rose significantly and finally, both agriculture and industry began to suffer from a lack of investment. Moreover, external conditions have changed from bad to worse: the Hungarian terms of trade deteriorated, which added further difficulties to the already existing budgetary problems and balance of payments.

Period 2: Co-existence and Nursing the Market Economy (1982–88)

To enable further economic progress and support political, economic and social transformation, in 1981 Hungary further liberalized its economy and became the first COMECON member state introducing SME legislation. Sole proprietorships and different forms of joint ventures (e.g., business associations within the industrial and services sectors, small co-ops in the agriculture) with income-related incentives broke up the rigid, centrally controlled wages paid by public firms. With merit-based incentives and increased individual responsibility, entrepreneurial spirit and attitude have been created, which resulted in about 35000 enterprises of these various types. The entrepreneurial culture was established and rapidly disseminated, co-existing with the 'socialist sector'.

In 1982, to strengthen the macroeconomic background, Hungary joined the International Monetary Fund (IMF) and World Bank, respectively. In 1986, the two-tier banking system (central bank + commercial banks) and shortly thereafter, the individual income tax along with the value added tax (VAT) were introduced. Essential laws on liquidation, commercial enterprises, the transformation of enterprises, corporations and cooperatives, as well as on foreign investments were enacted. The Law of Business Associations (LBA) of 1989 became the platform to processes that irreversibly changed the composition of economic stakeholders and proved to be crucial in promoting economic regime change. In retrospect, the LBA was of inestimable importance to the future development of the country and its enterprises.

Period 3: Free Market Economy (1989–)

Phase 1: broadening and stabilizing market economy (1989–2003)

After 1989, the combined effect of the new legislative framework, political changes (e.g., the dissolution of the Soviet Union) and the unfolding economic processes (both domestic and foreign, especially the dissolution of COMECON and the collapse of the socialist international market), led to a rapid transformation in the organizational structure of the economy. An overall deregulation was implemented in the legal system: the administrative barriers to a market economy were removed and economic legislation completed in 1996, which provided a new institutional foundation for the entire Hungarian economy.

The centre of the economic regime change has been the privatization legislation; the country turned from a socialist economy, based on absolute superiority of socialist state property, to a market economy based on the dominance of private property. Hungary was the earliest of the former socialist countries to start the privatization process in 1989. The LBA served as its legislative basis along with a new bankruptcy law. The first stage, 'spontaneous privatization' lasted about a year and affected about 2 per cent of the state sector. The second stage, the state-managed compulsory privatization based on the Privatization Law, between 1992 and 1997 transformed about 99 per cent of the remaining state-owned companies into joint stock or limited liability companies.

Slower transformation and stabilization processes followed the rapid change and by 1995 a new property, economic organizational structure came into existence; the new structure of the new Hungarian market economy was completely established and politically stabilized.

The transition process transparently demonstrated the weaknesses of the Hungarian economy: it led to surging inflation as an unwelcome result of the liberalization of prices and foreign trade, increased unemployment, budget imbalances and indebtedness, and made the social net more expensive. In 1995, as a response to the challenges, the government introduced a drastic stabilization programme that also accelerated structural reforms: a crawling peg, restrictive wage policy and tighter fiscal policies, further liberalization of consumer prices, and systematic pension reform. As a result of the stabilization programme, GDP growth rate increased driven by export growth, inflation decreased and the volume of foreign direct investment (FDI) rose again.

The national wealth, which had been nearly completely nationalized after 1945, became privately owned over one-and-half decades, which is historically a very short time. Privatization revitalized the market economy and dissolved the economic pillars of the one-party socialist political system. As a 'by-product' of the transformation, masses became unemployed and a significant portion of them became entrepreneurs from necessity. Old habits of insufficient work ethics and tax avoidance survived, and the shadow economy, including corruption, grew. Despite some negative tendencies, the early adoption of the legal framework of the market economy was an advantage for the country in the course of EU accession and legal harmonization. Around the millennium, the Hungarian economy had recovered, became healthy and satisfied the membership criteria of the EU, which it joined in 2004.

Phase 2: EU membership and integration (2004–08)

Joining the EU added new and real regional challenges and opportunities (to the already existing global ones) for the Hungarian government, businesses and society alike. The compliance with EU requirements required a continuous effort to compete on an open regional EU market and to learn to utilize the advantages and avoid the disadvantages provided by the institutional framework; it has been and still is a difficult undertaking. The fundamental changes of the economic environment included a continuously evolving multilevel regulatory environment, as well.

In 2005, Hungary adopted the new SME definition and followed the related EU economic policies, which underline the importance of the sector: 'Micro, small and medium-sized enterprises (SMEs) are the engine of the European economy. They are an essential source of jobs, create entrepreneurial spirit and innovation in the EU and are thus crucial for fostering competitiveness and employment' (European Commission, 2005, p. 3).

According to the EU law, the main factors determining an SME[5] are included in Table 17.1.

The European Commission's Small Business Act for Europe (SBA) (see European Commission, 2008) provides a comprehensive SME policy framework for the EU and its member states, to promote entrepreneurship and to strengthen competitiveness. The SBA implements a two-level (EU Commission and member states) regulation to eliminate impediments and support growth and job creation. The EU Commission annually monitors and assesses the progress of members states in implementing the SBA policies, based on a set of political measures, which are organized around ten principles.[6] Both the EU and the member states allocate financial resources to support policies, often bundling them for higher

Table 17.1 SME size class definitions

Company Category	Employees	Turnover (Million Euros)	Balance Sheet Total (Million Euros)
Medium-sized	< = 250	< = 50	< = 43
Small	< = 50	< = 10	< = 10
Micro	< = 10	< = 2	< = 2

Source: European Commission (2008).

efficiency. For eligible SMEs, the system offers two types of potential benefits: (1) participation in EU business support programmes (e.g., research funding, competitiveness and innovation funding) and (2) fewer requirements or reduced fees for administrative compliance.

Despite all efforts, the performance of Hungarian SMEs did not improve spectacularly after joining the EU; they did not measure up to the competition and were at a disadvantage on the Common Market. Neither revenue generation, nor employment improved significantly and the Hungarian SMEs lagged behind their EU competitors in different areas (e.g., management, organization, telecommunication techniques and self-organization). When joining the EU in 2004, Hungary was economically one of the most advanced among the new member states, however, its extremely open economy, high level of fiscal and balance of payments deficit along with government, household and corporate debt (mostly denominated in foreign currencies) made the country financially vulnerable. With the global financial crisis of 2008 investors became sceptical about the prospects and ability of the Hungarian economy and investors hastily left the market (Figures 17.1 and 17.2). In order to defend its currency, the central bank hiked the key lending rate to 11.5 per cent, and became the first EU country to be rescued. In the fourth quarter of 2008, the country entered recession, the worst since 1991.

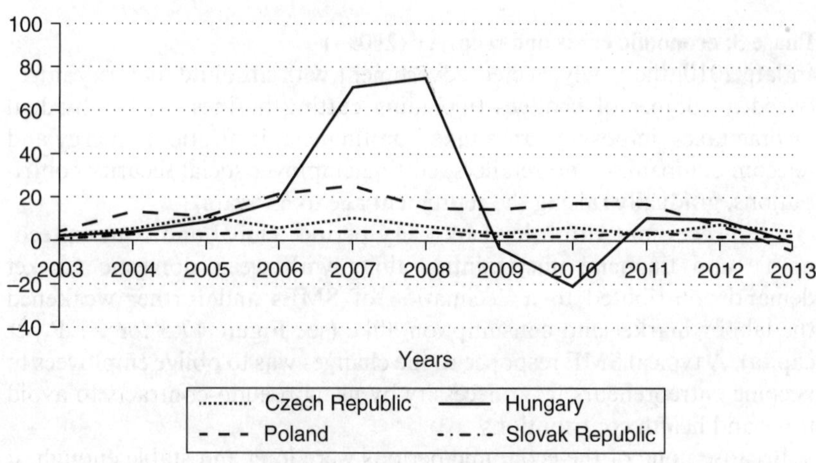

Source: European Commission (2014c).

Figure 17.1 Foreign direct investment of Hungary and its major regional competitors (net inflows, billion USD)

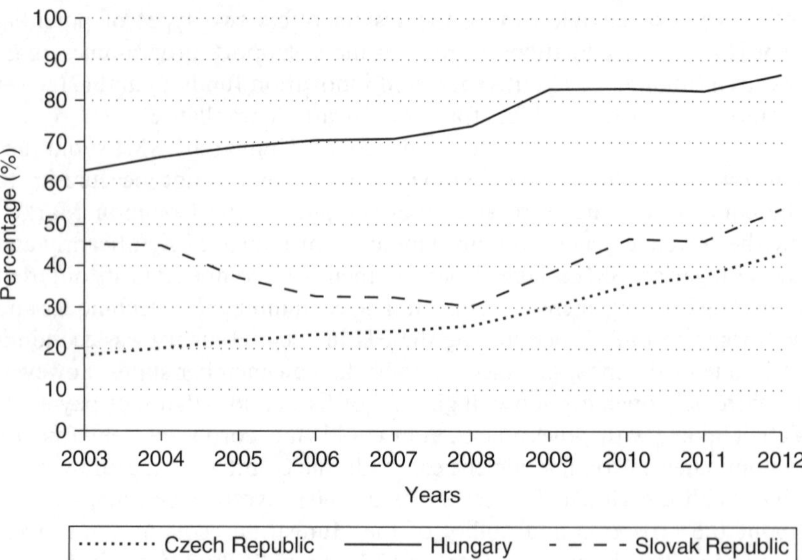

Source: European Commission (2014c).

Figure 17.2 The debt of the central government of Hungary and its major regional competitors (% of GDP)

Phase 3: economic crisis and recovery (2009–)

In late 2010, the newly elected government with absolute majority introduced a number of changes (including cutting business and individual income taxes, imposing 'crisis taxes' on financial institutions, energy and telecom companies, and retailers, cutting employer social security contributions, gradually raising the retirement age to 65 years).

Deep recession with a long recovery period, global and regional economic and financial uncertainties along with weak domestic market demand contributed to a decimation of SMEs and further weakened the labour market and consumption alike (see Figure 17.3 for GDP per capita). A typical SME response to the changes was to oblige employees to become entrepreneurs from necessity by using pseudo-contracts to avoid taxes and health contributions.

Because none of the economic periods were long and stable enough, it became impossible to accumulate a sufficient amount of capital, while the changing periods of market economy and socialist or nationalized state economy made the establishment of a multigenerational entrepreneurship culture impossible. A direct consequence of the missing accumulated

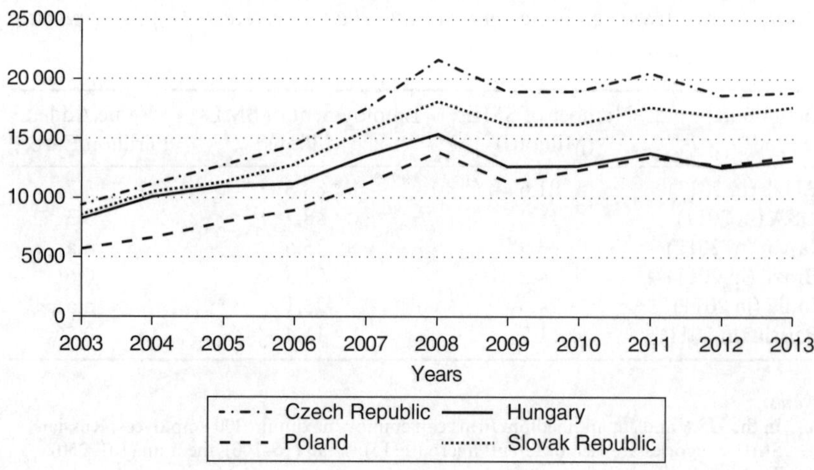

Source: European Commission (2014c).

Figure 17.3 GDP per capita of Hungary and its major regional competitors (current US dollars)

capital is that from time to time, political powers replaced the historically evolving capital accumulation with a forced redistribution of national resources, which were then used inefficiently, making the economy permanently dependent on foreign capital. The redistribution of national resources by the political elite is acknowledged by the empirical study by Róbert (1999, p. 403), which considers political embedding and even party membership a key factor in the career path to entrepreneurship. In the absence of multigenerational entrepreneurship culture, only education could have helped to develop proper management skills.

Methodological Remarks

The Hungarian case shows that SMEs do not flourish without a supportive regulatory environment. It is also apparent that any regulatory strategy assumes timely, clear and definite signals delivered by a proper information system (first of all data and methodology to process these data), based on which quick assessment and re-definition of goals and/or regulations along with resources can be defined. There is certainly a minimum set of data required for longitudinal data analysis for SMEs (e.g., number, size, age, sector affiliation, revenue and/or added value, market penetration). It should be mandatory to define, collect and publish these national and regional SME data to make proper assessments possible.

Table 17.2 Major global economies and their selected SME performance indicators

Economies	Number of SMEs (Millions)	Employment of SMEs[a] (Millions)	Value Added (Trillion Euros)
EU28 (in 2013)	21.6	88.8	3.7
USA (in 2011)	18.2	48.7	3.3
Japan (in 2012)	3.9	33.5	n.a.
Brazil (in 2011)	4.2	23.3	0.6
India (in 2011)	24.5	73.1	n.a.
Russia (in 2011)	1.7	11.4	0.7[b]

Notes:
a. In the USA and Japan, medium firms can employ maximum 300 employees. Russian SME categories are also different: micro (0−15), small (16–100), medium (101–250).
b. Turnover.

Source: European Commission (2014a).

HUNGARIAN SMEs BETWEEN 2008 AND 2013

An EU Perspective

In the EU-28, the non-financial business sector[7] the 21.6 million SMEs (more than 99 per cent of all businesses) employed 88.8 million people (two-thirds of all employees), generating 3.666 trillion euros in value added (58 per cent of value added per euro). Under the circumstances of a slower than expected recovery, the major performance indicators show the importance of SMEs in the EU economy (Table 17.2).

The aftermath of the 2008 crisis created clear fractures across SME size classes, economic sectors and EU member states. The EU SMEs have only partially recovered; in terms of value added and of number of firms, recovery can be considered as complete, but in terms of employment, in 2013 enterprises of all SME class sizes were still well below the 2008 level. While the number of EU microenterprises increased, the number of small and medium enterprises decreased. SME performance in terms of value added has been driven by medium enterprises. By now, five key economic sectors ('manufacturing', 'construction', 'professional, scientific and technical activities', 'accommodation and food' and 'wholesale and retail trade, repair of motor vehicles and motorcycles') account for approximately 78 per cent of all SMEs, about 71 per cent of value added and 79 per cent of total SME employment in the EU, but only the 'business services', the 'other SMEs' and the 'accommodation and food' sectors achieved significant growth, while 'manufacturing', and 'construction' did not recover at all during the 2008–13 period. Based on their SME performance, the member states can be placed into the following groups: 'front runner', 'solid performer', 'no change', 'weak' and 'very weak'. Hungary is in the very weak performers' group along with Croatia, Cyprus, Czech Republic, Greece, Ireland, Portugal, Romania, Slovenia and Spain (see European Commission, 2014a). As EU-wide most of the SMEs operate on domestic markets, they did not use the opportunities of the expanding extra-EU markets, despite the fact that further recovery would depend on the utilization of export benefits and the general macroeconomic recovery.

The business environment, in which the EU SMEs operate, is regularly analysed using the Survey on Access to Finance of SMEs in the Euro Area (SAFE) and the Innobarometer, run by the European Commission (EC) and the European Central Bank (ECB). The SAFE survey connects the following key issues and challenges to SME performances by asking for ranking of:

- access to finance;
- availability of skilled staff or experienced managers;
- competition;
- cost of production;
- finding customers;
- regulation.

Market demand is the most pressing problem across the board of EU SMEs, but other issues are considered as equally important. SME class size, however, largely determines the individual answers. The barriers to the access of financial resources and bureaucratic hurdles to access EU funds were perceived as less important by the SMEs than by the microenterprises, contrary to the availability of skilled staff and/or experienced managers. Competition – especially on the supply side – is a special concern of medium-sized enterprises. In general, the better the SMEs' business environment is and the better they perform, the more they are concerned with the still existing difficulties. The 2014 Innobarometer survey[8] shows that access to R&D funding is the main obstacle to the commercialization of innovative products or services.

The European Commission's Directorate-General for Enterprise and Industry (EC DG ENTR) produces the annual SBA country fact sheets, for example, European Commission (2014b) and an annual SBA EU report, for example, European Commission (2014a), which serve as an additional source of information designed to improve evidence-based

Table 17.3 Rationale of SBA principles

SBA Principle		Rationale
I	Entrepreneurship	To create an entrepreneur friendly and rewarding environment
II	Second chance	To ensure that honest, but bankrupted entrepreneurs get a second chance
III	Think small first	To design rules according to the 'Think small first' principle
IV	Responsive administration	To make public administrations responsible to SMEs' needs
V	State aid and public procurement	To facilitate SME participation in public procurement and better use of state aid possibilities for SMEs
VI	Access to finance	To facilitate SME access to finance and develop an environment that supports timely payments in commercial transactions
VII	Single market	To benefit more from the single market
VIII	Skills and innovation	To promote skills upgrading and all forms of innovation
IX	Environment	To enable SMEs to turn environmental challenges into opportunities
X	Internationalization	To support SMEs to benefit from the growth of markets

Source: European Commission (2008).

policy-making. The data of 68 indicators are organized around ten principles as presented in Table 17.3.

At the EU level, there are considerable differences among SBA principles in terms of policy dynamics. Most countries are performing well on principles III (think small first), IV (responsive administration) and VI (access to finance), but score poorly on V (state aid and public procurement) and VIII (skills and innovation). A high spread of achievement can be observed regarding principles II (second chance), VII (single market), and X (internationalization). Well-performing member states exhibit less variability in terms of underlying indicators, while member states with lower-level achievements often have performance gaps between EU average and particular indicator values, while showing better performance in others (e.g., principles III [think small first], IV [responsive administration], VI [access to finance], IX [environment] and X [internationalization]). The results clearly show that there is a need to develop EU-level transformational policy processes, spread best practices and improve the overall evidence-based policy-making process. According to the European Commission (2014a), EU-level efforts will focus on five SBA foundations: I (entrepreneurship), IV (responsive administration), VI (access to finance), VIII (skills and innovation) and X (internationalization). The EU-level efforts result in certain policy implications, which have a significant impact on the member states' strategies as will be discussed later.

An additional survey about SBA principles has been conducted in relation to the *Annual Report on European SMEs 2013/2014* (see European Commission, 2014a). The results illustrate that principle VI (access to finance) achieved the highest policy progress followed by I (entrepreneurship) and VIII (skills and innovation), while VII (single market) and II (second chance) were the two lagging principles.

Hungarian SMEs in 2013

Based on the classification criteria of 'legal form', in 2013 there were about 1 828 000 registered economic corporations and unincorporated enterprises in Hungary (Figure 17.4). In a country with a population less than 10 million, there are over 1 million sole proprietors, more than 400 000 limited liability companies and about 160 000 corporations without legal entity in the form of limited partnership. However, our focus will be on SMEs from the non-financial business sector.

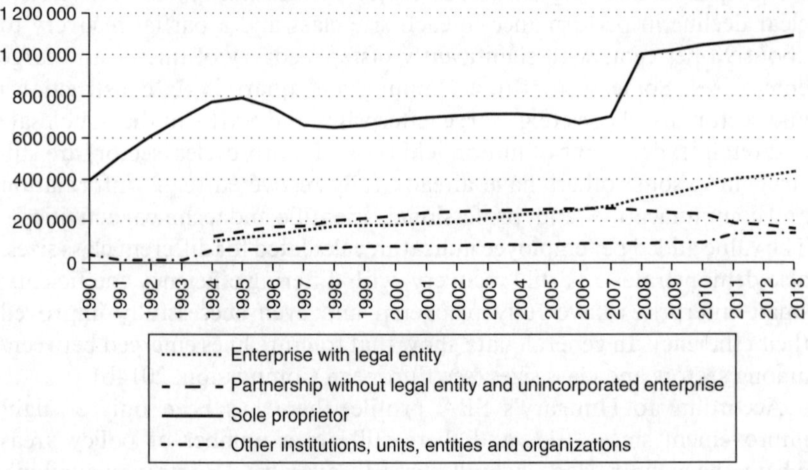

Source: Hungarian Central Statistical Office.

Figure 17.4 Legal form of enterprises between 1990 and 2014

Amidst an EU economic crisis, on the way to a fragile and partial recovery, the key performance indicators of the Hungarian SMEs in 2013 are presented in Table 17.4 (see also Figures 17.5 and 17.6). Based on these indicators, the importance of SMEs is clearly visible; most of the Hungarian enterprises (99.8 per cent) are SMEs, which employ more than two-thirds (70.8 per cent) of the employees and generate more than half (50.3 per cent) of the value added at factor cost.

The geographical dispersion of SMEs over the different Hungarian regions is uneven; one-third of the SMEs are located in the capital city area of Budapest, and about half of them in the central region of the country (which also includes Budapest).

The slow economic recovery and the extremely tough conditions are clearly reflected in the business demographics data; increasing SME death and decreasing birth rates can be observed, which in the 2008–13 time period resulted in an overall decreasing number of SMEs. Currently, about two-thirds of the SMEs are active, one-third (mainly microenterprises) have suspended – but not (yet) discontinued – their business activities. The average age of enterprises in 2013 is about ten years. In 2010 the proportion of enterprises surviving the five-year period was about 40 per cent of that measured in 2005. The ability to survive is determined by the sector and the size of the enterprise, and considered as very low.

The SMEs were the last resort during the financial crisis and are playing a crucial role in the recovery phase. Unfortunately, the recovery is only partial and very slow. The major performance indicators show a clear decline in performance in each size class and a partial recovery to about 90 per cent, with significantly faster recovery of micro- and large enterprises. Some sectors (e.g., 'mining and quarrying', 'construction') and sector size classes (e.g., large enterprises and SMEs in the 'wholesale and retail trade, repair of motor vehicles and motorcycles' sector) are still struggling, some others have already fully recovered (e.g., 'information and communication' and 'professional, scientific and technical activities'). The value added per employee indicator, calculated for different class sizes, also demonstrates a partial recovery, with differing efficiency coefficients; small enterprises have fully recovered and even successfully improved their efficiency. In general, data show that fracture lines emerged between/among sectors and class sizes (see European Commission, 2014b).

According to Hungary's SBA profile, there has been only a slight improvement since 2013, and there still are a number of policy areas where the country lags behind the EU average: I (entrepreneurship), II (second chance), VIII (skills and innovation), IX (environment) and X (internationalization). Hungary performs at average on principles VII (single market), VI (access to finance) and IV (responsive

Table 17.4 2008–13 performance indicators of Hungarian SMEs

Performance indicators	Size class	2008	2009	2010	2011	2012	2013	Recovery %
Number of enterprises	0–9	533 712	519 427	518 355	514 478	489 989	497 947	93.30
All sections B–J, L–N	10–49	26 920	23 467	24 539	23 921	23 861	23 906	88.80
	50–249	4 565	4 179	4 015	4 069	4 056	4 064	89.03
	250+	886	792	804	796	805	829	93.46
	Total	566 084	548 865	547 743	543 264	518 711	526 746	93.05
	All SMEs	565 197	548 073	546 939	542 468	517 906	525 917	93.05
Number of persons employed	0–9	920 111	874 910	877 776	870 499	858 961	867 316	94.26
All sections B–J, L–N	10–49	512 978	467 128	462 319	448 987	448 800	447 932	87.32
	50–249	448 978	410 114	400 296	405 180	406 367	404 374	90.14
	250+	756 825	672 667	685 235	699 339	697 671	708 457	93.61
	Total	2 638 505	2 424 819	2 425 626	2 424 005	2 411 799	2 428 079	92.02
	All SMEs	1 881 680	1 752 152	1 740 391	1 724 666	1 714 128	1 719 622	91.39
Value added at factor cost (100 000 euros)	0–9	9 290	8 063	8 863	9 370	8 590	8 570	92.25
All sections B–J, L–N	10–49	8 592	6 975	7 485	7 603	7 614	7 528	87.62
	50–249	9 869	8 490	8 637	8 993	8 896	8 874	89.92
	250+	23 403	19 073	21 095	22 437	21 361	21 365	21.29
	Total	51 153	42 601	46 081	48 403	46 460	46 337	90.58
	All SMEs	27 750	23 528	24 986	25 966	26 099	24 972	89.99

Source: SME Performance Review 2013/2014 Eurostat SBS database.

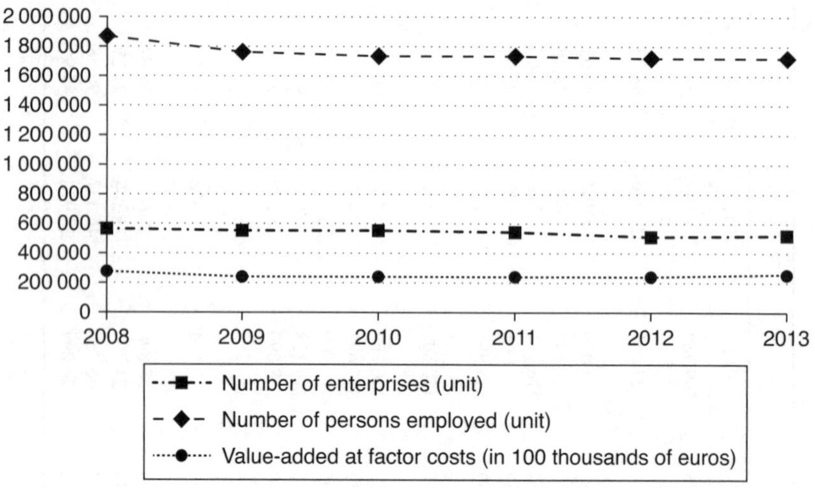

Source: European Commission (2014c).

Figure 17.5 2008–13 Performance indicators of Hungarian SMEs

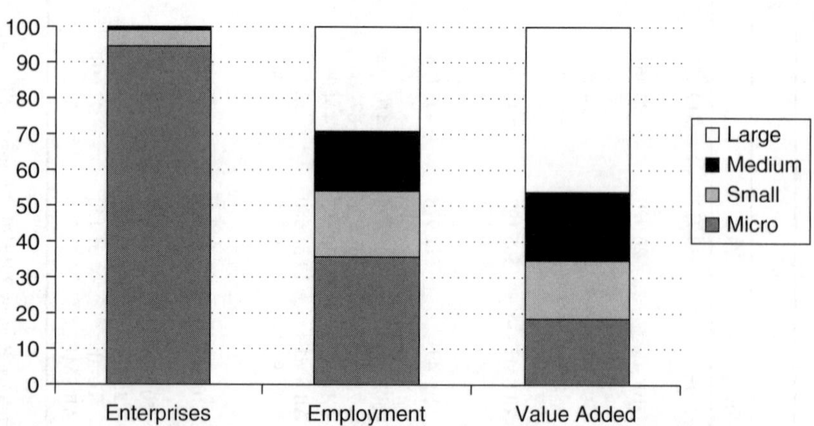

Source: European Commission (2014c).

Figure 17.6 Share of Hungarian SMEs and large enterprises in 2013 (%)

administration), but scores only on V (state aid and public procurement) above average. Over the past six years about half of the SBA principle areas improved, only II (second chance), VII (single market), IX (environment) and X (internationalization) did not.

Competitiveness and Competitors

The authors' understanding is that business competitiveness is the ability and performance of an enterprise, or a set of enterprises (e.g., defined by economic sector, geographic location), which try to achieve its/their strategic goals in a contest[9] (e.g., for markets, resources, technology, goods, partners, recognition or status) with other enterprise(s) acting on the same market. This working definition provides enough room to integrate the different approaches used for measuring competitiveness and accept the results of related theoretical discussions between Krugman (1994) and Dunn (1994).

The impact of SBA implementation on the competitiveness status of the EU member states has been investigated using the Global Competitiveness Index (GCI) and the Europe 2020 Competitiveness Index created by the World Economic Forum (WEF) (see Schwab and Sala-i-Martín, 2014). Competitiveness is defined by the WEF as 'the set of institutions, policies and factors that determine the level of productivity of a country' (ibid., p. 4). The different competitiveness indicators are grouped in 12 pillars, which compose the GCI. The index is used for classification of countries into factor, efficiency and innovation-driven classes of economies. Hungary is identified as one of the high-performing countries in terms of SBA implementation (high performing in at least two out of five key SBA principles) and was ranked according to the GCI classification in the group of 'transition from stage 2 (efficiency driven) to stage 3 (innovation driven)'[10] (ibid.).

Another indicator is *Doing Business*, which is an annual report of the World Bank, benchmarking the regulations that affect SMEs (see World Bank, 2013). *Doing Business* is based on assessments of business regulations of 11 different lifecycle areas (including starting a business, dealing with permits, getting credits, paying taxes, trading across borders, etc.). The index does not include a full range of factors, policies and institutions (e.g., security, corruption, macroeconomic stability). The ranking is based on the 'distance to frontier' score.

In addition, the International Institute for Management Development (IMD) regularly releases the *World Competitiveness Yearbook*, which creates a global competitiveness ranking of nations, based on four components; economic performance, infrastructure, government efficiency and business efficiency (see IMD WCC, 2014).

All major rankings demonstrate a weakened competitive position of

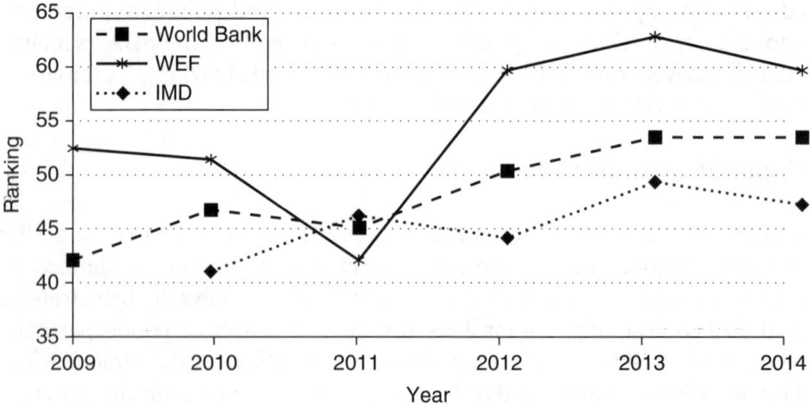

Sources: World Bank (2013), Schwab and Sala-i-Martín (2014) and IMD WCC (2014).

Figure 17.7 Ranking changes of Hungarian competitiveness

Hungarian SMEs between 2008 and 2014 (Figures 17.7 and 17.8). Low performance and insufficient competitiveness are caused by different factors, among others low productivity due to obsolete technology, insufficient use of modern ICT, low levels of innovation and R&D activity, lack of capital and/or continuous liquidity problems, missing cooperation among SMEs (including joint innovation and product development). The current business environment also constitutes problems, which worsened during the past few years and cannot be resolved easily (e.g., high administrative burdens, regulatory volatility, and administratively limited competition, [in]direct political involvement in economic/business affairs). Hence, the Hungarian SME sector is not expected to experience considerable short-term growth.

The major competitors of Hungary are those Central Eastern European countries that joined the EU in 2004; the Czech Republic, Poland, Romania, Slovak Republic. The multifaceted and multilevel competition includes not just the EU and the global market, but also the financial resources available globally and in the EU in the form of FDI and/or diverse EU funds. The Hungarian economic and political problems are similar to those of other competitors, but datasets demonstrate clearly that Hungary lost its competitive edge after 2008 and will have a hard time to improve or even maintain it in the future (Figure 17.9).

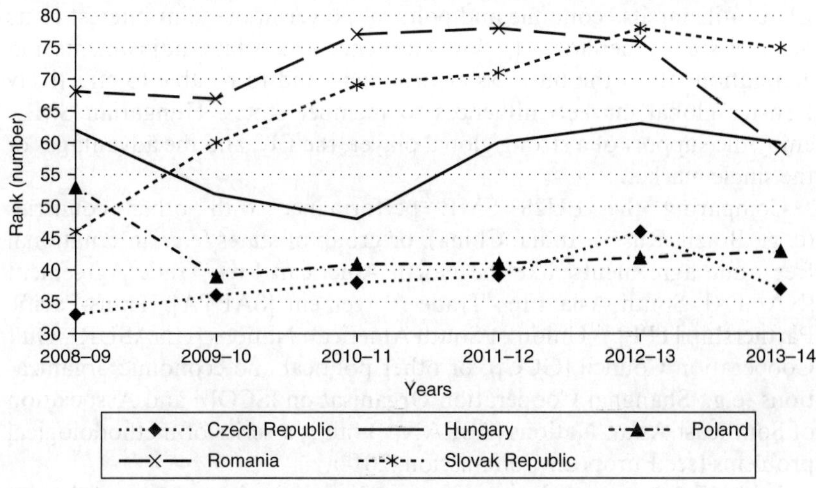

Sources: World Bank (2013), Schwab and Sala-i-Martín (2014).

Figure 17.8 Global competitiveness index of Hungary and its major regional competitors

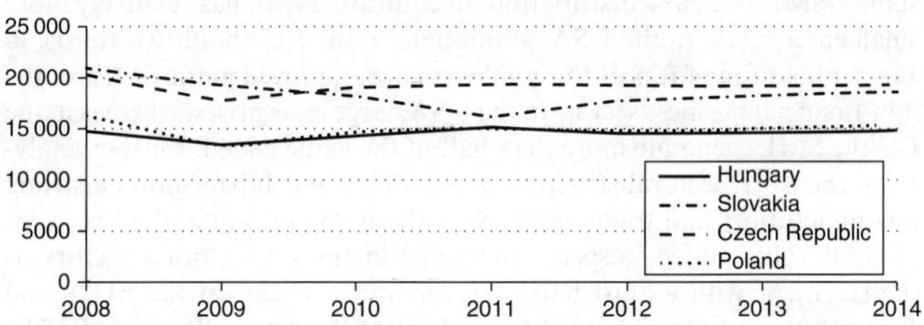

Source: European Commission (2014c).

Figure 17.9 SME value added per employee in Hungary and in the major regional competing countries (in 1000 euros per employee)

The global position of the EU

The EU appearance on the global market established a large regional market, a single market with individual member states, which is regulated by the institutions of the EU, therefore can be considered as a single politico-economic entity and global player on the global market. The

EU is utilizing its economic and political power in the joint interest of its member states; therefore, its global presence necessitates adjustments and adaptations to fit the business environment and to be able to effectively transfer global market influences to member states. Hungarian SMEs enjoy the support of a strong global player, the EU, and the advantages of the single market.

Comparing the EU28 SME performance with other countries (e. g., Brazil, Russia, India, China), or group of states (e.g., international free trade agreements, like the North American Free Trade Agreement [NAFTA], South Asia Free Trade Agreement [SAFTA], Trans-Pacific Partnership [TPP],[11] Union of South American Nations [UNASUR], Gulf Cooperation Council [GCC]), or other political and economic organizations (e.g., Shanghai Cooperation Organisation [SCO][12] and Association of Southeast Asian Nations [ASEAN][13]) raises a series of methodological problems (see European Commission, 2014a).

Table 17.2 does not take into account the relative importance of the size of the respective economies. In developed economies, SMEs account for the vast majority of enterprises. The adjusted indicator of the number of SME/GDP shows that the relative number of SMEs in the EU28 is very similar to the USA, while in Japan there are relatively much fewer SMEs, which employ relatively more employees. The EU28 and USA have a similar SME size class distribution; in contrast, Japan has relatively more small enterprises. In the USA, about half, in the EU about two-thirds, in Japan about four-fifths of the employees are employed in the SMEs of the non-financial business sector. In the USA, large enterprises, whereas in the EU the SMEs generate more than half of the value added. Further analysis of the SME sectoral structure of the EU28 and Japan shows a strong 'manufacturing' and trade sector with about 25 per cent and 20 per cent of total value added, respectively, while in the USA, 'other sectors' is the strongest with almost half the total value added (in the EU28 and Japan, 'other sectors' account for a third of the total value added). The approximately 10 per cent of the total value added performance of the 'information and communication' sector in the USA is remarkable.

The transitional economies of BRIC countries showed a considerable performance growth and a notable resilience during the observation period of 2008–13. Two-digit growth rates in terms of the number of SMEs (e.g., Brazil and Russia with 10 per cent and 35 per cent, respectively) or number of employees (e.g., Brazil and India with about 18 per cent and 10 per cent respectively) are considered 'normal'. Moreover, SMEs recovered in the BRIC more quickly and strongly then their EU28 counterparts (e.g., in Brazil, Russia). Despite the fact that no data are available (e.g., China) or if they exist then in a different structure (e.g., Russia, Brazil) or level of detail (e.g., India), one can say that the BRIC countries must be considered as global competitors on the global SME market.

Global competition and the globalization process itself motivates leading economies (e.g., USA, China, EU) to create a more friendly global economic environment, cement current economic positions and expand them, while containing competitors by using newly established international organizations, trade partnerships, free trade zone agreements, or direct political means (e g., embargo, local conflicts, regional wars). The dialectics of competition and cooperation is prevalent also in recent developments.

Internationalization and Business Networks

Internationalization

The authors' understanding is that internationalization is a process, which can include all/any meaningful activities of a business relationship with a foreign partner: exports, imports, foreign direct investment, international subcontracting and international – mainly technical – cooperation.

Based on the location of the business of foreign partners, two market segments can be distinguished: intra-EU and extra-EU market. Both intra-EU import and export figures, furthermore, the costs of intra-EU exports and imports, show that the trading performance of Hungarian SMEs is over the EU average. Moreover, all indicators measuring aspects of transposing EU directives into national law are also above EU average, showing a positive picture of Hungary creating an enabling environment for trading within the single market. Regarding extra-EU internationalization, Hungary has not improved its performance and remains below the EU average; there have been some improvements, especially in relation to the costs of foreign trade (both imports and exports) but other indicators, especially the time required for or the complexity of administrative procedures related to trading have not improved. In harsh contrast to the intra-EU trade, trade with non-EU countries declined to a rather low level.

The EU conducts regular surveys about SME internationalization.[14] Based on the survey results, both the EU and the Hungarian SMEs are about at the same stage of internationalization. About 25–30 per cent of the SMEs are engaged in intra-EU export and import activities, while about only 13–15 per cent in extra-EU activities. Only a small portion (far below 10 per cent) of SMEs are involved in cooperation, bidirectional subcontractor relationships, or taking part in foreign direct investment. This focus is understandable; the single market is one of the main driving forces of the European economy, which provides for market integration and removes obstacles to the free movement of capital, goods, services and people.

The survey data show positive correlation between SME size, SME age and internationalization. There is negative correlation between SME country size, country population and internationalization. The sectors 'wholesale and retail trade, repair of motor vehicles and motorcycles', 'manufacturing', 'transportation and storage', 'information and communication', and 'professional, scientific and technical activities' are the most internationalized.

SMEs start their international activities most often by importing, even if export activities are more supported EU-wide. Partners are enterprises mostly from other EU countries, but the relations with BRIC countries are improving rapidly. Only a marginal share (about 5 per cent) of internationally inactive SMEs are planning to start international activities in the foreseeable future. However, the Internet made it easier for SMEs of all sizes to overcome internationalization barriers (e.g., size, capital) and get involved in diverse e-commerce activities.

In general, international EU SMEs create more jobs and higher turnover growth, are more innovative, and more internationally active than US and Japanese SMEs. Despite evidence of international success, SMEs' public financial support goes largely unnoticed (unutilized), while the internal and external barriers[15] of internationalization are clearly perceived and overstated by the EU SMEs (see European Commission, 2010, p. 57).

Business networks and multinational enterprises (MNEs)

The terminological uncertainties are clearly reflected in the variety of different definitions used to describe the same phenomenon/subject, called business network. The authors consider business network a large social network, consisting of business-related entities, including but not restricted to business organizations (e.g., SMEs, large enterprises, chambers of commerce), and customers. The EU defines the same term in a more restricted way (Spanikova et al., 2014, p. 7).

According to the EU, two types of business networks are distinguished and regularly monitored: (1) business associations, which provide a platform and proper conditions for cooperation, while the actual decision is left with the association members, and (2) company aggregations, which already decided to cooperate and aggregate, based on a concrete, jointly set objective, which must be achieved.

Both the longer- and shorter-term objectives[16] should serve the interest of the participating enterprises and add value. According to EU experience, internationalization, however, is not an automatic development of business networks, therefore must be proactively supported.

Internationalization in Hungary is promoted by the Hungarian Chamber of Commerce and Industry (HCCI). The HCCI is a national business network of business association types. The size of the Hungarian enterprises and market did not necessitate to separately establish business networks of company aggregations. Members of HCCI are divided into 23 regional chambers, all of which are operating independently and which have altogether 412 000 members. Hungarian companies are direct members of the regional chambers and not of the HCCI. The regional chambers have 412 000 members. Two types of membership exist: voluntary and mandatory, the latest since 2012. The services offered by the regional chambers include tax, legal, export, and credit advice, as well as assistance with business partner search. The chambers also provide regular information for their members about possible tender competition; organize business trips and exhibitions, seminars, conferences and training about 'hot topics' (e.g., changing legislation and administrative rules). To support the internationalization of companies, the HCCI – along with other centres – works closely together with the Enterprise Europe Network (EEN), which has 20 contact points in Hungary, located in the premises of the regional chamber offices. The EU-level mechanisms, which further support internationalization, assuring the realization of common terminology, rules and objectives and fostering cooperation of companies through business networks, would serve as an interface between business networks (e.g., HCCI) and the EC DG Enterprise and Industry.

At the current size and organizational level, there are only a few Hungarian SMEs, which are multinational enterprises (MNE)[17] or global multinational enterprises (GMNEs). MNEs and GMNEs operate, produce goods or services, in one or more countries, regions other than the home country (if any), or even on a global scale. The applied attribute to define 'global' enterprises is based on the arbitrary criteria of generated sales revenue; at least 20 per cent of the enterprise sales revenue must be generated in each of at least three different continental markets. Because of the SME definition of the EU, problems of moral and legal behaviour (e.g. taxation, conflict of laws) of SME (G)MNEs and the related problems of globalization are neglected and considered as insignificant.[18]

The 'information and communication' sector of the Hungarian SMEs demonstrates vitality, dynamic and successful MNEs, even a few 'born globals' are on the rapidly changing market, among others, KÜRT ('lost data' recovery), Interactive Net Design (web design), IND Group (financial data software for the banking sector), Appello (location-based services provider), Kulcs-Soft (business software through mobile phones), Prezi (presentation software) and Team Distinction (mobile software development).

Multilevel Regulations

EU Focus of regulatory actions

The economic role of SMEs in the EU and the rapidly growing globalization requires multilevel (EU and national) actions, which will have long-term economic and political impacts. The premises include the following:

- Both EU and national economic growth depend to a large extent on the SMEs' performance.
- SMEs need adequate support to access international markets. Awareness and use of business support programmes (both financial and non-financial) must be raised among SMEs.
- The positive relationship between internationalization and innovation, as well as internationalization and competitiveness must be strengthened.
- The cooperation between member states and EU-level institutions in collecting and analysing information on market developments and the legal and institutional environment (statistical and marketing information systems, standards and compliance certification) must be strengthened; efficiency gains could be obtained by (re)-organizing EU level institutions.

The EC response to the challenges of laying the foundation for future sustainable growth is the *Entrepreneurship 2020 Action Plan* (see European Commission, 2013). The action plan intends to reignite entrepreneurial spirit in Europe and considers entrepreneurship the main driving force of economic growth and job creation. In order to achieve this goal, a cultural change is necessary along with a 'bold and coordinated action by all administrations at European, national and regional levels' (ibid., p. 5), which would be able to fully transform the EU. The key areas, the EC proposals, member state recommendations, implementation resources and time frames are presented in Table 17.5.

The EU-level regulations, financed by the dedicated programmes, provide a highly cooperative business environment, but at the same time establish for the member states an area of competition for financial resources. National regulations must adapt to EU policies and regulations and add new target areas to the EU level regulations, finance and assess them accordingly, either by using EU funds or national resources.

Hungarian national assessment, strategy and regulations

The main goals of the Hungarian SME strategy during the financial framework of 2007–13 have been to:

Table 17.5 EC key actions to the Entrepreneurship 2020 Action Plan

Key areas	EEC proposal	Implementation
Entrepreneurial education and training to support growth and business creation		
Education and training	Pan-European entrepreneurial learning initiative	2013–15
	EU–OECD joint framework for entrepreneurial schools and vocational education and training	2013–14
	Entrepreneurial university framework for EU Higher Education Institutions	2012–13
	Create mechanisms of university-driven business creation (spin-offs etc.) and university–business	
	Ecosystems	
Create an environment where entrepreneurs can flourish and grow		
Access to finance	Further development of the microfinancing market in EU, through Programme for Social Change and Innovation (PSCI) and Joint Action to Support Microfinance Institutions (JASMINE) via the European Social Fund (ESF) or the European Regional Development Fund (ERDF)	2014–
	Facilitating the direct access of SMEs to the capital market (review of the Market in Financial Instruments Directive [MiFID])	Ongoing
Support of lifecycle phases of new businesses	Creating more entrepreneur-friendly fiscal environment in the member states	Ongoing
	Prohibiting misleading marketing practices	2013
	Integrated support schemes for new entrepreneurs, financed by ESF	2013
Unleashing 'digital age' business opportunities	Knowledge base creation on major trends and innovative business models in the digital sector	2013–on

Table 17.5 (continued)

Key areas	EEC proposal	Implementation
	Information campaign for SMEs on ICT benefits and creation of a European network of web businesses	2013–on
	Creation of a European Mentors Network for training and match-making	2014
	Initiatives for web entrepreneurs as Start-up Europe Partnership and Leaders Club, strengthening the web entrepreneurial culture, and creating Massive Online Open Courses along with technological platforms	2013
	Strengthen competences and skills i.e. e-skills, scientific and creative skills and managerial and entrepreneurial skills	Ongoing
Transfers of businesses	Make business transfers easier, removing remaining possible barriers to cross-border business transfers	2013–14
Second chance for honest bankrupts	Communication on a new European approach to business failure and insolvency, including on giving honest bankrupts a second chance	2013
Regulatory burden: clearer and simpler rules	Legislation for further simplification of cross-border business administration within the internal market	2013
	Assessing specific needs of liberal profession entrepreneurs	2013
	Ensure help through SOLVIT in case of misapplied internal market law	2013

Role models and reaching out to specific groups		
Entrepreneurs as role models	Present entrepreneurs as role models for students of secondary education	2013
Women	Create online business network platform for women entrepreneurs	2013–15
Seniors	Support mutual and intergenerational mentoring between entrepreneurs	2013–15
Migrant	Facilitate entrepreneurship among migrants, attract migrant entrepreneurs	2014–17
	Remove legal obstacles to qualified immigrant entrepreneurs establish a business and obtain a stable residence permit	2013
Unemployed	Target vulnerable groups (incl. unemployed) with microfinance facility under the PSCI	2013
	Provide technical assistance through ESF for young entrepreneurs	2013
	Promote entrepreneurship in the green economy	2013
	Promote 'self-employment'	2013

Source: European Commission (2013).

- improve the regulatory environment;
- facilitate financing;
- develop the knowledge and entrepreneurial infrastructure.

At the end of the period of the EU financial framework of 2007–13, the Hungarian authorities assessed the SME-related problem issues. The following general and specific problems were acknowledged:

- General problems:
  - lack of public trust in government authorities;
  - negative attitude towards political decision-makers;
  - unrestricted spread of corruption.
- Specific problems:
  - the performance, capital and asset base is far below the EU average;
  - high taxes and administrative costs, which are disadvantageous for competitiveness and nourish the shadow economy;
  - financial crisis: decreasing demand and lack of financial liquidity;
  - there are too many micro and only few strong medium-sized SMEs;
  - SMEs lag far behind the EU in SBA principle skills and innovation;
  - low-level entrepreneurial culture, many entrepreneurs from necessity;
  - low level of export and suppliers' inability to cooperate;
  - low quality public services (incl. education and training); excessive commitment towards large multinational enterprises; and
  - effects of social-political inequality.

Based on a complex SWOT analysis (Box 17.1) and key national and EU documents[19] a new SME strategy has been developed and published (Ministry for National Economy, 2013) for the period of 2014–20 EU financial framework programme. The Hungarian SME strategy, however, has not passed all the administrative hurdles yet, and as of now, there is unfortunately no well known national SME strategy elaborated and approved by the government institutions.

Without sophisticated national SME policies and regulations, without timely and proper synchronization with the EU, Hungarian SMEs will not be able to fully utilize all the competitive advantages. Timely and efficient correction of decisions and additional resources are key to a policy response and eventual reorientation.

BOX 17.1 SWOT ANALYSIS OF THE HUNGARIAN SMEs

Strengths

Minimal administrative burdens using the one-stop-shop system for new SMEs.
There is a legislative framework present for establishing SMEs.
Entrepreneurs are flexible and adapting quickly to the new circumstances.
New entrepreneur generation entering the market.
Simplified corporate tax.
EU Info Centre services are available.
Business incubator system established.
Improvement in loan facilitation.
Factoring services.
Simplified current asset financing.
Wide range of experts with scientific background available.

Weaknesses

Dual economic structure: strong multinational corporations, weak and vulnerable SMEs.
Disadvantageous structure of the labour market.
Unpredictable economic policies and complex tax system with increasing taxes.
Large portion of the SMEs are inefficient and under-capitalized. Insufficient capital accumulation.
Indebtedness, including circular indebtedness.
Costly administrative burdens (e.g., tax).
Lack of innovation and ability of cooperation.
Risk avoidance and low-level entrepreneurial culture.
Corruption, black market and blackleg workers.
Non-transparent state pork-barrel spending.
No parliamentary activities and legislation.

Opportunities

Inter-EU market advantages.
R&D and innovative solutions create advantages against low labour costs EU competitors (Croatia, Romania, Serbia).
Further decrease of administrative costs, based on the EU SME Charter.
Utilization of the EU Financial Framework Programmes of 2014–20.
Facilitating networking using public–private partnership (PPP) to support suppliers.
Improving competitiveness using consultancy centres.
Entrepreneurship programmes for minorities.

Threats

The SME development slowed down, while already at a disadvantage compared to competitors.
Disadvantageous macroeconomic processes (national debt, budget restrictions), slow convergence, low level market demand.
Better economic environment attracts enterprises to move into the neighbourhood countries.
Non-profitable enterprises tend to be eliminated; the number of SMEs is decreasing.
No tolerance policy and strict enforcement of complex regional and local community regulations.
Microfinance does not help self-employed entrepreneurs accessing the markets.

Opportunities	*Threats*
Effective technology transfer and R&D&I in ICT and knowledge-based SMEs.	Short-term profit interest motivates the neglect of sustainability. No international embedding, non-preparedness for internationalization. Insufficient information and management consultancy creates difficulties in competition.

Source: Created by the authors using Ministry for National Economy (2013).

Some Methodological Issues

With rapid globalization, the worldview, based on national-level data collection and regional/global aggregation, must be revisited. Data synchronization and methodology harmonization are required, while global analysis for special purposes (e.g., preparation of policy decisions, crisis management) necessitates accurate and fast information systems. Unfortunately, there is no generally accepted methodology and internationally accepted regular dataset that could be used for analysis. Data at national level are considered by the authors to be more accurate; therefore a bottom-up processing is suggested. Metadata and data aggregations should use globally standardized methodology and data collection.

There is an urgent need to introduce new methodologies to analyse global and regional business networks, apply indicators used in social network analysis. Creating methodological clarity and proper data analysis to define the applied terms (e.g., business network) are early and vital steps in this modernization process, because inconsistent terminology often results in incompatible datasets and methodological problems (e.g., for longitudinal SME analysis). The new terminology and methodology must be able to integrate and describe the new market developments (e.g., global e-commerce) in the form of data collected. New data and methodology along with new applied IT (e.g., business networks including customers analysed using social network analysis and related software tools) is a vehicle to improve SME performance globally.

The authors recognize two extreme contemporary data processing and exchange solutions. The first one is used in China, with no or very little data published and exchanged. The second one is used in the EU, with a systematically developed evidence-based policy-making, which is widely published and exchanged also outside of the EU (e.g., European Commission, 2014d). There is no question, the second solution serves global needs better and helps more to improve global SME performance.

However, there is still room for improvement also in the EU in streamlining data exchange and synchronization, furthermore speeding up knowledge generation to effectively respond to new challenges (e.g., economic downturn).

CONCLUSIONS

Global economy requires global thinking and a global worldview. The Hungarian case demonstrates clearly that successful SME policy and regulation enable and support performance growth. Multilevel policy-making and regulations of the EU provide new opportunities to improve SME performance globally. The authors think that this improvement could be more significant than those competitive strategies SMEs have pursued on their own (e.g., innovation strategy, IT strategy, niche strategy, network strategy, cluster strategy and FDI strategy). Beyond the global SME management, there are still a series of areas where SMEs could develop powerful examples and achieve performance growth (e.g., management of SME growth (conversion and/or transformation)) across SME class sizes, and develop new cooperative business models.[20] The new IT solutions will further improve SME performance globally and open the way for a more stable global economic, political and social development.

NOTES

1. Similar periods were introduced in Róbert's paper (1999).
2. After the Paris Peace Treaties of 1919–20, the newly created state of Hungary, which has been earlier a part of the Austro-Hungarian Empire, was unable to recover from the impacts of World War I, including the loss of about two-thirds of its territory, about one-third of population (left outside of the new borders), and its direct access to the Mediterranean Sea. Furthermore, the country had to pay war reparations, faced trade barriers and suffered a chronic lack of accumulated capital.
3. Western countries were not members of the Council for Mutual Economic Assistance (COMECON).
4. Kornai (1980, p. 147), referred to diverse sources considered to be the most authentic on this subject in the Hungarian literature.
5. The rules apply to individual firms only. The statistical definition considers only the employees. Other nation's definition might be different (e.g., USA).
6. Annual report on European SMEs and member state fact sheets. Also available: Survey on Access to Finance of SMEs in the Euro Area (SAFE), SME Economic Activity Index Survey, and the Innobarometer.
7. The non-financial business sector includes the following industrial sectors: 'mining and quarrying', 'manufacturing', 'electricity, gas, steam and air condition supply', 'water supply, sewerage, waste management and remediation activities', 'construction', 'wholesale and retail trade, repair of motor vehicles and motorcycles', 'transportation and storage', 'accommodation and food services', 'information and communication', 'real

estate activities', 'professional, scientific and technical activities' and 'administrative and support services'.

8. The survey was devoted to the commercialization of innovation.
9. In contrast to cooperation.
10. The key pillars of country's competitiveness in stage 2 are higher education and training, market efficiency for trading in goods, labour market efficiency, financial market development, technological readiness, and market size. The key pillars of country competitiveness in stage 3 are business sophistication and innovation.
11. Member states: Australia, Brunei, Canada, Chile, Japan, Malaysia, Mexico, New Zealand, Peru, Singapore, the United States and Vietnam.
12. Member states: China, Kazakhstan, Kyrgyzstan, Russia, Tajikistan and Uzbekistan.
13. Member states: Indonesia, Malaysia, Philippines, Singapore, Thailand, Brunei, Cambodia, Laos, Myanmar (Burma) and Vietnam.
14. The 2009 survey is based on data of 9480 SMEs in 33 European countries (see European Commission, 2010).
15. Internal barriers: product or service price and high cost of internationalization. External barriers: lack of capital, of adequate information, and of adequate public support; furthermore, transport administration costs.
16. Longer-term strategic objectives: strengthening innovation, internationalization and foreign match-making. Shorter-term operational objectives: information sharing, resources pooling, creation of new business opportunities and international markets, provision of legal and financial services (see Spanikova et al., 2014, p. 7).
17. Also called multinational corporations (MNCs), international corporations, or 'transnational corporations', or stateless corporations (without any identified national home).
18. It is obvious that recent developments, especially the negotiations of the Transatlantic Trade and Investment Partnership (TTIP) can significantly change even the current definitions. TTIP is a trade agreement, which is presently being negotiated and aims at removing trade barriers in a wide range of economic sectors between the EU and the USA.
19. *Europe 2020 Strategy*, *Entrepreneurship 2020 Action Plan*, *EU Cohesion Policy 2014–2020*, *National Reform Program 2020*, *National Development 2020* and partnership agreements.
20. A good example is the MONDRAGON Corporation, which is a corporation and federation of worker cooperatives based in the Basque region of Spain.

REFERENCES

Berend, I.T. (1999), *Central and Eastern Europe, 1944–1993: Detour from the Periphery to the Periphery (Cambridge Studies in Modern Economic History)*, Cambridge, UK: Cambridge University Press.

Berend, I.T. (2006), *An Economic History of Twentieth-Century Europe: Economic Regimes from Laissez-Faire to Globalization*, New York: Cambridge University Press.

Dunn, M.H. (1994), 'Do nations compete economically?', *Intereconomics: Review of European Economic Policy*, **29**(6), 303–8.

European Commission (2005), *The New SME Definition User Guide and Model Declaration*, Brussels: Publication Office, Enterprise and Industry Publications.

European Commission (2008), *'Think Small First' A 'Small Business Act' for Europe, Communication from the Commission to the European Parliament, the Council, the European Economic and Social Committee and the Committee of the Regions*, Brussels: European Commission, accessed 27 May 2015 at http://eur-lex.europa.eu/LexUriServ/LexUriServ.do?uri=COM:2008:0394:FIN:EN:PDF.

European Commission (2010), *Internationalisation of European SMEs Final Report*, Brussels: European Commission.

European Commission (2013), *Entrepreneurship 2020 Action Plan. Reigniting the Entrepreneurial Spirit in Europe, Communication from the Commission to the European Parliament, the Council, the European Economic and Social Committee and the Committee of the Regions*, Brussels: European Commission.

European Commission (2014a), *Annual Report on European SMEs 2013/2014 – A Partial and Fragile Recovery, Final Report – SME Performance Review 2013/2014*, Brussels: European Commission.

European Commission (2014b), *Enterprise and Industry 2014 SBA Fact Sheet Hungary*, Brussels: European Commission.

European Commission (2014c), 'Small and medium-sized enterprises (SMEs)', accessed 30 November 2014 at http://ec.europa.eu/enterprise/policies/sme/index_en.htm.

European Commission (2014d), 'Implementation of the 'Small Business Act' for Europe in the Mediterranean Middle East and North Africa 2014', *Briefing Note*, Brussels: European Commission.

IMD WCC (2014), *IMD World Competitiveness Yearbook 2014 – Main Results*, accessed 29 May 2015 at http://icegec.hu/download/publications/imd-icegec-pressrelease2014_eng.pdf.

Kornai, J. (1980), 'The dilemmas of a socialist economy: the Hungarian experience', *Cambridge Journal of Economics*, **4**(2), 147–57.

Krugman, P.R. (1994), 'Competitiveness: a dangerous obsession', *Foreign Affairs*, **73**(2), 28–44.

Ministry for National Economy (2013), *A Kis- és Közép-vállalkozások fejlesztésének stratégiája 2014–2020* [SME Development Strategy for 2014–2020], Budapest: Ministry for National Economy.

Róbert, P. (1999), 'Kikbõl lettek vállalkozók? A vállalkozóvá válás meghatározó tényezõi Magyarországon a kommunizmus elõtt, alatt és után' [Who became entrepreneurs? Key factors determining the process of becoming an entrepreneur in Hungary, before, during and after the communism], *Közgazdasági Szemle*, **46**(5), 403–27.

Schwab, K. and X. Sala-i-Martín (2014), *The Global Competitiveness Report 2014–2015: Full Data Edition*, Switzerland: World Economic Forum.

Spanikova, V., L. Birkman and C. Besseling (2014), *Business Networks, Final Report*, Rotterdam: ECORYS, EC DG ENTR.

World Bank (2013), *Doing Business 2014: Understanding Regulations for Small and Medium-Size Enterprises*, Washington, DC: World Bank Group.

18. Conclusions and future research

V.H. Manek Kirpalani and Pervez N. Ghauri

INTRODUCTION

Since the end of World War II trade in the international marketplace has increased at almost double the rate of growth of world GDP. The causes are many. The leaders of the leading victor nations in World War II decided wisely to set up some major institutions that would facilitate the growth of world trade directly and indirectly and through this also the growth of world economies. These institutions were the United Nations, General Agreement on Tariffs and Trade, the International Monetary Fund and the World Bank. Further, the intelligentsia of the time, people such as Keynes, Samuelson, Stiglitz and others introduced ideas designed to encourage growth of markets and international markets. In addition, the business leaders addressed issues such as building a European Union and this was followed by others who developed the Warsaw Pact and the North American Free Trade Agreement. The outcomes were large free trade areas, some common markets, lower tariffs globally, a number of favourable interventions by the International Monetary Fund, and a significant amount of World Bank help. Also it led to the rise of multinational enterprises (MNEs), which could operate more easily in larger markets, and to the energizing of the small and medium-sized firms (SMEs). Much of this occurred at the same time as technology advanced and the Internet with its vast communication ability came into being. Through all this, with advancing educational ideas, entrepreneurship has come into its own right. It was further fuelled by enterprising individuals who grew up and led the movement of emigration from poor to richer lands where many could contribute more and some founded innovative firms.

The above is the broad background of our interest in this book: *Handbook of Research on International Entrepreneurship Strategy: Improving SME Performance Globally*. It is well recognized that most employment arises out of the SMEs and that these firms are the ones that are important to grow because of their impact on the rest of the economies that they reside in. SMEs constitute more than 90 per cent of the firms in most countries and are in total the largest employers in the private sectors of their country economies. For an example, we refer the reader to

Chapter 11 on the 'Internationalization of European SMEs' (Irene Mandl and Funda Celikel Esser).

Internationalizing SMEs used to be a traditional lot, mainly doing business across their borders in psychologically close regions. This was also how the first theories of their international activities were thought out by the 'Uppsala' group (Johanson and Vahlne, 1977 and Johanson and Weidersheim-Paul, 1975) who displayed internationalization as an evolution through discrete stages, as firms learn to operate in foreign markets and accumulate resources. This incremental multi-stage process of internationalization was soon challenged by others, who argued for a more complex process of rapidity (Oviatt and McDougall, 1994). More recent authors point to the new phenomenon of 'born globals' (BGs) (Gabrielsson and Kirpalani, 2004 and 2012) wherein some SMEs internationalize very rapidly from the beginning. These are founded by entrepreneurs with strategic vision, specific global products, and have the entrepreneurial prowess to gather sufficient resources or join networks of established firms with far-reaching limbs. Tables 18.1 and 18.2 depict how SMEs can be segmented into different types for purposes of researching their internationalization capacity and performance. There are BGs, then born regionals (BRs), followed by born again globals (BaGs), born again regionals (BaRs), international new ventures (INVs), and internationalizing SMEs (ISMEs). Red Bull and Angry Birds are

Table 18.1 Research grid of BG/SME enterprises and internal areas of study

Areas of Study/Types of Enterprise	BG	BR	BaG	BaR	INV	ISME
Rapid globalization/internationalization						
International entrepreneurship						
Internet						
International new ventures[a]						
Knowledge acquisition, application, dissemination, management						
Market orientation						
Networks, joint ventures and large channels						
Organizational learning						
Resources: finance and other						
Strategy						

Note: a. INV (international new venture) = venture capital and/or joint venture with firm in BG-related group.

Source: Adapted from Gabrielsson and Kirpalani (2012, p. 102).

Table 18.2 Research grid of BG/SME and selected external variables that directly interact and/or impact them

Areas of Study/Types of Enterprise	BG	BR	BaG	BaR	INV	ISME
Culture						
Institutional perspective: entrepreneurial capabilities						
Institutional perspective: resources and decision-making processes						
International new ventures[a]						
Large channels						
Networks/strategic alliance						
Public policy on SMEs						
Public policy on R&D						
Resources: finance and others						
Social capital						

Note: a. INV (international new venture) = venture capital and/or joint venture with firm in BG-related group.

Source: Adapted from Gabrielsson and Kirpalani (2012, p. 113).

examples of born globals, Zara may be termed a born regional, born again globals are firms that have retreated from the global scene and then have later gone forth again, as is the case with born again regionals. The international new ventures are firms that have received encouragement from abroad either through imports of components that are then re-exported in more finished goods or completely assembled final products or are networks of local and foreign people, with the latter including locals who have emigrated abroad. The most successful firms in the latter area are probably those who have emerged out of the Silicon Valley and joined forces with firms in other countries. The last category is the traditional SMEs who are advanced internationalizing firms that have done cross-border business for many years.

There is a very large literature on the internationalization of the SME. The traditional view was that put forward by Johanson and Vahlne (1977) that internationalization is an evolutionary process manifested in stages. The outcomes of each stage became the inputs for the next stage. Market knowledge and commitment affect the allocations of current resources, which in turn effects future market knowledge and leads to an increasing commitment of resources as the internationalization grows (Andersen, 1993). In today's world this culminates in a business network internationalization model where partners share knowledge during a trust-building process (Johanson and Vahlne, 2009). This is a competitive capability supplemental to the resource-based view since the SME involved in this grows relationships with agencies, distributors, suppliers and other organizations. Other researchers have favoured a behavioural theory of the firm where SME managers find low involvement modes such as exporting agents to test new markets, which when successful leads to more involvement with those foreign markets and an evolutionary process of stepwise greater internationalization (Johansson and Vahlne, 1977 and 2009).

In more recent times research has shifted to study the SME as an actor embedded in business networks that connect it to its distributors, suppliers, other collaborators, competitors and customers (Johansson and Mattsson, 1993). Their viewpoint draws on theories of social exchange and resource dependency, which lead to internationalization proceeding as a consequence of externalities from the SME network of customers, relatives and friends abroad, and others who expand the boundaries of the firm's relationships. From this network perspective, the SME's network expands through international extension with another country/region network, penetration of those networks, and international integration through mutual connections.

Recently moreover, knowledge-intensive SMEs have entered domestic and international markets concurrently, or even gone international before entering domestic markets, which has led to the growing number of 'born global' SMEs (Gabrielsson and Kirpalani, 2012). Overall, however, compared to the conceptual and theoretical work in the SME sector, empirical work has been especially limited. All of this background led us to write this *Handbook of Research on International Entrepreneurial Strategy: Improving SME Performance Globally*.

SUMMARY AND ANALYSES OF THE CONTRIBUTIONS

Part I of our book began with the definition of important terms that are frequently used in the published literature so that the readers, contributors and ourselves should be more or less on the same page. Thus, future researchers may also follow the same definition tracks and thereby the whole field might gain. The chapter immediately following the overview chapter is by Lazaris, Ngasri and Freeman. Positioned within the field of international entrepreneurship, this chapter argued that observed internationalization patterns of SMEs relate to two distinct entrepreneurial approaches: causation and effectuation. The first path, causation – consistent with a planned approach – describes a situation where international businesses opportunities are recognized and pursued based upon a plan. This has been the foundation of most previous research. The second path, effectuation denotes an emergent strategy, whereby founders experiment and make decisions based on loss affordability and flexibility (Sarasvathy, 2001; Chandler et al., 2011).

Effectuation theory can be drawn upon to explain proactive and reactive internationalization behaviours in terms of two salient and widespread factors: the knowledge and networks of modern SME founders. We identify effectuation theory as a relevant and valuable emerging theory in international entrepreneurship. We argue that effectuation logic prevails during initial internationalization of 'born global' SMEs. Lazaris et al. state, however, that in their findings, internationally experienced managers are more likely than inexperienced managers to engage in proactive behaviours, supported by causation logic, thereby employing both approaches simultaneously. We agree that these findings are consistent with what we would reasonably expect.

Shneor and Efrat (Chapter 3) point out that much of the research on BGs has focused on the early stages of international new venture creation, as well as on the motivations and drivers for its creation and emergence (Kirpalani and Gabrielsson, 2012; Leonidou and Samiee, 2012). More specifically, when considering international marketing strategy of international new ventures, a review by Aspelund et al. (2007) has revealed that research has mainly focused on:

- the speed of the internationalization process;
- niche versus commodity focus in product strategy;
- entry into few versus multiple markets simultaneously;
- elements influencing market selection choices;
- entry mode decisions.

Surprisingly enough, however, it largely ignores the critical international marketing strategy question, concerning the standardization versus adaptation/localization of marketing mix elements. Shneor and Efrat emphasize that this question is of particular importance, due to the effect standardization and/or adaptation strategy has on firm performance in particular. Based on the analysis of survey data collected from Israeli born globals, the study reveals that marketing adaptation efforts with respect to sales force significantly impacts their performance. In addition, the study also shows that marketing intelligence generation also has significant impact on their performance.

Julkunen, Gabrielsson and Raatikainen (Chapter 4) emphasize that

Finnish firms are almost entirely SMEs and that government support for technology-led business has been strong; and especially in modern times, for Internet video games Finland is a small medium open economy (SMOPEC) and firms are thus pushed towards internationalization. The number of new international ventures and growth-oriented firms is larger in Finland than elsewhere in Europe in general (Eurofound, 2012). Further, strong bilateral partnerships between MNEs and SMEs are crucial for the international growth of the SMEs. The authors document case studies that show how the INV cases have taken to entrepreneurial strategies to both ally and distance themselves from their MNE partners in order to establish their own products and brands. They propose that more longitudinal research studies be done to support their findings.

Kimiagari, Gabrielsson, Gabrielsson and Montreuil (Chapter 5) continue with another case study of an INV's internationalization. They conclude that effectuation logic relies less on planning market strategy and facilitates country and customer diversification, by relying more on learning from newness.

Gripsrud, Hunneman and Solberg's study (Chapter 6) from Norway study covers 2390 Norwegian new ventures and the research question of whether the speed of export start-up matters for the firm's future success and expansion. The answer is YES, and their conclusion is that it effects the betterment of the firm's resources in terms of management, products and network. Moreover, their study raises the question of whether the Uppsala school approach (Johanson and Wiedersheim-Paul, 1975; Johanson and Vahlne, 1977, 2009), which most new ventures follow of starting exports to countries with closer psychic distance, is the most effective strategy. Furthermore, they put forth the idea that the experiential knowledge acquired in the home market by those firms that export later restrains their search for opportunities abroad and makes them less prepared to engage in exporting. In turn, this leads to questioning whether government export promotion programmes should not be specifically more oriented towards encouraging early export start-ups.

Martins, Rialp-Criado and Vaillant's study findings in Chapter 7 show evidence from each innovativeness dimension, namely considering the influence of innovativeness and uniqueness in product and/or service as well as in process/technology. In summary, the better the firm's ability to innovate in product or service, the better it constitutes an essential driver to face international challenges. Equally important, the findings also suggest that knowledge and learning obtained by means of gaining experience in foreign markets may also help firms increase their capacity to innovate. The ability of a firm to assimilate, learn and apply its export-related experience to commercial ends is critical to developing its innovative capabilities.

Stoian and Ghauri (Chapter 8) focus on the importance of network development for increasing internationalization. They delve more deeply into network structure, content and governance. Their findings are based on a study of three cases, where the methodology applied is explicitly validated. Their results point to the efficacy of a proactive management attitude based on trust building over time. They also suggest the importance of further research in both developed and emerging countries in this important field.

Crespo, Simões and Fontes (Chapter 9) open the 'black box' on the new ventures' internationalization processes: the organizational processes through which antecedents – such as entrepreneurs' demographics, venture characteristics and environmental factors – are related to internationalization and performance outcomes. Their framework encompasses managerial decisions related to absorptive capacity, competitive generic strategies, entrepreneurial alertness and networking, together with environmental, industry and market-wise moderating forces. The framework is expected to contribute to stimulate further research along these lines. This will enable us to enhance our knowledge about how new ventures' internationalization processes develop.

Nowak (Chapter 10) explains how SMEs have increasingly become a driving force in the European economy and an even greater force in the Polish economy. In addition, he delves into the many ways in which the EU is helping their growth. Furthermore, he illustrates how the Polish authorities are trying to help SMEs to be more proactive in development and move towards the formation of clusters of large and small businesses in regions. He points out how Polish educational systems can join efforts with businesses to raise the training and skills of the workforce. All in all, Poland is far advanced in its thinking of ways to make its SME sector more useful in the cause of economic growth.

Part II of the book began with Chapter 11 by Mandl and Celikel Esser, which complements the Nowak depiction by adding further information and analysis from the entire EU zone. They lament the lack of internationalization by the EU SME sector in not internationalizing outside the EU zone in a more aggressive and purposeful way. Also they point out the need to focus programmes on specific needs of SMEs; differentiated by size, configuration of resources and other needs related to awareness and development towards entrepreneurship. They also propose that SME employees and potential employees be given internships by businesses. Furthermore, they recommend simplification of the various rules and regulations that impinge on SME activity and the search for information and resources.

Chapter 12 by Leonidou, Samiee and Geldres focuses on the instrumental role of national export promotion programs in helping SMEs to enhance their international entrepreneurial initiatives. Drawing a parallel between innovative behaviour, entrepreneurship and the exporting process, they identify the critical roles of risk-taking, innovativeness and a proactive posture in successfully instilling an entrepreneurial spirit in exploiting export markets. They then illustrate how government export assistance, focused in terms of financial, informational, education/training, legal, market targeting, marketing, and miscellaneous programmes, can help firms overcome international entrepreneurship hurdles and achieve superior export performance.

The next piece by Jang, Kim and Ohn (Chapter 13) is about South Korean SME ventures and how government can successfully support these activities in countries that have emerging economies and markets. Characteristics of the South Korean economy, especially in regard to entrepreneurial firms, are investigated, supporting the theory that these ventures are essentially nurtured by the South Korean national and local governments. The literature review and case analysis provide that these major institutional factors act as mechanisms that contribute to the birth of high-tech firms, resulting in innovative results and new value creation. The study shows how an emerging country has had to develop a stronger foundation since they start from a weaker base of skilled human resources and institutional infrastructure. They recommend a multi-pronged attack:

- Students should be provided with the knowledge of their capabilities in creating their own businesses so that it would make them more inclined to favour new ventures.
- Clarification on the standards of how to measure the successes of entrepreneurial funds or projects is required. The priorities of entrepreneurial efforts should lie in creating new ventures that can last at least three years or until the time of attaining the complete return of investment.
- Both practitioners and scholars in the field of entrepreneurship need to examine how to evaluate the economic conditions and outcomes that act as supporting activities, as well as the government and social factors that all influence the direction of entrepreneurs.

Kuivalainen, Saarenketo, Torkkeli and Puumalainen (Chapter 14) delve into international entrepreneurship among Finnish SMEs. They segment the internationalizing SMEs into four types: the born globals, born again globals, born internationalizers and the traditional internationalizers. Then they outline their respective internationalization paths, and point out that a number of these firms tend to sell out to foreign firms sooner or later. They recommend that Finland as a small country should be careful not to lose such firms. Therefore when government and linked agencies are giving support to SMEs they should also probe into the future objectives of the firms.

Zucchella and Hagen's study (Chapter 15) is about the internationalization of SMEs in Italy. It points out that the SME sector is much above the EU average in its contribution to GDP and employment. Moreover, Italy is characterized by traditional SMEs or those that specialize in industries, which have achieved international competitiveness notwithstanding the prevailing small scale of their businesses. A second specificity is represented by the frequent concentration of economic activities, especially of smaller firms, in districts and local clusters. The spatial organization of economic activities in Italy provides a very interesting perspective about how SMEs cope with the liability of smallness. After stressing the advantages of regional governmental help and of clusters, they make two practical suggestions for regional governments. One, to develop one-stop shops where SMEs can go for help. Two, to grow a 'voucher' system where SMEs can use vouchers given by the authorities to select amongst competing providers of internationalizing services.

Li and Jones's contribution (Chapter 16) is about Scottish SMEs. Scotland has a considerable number of SMEs and its export figures through them mirror more or less what the rest of the UK does. The bulk of the trade is with North America and a few of the northern EU countries. The government is trying to expand trade with China and lends support to SMEs who are interested in the same region. The author(s) propose an ACE model, where the A stands for Ambition & Awareness, C for Capability & Capacity, and E for Extension & Expansion. Scotland has a high level of education and its people have a natural entrepreneurial spirit developed through emigration and successful achievement in other countries.

Molnár and Belyó (Chapter 17) emphasize the environment of Hungarian SMEs and the political and economic system that supports them in global competition. The case of the Hungarian SME is discussed from the historical, national, EU and global perspective. The authors argue for the most appropriate level of policy intervention based on fact-based decision processes. They argue for the proper level of financial support, education, training and information technology.

RECOMMENDATIONS AND FUTURE RESEARCH

Our conclusions and recommendations from this book, as authors, are succinct and definitive. As outlined in the introduction to this chapter, the world is changing into a global market where technology is forcing the advance through ICT plus every other product and service. Under this canopy, entrepreneurship and international entrepreneurial activities are and will continue to thrive. This leads to the obvious conclusion that only industries with sustainable competitive advantage can survive in the long run. Governments therefore have to back such industries in order to keep up the GDP of their countries and the incomes of their people.

From this it follows that governments must support growth in their internationalizing SMEs. The macro-picture demands that tax policy actively support the state social and economic policy and favour the pursuit of its goals. This approach is vastly more advantageous to the SMEs. Furthermore, the following areas should be pursued in future research projects:

- Industries with sustainable competitive advantage (SCA) must be selected and supported.
- Governments must segment internationalizing SMEs and cater to the specific needs of each segment.
- SMEs must be encouraged to expand their networks and be taught networking skills.
- SMEs need to learn marketing techniques such as branding and competitive strategies.
- Governments must encourage MNEs in industries with SCA to bring SMEs into their networks.
- Governments must move towards developing clusters in which SMEs can thrive and help each other and the common good.
- Governments have to link the sectors of academicians/practitioners/government officials more cooperatively to work towards 'mainstream' (the broader economy, social fields and climatic stabilization) gains for the good of the people.

The responsibility thus lies not only on company managers but also on politicians and policy-makers.

REFERENCES

Andersen, O. (1993), 'On the internationalization process of firms: a critical analysis', *Journal of International Business Studies*, **24**(2), 209–31.

Aspelund, A., T.K. Madsen and Ø. Moen (2007), 'A review of the foundation, international marketing strategies, and performance of international new ventures', *European Journal of Marketing*, **41**(11–12), 1423–48.

Chandler, G.N., D.R. DeTienne, A. McKelvie and T.V. Mumford (2011), 'Causation and effectuation processes: a validation study', *Journal of Business Venturing*, **26**(3), 375–90.

Eurofound (2012), *Born Global: The Potential of Job Creation in New International Businesses*, accessed 5 May 2014 at www.eurofound.europa.eu/pubdocs/2012/65/en/1/EF1265EN.pdf.

Gabrielsson, M. and V.H.M. Kirpalani (2004), 'How to reach new business space rapidly', *International Business Review*, **13**(5), 555–71.

Gabrielsson, M. and V.H.M. Kirpalani (2012), 'Overview, background and historical origin of born globals: development of theoretical and empirical research', in M. Gabrielsson and V.H.M. Kirpalani (eds), *Handbook of Research on Born Globals*, Cheltenham, UK and Northampton, MA, USA: Edward Elgar Publishing, pp. 3–15.

Johanson, J. and J.-E. Vahlne (1977), 'The internationalization process of the firm – a model of knowledge development and increasing foreign market commitments', *Journal of International Business Studies*, **8**(1), 23–32.

Johanson, J. and J.-E. Vahlne (1990), 'The mechanisms of internationalization', *International Marketing Review*, **7**(4), 11–24.

Johanson, J. and J.-E. Vahlne (2009), 'The Uppsala internationalization process model revisited: from liability of foreignness to liability of outsidership', *Journal of International Business Studies*, **40**(3), 1411–31.

Johanson, J. and F. Wiedersheim-Paul (1975), 'The internationalization of the firm – four Swedish cases', *Journal of Management Studies*, **12**(3), 305–22.

Kirpalani, M.V.H. and M. Gabrielsson (2012), 'Born globals: research areas that still need to be covered more fully', in M. Gabrielsson and M.V.H. Kirpalani (eds), *Handbook of Research on Born Globals*, Cheltenham, UK and Northampton, MA, USA: Edward Elgar Publishing, pp. 99–127.

Leonidou, L.C. and S. Samiee (2012), 'Born global or simply rapidly internationalizing? Review, critique, and future prospects', in M. Gabrielsson and M.V.H. Kirpalani (eds), *Handbook of Research on Born Globals*, Cheltenham, UK and Northampton, MA, USA: Edward Elgar Publishing, pp. 16–35.

Oviatt, B.M. and P.P. McDougall (1994), 'Towards a theory of international new ventures', *Journal of International Business Studies*, **25**(1), 45–64.

Sarasvathy, S.D. (2001), 'Causation and effectuation: toward a theoretical shift from economic inevitability to entrepreneurial contingency', *Academy of Management Review*, **26**(2), 243–63.

Index